The Rise and Fall of Money Capitalism

The book studies the trends that led to the worst financial crisis since the Great Depression, as well as the unfolding of the crisis, in order to provide policy recommendations to improve financial stability. The book starts with changes in monetary policy and income distribution from the 1970s. These changes profoundly modified the foundations of economic growth in the U.S. by destroying the commitment banking model and by decreasing the earning power of households whose consumption has been at the core of the growth process.

The main themes of the book are the changes in the financial structure and income distribution, the collapse of the Ponzi process, and actual and prospective policy responses. The objective is to show that Minsky's approach can be used to understand the making and unfolding of the crisis and to draw some policy implications to improve financial stability.

A highly relevant and topical study, this book will be of interest to researchers, economic analysts, and all those working in the field of economic causation.

Eric Tymoigne is an Assistant Professor of Economics at Lewis & Clark College, Portland, Oregon, USA. His book *Central Banking, Asset Prices, and Financial Fragility* was published by Routledge in 2009.

L. Randall Wray is a Professor of Economics at the University of Missouri-Kansas City, USA.

Routledge Critical Studies in Finance and Stability
Edited by Jan Toporowski
School of Oriental and African Studies, University of London, UK.

The 2007–2008 Banking Crash has induced a major and wide-ranging discussion on the subject of financial (in)stability and a need to revaluate theory and policy. The response of policy-makers to the crisis has been to refocus fiscal and monetary policy on financial stabilization and reconstruction. However, this has been done with only vague ideas of bank recapitalisation and "Keynesian" reflation aroused by the exigencies of the crisis, rather than the application of any systematic theory or theories of financial instability.

Routledge Critical Studies in Finance and Stability covers a range of issues in the area of finance including instability, systemic failure, financial macroeconomics in the vein of Hyman P. Minsky, Ben Bernanke, and Mark Gertler, central bank operations, financial regulation, developing countries and financial crises, new portfolio theory, and New International Monetary and Financial Architecture.

1   **Banking Systems in the Crisis**
    The faces of Liberal Capitalism
    Edited by Sue Konzelmann and Marc Fovargue-Davies

2   **Post-Keynesian Views of the Crisis and its Remedies**
    Edited by Óscar Dejuán Asenjo, Eladio Febrero Paños and Jorge Uxo Gonzalez

3   **The Rise and Fall of Money Manager Capitalism**
    Minsky's half century from World War Two to the Great Recession
    Eric Tymoigne and L. Randall Wray

/

The Rise and Fall of Money Manager Capitalism

Minsky's half century from World War Two to the Great Recession

Eric Tymoigne and L. Randall Wray

LONDON AND NEW YORK

First published 2014
by Routledge
2 Park Square, Milton Park, Abingdon, Oxfordshire OX14 4RN

Simultaneously published in the USA and Canada
by Routledge
711 Third Avenue, New York, NY 10017

First issued in paperback 2016

Routledge is an imprint of the Taylor & Francis Group, an informa business

British Library Cataloguing in Publication Data
A catalogue record for this book is available from the British Library

Library of Congress Cataloging in Publication Data
A catalog record has been requested for this book

ISBN 13: 978-1-138-65016-9 (pbk)
ISBN 13: 978-0-415-59193-5 (hbk)

Typeset in Times New Roman
by Wearset Ltd, Boldon, Tyne and Wear

Contents

Figures

Tables

Acknowledgments

This book was made possible by the support of the Ford Foundation and the Levy Economics Institute of Bard College. We thank Leonardo Burlamaqui at the Ford Foundation, and Dimitri P. Papadimitriou and Jan A. Kregel at the Levy Economics Institute for providing us the financial and technical supports that have facilitated the completion of this book. This book also benefited from discussions with many individuals; among them are Scott T. Fullwiler, William K. Black, John F. Henry, Marc Lavoie, and Steven Fazzari. Special thanks to Eric Tymoigne's students, Erin Haswell and Preetham Sridharan, for carefully reading the book proof.

Introduction

The growth of financial fragility and the Great Recession

The 2007 global financial crisis, also called the Great Recession, was the worst recession of the developed world since the Great Depression. Governments had to respond decisively on a large scale to contain the destructive impact of a massive debt deflation. Still, large financial institutions such as American International Group, Bear Stearns, Lehman Brothers, Countrywide Financial, Washington Mutual, Wachovia, Northern Rock, and Landsbanki collapsed; thousands of small-to-medium financial institutions failed or needed to be rescued; millions of households lost their retirement savings, jobs, houses, and communities; numerous nonfinancial businesses closed.

Five years later, we are still experiencing the effects of the crisis. In the United States, financial institutions are still failing and, as of December 2012, almost 470 Federal Deposit Insurance Corporation (FDIC)-insured banks have failed since 2007. The employment–population ratio has dropped sharply. Nine million jobs were lost from the peak of January 2008 and, at the current pace of sluggish job creation, it will take at least seven-and-a-half years to regain them. Only in the Great Depression did it take longer for employment to recover in the U.S. Worldwide, as of May 2012, fifty million jobs are still missing compared to the pre-2008 crisis level according to the International Labor Organization and they are not expected to be regained until late 2016.

Prior to the Great Recession, developed economies experienced a long period of stability in terms of inflation and economic growth, which prompted U.S. economists to call this period the "Great Moderation." On the financial side, however, things were not as smooth, as the financial fragility of the economy increased and several financial crises occurred. Focusing strictly on the U.S., there was the Savings and Loan (S&L) crisis, the Long-Term Capital Management crisis, and the dot-com bubble. However, the effect of these crises on the economy was contained through government interventions that had been growing in size since the 1960s. Given the limited impact of these crises, it looked like finance was not a relevant factor that influenced the rest of the economy so it could be ignored. Thus, a majority of economists did not pay attention to the building up of financial fragility until it was too late.

Hyman P. Minsky knew better. He noted that at the same time that financial fragility was increasing in the financial sector, the finances of households also were worsening as their wages stagnated and indebtedness grew and as their retirement became more dependent on the whims of financial markets. Fiscal retrenchments of the 1990s compounded the problems as they ultimately led the private sector into a deficit in several developed countries.

During the Great Recession, the relevance of finance for the direction of the economy was brought to light. Minsky, who devoted his entire academic career to the understanding of the impact of finance on the rest of the economy, came into fashion once again—as it already had following the S&L crisis. Following the collapse of Lehman Brothers in September 2008 and the ensuing panic, the crisis was named the "Minsky Moment" and Minsky's work became associated with mania, panic, and crash, in the words of a famous book by Charles P. Kindleberger. This is unfortunate because the work of Minsky is much richer. If those elements were the only things that Minsky's framework had to offer its relevance would be limited.

In the Minskian framework, the most relevant instability is upward, not downward. The mechanisms underlying a debt deflation have been well understood since at least 1932 with Irving Fisher's *Booms and Depressions* so it is not Minsky's main contribution. Similarly, the focus on boom, with its manias and irrationality, to explain the cause of a crisis has been quite common and is not original to Minsky. While the boom does play a role in the Minskian framework, it is only the last stage of the transformation of the economy during a period of sustained economic growth. His characterization of financial fragility in terms of hedge/speculative/Ponzi finance and the move away from hedge finance and toward Ponzi finance was based on an explanation that goes beyond psychological propensities to make foolish decisions and does not require the latter. Instead of focusing on individual decisions, Minsky focused mostly on the characteristics of the economic system itself and argued that capitalist economies are prone to financial instability either in terms of inflation or in terms of depression. Minsky noted that with a "big government" and a "big bank," deep depressions were no longer a concern and instead the main concern was inflation and potential moral hazard.

Beyond the Financial Instability Hypothesis, Minsky also worked on issues of employment, poverty, and institutional changes. Minsky developed a stages approach to the study of capitalism centered on the evolution of finance over the past centuries. When combined, the institutional framework (stages approach) and the theoretical framework (Financial Instability Hypothesis) provide a powerful analytical tool.

This book continues in the same tradition by focusing on the financial implications of the economic trends that developed over the past half century. This book argues that Minsky's framework helps us to understand what has happened over the past half century instead of merely explaining the recent boom and crisis.

The first chapter presents the analytical framework that will be used in the rest of the book. Minsky's premise is that capitalism is a monetary-production economy not a real-exchange economy. Commodities need to be produced before they can be exchanged, and production is undertaken with the expectations of selling output, needs to be financed, takes time to be implemented and completed, gathers groups with different economic interests, and involves irreversible decisions. All this is done in the context of a competitive environment that requires monetary accumulation and imposes monetary return targets. Thus, capitalism has two salient features: it pushes individuals to anticipate an uncertain future in order to get an edge against competitors, and financial considerations are at the heart of the system. Consequently, money influences the allocation, production, and distribution processes, and capitalism is a highly dynamic and forever changing economic system—stability is inconsistent with the principle of competition through constant innovations.

Minsky argued that "stability is destabilizing," i.e., prolonged economic growth generates financial fragility that results in "serious" business cycles that are mainly "due to financial attributes that are essential to capitalism" (Minsky 1986a: 173). One should be careful to distinguish that statement from the idea that capitalist economies are prone to asset-price bubbles. The Financial Instability Hypothesis is not bubble economics, it is an explanation of how financial fragility grows during periods of economic stability.

Minsky noted that financial crises are not rare events. Since the 1960s, they have grown in frequency and size, and have required growing government interventions to contain their negative impacts on the economy. Thus, even though stability is destabilizing, it does not mean that government intervention cannot help to stabilize the economic system. It can. One should not abandon all hope to be able to promote a more stable and fair capitalist economy. The point is that one needs to work at it. Promoting stability is always a work in progress.

Indeed, the effectiveness of given regulations will erode overtime and Minsky was highly critical of the "Keynesianism" that prevailed after World War Two because it did not account for the side effects of government fine-tuning on the economy. Instead, Minsky promoted a more structural/permanent government program to deal with full employment, price stability, and moral hazard in a more coherent way than fine-tuning. He was also highly critical of existing banking regulation and aimed at refocusing regulation toward the analysis of bank cash flows, underwriting, and financial innovations.

The second chapter explains how capitalism in developed countries progressively moved from a more stable form of capitalism that Minsky called Managerial Capitalism to a more unstable form called Money Manager Capitalism. Managerial Capitalism emerged out of the Great Depression and was characterized by a big government, an originate-and-hold banking model, and labor conditions that promoted sustained shared prosperity. Given its institutional characteristics, Managerial Capitalism was less prone to financial instability. As a consequence, it took longer for financial fragility to grow, which it did under the combination of psychological, economic, and policy factors. Not only did the private sector become more dependent on the use of debt to sustain economic activity, but policies actively promoted the dismantling of the labor and banking models of Managerial Capitalism. The 1980s S&L crisis put the final nail in the coffin of Managerial Capitalism as the system moved to Money Manager Capitalism (MMC). In addition, the "Golden Age" favored the emergence of money managers because households were able to save substantial amounts of money, and the provision for retirement increasingly became the responsibility of each individual.

MMC is characterized by the rise of a predatory state, the disengagement of the government, the return of a pro-market mentality, and a growing role of financial markets in determining economic outcomes. In this sense, MMC shares quite a few similarities with Finance Capitalism that prevailed until the Great Depression. However, one of the main differences is that the government is still much more involved in the economy than it had been prior to the 1930s, so debt-deflation tendencies can be short-circuited. At the same time, the availability of a safety net through big government and big bank has not been matched by a regulatory oversight that could prevent the growth of moral hazard and the loosening of lending standards.

The third chapter focuses on the past thirty years to explain how the Great Recession was made possible and critically reviews the policies used to deal with the crisis that began in 2007. Beyond the trends presented in Chapter 2, Chapter 3 identifies two main factors that contributed to the Great Recession: pro-market policies and the decline in underwriting standards on loans and securities. Both contributed to the growth of indebtedness in the private sector and to the change in the quality of this indebtedness for the worse. This change in quality manifested itself primarily through a move toward collateral-based lending, i.e., lending based on growing asset prices instead of income. The chapter concludes that the Great Recession was not a liquidity crisis but rather a solvency crisis. Unfortunately, most policies that have been implemented in the aftermath were aimed at solving the liquidity crisis that occurred after the fall of Lehman Brothers. Nothing substantial has been done to address the underlying solvency problems. Millions of mortgages are still delinquent in both the prime and non-prime sectors, asset-backed securities are trading at a deep discount, and bad assets are burdening banks—especially big banks that were involved in promoting the lending and securitization frenzy. Instead of dealing with these issues, the government has allowed banks to hide losses through accounting manipulations or through purchases of bad assets at par, has lent reserves at a near zero rate against toxic assets, and has not prosecuted any top managers despite the abundant evidence of frauds.

Instead of hiding losses and supporting poor management, the government should promote an orderly liquidation of banks. In addition, a better road toward recovery would be to deal with the source of the lingering problem, which is the fact that borrowers cannot pay their mortgages. While some borrowers will not be able to repay under any condition because they were never able to afford a house in the first place, millions would benefit from mortgages with permanently lower interest rate and lower principal outstanding. In addition, the government could help to sustain households' income by promoting full employment through a national jobs program. By lowering debt services and sustaining income, the delinquency rate on mortgages would decline which would sustain loans and securities. However, bankers do not currently have an economic interest in going that route and find foreclosure more immediately profitable.

The last two chapters deal with policy implications for finance and employment. Capitalist economies are, by nature, unstable. The last recession was particularly deep because the financial characteristics of some developed economies were such that the excessive size and low quality of private sector indebtedness promoted financial instability. A debt deflation was set in motion in 2007 and required large government involvement to be stopped. While containment was successful, the underlying problems have not disappeared. In addition, Eurozone countries have been limited in their capacity to respond because of constraints on the fiscal operations of their national governments. Layering needs to be simplified and governments should be able to smooth that process through active intervention in the economy. This book argues for regulatory and supervisory intervention to promote stable and productive banking, and for structural programs that promote full employment and price stability.

In terms of finance, the main goal is to stabilize finance and to reorient it toward promoting economic development and financial security. A strong emphasis is put on the regulation of bank cash flows and underwriting in order to promote hedge finance. In addition, the structure of banking should be reorganized. No institution that is insolvent should be rescued, regardless of size, and top management should be fired, the company should be put in receivership and the least costly solution should be found to dissolve the company. Banking used to be a simple boring job; it needs to go back there. One way to do that is to promote localized banks like community banks. Finally, retirement is too important an issue to be subject to the whims of financial market; if people are willing to gamble with their money they can, but Social Security benefits should be large enough to allow a decent standard of living without relying on money managers' speculation.

The best way to sustain national income in a capitalist economy is to sustain employment. Over the past forty years, the capacity of the U.S. economy to recover from a recession has weakened. It has taken more and more time for employment to return to its pre-recession level, duration of unemployment has risen, and economic growth has declined both in absolute terms and per capita. The last chapter of the book argues that the government has a role to play in promoting and maintaining full employment. The government should stand ready to hire anybody willing to work at the basic wage offered by the government. A job guarantee program promotes full employment as well as price stability. It also provides projects that are complementary to the private sector while tackling issues of structural employment through training and involvement in the labor force that increases the employability of workers. Finally, it helps to smooth aggregate demand through countercyclical fluctuations of the pool of people employed over an expansion and a recession.

The current recession was not an accident, it was the product of a specific form of capitalism that promoted leveraged speculation and fraud. Making capitalism more stable requires a broader involvement of the federal government, in terms of quantity and quality, to complement the benefits of market forces and to offset their destabilizing impacts.

1   The Minskian framework

This chapter presents the theoretical framework that will be used in the entire book to analyze the causes, unraveling, and consequences of the Great Recession. Following the crash, the work of Hyman Minsky gained some attention among academics and the popular press. They have especially acknowledged the relevance of the Financial Instability Hypothesis (FIH) to explain what happened in the late 2000s. However, as one may expect, most of what has been retained from the FIH is a narrow, and rather simplistic, narrative based on bubble, greed, and irrationality that is best illustrated by Kindleberger's *Manias, Panics, and Crashes*. If that was the only thing that Minsky had to offer, his contribution to economic theory would be marginal given that many authors have made those claims long before him. The point of this chapter is to provide a more detailed presentation of the Minskian framework from its hypotheses, to its logic, and, finally, to its policy implications. As shown in the rest of the book, this framework helps to build an understanding of what happened over the past fifty years rather than only what happened in the past five.

In the concluding chapter of the *General Theory*, Keynes noted that the "outstanding faults of the economic society in which we live are its failure to provide for full employment and its arbitrary and inequitable distribution of wealth and incomes" (1936: 372). Minsky took this conclusion to heart but also noted that

> although the obvious flaw in capitalism centers around its inability to maintain a close approximation to full employment, its deeper flaw centers around the way the financial system affects the prices and demands of outputs and assets [...] so that conditions conducive to financial crises are endogenously generated.
>
> (1994b: 19)

As a consequence, Minsky aimed at providing policy solutions to deal with those issues in order to promote stable lasting full employment. In order to do so, he developed a theoretical framework that synthesizes the work of John Maynard Keynes, Joseph Schumpeter, and Irving Fisher. In a nutshell, the central message of the Minskian framework is that, over time, capitalist economies are intrinsically financially unstable even if people are rational, even if the economy is regulated properly at a point in time, and are even more unstable if market mechanisms are left alone. Stated alternatively, the economic system, rather than the morality and intelligence of individuals or the state of market structures, is at the source of most of the economic problems we face today. Government intervention can help to limit the instability of the system but, over time, the effectiveness of a given set of policies tends to erode and the policy arrangements may even promote instability. Thus, in order for capitalist economies to promote durable prosperity, government intervention must be highly proactive and constantly keep up-to-date with what goes on in the rest of the economy.

The nature of capitalism

Minsky was highly influenced by Institutional Economics and believed that an economic theory must be rooted into the institutional structure of the economic system it tries to explain. He rejected the idea that an economic theory can apply to all economic systems past and present, and argued that a careful analysis of the existing socio-political-economic institutions is necessary to formulate a meaningful analysis of existing economic problems. As a consequence, Minsky's theoretical framework is not valid for all economic systems; it is a theory of capitalism built through a detailed observation of the capitalist financial system gained partly by sitting on the executive boards of banks. This led him to characterize capitalism in the following way: "A capitalist economy [...] [is] an integrated production, trading, and wealth owning system, with a structure of financial claims and commitments, [that] operates through real world and irreversible time" (1983b: 106). The central goal is, therefore, to include these elements into a coherent theoretical framework. As shown below, this has serious implications in terms of the core concepts and of the methodology that will be used to do economics.

Real-exchange economy vs. monetary-production economy

Keynes noted that there are two points of departure when practicing economics: real-exchange economy (or cooperative economy) and monetary-production economy (or entrepreneur economy). Each point of departure has a specific understanding of what capitalism is and begins from specific concepts that it uses to analyze this economic system. As a consequence, each point of departure has a specific understanding of the main problems that are recurrent in capitalism and so a specific view of the means to use to deal with those problems.

Real-exchange economy

Most academics practice economics within a real-exchange economy which is at the core of Robins' famous definition of economics: "Economics is the science which studies human behavior as a relationship between ends and scarce means which have alternative uses" (Robins 1945: 16). This framework of analysis starts with three central premises: resource scarcity, efficient market theory, and rational agents. It argues that the study of exchange in a barter economy with small independent producers is a good proxy to understand the basics of capitalism:

> Despite the important role of enterprises and of money in our actual economy, and despite the numerous and complex problems they raise, the central characteristic of the market technique of achieving co-ordination is fully displayed in the simple exchange economy that contains neither enterprises nor money.
>
> (Friedman 1962: 13)

Money can be added to the story but it does not substantially change anything. It merely smoothes exchange and is not sought for itself, and so does not influence allocation, production, and distribution. In this context, the central goal of economics is to study exchange mechanisms in order to find the most effective means to manage scarcity.

According to this framework, since human beings have existed they have had to deal with scarcity of resources. Scarcity means that limited resources are available to satisfy unlimited wants/preferences. In this context, the central goal of markets is to allocate scarce resources to the most efficient economic endeavors (i.e., the ones that produce the most output given inputs). In order to do so, prices must be able to move freely to eliminate shortages and surpluses, and market participants must strive to discover and undertake the most productive activities. Under strong market efficiency, these market adjustments are instantaneous and prices reflect all the relevant information (also called "fundamentals") about whatever is traded—productivity, time preference, available resources (Fama 1970). As a consequence, there can never be any bubble (i.e., times when prices do not reflect fundamentals) or misallocations of resources and so financial crises are impossible.

For market mechanisms to work efficiently, several conditions must be met. A first condition concerns the market structure: perfect competition must apply. Perfect competition requires that five criteria be met: atomicity, transparency, homogeneity, free entry/exit, and perfect mobility. Atomicity means that no market participant has market power, i.e., no buyer or supplier has any bargaining power to set prices. Transparency means that all information that needs to be known about whatever is traded is known and costless to obtain. Neither buyers nor sellers have private information that can be hidden. Thus, when a borrower goes to a bank, the bank knows everything about the borrower's project who cannot hide any negative information or embellish positive information. Homogeneity means that all the goods traded in a market and serving the same purpose are exactly the same. In financial markets, this means that all financial securities trade in organized exchanges. Free entry and exit means that market participants can come and go as they wish in the market, i.e., financial markets are perfectly liquid. Perfect mobility means that labor and capital can move freely anywhere in the world immediately and at no cost; there is no such thing as capital controls or market barriers.

Assuming that pure and perfect competition applies, a second condition for markets to work properly concerns the behaviors of individuals—they must properly account for market mechanisms. For example, financial-market participants must follow a long-term fundamental approach to asset pricing, i.e., they must ignore changes in monetary returns that are unrelated to "real" changes such as capital and labor productivities, and leisure and time preferences. This means that they must be able to select and acquire all relevant information and to compute it in order to make a decision; having highly powerful computers, and a good education help to make this a reality. Individuals must also be free of "biases" like monetary illusion, over-optimism, being influenced by the way the information is provided, and other traits that are not typical of *homoeconomicus*. Individuals take market information as an input immediately usable without interpretation, and do not care about what others think or how others behave. All this ensures that market participants use price signals to allocate resources to the most productive activities.

A third condition for markets to work properly is that government should not interfere with perfect markets. Price variations should not be influenced by government because this would violate atomicity; usury laws and minimum wage laws are bad policies that interfere with voluntary contracting. Similarly, the government should not provide any financial help to individuals who want to get an education, to acquire a house, or to start a small business. Doing so would violate atomicity again so prices would not reflect only available information about fundamentals. As a consequence, prices would provide wrong signal inputs to market participants who would then make inappropriate decisions, leading to an oversupply of goods in some markets and an under-supply in others.

Any deviation from this ideal state is called an "imperfection." This imperfection can come from markets (price rigidity, asymmetry of information, or others), or from individuals (irrational, i.e., non-*homoeconomicus*, behaviors). Imperfections are sufficient, but not necessary, sources of market inefficiencies and so the point becomes to study potential sources of inefficiencies and to correct them (Fama 1970). The effects of imperfections may be compounded by perverse market incentives induced by market dynamics and externalities. These market failures lead to misallocations of resources and the closures of sound companies. Thus, in some cases, market discipline punishes market participants indiscriminately, promotes highly destructive debt-deflation processes (Fisher 1932, 1933), and undersupplies or oversupplies some economic activities. In these cases, there is a role for government regulation to compensate for market failures (Stiglitz 2010). This broad theoretical framework has been used by many different schools of thought to explain financial crises, from the Monetarists to the Behavioralists.

Monetary-production economy

Marx (1894), Veblen (1904), and Keynes (1933a, 1933b, 1933c, 1936) were three prominent authors who argued that capitalism is a monetary-production economy and Minsky followed their paths. The central aspect of this type of economy is that commodities need to be produced before they can be exchanged. Production is planned with the expectations of selling output, needs to be financed, takes time to be implemented and completed, gathers groups with different economic interests, and involves irreversible decisions. All this is done in the context of large-scale capital-intensive businesses evolving in a competitive environment that seeks monetary accumulation and imposes monetary return targets. Thus, capitalism cannot be approximated by a barter economy with money simply serving as a medium of exchange and with small independent producers.

The framework of analysis described in the previous section emphasizes the role of market exchange in the allocation of scarce resources while giving minimal attention to production. Those who adopt the monetary-production approach have three main problems with the real-exchange approach. First, they argue that scarcity is not natural but rather is institutionally created and rarely an issue—abundance should be the point of departure, not scarcity (Dugger and Peach 2008). Indeed, unlimited wants are not intrinsic characteristics of human beings but rather have been manufactured by capitalists in order to open new markets (Galbraith 1958, 1967).[1] Second, scarcity is rarely an issue because unemployment and excess production capacities are usual states of capitalism; instead, poverty (i.e., incapacity to satisfy limited basic needs) amid plenty is the core problem of developed capitalist economies. Third, beyond scarcity, the socio-economic aspects of production must be analyzed in detail because they are seen as crucial to explain the dynamics of capitalism. Indeed, production gathers two broad classes, workers and capitalists (with subdivisions in each), that have opposite core interests in the production process. This generates inter- and intra-class conflicts over methods of production and income distribution. As a consequence, income distribution is not based mainly on productive efforts but on relative powers.

In addition to studying production and distribution, one must understand how money affects the dynamics of capitalism. Money is not something that can be added as an afterthought to lubricate exchange. Business activities must be financed before they can be started and production is only undertaken if it is expected to be profitable *in money terms*. A business does not have to be productive, efficient, or useful, the only thing that matters is that money can be generated, which may entail a sabotage of production by capitalists in order to maintain artificial scarcity (Veblen 1921). Thus, the activities that generate the highest expected monetary returns, rather than the highest output, will be implemented, and capitalists may promote shirking and destroy capital if it is too productive. Businesses and households that do not comply with this rule and do not succeed in generating the expected return are ruthlessly eliminated, forcing workers and entrepreneurs to focus on monetary issues even if they have greater aspirations—high quality, durability, craftsmanship, great engineering, etc.—when starting an activity. Their socio-economic survival depends on submitting to the imperative to generate, not only a profit, but the profitability norms set by the competitive setup in their sector. This implies constant innovation and growth, and the result is that growth for the sake of growth (rather than for the sake of improving standards of living) becomes a central goal to achieve. It also becomes a central element of policy discussions as capitalists push for an economic agenda focused on economic growth and laissez-faire.

Note, however, that when a business venture is started there is no certainty that it will succeed. In addition, once decisions are made, they are impossible or highly costly to change—especially for capital-intensive businesses—so free entry and exit is not only unrealistic but also unachievable. While liquidity can be achieved through financial markets, it is limited and ends up affecting decisions. Thus, instead of a cold calculation of benefits and costs, individuals rely on conventions, psychological instincts, and heuristics. However, these behaviors are not irrational but, rather, perfectly normal given the institutional framework in which individuals must operate (Keynes 1936: 147ff.).

In the end, capitalism has two salient features, it pushes individuals to attempt to anticipate an uncertain future in order to get an edge against competitors, and financial considerations are at the heart of the system and so influence the allocation, production, and distribution processes; money is never neutral. Another consequence is that capitalism is highly dynamic and forever changing; stability is inconsistent with the principle of surpassing others through constant innovations. As a consequence, a monetary-production economy is inherently unstable.

This conceptual framework has some far reaching implications for theorizing. Economics becomes the science of social provisioning instead of the science of market allocation (Dugger 1996). Market efficiency is no longer the central concern and issues of equity and participation in social-economic activities become of concern. Proponents also tend to put forward income effects (production) rather than substitution effects (exchange) (Lavoie 1992), and to focus on studying the consequences of these income effects: high unemployment (low aggregate demand generates a shortage of jobs regardless of qualifications and frictions in the labor market), paradox of thrift (higher saving propensity does not raise aggregate saving), paradox of cost (lower wages increase unemployment), and many others. This framework also does not take individuals' preferences as given but rather considers them to be shaped by envy and emulation (Veblen 1898, 1899), and, more importantly, by producers themselves (Galbraith 1958, 1967). This is important because a central premise behind the real-exchange economy is that individuals have given preferences that are intrinsic to them. This is central to argue for the constant search for economic growth in order to meet as many wants as possible and helps to justify why the market, rather than government, can always respond best to the wants of individuals. If wants are not intrinsic to individuals but rather are manufactured by producers through advertizing and emulation, the urgency of economic growth and the incapacity of government to respond to wants are no longer convincing narratives. Government can shape individuals' preferences, define its own criteria of success, and may respond to the wants of individuals more appropriately. Improving well-being and constantly increasing production may not be similar goals. Government instead may strive to promote activities that lower consumerism, preserve the environment, and promote leisure or redirect efforts toward fulfilling crucial needs that may have very high fixed cost and very low, or no profitability. There is no reason to assume that firms should have a monopoly over directing what activities should be implemented, or that profitability should guide all economic activities.

Overall, a commonality among schools of thought in this framework is that market mechanisms do not automatically promote stability, or efficient allocation, production, and distribution. The reason for this is not mainly imperfections so promoting perfect competition, better education, and better incentives will not solve the problem of instability and crisis. Thus, at least some specific government involvement is needed that goes beyond accounting for market failures and that involves guaranteeing full employment, a proactive supervision of business practices and innovations, and performing the core economic activities that a society needs without reference to profitability.

Some key characteristics of a monetary-production economy

Economic behavior: the Wall Street view

If one starts at the microeconomic level, a main economic concern of economic units is to determine the structure of their balance sheet, i.e., to decide which assets to acquire and how to fund the positions in those assets. Economic units make arbitrages among all assets (physical and financial) on the basis of their expected rate of return from income and capital gains. In order to do so, they have to determine a portfolio horizon, set a targeted rate of return, make expectations about future returns, and determine what they believe to be an appropriate proportion of external funding. Unfortunately, there are no a priori hard facts, or so-called "fundamentals," that allow them to determine what the optimal value of all these elements should be. Indeed, the future is uncertain and future outcomes change depending on present decisions that depend on current and past expectations about the future.

In this context, Minsky notes that an individual's decision-making process is quite different from the one assumed in risky environments. Indeed, a probability calculus is not as reliable (or not reliable at all) and people tend to complement it (or to replace it) by simple rules like anchoring and adjustment (e.g., extrapolation of the recent past) and representativeness (e.g., a chartist approach in finance). These psychological factors have been studied extensively by Kahneman and Tversky (Tversky and Kahneman 1974; Harvey 1998). Psychological factors are complemented by sociological factors because, under uncertainty, individuals tend to look for the approval of others. This leads to the creation of economic conventions, i.e., mental models commonly agreed upon by a group of economic units. Conventions are institutions that exist to face uncertainty and manage complexity. They create "a significant degree of continuity, order and conditional stability [...] in spite of the potential for chaos and perpetual instability seemingly inherent in the assumption of true uncertainty" (Crotty 1992 [1993]: 64). The "New Economy" of the 1990s was a famous convention. A convention gives confidence to individuals to implement their decisions in a situation of uncertainty because it gives them an interpretation of the current situation, it defines the appropriate ("rational" or "reasonable") mode of behavior to adopt, and it provides an objective that reduces the darkness of the future (a projection of the future that society would like to create).

Conventions are the product of social interactions instead of hedonist behaviors, that is, the rationality of economic agents in an uncertain world is different from the rationality used in the real-exchange economy in which markets are complete, preferences are known, and the future is known at least in probabilistic terms. This position has been held for a long time in other disciplines like psychology or sociology (Wärneryd 2001: 80), and Veblen (1898) already criticized the utilitarian approach on such a point:

> Most social influences and interactions are by definition incompatible with economic rationality [...]. Social influence may mean to follow a market leader, to react simultaneously with other investors on identical information, or simply imitate behavior, spurred directly by one's own observations or indirectly by mass media reports on what significant other people are doing [...]. Social influence is not only the strongest when the individual feels uncertain and finds no direct applicable earlier experience of her/his own, but such situations may lead to an active search for some kind of *social support* and confirmation.
>
> (Wärneryd 2001: 203)

Thus, in an uncertain world, in which future is unknown and cannot be known, it is rational for individuals to look at what others do, and so a social behavior is rational (Glickman 1994; Orléan 1999; Keynes 1936, 1937a [1973]: 114).

The fact that it is rational to look at what other individuals do is reinforced by the existence of institutional factors that promote this kind of behavior. Indeed, the institutional set-up of capitalist economies implies that economic units look toward the future. They act in an uncertain world and are subject to the "unseen pressure of society" to valuate monetarily an "unseen future" (Commons 1934 [1959]: 440). This implies that the market mechanisms depend on confidence, speculation, manipulations, propaganda, the banking system situation, and sentiments (concerning liquidity, solvency, economic situation, etc.) (Commons 1934 [1961]: 455, 602). In this context, speculative behaviors are a rational response rather than an aberration (Orléan 1999: 50).

Conventions play a central role in Minsky's analysis. In normal time, there is always a "consensus" (Minsky 1972: 214) that exists and stabilizes the decisional process by playing the role of "certainty equivalent" (Minsky 1975a: 66). Those conventions do not need to rest on any objective criteria but may rest on the "prevailing mood of bankers, the users of their liabilities, and the regulatory authorities as to the safety of various types of assets" and methods of financing and funding (Minsky 1975b: 334). Ultimately, social conventions define norms of behaviors that determine what the "proper/acceptable/sensible" leverage and asset mix are, and they may express themselves through normal loan-to-value ratio, normal debt–service ratio, norms of profit rate, among other measures. Anybody who is ahead of the norm is seen as reckless and anybody who is behind the norm will lose market share in a competitive environment. As Wojnilower notes about bankers:

> In the 1960s, commercial bank clients frequently inquired how far they could prudently go in breaching traditional standards of liquidity and capitalization that were clearly obsolescent. My advice was always the same—to stick with the majority. Anyone out front risked drawing the lightning of the Federal Reserve or other regulatory retribution. Anyone who lagged behind would lose their market share. But those in the middle had safety in numbers; they could not all be punished, for fear of the repercussion of the economy as a whole. [...] And if the problem grew too big for the Federal Reserve and the banking system were swamped, well then the world would be at an end anyhow and even the most cautious of banks would likely be dragged down with the rest.
>
> (1977: 235–236)

John Maynard Keynes (1936: 157) understood this phenomenon. More than eighty years ago, he wrote: "Worldly wisdom teaches that it is better for reputation to fail conventionally than to succeed unconventionally."

In the end, therefore, capitalism combines the individual search for accumulation with a social base of justification. This rationality is determined through an imitation process that rests, not on following the previous behavior of individuals (irrational approach, cascade of information theory), but on anticipating the average opinion regarding the appropriate behavior—Keynes's beauty contest. Hence, the convention provides an alternative to "inherent" fundamentals in providing a point of reference for decisions. When the consensus is broken, there is no longer a point of reference and economic decisions are frozen as perceived uncertainty increases.

These types of behavior are "irrational" if one follows the straight-jacket of the real-exchange economic framework. However, the hypotheses underlying rationality in the latter framework are either those of pure and perfect competition (which implies perfect and costless information), or of risky and imperfect environments (probability distributions are well established or can be established over time with additional, albeit costly, information). In an uncertain world, in which the future is unknowable, behaving as if everything is known, or could be known, leads to dangerous consequences for individuals. In addition, in an uncertain world, more information does not necessarily lead to a better decision-making process. In fact, psychologists have shown that the quality of decisions declines above a certain amount of information and that only confidence is positively related to more information (Wärneryd 2001: 168). Finally, information is subject to interpretation (through the psychological and social factors cited above) and the latter is what matters rather the information itself.

The centrality of money and finance

Capitalism is a monetary economy, not because money is used in market exchange, but because money is at the center of the decision-making process of the economic units at the heart of the capitalist system: entrepreneurs. Money is present both at the beginning and at the end of the economic process involving entrepreneurs: "The firm is dealing throughout in terms of sums of money. It has no object in the world except to end up with more money than it started with. That is the essential characteristic of an entrepreneur economy" (Keynes 1933b [1979]: 89). "Only that which is financed can happen" (Minsky 1990c: 66), and the aim of any economic activity is to make a net *monetary* gain in order to stay liquid and solvent. "Money isn't everything, it is the only thing" (Minsky 1990a: 369). Thus, contrary to a real-exchange economy, in a monetary economy, "money plays a part of its own and affects motives and decisions" (Keynes 1933a [1973]: 408). Pecuniary emulations and invidious comparisons are at the center of economic dynamics, and the primary goal of businesses is "vendibility," not productivity (Veblen 1899, 1904). The economic system is not ultimately driven by physical conditions but rather hangs on a state of expectations about the future monetary profitability (and so, ultimately, on a given initial state of expectations). This state of expectations affects current decisions about consumption, investment, and employment, and so influences current and future economic conditions (employment, productivity, techniques of production, etc.), which, in turn, affects back the state of expectations (Kregel 1976, 1986; Tymoigne 2012b).

Beyond the role played by uncertainty, the core reason why money plays such a central role is because most economic debts—bank loans, taxes, and fees, among others—require a monetary payment. This centrality of money as a unit of account and means of payment leads economic units to judge the relevance of their economic activity in relation to monetary gains. Thus, people care about nominal value when making decisions. This does not mean that they do not adjust for expected inflation, taxes, and other considerations that they may have, but most economic calculations are made using nominal value, and the latter are not derived from real variables like productivity or time preference:

> The classical theory supposes that [...] only an expectation of more *product* [...] will induce [an entrepreneur] to offer more employment. But in an entrepreneur economy this is a wrong analysis of the nature of business calculation. An entrepreneur is interested, not in the amount of product, but in

the amount of *money* which will fall to his share. He will increase his output if by so doing he expects to increase his money profit, even though this profit represents a smaller quantity of product than before. [...] Thus the classical theory fails us at both ends, so to speak, if we try to apply it to an entrepreneur economy. For it is not true that the entrepreneur's demand for labour depends on the share of the product which will fall to the entrepreneur; and it is not true that the supply of labor depends on the share of the product which will fall to labour.

(Keynes 1933c [1979]: 82–83)

Of course, economic agents are happier if their purchasing power increases but that is a different proposition from stating that productivity and time preference determine nominal variables. Economic agents select economic activity according to their monetary profitability instead of their productivity, and the latter does not imply the former. In addition, economic agents pay a lot more attention to protecting themselves against insolvency rather than concentrating on the narrow problem of the purchasing power of their monetary hoards or income gains.

Many economic activities can be classified into two different categories, the production of assets and the carrying of assets. These economic activities are supported by a financial system so the financial and the production sides of a theoretical framework must be developed explicitly at the same time: "It is impossible to draw a meaningful investment demand function without simultaneously specifying the liabilities that will be emitted" (Minsky 1967b: 47). "A commandment for creating economic theory that is relevant for capitalist economies is: 'Thou shalt not dichotomize' between the presumably real and the financial spheres of the economy" (Minsky 1990b: 212).

Given the importance of financial needs in order for the economic process to start, financial institutions are essential components of the system at all stages of the economic process in order for the economy to grow properly. However, the financial sector may also promote financial instability and so needs to be regulated and supervised.

In any bank, defined in a broad sense as "the various classes of dealers (position-takers) and brokers that intermediate and facilitate financing" (Minsky 1984a: 41, n. 16), there are two essential operators: the loan officer and the position-making desk. One central role of the banking system is to evaluate the creditworthiness of borrowers: "Bankers are 'specialists' in 'determining' the likelihood of success of money-making business schemes that require external finance" (Minsky 1984b: 236). "Loan officers of banks are professionals, skilled in the evaluation of privately submitted and often confidential information about the operations of businesses, households, and government units that require financing" (Minsky 1994a: 9). Loans officers represent the conservative side of a bank and examine each project presented to them in great detail to "transform the optimistic views of profit expectations put forth by potential borrowers into realist expectations" (Minsky 1994a: 9). They are the "designated skeptics" (Minsky 1994a: 10) in the game of guessing the future, and help to contain the potential fragility of the economy (Minsky 1986a: 212; Kregel 1997). Loan officers are, thus, essential to the stability of the capitalist system, even though their skepticism may be eroded over a prolonged expansion.

The conservative side of banks is complemented by its opposite. Indeed, bankers "are sceptics as 'underwriters' and enthusiasts as 'sellers'" (Minsky 1996: 76), that is, bankers assume that they will usually be able to refinance or sell their positions at a cost low enough not to compromise the profitability of granting advances; or that they will be able to transfer the financial cost on their cash-inflow-generating activities to their customers (increase in interest rates, fees, and other sources of funds). Banks are "profit maximizing, highly levered, speculative enterprises" (Minsky 1975b: 330) because the maturity of their debts is shorter than the maturity of their assets, so there is a refinancing cost upon which they have to speculate (Minsky 1977a: 19–20).

As shown later, the structure of banking is a major source of instability. Moreover, the changes in the banking structure over the past forty years have promoted the position-making desk and reduced the role of the loan-officer desk, which has increased the instability of the financial system.

Macroeconomic accounting

In order to get a solid macroeconomic theoretical framework, one must not only theorize from a solid knowledge of the underlying institutional set up, but one must also be aware of the double-entry accounting rules that apply at the aggregate level. Minsky was well aware of the work of economists like Wynne Godley who understood the great economic insights that one can get from understanding macroeconomic accounting (Godley and Lavoie 2007). In the following, we will take the example of the macroeconomic accounting system of the United States but the same accounting rules apply to all countries.

At the aggregate level, the national income and product accounts (NIPA) managed by the Bureau of Economic Analysis (BEA) record all economic operations on goods and services. NIPA shows us that the expenditure approach to gross domestic product (*GDP*) holds as a matter of accounting:

$$GDP \equiv C + I + G + NX$$

The gross domestic product is the sum of all final expenditures on goods and services, including domestic private final consumption (*C*), domestic private investment (*I*), government spending on goods and services (*G*), and net exports (*NX*), i.e., exports minus imports. We also know that the income approach to *GDP* holds as a matter of accounting:

$$GDP \equiv Y_D + T$$

That is, with minor discrepancies, the gross domestic product is the sum of all gross incomes, or, stated alternatively, the sum of all domestic disposable incomes (Y_D)—wages, profits, interest, and rent—and the amount of overall taxes (net of transfers) on income and production (T). This means that:

$$Y_D + T \equiv C + I + G + NX$$

We also know that, when accounting for international income sources, the U.S. international transactions accounts (USITA) (that accounts for the relation between the U.S. and the rest of the world also called the foreign sector) tells us that:

$$CAB_{US} \equiv NX + NRA$$

The current account balance (CAB) is the sum of the trade balance (net exports) and net revenue from abroad (NRA) (net of unilateral current transfers). In addition, as a matter of accounting, USITA tells us that:

$$CAB_{US} + KAB_{US} \equiv 0$$

That is, the sum of the U.S. current account balance and the U.S. capital account balance (KAB_{US}) must be zero. All this is saying is that if the U.S. net financial gains from trade or income are positive ($CAB_{US} > 0$), it implies the rest of the world must have provided to the U.S. a net amount of funds ($KAB_{US} < 0$), that is, the rest of the rest world must have a net financial loss from trade or income ($CAB_F < 0$).

If we combine the NIPA and USITA and now includes in T the taxes earned on foreign income we get the following:

$$Y_D + NRA_D + T \equiv C + I + G + CAB_{US}$$

We also know that, in the NIPA, aggregate saving (S) is defined as the difference between disposable income and consumption, $S \equiv Y_D + NRA_D - C$, therefore:

$$(S - I) + (T - G) - CAB_{US} \equiv 0$$

Or, given that for every net exporter there is a net importer ($CAB_F = -CAB_{US}$):

$$(S - I) + (T - G) + CAB_F \equiv 0$$

For the following chapters, this identity is very important. It tells us that the sum of domestic private financial balance ($S - I$), the government fiscal balance ($T - G$), and financial balance by the rest of the world must be zero as a matter of accounting rules.

Given the importance of this accounting identity for the rest of the book, it is good to spend a bit more time understanding what its implications are. To simplify, let us assume that $CAB_F = 0$, therefore:

$$(S - I) \equiv (G - T)$$

That is, for the private domestic sector (households and private companies) to be able to record a surplus, the government must run a fiscal deficit. When the government spends, it injects dollars in the domestic economy, and when it taxes it withdraws dollars from the economy. If the government spends more than it taxes, there is a net injection of dollars by the government into the economy and this net injection must be accumulated somewhere. In the simple case, it is the private domestic sector that must accumulate the dollars injected. The reverse logic applies when the private sector runs a deficit, i.e., it injects a net amount of dollars into the economy; in that case the government must run a surplus. A powerful consequence of this simple accounting rule is that it is impossible for both sectors to run a surplus simultaneously, as one of the domestic sectors (private or government) must be in deficit in order for the other sector to be in surplus. Moreover, government surpluses or even declining deficits negatively impact the growth of nominal net wealth of the private sector.

No theory, behavioral equation, or causality, was used above to explain this identity, which simply states that a net injection of funds by a sector must be accumulated in another sector. Every dollar must come from somewhere and must go somewhere. This accounting identity can be expanded to include the rest of the world. In this case it shows that, for the rest of the world to accumulate U.S. dollars, the domestic economy must run a current account deficit, which implies that either the government or the private sector, or both, are injecting dollars outside the U.S.

This basic accounting identity can be combined with causalities and behavioral equations to form a theory. Without going into complex theory, the identity tells us that, given a balanced current account, if the government wants to run a surplus, it must imply that the private sector must be willing to go into deficit and so borrows and/or runs down its hoards. Otherwise aggregate income will adjust downward as the private sector cuts spending and tries to return to a surplus, which makes the government's attempt to run a surplus futile. Our position in this book is that, in a monetarily sovereign country, the government balance (surplus or deficit) is ultimately set by the desired balance of the domestic private sector and rest of the world. Usually the last two sectors desire to be in surplus; therefore the government balance will be in deficit most of the time (Wray 2012).

Another way to look at these relationships is to use the flow of funds accounts that focus on financial operations. This accounting approach uses balance sheets to analyze the three main economic sectors of an economy: the domestic private sector (DP), the government sector (G), and the rest of the world/foreign sector (F) (Ritter 1963). A balance sheet is an accounting document that records what an economic unit owns (assets) and owes (liabilities) (Table 1.1).

Financial assets are financial claims on other economic units and real assets are things that have been produced, which for our purpose can be reduced to physical things (cars, buildings, machines, pens, desks, inventories, etc.). Financial liabilities are claims of other economic units on the economic unit. A balance sheet must balance, that is, the following equality must hold all the time:

Table 1.1 A basic balance sheet

Assets	Liabilities and net worth
Financial assets (FA)	Financial liabilities (FL)
Real assets (RA)	Net worth (NW)

$FA + RA \equiv FL + NW$ or $NW - RA \equiv FA - FL$. Each macroeconomic sector has a balance sheet (Table 1.2).

Given that financial assets are claims of an economic sector on the two other economic sectors and financial liabilities are the claims of the two other economic sectors on an economic sector, it must be true that the sum of all financial assets and liabilities across sectors is zero. For every lender there is a borrower, and if one adds together the claims of the lender and the borrower they must cancel out:

$$(FA_{DP} - FL_{DP}) + (FA_G - FL_G) + (FA_F - FL_F) \equiv 0$$

Thus, summing across sectors, it is true that the sum of all net worth equals the sum of real assets, that is, only real assets are a source of wealth for an economy.

$$(NW_{DP} - RA_{DP}) + (NW_G - RA_G) + (NW_F - RA_F) \equiv 0$$

Given that the previous identities hold in terms of levels, they also hold in terms of changes in levels ("flows"):

$$\Delta(FA_{DP} - FL_{DP}) + \Delta(FA_G - FL_G) + \Delta(FA_F - FL_F) \equiv 0$$

And, knowing that saving represents the change in net worth ($S = \Delta NW$) and investment is the change in real assets ($I = \Delta RA$), it is also true that:

$$(S_{DP} - I_{DP}) + (S_G - I_G) + (S_F - I_F) \equiv 0$$

This last identity is similar to the NIPA identity $(S - I) + (T - G) + CAB_F \equiv 0$ presented above (the flow of funds identities also includes capital gains and losses while the NIPA identity does not). Let us focus instead on the side of the balance

Table 1.2 Balance sheet of each macroeconomic sector

A_{DP}	L_{DP}	A_G	L_G	A_F	L_F
FA_{DP}	FL_{DP}	FA_G	FL_G	FA_F	FL_F
RA_{DP}	NW_{DP}	RA_G	NW_G	RA_F	NW_F

Note
DP is the domestic private sector, G is the government sector, F is the foreign sector also called the rest of the world.

sheet that deals with financial claims. Given that $NW - RA \equiv FA - FL$, it must be true for each sector that $(S - I) \equiv \Delta(FA - FL)$. The operations on goods and services are mirrored by financial operations. $\Delta(FA - FL)$ is called net lending so the following identity holds for an economy as a whole:

> Domestic Private Net Lending + Government Net Lending + Foreign Net Lending $\equiv 0$

If an economic sector accumulates more claims on the two other sectors than the two other sectors accumulate claim on an economic sector, the economic sector is a net lender: $\Delta(FA - FL) > 0$. Otherwise, the sector is a net borrower. It is quite straightforward to notice that not all sectors can be a net lender at the same time. At least one sector must be a net borrower if one sector is net lender. For every lender there must be a borrower. Most of the time the domestic private sector is a net lender and the government sector is a net borrower.

The Financial Instability Hypothesis

The Financial Instability Hypothesis (FIH) is at the core of the Minskian framework of analysis and is an alternative to the Efficient Market Hypothesis (EMH). The latter states that markets tend to allocate scarce resources efficiently (i.e., toward the most productive economic activities) and to allocate financial risks toward economic entities that are most able to bear them. The EMH also states that market mechanisms tend to self-correct and to eliminate any disequilibrium such as bubbles or crashes. The EMH has been at the core of economic thinking and financial regulation over the past forty years. For example, the 2005 Basel accords emphasize market discipline and self-regulation of large banks as core pillars of international financial regulation. The FIH rejects this view and is rooted in a theoretical framework that encompasses all the elements of a monetary-production economy, in order to explain some of the economic dynamics that occur during a period of economic stability, and why and how market forces actually lead to financial instability.

Financial fragility and financial instability

In order to understand the FIH, one must first provide a conceptual framework that allows for financial fragility and financial instability. There are macroeconomic and microeconomic aspects to financial fragility. At the microeconomic level, financial fragility broadly means that elements on the liability and/or asset side of the balance sheet (plus off balance sheet assets and liabilities) are highly sensitive to changes in interest rate, income, amortization rate, and other elements that influence the liquidity and solvency of a balance sheet. In this case, not-unusual fluctuations in these variables create large financial difficulties. The flip side of this high cash-flow sensitivity is a high reliance on refinancing sources (high refinancing risk) and/or asset liquidation at rising prices (high liquidation risk) in order to pay debt commitments.

At the macroeconomic level, financial fragility can be broadly defined as the propensity of financial problems to generate financial instability, that is, large disruptions in the financial systems that ultimately manifest themselves in the form of a debt deflation. A debt-deflation is an economic situation that is characterized by a downward spiral of debts and asset prices in which indebted economic units desperately try to pay their debts by selling many assets at once, resulting in a massive drop in asset prices and so increasing the difficulty in obtaining enough funds to pay debts, leading to further distress sales. The large declines in asset prices negatively affects the net worth of otherwise sound economic units and so may propagate to economic sectors that were not previously in difficulty. Thus, financial fragility can be defined as the propensity of financial problems to generate a debt deflation.

Analytical definition of financial fragility

These broad microeconomic and macroeconomic definitions can be made more precise by taking the analytical definition developed by Minsky. He noted that there are three different degrees of financial fragility when economic units are indebted: hedge finance, speculative finance, and Ponzi finance.

Hedge finance means that an economic unit is expected to be able to meet its liability commitments with the net cash flow it generates from its routine economic operations (work for most individuals, going concern for companies) and monetary balances. Even though indebtedness may be high (even relative to income), an economy in which most economic units rely on hedge finance is not prone to debt-deflation processes, unless unusually large declines in routine cash inflows and/or unusually large increases in cash outflows occur. Even then, cash reserves and liquid assets are usually available in a large enough amount to provide a buffer against unforeseen problems.

Speculative finance means that routine net cash-flow sources and monetary balances are expected to be high enough to be able to pay the income component (interest, dividend, annuities, among others) but too low to pay the capital component (debt principal, margin calls, cash withdrawals, and insurance payments, among others) of liabilities. As a consequence, an economic unit needs either to borrow funds or to sell some less-liquid assets to pay liability commitments.

Ponzi finance, also called interest-capitalization finance, means that an economic unit is not expected to generate enough net cash flow from its routine economic operations, or to have enough liquid assets that can be converted into cash to pay the capital and income service due on outstanding financial contracts. As a consequence, Ponzi finance involves an expectation of borrowing money and/or selling non-monetary assets in order to pay interest and principal payments on debts. At the microeconomic level, an economic unit that uses Ponzi finance to fund its asset positions is highly financially fragile. At the macroeconomic level, if key economic units behind the growth of the economy are involved in Ponzi finance, the economic system is highly prone to a debt deflation.

Note that this categorization is not a measure of the use of external funding, i.e., of the size of leverage; but rather, a measure of the quality of the leverage. At the core of this analytical definition is an analysis of the financial means that are expected to be available for economic units in order to fulfill their financial contracts. The more an economic unit is expected to need defensive position-making operations, the more financially fragile it is. Position-making operations are portfolio transactions (buying/selling assets, borrowing/lending) induced by the existence of an excess or a shortage of cash relative to the needs of an economic unit. Minsky especially focused on a situation of shortage of cash (i.e., "defensive/forced" position-making operations), in which case position-making is the act of meeting financial commitments by borrowing funds (refinancing) and/or by selling assets (liquidation). Position-making occurs when internal sources of cash have been exhausted (i.e., net cash inflows from routine/strategic operations are too low relative to debt commitments and cash reserves have been drained), which leads to a need to acquire more cash. The safest position-making sources are central-bank refinancing channels (at least when a government is monetarily sovereign), long-term contractual credit lines, and unencumbered highly liquid assets (cash reserves are not part of this because position-making is concerned with meeting debt commitments with the help of an external agent, i.e., once cash reserves have been exhausted). The most unreliable position-making sources are illiquid encumbered assets and short-term contingent credit lines. In the first case, assets are hard to sell and, in the second case, credit lines can be withdrawn.

Hedge finance is a financial position in which no defensive position-making operations are expected. If position-making operations are unexpectedly needed, channels to do so are highly reliable. Speculative finance is a financial position that is expected to require a rolling-over of outstanding debt and/or liquidation of assets at a given price. This state of financial fragility is especially common among economic units whose business model involves funding the ownership of long-term assets with short-term external sources of funds, and so requires constant access to reliable refinancing sources to work properly. Commercial banks fall into this category. Ponzi finance is a financial position that is expected to require a growing use of position-making operations (NCF_{PM}). More precisely, Ponzi finance relies on an expected growth of refinancing loans (L_R), and/or an expected full liquidation of asset positions at growing asset prices (P_A) in order to meet debt commitments on a given level of outstanding financial contracts (L).

$$E(NCF_{PM}) = \Delta L_R + \Delta(P_A Q_A) > 0 \text{ and } d(E(NCF_{PM})/L)/dt > 0$$

Ponzi finance is an unsustainable financial process. Indeed, in order to persist it requires an exponential growth of financial participation, which is not possible because, ultimately, there is a limited number of economic agents that can or will participate. Ponzi finance creates strong pressure to perform because creditors must be paid (to avoid immediate legal, reputational, and financial costs),[2] which gives strong incentives to debtors to take more risk and, potentially, to be involved in fraud to hide risk, debt, and losses with hope that the scheme will work out and solve financial problems.

The higher the need to use (defensive) position-making operations, the greater the adverse consequences are for an economic unit if refinancing channels close or if asset prices start to decline (or rise if an economic unit took a short asset position). When position-making needs are growing, rising asset prices are a requirement in order to maintain the net worth of an economic unit and to allow the unit to refinance the same or a growing amount of outstanding debt. If asset prices decline and lead to a decline in net worth, bankers will refuse to rollover existing loans and will demand a bigger down payment given the loan-to-value ratio. For example, say that a home is worth $100 and that the acceptable loan-to-value ratio is 80 percent. This means that someone who wants to buy the home must provide a downpayment of $20 in order to receive $80 from a bank. Now let us assume that Paul did buy the house but an economic downturn creates a difficulty in making payments on the mortgage. Paul decides to refinance the $80 mortgage to get more affordable terms. Unfortunately, as a result of the downturn, the price of his home declined by 10 percent to $90. In this case, the bank will only grant a loan of $72 to Paul who must now come up with $8 to be able to avoid foreclosure. Declining asset prices are detrimental for borrowers who need to refinance. What applies in the housing market also applies to any other economic activity in which secured lending is used. For example, maintenance margins (nicknamed "haircuts") played a central role in the dynamics of financial markets and were at the center of financial instability in 2008 as discussed in Chapter 3.

One should note that the H/S/P category does not apply to monetarily sovereign governments, i.e., governments that issue their own nonconvertible currency and securities denominated in their currency. Examples of monetarily sovereign governments are the United States Federal Government under the current monetary system, the Japanese National Government, the United Kingdom National Government, the Chinese and Mexican Central Governments. Examples of non-monetarily sovereign governments are national governments of the Eurozone, the United States under the gold standard before 1933, state and local governments in the United States, and any country that issues securities denominated in a foreign currency. When a government is monetarily sovereign, it has a monopoly over the currency supply and so always can meet payments denominated in its currency as they come due; there is no hard budget constraint. A government may impose budgetary constraints on themselves (debt limits, budgetary procedures, etc.) but these are artificial constraints because they are self-imposed. Governments can also peg or manage their exchange rates but again that is self-imposed and can be dropped as necessary. Thus, default is impossible and liquidity problems are also impossible, at least for economic reasons. Hedge finance applies to all sovereign government that issues its own currency.

More detailed explanation of Ponzi finance

For the rest of our analysis, the concept of Ponzi finance will be crucial; therefore, it is important to take the time to make sure that this concept is understood thoroughly. The central point is that the previous classification was based on the means used to service financial contracts. No special assumption was made about the "proper" pricing of assets (P_A), nothing was said about the legality of the economic activities sustained by the different financial positions or about the type of credit risk, and no assessment was made about the purpose of holding assets. Thus, Ponzi finance is different from bubble, fraudulent activity, poor credit, or speculation; it may coexist with them but it is independent from them.

Ponzi processes (i.e., economic activities sustained by Ponzi finance) may not be masterminded solely by a single individual, or a small group of individuals, but, rather, may be sustained, and approved, by the entire society. In the recent housing boom, this approval included an endorsement by Alan Greenspan of the financial innovations in the mortgage industry and elsewhere, on the basis that they promoted homeownership. In the short run, Ponzi finance may raise standards of living, and maintain economic growth, employment, and competitiveness. In any case, those already in the Ponzi process have an incentive to create and hold a good view of the future to entice others to join the process. This is reinforced by the seemingly great returns that the Ponzi scheme may have provided in the past, which, combined with competitive pressures and social pressures, give additional incentives to join (Galbraith 1961; Shiller 2000).

Some forms of Ponzi finance are more dangerous than others, depending on the way the economic units ultimately plan to service their debts. This, in turn, depends heavily on the types of assets involved in the Ponzi process. The most dangerous of all Ponzi processes are those for which continuous liquidation and/or unlimited growth of refinancing are necessary for the process to continue, also called pyramid schemes; there is no way to terminate the process without a collapse or widespread restructuring of financial commitments. This type of Ponzi process usually involves the funding of assets that do not produce any cash flow from operation (e.g., home of residence), or that generate cash flows over which the owner has very minimal or no control (e.g., shares of companies) and so cannot be adjusted to meet the demands of debt services. More broadly, it involves the funding of economic activities for which the borrower is never expected to be able to draw an operational income high enough to service debt. Examples of those processes are the mortgage practices of the 2000s and the Madoff scheme.

The least dangerous Ponzi financial practices involve the temporary use of growing refinancing before net cash flows from core economic operations are expected to become large enough. This usually implies that the economic units involved in the Ponzi process have some market power and that the underlying asset is expected to provide reliable and high enough net cash flows from its operation. For example, the construction of investment goods takes time and must be financed; however, they do not generate any cash inflows from operation (for the producer and the acquirer) until they are finished and installed in the production process. Thus, a producer's (and his creditors') profitability depends on the capacity to sell the finished investment good at a high enough price, and the acquirer's profitability depends on its capacity to influence the cash flow received from the output produced by the investment good. This may put both the producer and the acquirer in a state of Ponzi finance if they do not have any other profitable economic activities. A start-up company will often be in that case. From the point of view of systemic stability, both types of Ponzi finance (pyramid/collateral based or production/income based) are a source of concerns for long-term economic growth because, as long as they exist, the economy is potentially subject to a debt deflation.

As the position-making formula above shows, the notion of Ponzi finance does not require the existence of a bubble (i.e., that P_A be above its fundamental value; however defined), it just requires expected rising prices of collateral assets or other assets held by the entity involved in a Ponzi process. The latter condition is required for cheap refinancing to occur and/or to liquidate at a price that covers debt services.

Thus, an economy may be highly fragile even if there is no bubble, and a bubble may exist but financial fragility may be limited because of the limited recourse to external funding. In that case, a debt deflation is not possible given that debt is not involved or is limited. An example of this would be the current housing bubble in China, which seems to be mostly self-funded; a decline in home price will have an impact on the economy but it will be limited, and the size of the decline itself may be limited given the limited need to sell houses to pay outstanding debts.

Ponzi finance is different from speculation and is not generated necessarily by greed or fraud. Speculation is defined as taking an asset position with the expectation of making a capital gain from selling the asset. In a speculative deal, liquidation is a means to make a monetary gain, whereas, in a Ponzi process, liquidation is a means to service financial commitments, without necessarily requiring or expecting a gain from liquidation. In fact, people involved in a Ponzi process may hope that they will never have to liquidate their asset positions (at least in net terms) because this would lead to a collapse of the process. Gains for the individuals involved in the process come from holding the asset (e.g., a home), fees from managing the schemes, and other monetary and non-monetary compensation funded by attracting additional participants. Speculation with borrowed money is a form of Ponzi finance; however, Ponzi finance occurs in speculative and non-speculative activities. For example, the recent mortgage boom was sustained by a Ponzi process that involved prime borrowers who truly wished to stay in their homes.

Ponzi finance is also different from fraudulent and "abnormal" liability practices because some individuals may enter Ponzi processes while playing by the rules of law, and while following the financial norms of behaviors established by society. As stated above, investment by firms may involve some routine income-based Ponzi financing. In addition, fraudulent activities can occur at all three stage of financial fragility with hedge finance based on stated income, jobs, and/

or assets (also known as "liar loans"). Thus, everybody may behave "wisely" or "properly" but still may contribute a great deal to a rising financial fragility. It is a central point of Minsky's approach that lending norms loosen over time and that what was previously considered excessively risky funding methods may become commonly accepted. This change in norms, however, does not make Ponzi finance harder to detect because it is defined independently of those norms.

Ponzi finance should also be differentiated from poor credit, i.e., high probability of default and expected losses. Prime borrowers can be involved in Ponzi finance; Chapter 3 will provide a clear example of this possibility. If, when signing a loan contract, a banker and a borrower expect that the delinquency risk will be low because they expect to be able to refinance or to sell assets to service both the interest and principal due, they are involved in Ponzi finance.

Finally, Ponzi finance may not result from choice but may be forced on individuals by exogenous shocks that adversely affect cash inflows and cash outflows. In two extensive studies Minsky (1964: 252–262; 1975a: 73, 87–88, 115) suggested several exogenous/accidental sources of growing fragility: unexpected losses of income (e.g., an individual may become unemployed or very sick, or one of the members of a household may die, or a business may record a large decline in customers due to a recession); rising operation costs (e.g., energy costs, labor costs); higher cost of refinancing; exercise of demand options (e.g., run on a healthy bank); exercise of contingent liabilities (e.g., a major natural catastrophe leads to huge payments by insurance companies); decline in asset prices or malfunctioning of a market (e.g., technical malfunction, or war, leading to a huge drop in prices). In cases of accidental use of Ponzi finance, loan modifications, lender of last resort, and government spending to restore routine cash flows can be of great help to restore sound financial footings.

Overall, therefore, the economic system may be highly prone to a debt deflation even if there is no bubble, no fraud, no speculation, no poor credit, and no unusual level of greed. Of course, the fact that Ponzi finance is different from bubbles, speculation, poor credit, and fraud, does not mean that the latter are not relevant to explain financial instability; that is, expectations about the size of position-making needs is not the only source of financial instability. Indeed, hedge finance can be subject to fraud and excessive optimism in the valuation of net cash flows from operations. However, the main point of the Minskian classification above is to show that the way economic units plan to meet their liability commitments is a central determinant of financial instability; it reinforces tremendously the effect of small and localized financial problems.

Stability is destabilizing

Two phases to instability

The main claim of the Financial Instability Hypothesis is that periods of economic stability are a fertile ground for the growth of financial fragility and that significant business cycles are mainly "due to financial attributes that are essential to capitalism" (Minsky 1986a: 173). More technically, during a period of prolonged expansion, the proportion of economic units involved in speculative and Ponzi finance grows and so the risk of a debt deflation increases. Two phases are involved in this process of fragilization:

> Even though a prolonged expansion, dominated by private demand, will bring about a transformation of portfolios and changes in asset structures conducive to financial crises, the transformations in portfolios that take place under euphoric conditions sharply accentuate such trends. [...] Thus, the theory of financial stability takes into account two aspects of the behavior of capitalist economy. The first is the evolution of the financial structure over a prolonged expansion [...]. The second consists of the financial impacts over a short period due to the existence of a highly optimistic, euphoric economy; the euphoric economy is a natural consequence of the economy doing well over a prolonged period.
>
> (Minsky 1972: 119)

There are several important points in this quote. First, a period of prolonged expansion is necessary for financial fragility to develop. This period of expansion may record minor recessions, like the 1991 and 2000 downturns, that do not significantly alter the state of expectation of private economic units and so do not significantly reduce the level of financial fragility. If that is the case, the longer the period of economic stability goes on, the more the dynamics that lead to fragility will prevail.

Second, for financial fragility to increase, it has to be led by the private sector or governments that are not monetarily sovereign so that the move to Ponzi finance is possible. Economic growth, therefore, will not generate a weakening of the financial positions of private units if it is based on federal/national government programs that continuously increase the surplus of the private sector and inject safe assets into the balance sheets of private units (Minsky 1980b: 518; Lavoie 1986). This last point is very important: "During a protracted expansion dominated by household and business deficits the ratio of household and business financial commitments to income rises, whereas in an expansion dominated by government deficits the ratio of private commitments to income decreases" (Minsky 1963: 412).

As explained previously, if the government deficit spends, it allows the private sector to be in a surplus, that is, it allows companies to increase their profitability (the government is a customer like any other economic unit, so if it spends more on companies' products, companies receive greater revenue), and it allows households to improve their income earnings by sustaining employment. In addition, the federal government may provide treasury bonds and other default-free liquid securities that boost the liquidity of the balance sheets of the private sector. The long period of financial stability in the United States after World War Two is an example of the impact of highly liquid balance sheets in the private sector due to large government deficits during World War Two that flooded the private sector with safe assets (Minsky 1983a: 272).

While federal-government-led economic growth helps to improve the financial positions of the private sector, it does not lead to an increase in the financial fragility of the government provided that it is a monetarily sovereign government. This is so regardless of the size or growth rate of the fiscal deficit and/or the size or growth rate of the public debt. As explained earlier, this economic unit is always engaged in hedge finance because it can always meet payments due to its creditors without resorting to any position-making operations as long as those payments are denominated in the domestic currency.

All this of course does not mean that the government should take over the economy or that a growing size of the government may not generate economic problems. As explained below, government can be too big and so can be a source of inflation and moral hazard; it also can implement policies that are highly ineffective at tackling a problem. In fact, Minsky had his own criteria to determine what the appropriate size of the government should be and what specific policies should be implemented to tackle unemployment, inflation, and investment instability (Tymoigne 2010). The argument above is only saying that, from a pure financial aspect, i.e., leaving aside all potential issues that might occur on the real side of the economy, government-led economic growth is more prone to financial stability (Wray 2012).

So far, we have tackled issues surrounding the period of prolonged expansion and we have seen what "prolonged expansion" means and how different the consequences are for financial stability depending on who leads the expansion. The next section will spend more time exploring the sources of financial fragility during the period of prolonged expansion. It is now necessary to tackle the second phase of the FIH; the euphoric period.

It is important to note that the euphoric period is not what causes financial instability, that is, a period of "over-optimism," "irrational exuberance," "mania," "bubbles," or whatever else one may call it, is not necessary to explain how the growth of financial fragility came to exist. Fragility emerges during the period of prolonged expansion so the main goal of the FIH is to explain how financial fragility can emerge and grow when economic units are making reasonable decisions based on conventions and when businesses are involved in routine business activities rather than speculation or leverage buy-outs: "The fundamental instability is the way in which a period of steady growth evolves into a speculative boom" (Minsky 1974: 267). The boom just amplifies the dynamics that emerged previously.

However, the analysis of Minsky's theoretical framework would not be complete without referring to the boom period. This is a short-term phenomenon that "lives a precarious life" (Minsky 1975a: 115), during which a market economy is close to full employment and euphoria in cash flow expectation spreads to economic units engaged in hedge finance. For Minsky, even if this period is short, it is essential:

In this interpretation the boom is critical; it builds an ever-more-demanding liability structure on the base of a cash-flow foundation consisting of the prospective yields of capital assets, which are, because of technology and the limited ability to squeeze workers' real wages, at best constrained ultimately to grow at a steady rate in real terms. The debt base, which grows at an accelerating rate during a boom, is not so constrained.

(Minsky 1975a: 142–143)

The idea behind the boom period is, therefore, that the sum of the net cash inflows from routine operations cannot grow as fast as the cash outflows from financial commitments without generating inflation in output and/or asset markets. This inflationary pressure will be built up in financial contracts, and the economy will become more sensitive to the realization of asset-price and output-price expectations. Coupled with euphoria, this high sensitivity leads to a major crisis when the expectations are not realized and refinancing needs cannot be met.

Another factor that enters into consideration during the boom is the widespread use of external funding of purely financial activities like "corporate maneuverings, takeovers, mergers and conglomerate expansions that characterize the boom" (Minsky 1975a: 89). Also, during this period, "households will become more willing to use more debt to own shares, bankers will be more willing to finance such 'margin' purchases of shares" (Minsky 1975a: 112). These kinds of activities increase the amount of cash commitments without financing or funding any potential increase in national income. They are based on collateral-oriented loans rather than income-oriented loans. The capacity to meet cash commitments rests on an expected realization of capital gains. Thus, price speculation may spread to all sectors of the economy as both product markets and financial markets become more dependent on the realization of a bonanza via capital gains from asset-price and output-price increases. Therefore, the boom period is essential to explain the increase in the proportion of collateral-based Ponzi finance, while income-based Ponzi finance may start to grow much earlier during the prolonged expansion. A growing proportion of economic projects will tend to be collateral-based Ponzi financed rather than income-based Ponzi financed, which creates greater fragility.

Finally, the boom also matters because it makes hedge and speculative positions more fragile by making them more dependent on the realization of unreasonable expectations given past experiences (Minsky 1977c: 144). For example, all investment projects may be highly profitable, may be expected to be highly profitable, and may be hedge financed even late during the boom. However, if this profitability rests heavily on the continuation of output inflation (even moderate) rather than growth in customers, and if, for example, the Treasury starts to tighten its policies to fight inflation, some projects suddenly will become speculative or even Ponzi.

Dynamics

Now that we know what the FIH is and what it aims at explaining, it is possible to bring forward and combine the reasons why financial fragility grows during a period of prolonged expansion. The instability of a capitalist economy is not mainly the result of irrational choices, asymmetries of information, or other "imperfections" of markets and individuals. Instead, it is the result of psychological, sociological, economic, and policy factors that a capitalist economy tends to exacerbate.

SOCIO-PSYCHOLOGICAL ASPECTS

As noted previously, under uncertainty, individuals use socio-psychological mental tools (norms and heuristics) to make decisions. Minsky was keenly aware of the relevance of socio-psychological elements for the FIH and noted that "acceptable liability structures are based upon some margin of safety" (Minsky 1977b [1977]: 24) and that:

> The fundamental instability is the way in which a period of steady growth evolves into a speculative boom. Central to this evolution is the endogenous determination of the accepted or desired liability structure of not only ordinary business firms (corporations) but also banks.
>
> (Minsky 1974: 267)

Over a period of prolonged expansion, the normal/acceptable margins of safety (amount of liquid assets relative to outstanding debt, maximum debt service ratio, and net worth) used in banking and among entrepreneurs and households loosen. As a consequence, private economic units are willing to take on more risk on their liability side, i.e., to take on more leverage and to decrease the quality of this leverage.

Psychological and sociological factors contribute to this trend in several ways. First, the longer a period of expansion, the more people think recessions are a thing of the past and so the more indebted and the less liquid they are willing to be. Second, once a convention is formed economic units will tend to ignore information that does not fit in the prevailing convention, to discard individuals that have a contrarian view, and to interpret negative information as positive information. Third, prolonged expansion means a history of successes and so more favorable data inputted into the decision process, as well as a common agreement among the economic community about the "most profitable" and "less risky" projects (Kregel 1997): "As we learn from the past and as horizons are short, a run of success or failure will feed back quickly into the evaluation of risks" (Minsky 1967a: 288).

> The determination of the cash to be expected by the borrower depends upon the loan officer's views of what business conditions over the time of the

contract will be; these views, even in an era where loan officers use fore-
casts of the economy, are seriously affected by the performance on outstanding loans.

(Minsky 1984b: 238)

Thus, given the way decisions are made in an uncertain world, a period of good
times will lead economic units to change their views about the future and to
become more optimistic; not because they are irrational but because current and
past results seem to justify an improvement in the state of mind. While a simple
fix to this problem seems to be an increase the timeframe inputted in the decision
process (say the last fifty years of data including the worst past crises), there is a
tendency to discount past information and there are competitive pressures and
internal incentives not to do so:

> To some extent [...] all risk management tools are unable to model/present
> the most severe forms of financial shocks in a fashion that is credible to
> senior management [...]. To the extent that users of stress tests consider
> these assumptions to be unrealistic, too onerous, [...] incorporating unlikely
> correlations or having similar issues which detract from their credibility, the
> stress tests can be dismissed by the target audience and its informational
> content thereby lost.
>
> (Counterparty Risk Management Policy Group III 2008: 70, 84)

ECONOMIC ASPECTS

There are several economic aspects that promote instability. First, competition
for monetary accumulation pushes economic agents to try to guess the uncertain
future in order to obtain a bigger monetary profit relative to their competitors.
This race toward the future is the source of the productivity of the capitalist
system, but also of its instability. Indeed, it forces individuals to forget about the
big picture concerning where the economy is heading, and to narrow their effort
on beating the competition by all means (sometimes illegal) because their own
economic survival is at stake. One of these means is the use of debt; for example,
managers are not rewarded for managing a stable business but for an aggressive
expansion. All this can be understood by decomposing the profit rate of companies (Minsky 1975b, 1977a; 1986a: 234–238):

$$\frac{\Pi}{E} = \frac{\Pi}{A} \times \frac{A}{E}$$

The profit before distribution relative to equity is equal to the return on assets
multiplied by leverage ratio. As an economic expansion proceeds, the rate of
return on equity tends to decline because profit is added to equity and the growth
rate of profit tends to decline over time as markets saturate. If, due to competitive
pressures and demands from shareholders, companies have to meet a given

targeted net profit rate, they respond to the decline in net profit rate in two ways. The first method is to increase the net return on assets, which is done, given operating costs and the size of total assets in portfolio, by finding cheaper sources of funds (liability management) and/or by switching toward more profitable assets (asset management). In the former case, this usually means finding shorter-term sources of funds that provide more guarantees to the lender in case of problems. The second method to raise the net profit rate is to increase the asset-to-equity ratio. This method increases leverage and so position-making risk rises.

A second economic factor that promotes instability is financial innovation. Innovations are essential in the dynamics for all industries and help financial institutions to maintain their profitability because, like for any other industry, the market for a given product is always eventually saturated. Financial innovations end up promoting instability in two ways. Over a period of enduring expansion, innovation involves extending the use of existing financial products to more risky projects and the creation of financial products with higher embedded leverage (leverage on leverage)—this will be illustrated in Chapter 3 with securitization. In addition, new financial products are marketed as sophisticated products that are better able to measure and/or to protect against risks associated with leverage, which tends to let people believe that the use of debt is safer than in the past (Galbraith 1961). All this was observed very clearly over the past thirty years especially with the growth of securitization and derivative markets, and the belief that risk was better spread around in the system and allocated toward entities that could bear it best.

Third, competition is an essential ingredient in the formation of conventions and their wide use by economic agents. Indeed, given the fast pace, "in-the-present" world of entrepreneurial leadership, the previous sociological and psychological factors tend to be followed more closely. Also, competition pushes competitors to follow those who perform best, and to ignore information that is too costly to obtain or that could threaten a competitive position (Schinasi 2006: 221; Galbraith 1961; Morgenson 2008).

A fourth economic factor that promotes instability is the fact that the macroeconomy operates under different rules from the microeconomy so things that make sense at the individual level may be fallacious for the economy as a whole. This generates positive feedback loops peculiar to the capitalist system (Minsky 1986a: 227) that individuals are unaware of, or unwilling to take into account, because they are too complex to analyze. The paradox of thrift (higher thriftiness does not lead to higher aggregate saving) and the paradox of liquidity (financial markets are illiquid at the aggregate level) are examples of such aggregate economic processes. Another example comes from taking the identity:

$$S \equiv I + (G - T)$$

This identity can be used to develop a theory of aggregate profit based on Kalecki's (1971) equation of profit. Saving (S) is composed of workers' saving

(S_W) and firms' profit (Π) so, assuming that the causality runs from the right side to profit, we have:

$$\Pi = I - S_W + (G - T)$$

Thus, the more entrepreneurs invest, the more they earn in the aggregate, and so the more their expected earnings rise which encourages additional investment. This leads to the "paradox of debt" (Lavoie 1997) for which a higher willingness to go into debt leads to lower aggregate debt-to-equity ratio. This positive "frustration" of expectations reinforces entrepreneurs' optimism and so increases their willingness to use leveraged positions (Minsky 1986a: 213; 1975a: 114).

A fifth economic factor that promotes instability is the shortening of the maturity of debts and increased use of floating-rate liabilities. Over a prolonged period of time, the proportion of short-term debts (short relative to the maturity of the operations they fund) and of flexible interest rate loans tends to grow because they are less expensive and because refinancing operations grow. Shorter maturity compounds the effect of higher interest rate on debt-service payments by increasing the speed of repayment. Shorter maturity also creates a need to refinance and so make an economic unit more vulnerable to disturbances in the financial sector. As the recent crisis has shown, debts with flexible interest rate or payment shocks (interest rate resetting and change in amortization rate) that affect the amortization rate have played an important role in the growth of Ponzi finance.

POLICY ASPECTS

Finally, at the policy level there are, for Minsky, several aspects that may promote instability. They can be separated into macroeconomic policies and regulatory policies. In terms of the former, once a capitalist economy is booming and close to full employment, it tends to promote inflation. This pushes the central bank to raise its rate of interest based on the belief that higher rates slow economic growth, which generates an increase in interest payments. This is all the more the case if debts are based on flexible interest rates and short and medium maturities, and if a lot of refinancing operations are performed. While the central bank raises its interest rates, fiscal policy also becomes more restrictive, either for political reasons (reaching a budget surplus usually is part of the political agenda of many administrations), to limit inflationary pressures, or, more often, because automatic stabilizers lead to a decline in deficit during an expansion. This reduces the net incomes received by private entities and so further decreases their capacity to service debts, which leads to an increasing dependence on refinancing sources. Given everything else, the decline in net income induced by fiscal contraction also discourages spending and so further reduces income (Fazzari 1993). Thus, trying to fight inflation and reduce the deficit leads to an increase in financial fragility given everything else.

In terms of regulation and supervision, they will be effective at preventing the growth of financial fragility only if they are able to curtail the dangerous practices of financial institutions and if the government is willing to enforce them. In addition, a given set of regulations may rapidly become obsolete if they are not flexible enough to deal with financial innovations. Innovations are usually used by financial institutions to bypass existing rules so unless innovations can be accounted for as they appear, regulations will not work properly to prevent the growth of financial fragility induced by the growth of leverage and/or the decline in the quality of leverage: "As households, firms, government units and financial institutions learn how a new legislated financial system works they modify their behavior so that they can best profit within this new financial structure" (Minsky 1994b: 11). Moreover, inappropriate and outdated regulatory and supervisory institutions also will tend to promote instability. Notably, a regulatory system that is not flexible enough to account for new innovations and changes in behaviors may create competitive disadvantages and perverse incentives (Regulation Q in the 1970s is an example).

In addition to the lack of flexibility and an inappropriate regulatory and supervisory system, regulation and supervision may also promote instability if they promote self-regulation by financial institutions and if supervision and enforcement are minimal. This tendency may be more or less strong depending on the cultural background of a society and the relative power of financial institutions. For example, at the core of the culture of the United States is the idea that self-reliance and freedom of choice are to be promoted whenever possible, because individuals are mostly responsible for their own successes and failures. This idea was shaken during the Great Depression but a long period of economic stability progressively erased the memory of the past and a new generation was brought up within the cultural environment of U.S. society. Combined with economic stability and a systematic political organization to promote laissez-faire (Crockett 1995), the dismantling of the regulations put in place during the 1930s became a central theme of political life from the 1970s. Thus, a prolonged period of economic stability may lead to an increase in financial fragility because the regulatory body becomes more willing to relax "old" rules that prevent businesses from thriving and "deserving customers" from getting what they want. Combined with the socio-psychological aspects developed earlier, this cultural element may lead to a cycle between strong and weak regulation, or, if not weak regulation, at least weak supervision and enforcement by government. This tendency will be all the more strong if mega-financial institutions, with lobbying power and key positions in governments, can prevent the implementation of rules to curtail effectively the growth of financial fragility.

Over a long period of stability, this change in the state of mind leads to deregulation, desupervision, and deenforcement of existing laws, which promotes moral hazard. Thus, it is not the existence of a government and a central bank acting as lender of last resort that is the source of moral hazard. It is the fact that the laws that were put in place to deal with moral hazard are not implemented or are removed. For example, the preamble of the Federal Reserve act stipulates that an "elastic" currency is created but also that strong banking supervision must be implemented. Black (2005, 2009) shows how the return of free-market ideas has led to complacency, leniency, and ignorance of existing laws, leading to massive frauds and moral hazard. At the same time, under the guise of the virtues of free markets, contemporary conservatives have used the government for their own purposes, leading to a decline in the effectiveness of government and, effectively, to crony capitalism (Galbraith 2008).

IMPLICATIONS

In order for a greater proportion of the economy to move from hedge to Ponzi finance, it must be the case that the growth of net cash flow from routine economic operations grows at a slower pace than the growth of cash commitments on liabilities. Otherwise it is impossible for speculative and Ponzi finance to emerge from hedge finance, which is the whole point of the FIH. Without the framework of the FIH, the growth of Ponzi finance would be explained by relying on unexpected events (bad luck), fraud, or other exogenous "shocks," which certainly do play a role but tell a pretty narrow or unsatisfactory story of economic dynamics.

A good starting point to check the endogenous movement from hedge to Ponzi finance is the Kalecki equation of aggregate profit. If, for the sake of the argument, one assumed that profit earners do not consume, it is equal to:

$$\Pi = I - S_W + (G - T) + NX$$

Profit gives us a more or less reliable proxy of the net cash flow from the operation of businesses as going concerns (i.e., from holding and operating assets on the balance sheet). For the purpose of analyzing financial fragility, aggregate profit needs to be compared to cash commitments on liability contracts. These cash commitments (CC) are a function of income payment due (iL) and capital payment due (aL):

$$CC = (a + i)L$$

where a is the amortization rate that depends on the maturity of the debt (lower maturity means higher amortization rate), and i is the interest rate on outstanding liability contracts (L).

In a hedge finance position, aggregate profit is expected to be higher than cash commitments during the entire length of the liability contracts, $\Pi_t > CC_t \ \forall t$. In a Ponzi finance position, the reverse applies for at least part of the length of the debt contract. The point is, therefore, to explain how one goes from hedge to Ponzi. In order to do that, one must explain why profit (or income if one takes another sector of the economy) grows less fast than cash commitment:

$$g_\Pi < g_{CC}$$

which means to explain the conditions that lead to:

$$(g_I s_I - g_{S_w} s_{S_w} + g_G s_G - g_T s_T + g_X s_X - g_J s_J)/s_\Pi < g_u + g_L$$

Where $u = a + i$ is the average unit cost of debts, and s_h is the share of variable h in GDP. Let us start from the left side of the equation and see what happens during a period of prolonged expansion and the boom.

First, investment may grow at a slower pace or fall and the share of investment in the economy may decline. This may result because the cost of external funds goes up through higher interest rates, lower maturities, and other loan requirements; because optimism cannot maintain its impact on the growth of profit expectations and the decrease in the perceived risk; and/or because markets saturate. In addition, during the boom period, there may be a disconnection between profitability and investment because of the greater focus on trading assets instead of producing assets as a means to generate a profit. This leads not only to a decline in investment, but also to a disconnection between aggregate cash flow and aggregate investment, which Minsky observed during the period of Money Manager Capitalism (Minsky 1993a; Stockhammer 2004).

Second, as income goes up, the growth rate of saving of workers may accelerate and its share may rise. This second channel may not apply if consumption out of wealth is large enough and consumption is speculatively funded. For Minsky, consumption is usually hedge funded; however, with the development of credit cards and other forms of consumer loans, consumption has become more prone to speculative finance over the past thirty years (Minsky 1980a [1982]: 32; 1995; Palley 1994; Wray 2005). All this may lead to a negative growth rate of households' saving to the point where the share of saving in GDP becomes nil or even negative (Brown 2007; Tymoigne 2007a), which boosts aggregate profit. There is, however, a limit to the capacity of households to grow their indebtedness based on negative saving. In this case, Ponzi finance may grow in the household sector rather than the business companies. Later in the book, we will provide evidence that this channel was actually important during the Great Moderation.

The third factor that can put a downward pressure on profit is the trade balance. This influence will depend on what drives economic growth in the country. If the country has a strategy of export-led growth, with a positive trade balance there is no adverse effect on profit as the economy grows other than possible market saturation or adverse developments in other countries. Alternatively, if economic growth is led by consumption and investment, the share of imports may grow at a faster rate and may represent a bigger share of GDP than exports, which has a negative impact on profit growth.

Finally, one of the central forces that puts a downward pressure on aggregate profit is the tendency for the government deficit to go down during an expansion because of the political belief in the virtue of balancing the budget, or because sustained expansion leads to higher tax receipts and lower government expenditures due to the automatic stabilizers.

If one turns to the growth of cash commitments, one may decompose the cash commitments by the purpose of liabilities. Two main purposes can be identified, those created to support the production effort of the economy (L_O), and those related to pure financial activities like refinancing and speculation (L_{NO}). Pure financial activities add a debt burden without generating any actual or potential increase in Π (Minsky 1975a; Lavoie 1986).

$$CC = (a_O + i_O)L_O + (a_{NO} + i_{NO})L_{NO}$$

One can see that four factors affect the growth of cash commitments: two price-related factors that affect the growth of u—the unit cost of debt—and two volume-related factors that affect the growth of L.

If one starts with volume factors, as the economy grows, refinancing loans and other purely financial maneuvering activities may grow. Leaving aside the refinancing component of L_{NO}, during a long expansionary period and a boom period, there is a "reciprocating stimulus—a positive feedback—between speculation on the exchanges and speculation by firms" (Minsky 1975a: 90). The success on the production side of the economy leads to optimism in financial markets and higher leveraging of positions by borrowing from brokers, or by tapping into reserves and liquid assets (Minsky 1975a: 121–123; 1977c: 147). Concentrating on the refinancing side of L_{NO}, refinancing activities increase over time because of economic incentives (in terms of costs and rewards) to include refinancing operations in funding plans (Minsky 1975b: 317ff.; 1986a: 213; 1993b: 80–81).

A first incentive is the interest rate differential (Minsky 1986a: 201, 211) because a shortening of maturity (or a use of debt with a flexible interest rate and payment shocks) leads, for the same amount borrowed, to a lower interest payment ($\Delta iL < 0$) and a higher principal payment ($\Delta aL > 0$). As long as the maturity is not too short to offset completely the interest-payment gain obtained from borrowing short term, it is cheaper to use short-term credits. However, a shorter maturity implies that it is necessary to recontract more often so the sensitivity to adverse changes in financial conditions increases. These kinds of trends were observed during the Great Moderation with the proliferation of exotic mortgages and exotic derivative and securitization deals.

A second incentive is the nature of banks. Banks, because of the maturity mismatch in their balance sheet and competitive pressures, are speculative units and promote speculative financial structures: "Not only do banks engage in speculative finance, but they are the transmission belt toward speculative financing by others" (Minsky 1977a: 20). Indeed, in order to limit maturity mismatch on their balance sheet and due to competitive pressures, banks usually provide loans with a shorter maturity than the maturity of the positions that need to be externally funded (Minsky 1977a: 20), and banks have an incentive to encourage borrowers to substitute long-term debts for short-term debts (Minsky 1982: 26). In addition, given the limited pool of good borrowers and the limits that hedge financing imposes on market size, banks will expand their activities beyond these two barriers to maintain their profitability as competition lowers spreads on safest assets.

Thus, one may conclude that the growth of purely financial operations has both volume and price effects on CC by increasing L_{NO} and a. These financial operations do not need to be driven by speculative mania. They can be the results of the normal production process. Indeed, as the Circuit theory—that analyzes macroeconomics by analyzing the flow of funds induced by production and spending, and the resulting interrelations between different economic sectors—shows, in the simplest macro model, a sufficient condition for the emergence of refinancing needs for firms is households' desire to keep part of their savings in monetary form (Davidson 1978; Lavoie 1987, 1992; Parguez 1984). In this case, the short-term advances granted at the beginning of the production process to pay for wages and raw materials cannot be reimbursed completely. Banks must agree to rollover unpaid the short-term debts for the economic process to continue.

Turning to the price-related factors, as the economy and optimism grow, the amortization rate also grows for all types of economic activities (Minsky 1986a, 1995). Indeed, it is assumed by optimistic bankers and entrepreneurs that good results will come soon, and so that shorter maturity terms can be accepted. In addition, toward the end of the expansion if the liquidity preference of bankers increases, a also increases. A shorter maturity on loans raises debt service and increases interest-rate risk.

Finally, over a prolonged expansion, interest rates may tend to rise for all maturities. First, lending and borrowing activities are based on margins of safety, the latter being determined by conventions prevailing in the economy. If borrowers do not satisfy these margins, then, unless lending conventions change or financial innovations occur, there will be an increase in interest rates on debt contracts (lending will also been rationed on the quantitative side). Thus, one reason for the rise in interest rates would be that the convention of bankers has a tendency to loosen less rapidly than businesses. As shown earlier, bankers are the skeptics of the game.

Second, while the economy is still growing, earnings may fall short of what was expected. This, following Keynes (1930), puts an upward pressure on interest rates as bearishness spreads in financial markets (Erturk 2006, 2007). The more prolonged an expansion, the easier it is for results to fall short of Wall Street's expectations as market growth meets several constraints (Sterman 2000) and as expected results become less accommodative of a possible downturn, or even deceleration of growth, in sales.

A third factor that promotes a rise in interest rates is the inelasticity of loan demand to interest rates. Indeed, the refinancing process creates a need for funds whatever the rates of interest are. In a Ponzi position, this need grows over time, and it grows at an accelerating rate as interest rates increase and maturity decreases. In this kind of situation, unless the Ponzi process sustains an activity that ultimately will increase the cash generating power of a unit (and will grow this power at a rate superior to the growth of cash outflows), the accelerating deterioration of balance sheets will make banks more and more reluctant to lend given the banking convention.

Fourth, monetary policy plays an important role in the rise of interest rates as the expansion proceeds:

> For interest rates not to rise during an investment boom, the supply of finance must be infinitely elastic, which implies either that a flood of financial innovation is taking place or that the central bank is supplying reserves in unlimited amounts [to target the overnight rate].

(Minsky 1982: 33)

Because of inflationary pressures (real or expected), the central bank may tighten its policy. Given the state of financial innovations and the liquidity preference of banks and financial-market participants, this rise in policy rates is transmitted to other interest rates.

Overall, therefore, the growth of CC is due to a multitude of factors. Most authors in the Minskian tradition have focused on rising interest rates but that may not be the primary channel for the growth of financial fragility. Growing debt, change in debt composition toward financial purposes, increase in payment shocks, and declining maturity may be major contributors to the growth of financial fragility.

When one combines the cause of the decline in the growth of profit and the increase in the growth of cash commitment, the most dramatic situation that may generate an increase in financial fragility involves a move away from income-based activities to capital-based activities and a growing use of refinancing to sustain these types of activities. This debt-inflation process is most favorable to the growth of the most destructive form of funding methods: collateral-based Ponzi finance. As explained earlier, this move toward Ponzi finance may be voluntary as economic opportunities based on sounder financial practices get scarce or less profitable, so besides the changes in income and debt service presented above, changes in underwriting may directly lead to a situation where income is too small to meet debt services. This may not be true for the entire economy but, as long as a significant sector is affected, financial fragility will rise at the level of the economy. When a downturn occurs, the debt deflation generally will be stronger the longer collateral-based Ponzi finance has been allowed to last, and the more it has been allowed to spread to different sectors of the economy.

The investment theory of the cycle and Minsky's financial theory of investment

Minsky believed that Keynes's investment theory of the business cycle is incomplete because it did not really analyze how investment is financed when the marginal efficiency of some capital asset exceeds the expected return to holding money and other safe, liquid, assets. There seems to be an implicit assumption in the *General Theory* that the investment project will get funded. While Keynes did deal with this in a bit more detail in several publications after 1936, most of his effort went toward explaining why saving cannot be a source of finance. Hence, Minsky's most important contribution was to add the "financial theory of investment" to Keynes's "investment theory of the cycle." Figure 1.1 provides a graphical illustration of Minsky's theory. The two key building blocks are the "two price system," and the "lender's and borrower's risk." Following Keynes, Minsky distinguished between a price system for current output and one for asset prices. Current output prices can be taken as determined by "cost plus mark-up," set at a level that will generate profits so long as the administered price can be maintained with adequate sales. Current output covers consumer goods and services, investment goods and services, exports, and even goods and services purchased by government.

In the case of investment goods, the current output price is effectively a supply price of capital—the price just sufficient to induce a supplier to provide new capital assets (P_I). However, this simplified analysis can be applied only to purchases of capital that can be financed out of internal funds (such as sales revenue from ongoing operations). If external (borrowed) funds are needed, then the supply price of capital also includes explicit finance costs—most importantly the interest cost, but also all other fees and costs—that is, total supply price (P_{Is} in Figure 1.1) rises above the price administered by suppliers (P_I) due to "lender's risk" that is included in the costs of borrowed funds. This is represented by an upward slope in the P_{Is}-curve once investment is expected to require external funds. The quantity of investment goods that is expected to be purchased using expected internal funds is given by the distance from the origin to $E(O_{IF})$, the expected quantity of investment goods to be purchased with internal funds. The expected quantity of investment goods funded with external funds is equal to the distance from $E(O_{IF})$ to O_{Id}, the quantity of investment goods demanded. The nominal value of investment is the product $P_I O_{Id}$.

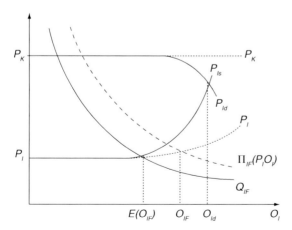

Figure 1.1 Macroeconomic determination of the level of investment.

There is a second price system for assets that can be held through time. Assets include capital assets and financial assets—essentially anything that can be held through time as a store of nominal wealth. Except for money (the most liquid financial asset), these assets are expected to generate a stream of income and possibly capital gains. The important point is that the prospective income stream cannot be known with certainty, thus it depends on subjective expectations. By taking the price of old capital assets (P_K) as a point of reference, we obtain a demand price for new capital assets (P_{Id}) from this asset price system: how much would one pay for the asset, given expectations concerning the future net revenues that it can generate?

Again, however, this is too simplistic because it ignores the financing arrangements. Minsky argued that the price one is willing to pay depends on the amount of external finance required—greater borrowing exposes the buyer to higher risk of insolvency. This is why "borrower's risk" must also be incorporated into demand prices. Unlike lender's risk, this "cost" is solely subjectively determined and is not written into any contracts. One can think of it as a "margin of safety": if one expects an asset to generate a stream of returns with a discounted value equal to $1 million, one would not be willing to pay more than perhaps $750,000 for the asset. The margin of safety provides a cushion ($250,000 in this case) to ensure that debt contracts created to finance the position in the asset can be serviced even if revenues turn out to be less than expected. That way, one will avoid bankruptcy unless the margin of safety proves to be too small. Obviously, there is no hard and fast rule governing the appropriate margin of safety because the borrower's risk cannot be calculated precisely for a future that is yet to unfold.

The quantity of investment goods purchased (O_{Id}) is determined where $P_{Id}=P_{Is}$, not when $P_K=P_I$. The latter equality is the explanation of investment developed by Tobin (1969). Tobin's explanation assumes away the importance of uncertainty and funding structure for the determination of investment. Note that in Minsky's version, the demand price declines with the level of investment demand, whereas the supply price increases with investment. This is due to Kalecki's principle of increasing risk, which states that, given expected internal funds and given conventions about the appropriate leverage-ratio, entrepreneurs and bankers assume that it is more and more risky to invest as the expected level of external funding increases. Thus, as the level of investment increases above O_{IF}, entrepreneurs become less willing to invest (the demand price declines as borrower's risk increases) and bankers become more and more stringent as external funding increases (the supply price increases as the lender's risk increases). Note that if there was no lender's or borrower's risk, then the level of investment determined by Tobin would be correct. P_I would rise as the economy gets closer to full employment.

Investment can proceed only if the demand price (adjusted for borrower's risk) exceeds the supply price (adjusted for lender's risk) of capital assets. Because these prices include margins of safety, they are affected by expectations concerning unknowable outcomes. In the beginning of a recovery from a severe recession, margins are large as expectations are pessimistic; over time, if an expansion generates returns that exceed the projections these margins prove to be larger than necessary. This leads to a reduction in the perceived borrower's risk and lender's risk, which generates flatter P_{Id} and P_{Is} curves and so increases the demand for investment goods. This, in turn, means that, given the expected flow of internal funds, bankers and entrepreneurs expect and accept a higher proportion of external funding and greater investment. Thus, margins will be reduced to the degree that projects are generally successful.

Attempts to raise leverage and to move to more speculative positions can be frustrated at least temporarily. Indeed, the actual level of internal funds (Π_{IF}) can be different from the expected level of internal funds (Q_{IF}). This has all the more chance to be the case as the actual level of internal funds depends on the level of investment, i.e., the more investment there is the higher the amount of internal funds (Kalecki's equation of profit). As a consequence, the quantity of investment goods that is actually internally funded (O_{IF}) may be much higher (or much lower) than expected. Figure 1.1 shows a situation where profit results turn out to be more favorable than expected, as a consequence entrepreneurs attempting to engage in speculative finance could remain hedge *ex post*. This added strength to Minsky's proposition that the fundamental instability in the capitalist economy is upward—toward a speculative frenzy, as investment generates profits, which breeds more investment.

Further, with the Kalecki view of profits incorporated in his investment theory of the cycle, Minsky argued that investment is forthcoming today only if investment is expected in the future—since investment in the future will determine profits in the future (in the skeletal Kalecki model). Because investment today produces profits to validate the decisions undertaken "yesterday" to invest, expectations about "tomorrow" affect ability to meet commitments that were made "yesterday" when financing the existing capital assets. While this might sound complicated, it just means that firms need to obtain profits "today" to satisfy the expectations they held in the past when they purchased capital. But, given everything else, profits "today" will be lower if firms are not investing now (perhaps because they are pessimistic about the future). So to validate the decisions made in the past, we need investment today that in turn depends on expectations about "tomorrow." There is thus a complex temporal relation involved in Minsky's approach to investment that could be easily disturbed. By linking this to the "two price" approach described above, Minsky made it clear that anything that lowers expected future profitability can push today's demand price of capital below the supply price, reducing investment and today's profits below the level necessary to validate past expectations on which demand prices were based when previous capital projects were undertaken. This also means that the margins of safety that were included in borrower's and lender's risk can prove to be inadequate, leading to revisions of desired margins of safety going forward. As margins rise due to disappointments, the demand price of capital falls below its supply price (appropriately adjusted for lender's and borrower's risk), leading to less investment and through the multiplier to still lower output and employment. The economy can spiral ever downward into a deepening recession.

Moreover, since today's financing of ownership of positions in capital assets sets up a stream of commitments to pay over a series of tomorrows, if production of investment goods does not take place in those tomorrows, the positions taken today will not be validated. "This intertemporal nature of the financial relations of a capitalist economy is the essential reason why capitalist economies are likely not to behave in a nice equilibrium seeking way and why markets need to be regulated and controlled" (Minsky 1993c: 40).

While Minsky mostly developed his theory in the context of investment by firms, the principles laid out above can be extended to other economic activity and other sectors. The only general point is to have an income that is endogenous to the expenditure. Households' aggregate investment (home purchase) could be analyzed with salaries as the main source of income. At the macroeconomic level, salaries are dependent on the level of employment which depends on the level of aggregate expenditures. Consumption, imports, the purchase of financial assets, and their respective funding can also be analyzed using this approach.

Different forms of capitalism: Minsky's stages approach

Socio-economic institutions are not fixed. Even though the intrinsic nature of capitalism—monetary-production economy—does not change, the ways in which it operates have changed dramatically over time and this has some important implications for its stability. Minsky developed his own analysis of the evolution of capitalism based on the changes in the role of finance in the economy. Thus, while Minsky's FIH is usually interpreted as a theory of the business cycle, he also developed a theory of the long-term transformation of the economy (Minsky 1986a, 1990c, 1992a, 1992b, 1992c, 1993a, 1993c; Minsky and Whalen 1996; Sen 2010; Wray 2008a, 2009; Whalen 1997, 2001).

The nineteenth century saw "Commercial Capitalism" where commercial banking dominated—banks made short-term commercial loans and issued deposits. Early in the twentieth century, Hilferding identified a new stage of capitalism—Finance Capitalism—characterized by complex financial relations and the domination of finance by investment banks that provided the finance for corporations (Hilferding 1910 [1981]).[3] He argued that the most characteristic feature of Finance Capitalism is rising concentration which, on the one hand, eliminates "free competition" through the formation of cartels and trusts, and on the other, brings financial capital and industrial capital into an ever more intertwined relationship (Hilferding 1910 [1981]: 21–22). Minsky also recognized this new stage of capitalism. Commercial Capitalism had been a stage in which firms used commercial banks to provide working capital (finance of production). However, plant and equipment had become so expensive that external finance of investment became necessary.[4] Thus, commercial banking was superseded by investment banking by the end of the nineteenth century. This fundamentally changed the nature of capitalism in a manner that made it much more unstable. Indeed, external finance of investment is a prior commitment of future profits. This creates the possibility of default and bankruptcy—the concerns of Minsky—while at the same time it opens the door for separation of ownership from control.

The financial structure became riskier. In addition, by the late 1920s, these big investment houses were mostly financing speculation in financial assets, particularly in equities issued by subsidiary trusts of the investment banks themselves. In truth, these were little more than pyramid schemes—speculating in essentially worthless shares, much like the infamous schemes of Charles Ponzi or the modern day Bernie Madoff. Goldman Sachs played a prominent role in the scams of the period, and warranted a whole chapter in the best account of the 1929 "Great Crash" by economist John Kenneth Galbraith. According to Minsky, the Great Depression marks the failure of Finance Capitalism.

The U.S. emerged from World War Two with a new form of capitalism, "managerial welfare-state capitalism" in which financial institutions were constrained by New Deal reforms, and with large oligopolistic corporations that financed investment mostly out of retained earnings. Private sector debt was small, but government debt left over from war finance was large—providing safe assets for households, firms, and banks. This system was financially robust, unlikely to experience deep recession. However, the relative stability of the first few decades after World War Two encouraged ever-greater risk-taking as the financial system was transformed into "Money Manager Capitalism," where the dominant financial players are "managed money"—lightly regulated "shadow banks" like pension funds, hedge funds, sovereign wealth funds, and university endowments—with huge pools of funds in search of the highest returns. Innovations by financial engineers encouraged growth of private debt relative to income, and increased reliance on volatile short-term finance.

There are many aspects to this transformation, and Minsky was certainly not the only one to notice it. Some called it "casino capitalism," others called it "patrimonial capitalism," many identified it as "financialization" (Strange 1986; Aglietta 1998, 2000; Epstein 2005; Coriat *et al.* 2006; Boyer 2000; van Treeck 2009; Foster and Magdoff 2009; Hein *et al.* 2009; Crotty 2009; Guttman 2008). In important respects, Money Manager Capitalism was similar to Hilferding's Finance Capitalism—with what were called "nonbank banks," or "shadow banks," rising to challenge the commercial banks. This book will study these trends in detail. The central point here is that the changes were not random; instead they were the result of internal dynamics of capitalism.

Broad policy implications

Following Keynes, Minsky argued that unfair distribution, economic instability, and unemployment are structural problems of market economies, and so he promoted a form of capitalism that significantly involves the "big government." Appropriate government policies can tame the instability of capitalism and redirect some of the productive potential toward fulfilling the needs of a nation. However, a set of policies also generates its own problems and the efficacy of a given set of regulatory measures erodes over time and may end up creating instability. As such, "there is no final solution to the problems of organizing economic life" (Minsky 1975a: 168) and capitalism requires a constant government involvement in order to make sure to have an economy "where freedom to innovate and to finance is the rule" (Minsky 1993b: 81).

Minsky was for establishing a big government (i.e., a large enough federal/national government) and a big bank (i.e., a central bank), and he promoted specific policies in order to intervene continuously over the business cycle, rather than sporadically during downturns and upturns. However, not all government intervention is good and the quality of spending matters as much as the quantity of spending and intervention. In addition, a big government and big bank come with their own set of challenges that need to be tackled. Finally, all the following recommendations presume that a monetarily sovereign government is in place so that it has the fiscal and monetary flexibility necessary to achieve the goals (Wray 2012).

Economic stabilization

The first role of the government (here taken in the broad sense to include the central bank) is to promote economic stability. Aside from proper regulation and supervision, stabilization comes through the cash-flow and balance-sheet impacts of governmental activities. In terms of cash flows, government expenditures and transfers provide some income to the private sector. The Keynesian multiplier is a common way to present the direct and indirect income impacts, but Kalecki's profit equation is more insightful to show the direct impact of government spending and taxing on the private sector. In terms of balance sheets, a monetarily sovereign government injects default-free liquid assets into the private sector as it spends. Government deficits also indirectly help to sustain asset prices that depend on the discounted value of expected future profits (that partly depend on current profits). Finally, the government also directly helps to sustain asset prices by acting as a lender of last resort whenever necessary. Effectively, the central bank establishes a floor price as it lends against discountable assets.

The main question then becomes to figure out how big the government should be. According to Minsky, the government should be big enough to ensure that it can stabilize the economy. In terms of macroeconomic policy, a rough idea of the appropriate size of the federal government is the size of aggregate investment relative to GDP. Given that investment is the most volatile component of GDP, government spending and taxes should be at least as big as the share of investment in GDP to be able to compensate for upward and downward swings, and so to stabilize the aggregate level of profit and so employment in the private sector.

If a big government is able to stabilize the system—a desirable property that a small government does not have—it also creates new problems. Indeed, by becoming too big it may generate inflationary tendencies, promote moral hazard, and dampen entrepreneurship.

In terms of inflationary potential, a big government can contribute to inflation by raising the wages of its employees, or the prices it pays for goods and services, too fast, by increasing spending too fast on goods and services, and by having a tax structure that contributes to a fast increase in corporate income taxes. Transfer payments may create additional inflationary pressures by growing disposable wage income and disposable net profit too fast. In addition, a big government in which political discretion over economic issues is high may prevent government spending and taxes from moving up or down as necessary to prevent inflation or recession. Finally, if the government mainly focuses its spending on defense and other unproductive expenditures, there is a greater chance that a big government will be inflationary (Han and Mulligan 2008).

In terms of potential moral hazard, by providing a safety net the government may achieve short-term stability at the expense of long-term instability. A first moral hazard is the tendency for businesses to take too many risks knowing that the government will rescue most of them in time of crisis. A second moral hazard is the potential decrease in labor force participation, especially if there are substantial income losses from going back into the work force and giving up transfer payments, which may affect production capacities of the country and so may compound the potential inflationary pressures over the long term.

In terms of entrepreneurship, a too tight control of the economy may remove the fun from entrepreneurship by limiting choices and constraining possibilities. As Keynes noted, investment activity is highly uncertain and risky, but uncertainty is also a factor that promotes investment by leaving some space for human creativity and imagination. Minsky was aware of this and noted that:

> Federal Reserve policy therefore needs to continuously "lean against" the use of speculative and Ponzi finance. But Ponzi finance is a usual way of debt-financing investment in process in a capitalist society. Consequently, capitalism without financial practices that lead to instability may be less innovative and expansionary; lessening the possibility of disaster might very well take part of the spark of creativity out of the capitalist system.
>
> (1986a: 328)

Overall, therefore, the government has to make sure to provide sound financing methods while also promoting a dynamic economy that can respond to the needs of society.

Structural policies

In order for the government to be able to intervene continuously over the cycle, it should put in place structural *macroeconomic*[5] programs that directly manage the labor force, pricing mechanisms, and investment projects, and should constantly monitor financial developments. Because these programs would be permanent and structural, rather than discretionary and specific to one administration, they would be highly isolated from the political cycle and political deliberations. Where politicians would have a way to influence long-term trends in government activities is by influencing the existing structural programs and creating new ones. In addition, policy makers would manage the goal directly, rather than indirectly through interest-rate manipulation, tax incentives, or indirect spending. All this eliminates problems of lags, credibility, and time inconsistency. However, this does not mean that the government should apply a rule blindly when implementing its policy; discretion is still possible within each program to make sure that it works best. For example, Social Security is a structural program but government employees still have large discretion to determine if someone qualifies for benefits. As shown below and Chapter 5, the same applies to the programs put forward by Minsky, in which human discretion is still possible within the set of rules and structures.

A first element that should not be determined by market mechanisms is the level of employment. Minsky promoted the creation of an "employer of last resort" (ELR), i.e., universal government employment programs similar to those of the 1930s. The programs would be permanent and decentralized, and would employ at a uniform wage (plus benefits) anybody willing and able to work, and would take individuals as they are, where they are. Recently, this program has attracted growing attention and it has been applied in a limited way in Argentina (Tcherneva and Wray 2007; Wray 2007; Kaboub 2008; Harvey 1999, 2000, 2011; Fullwiler 2007). There are several benefits to this program. First, by fixing the base wage at which one is employed, the program would help to keep in check the growth of the average wage rate, which can be a source of inflation. In addition, this program tends to eliminate the inflationary tendency of the existing welfare and unemployment insurance programs that provide an income even though no current economic contribution to society is made.[6] By contrast, ELR workers would contribute to the growth of the economy and help to sustain the productivity of workers; the latter is essential to maintain their employability by the private sector. Second, by acting as an income buffer for those who lost their jobs in the private sector, the program would act as an automatic stabilizer. This is a good way to eliminate lags and to limit political interests in fiscal activism because G and T would move automatically with the number of people employed in the ELR programs. Employment in the program would swing against the business cycle, and so would the national government budget. Third, this program would also contribute to a more harmonious society by decreasing income inequalities (the ELR wage would be a living wage), and by lowering crimes and other negative consequences (many of them non-monetary but socially significant) induced by unemployment.

A second element of the economy that should be controlled is the level and composition of investment. The government should socialize investment by fixing the reward received by entrepreneurs, and by allocating resources toward the most socially needed investment projects. This does not mean that all individual decisions would be removed because the government could just bring forward the areas that need investment and let the private companies propose solutions. The government (or special local committees including government representatives) would select the most appropriate projects without necessarily undertaking their construction or removing ownership from the private sector

(Keynes 1936: 378ff.; 1937b). The government could also leave frivolous investment projects to the private sector while housing, infrastructure, and other social needs would be supervised and funded by government. Minsky's proposal for community development banks is part of this project. The goals of this policy are threefold. First, investment projects would be allocated to sectors that need them; this would help to broadly improve level of development and living standards, and so would contribute to economic stability and well-being. Second, the proposal would help to promote financial stability because the positive macroeconomic feedback loop between investment and profit would be attenuated. Finally, given that the growth of investment may contribute to inflation, the socialization of investment would help to manage inflation. For example, the government could ramp up spending on public infrastructures in a slump and reduce it during expansion. This would require some form of planning ahead so that projects are ready to go when needed (Keynes 1937b).

A third element is the control of the growth of income through a generalized income policy. The ELR program and the socialization of investment already would help to control income growth by affecting the growth of wages and aggregate profit. Nevertheless, additional policies may be necessary that define general rules to respect in wage bargaining, as well as the pay-out ratios of firms. For example, Minsky proposed that the pay-out ratio of banks (percentage of profits paid in dividends) be controlled by regulators so that the retained earnings of banks do not grow too fast because this is a major cause of instability and inflation (Minsky 1975b; 1977a; 1986a: 234–238, 321). This policy has two essential benefits; the first one is to help to dampen inflationary pressures. Indeed, wage payments, interest payments, retained earnings, and other income payments may have an effect on inflation if they grow too fast (Tymoigne 2009). The second benefit is to promote financial stability by limiting the demand that stockholders can put on rates of returns that firms and banks should generate.

A fourth element that should be controlled is the growth and distribution of assets and liabilities of all financial institutions. The main way this should be addressed is by cash-flow-oriented regulation and supervision while also using a flexible capital requirement policy. Minsky, however, had a limited faith in the use of capital requirement, and preferred a much more proactive regulatory and supervisory framework focused on managing financial practices based on the needs for position-making operations (Minsky 1975c).

One may note that all these programs are coherently related and are meant to be permanent. They are not a patchwork of temporary discretionary policies. These programs are also largely independent of the political climate, and influence both production capacities and purchasing power. Their implementation would be done by government employees who would have some discretion within the rules set up by the programs. For example, an ELR worker may be fired if he or she does not perform, and, within the income policy, some sectors may be favored over others to encourage their development. Note also that the inflationary tendencies of a big government are constrained by controlling both public and private spending directly as well as indirectly. There is no doubt that all these programs will lead to changes in the behaviors of individuals and that unpredicted and unintended adverse consequences will appear, but these have to be dealt with as we go *and* in reaction to the changes in the structure of the economy. Again, there is no final solution to economic management in a society that is highly dynamic and that fosters individual decisions.

Conclusion

The Financial Instability Hypothesis is a rich theory founded on the premise that capitalism is a monetary-production economy. It aims at explaining what the sources of instability are in the capitalist economy and at deriving some policy implications. The core argument here is that market mechanisms push economic entities to behave in a financially unsustainable way in all good conscience even if they are of high morality, because yearning for monetary accumulation is necessary for their own economic survival:

> In this framework, crises are not due to the special characteristics of any institution; crisis-prone situations emerge out of the normal profit-seeking activities of borrowers and lenders [over periods of enduring expansion]. The shift in the financial posture of units from hedge to speculative (roll-over) and Ponzi (capitalizing of interest) characterizes the evolution from a robust financial structure, where most failures are due to idiosyncratic attributes, to a fragile one, where systemic conditions are responsible for a large number of failures.
>
> (Campbell and Minsky 1987: 25)

In addition, individuals may find comfort in the fact that in a boom everyone is taking on risk. Thus, the propensity for instability in the Financial Instability Hypothesis is not based on morality and "bad" behavior but one of systemic instability. Systemic instability can be further promoted by inadequate government regulation, supervision, and/or enforcement. Moreover, the interaction between private economic units and government may promote instability as profit-seeking actors innovate to bypass the barriers imposed by government, and the government does not react quickly enough to account for innovations.

2 From Managerial Capitalism to Money Manager Capitalism

Capitalism is a constantly evolving economic system that has gone through different stages, each characterized by an identifiable financial structure. The 1970s were
marked by changes that led to the emergence of a new form of capitalism—Money
Manager Capitalism (MMC)—in which money managers (pension funds, mutual
funds, hedge funds, brokers and dealers, and other portfolio managers) and the financial sector in general have played an unusually central role in the dynamics of
the economy. This new stage of capitalism is more prone to financial instability
because of its focus on capital gains as the central means to validate a heavy reliance on debt; that is, MMC not only promotes indebtedness but also collateral-
based lending over income-based lending. As a consequence, the dangerous
dynamics presented in the previous chapter will occur more frequently and rapidly,
and fast rising asset prices are a core requirement for this stage of capitalism to
perform well. This chapter explains what promoted the emergence of MMC and
presents its essential characteristics. It shows that the Minskian framework can help
us to understand the economic dynamics of the past sixty years.

The emergence of MMC was not an accident; it was the outgrowth of the
changes that occurred during the postwar stability of Managerial Capitalism.
This stability created dynamics that led economic units to take more risks on the
asset and liability sides of their balance sheet, and also made them more inclined
to trust the guidance of market mechanisms in economic affairs. Thus,

> a clear path of deterioration is discernible over the recent years, in part
> because of policies such as those which Reagan and Thatcher exemplify, in
> part because of the way in which protracted success leads to an acceptance
> of commitments to pay which erode the margins of safety that make capital-
> ist firms and financial institutions resilient.
>
> (Minsky 1994b: 21)

Prior to the 1970s: Managerial Capitalism

Characteristics of Managerial Capitalism

Managerial Capitalism emerged out of the Great Depression, and its set up was
such that an economic state prevailed that was characterized by stable high

economic growth and shared prosperity. Indeed, the twenty-five years following World War Two were called the "Golden Age" of capitalism. While that period was far from perfect, Minsky was of the opinion that "it might very well be a practical best" for capitalism (Minsky 1994b: 21).

Prior to the Great Depression, Finance Capitalism prevailed in the United States. It was characterized by a small government, little regulation of banking and finance (or anything else), and growing income and wealth inequalities. As a consequence, the economy was much more financially unstable and recorded numerous, frequent, and prolonged economic contractions (Pollin and Dymski 1994; De Long and Summers 1988). From 1931, the size of government spending progressively grew and, with the New Deal, a new stage of capitalism progressively emerged that more heavily involved the federal government in macroeconomic and regulatory affairs. Partly due to this involvement, the distribution of income and wealth narrowed and real income grew across all income categories. A broad range of households benefited from the prosperity and were able to increase and maintain their standard of living without recourse to debt. Finally, banking and finance were at the service of the rest of the economy and, while consumerism was strong, bankers did not entice households and companies to use a lot of leverage to improve their economic well-being. Bankers' profitability rested on a careful examination of the creditworthiness of borrowers and the establishment of long-term recurring relationships, rather than the aggressive expansion of their market by increasing debt loads.

Beyond the structure of banking and government, other important characteristics of Managerial Capitalism are the structure of the labor market and the politico-economic environment. We will not spend much time on these characteristics because they are not the focus point of the Minskian framework; however, they are important to explain the relative stability and shared prosperity of Managerial Capitalism. In terms of the labor market, union membership was at its peak in the United States in the 1950s with about a third of the employed and a quarter of the labor force in a labor union (Mayer 2004; Troy 1965). Union power was strengthened by limited globalization that prevented companies from finding a cheaper labor force abroad that could perform the same type of work. Finally, socialist countries were setting an example in which the workers had been treated decently since the early 1920s (at least it seemed so), which gave an incentive to businesses and governments to fulfill some of the demands of workers in capitalist countries. Taken together, these characteristics made Managerial Capitalism more prone to shared prosperity.

Big government and big bank

With the emergence of Managerial Capitalism, the economy became much more stable (Figure 2.1, Table 2.1). Recessions still occurred but they were much milder and shorter, and their frequency declined markedly. On average, postwar recessions have occurred every six years instead of every four years and the average size of decline in real gross national product (GNP) has been around

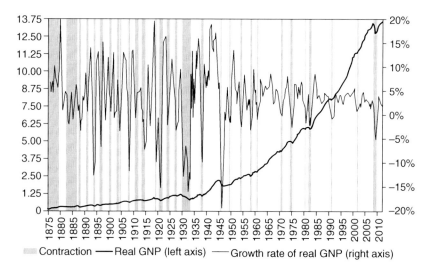

Contraction ⎯ Real GNP (left axis) ⎯⎯ Growth rate of real GNP (right axis)

Figure 2.1 Real gross national product of the United States, 1875–2010 (trillions of dollars, base: 2005) (sources: National Bureau of Economic Research (NBER); Gordon (1986); BEA).

1.8 percent instead of 5.8 percent prior to World War Two. In addition, the volatility of the growth rate declined markedly both on the upside and the downside, even though the growth rate has been about the same.

The decline in economic volatility was also accompanied by a decline in financial instability. Not only were financial crises less numerous during the postwar era but they were also milder. Bordo *et al.* (2001) show that, worldwide, the period 1945–1971 was a period of financial stability that recorded short and mild crises, mostly currency crises. They also note that the average duration of a crisis was 1.8 years, compared to around 2.5 years before and after the Golden Age (1945–1971). Finally, the authors show that the average cumulative decline

Table 2.1 Economic activity before and after the big government era

	Number of contractions	Average frequency (year)	Average length (month)	Average value of declines in real GNP	Average growth rate of real GNP	Average std. dev. of real GNP
1880–1939	16	3.8	19.1	−5.82%	3.15%	7.47%
1947–2010	11	5.8	11.1	−1.78%	3.23%	2.77%

Sources: see Figure 2.1.

Note
Average value of declines is based on all negative annualized growth rates recorded during each period even if there was no recession.

in real gross domestic product (GDP) during a financial crisis was 5.2 percent between 1945 and 1971, compared to 11.6 percent from 1880 to 1939 and around 8 percent after 1973.

In the United States, this economic and financial stability was achieved in large part because of the establishment of a big government and a big bank from 1933:

> The successful Capitalisms of the 1950's and 1960's are not the same as the failed Capitalisms of the 1930's. In general the 1930's system was a small government, gold standard constrained and essentially laissez faire capitalism. It was replaced by a big government, flexible central bank and interventionist capitalism. [...] The big government capitalisms that were put in place in response to the great collapse of 1929–33 [to protect] the economy from a severe fall in aggregate profits, such as occurred in the great contraction of 1929–33. This makes the collapse of asset values, which was so critical to the great collapse, impossible.
>
> (Minsky 1993d: 11–12)

Prior to 1933, the Federal Reserve operated under a gold standard domestically and externally, and it was constrained in its discounting operations by the Real Bills Doctrine. From March 1933 to January 1934, several Executive Orders, later made permanent by the Gold Reserve Act of 1934, removed any obligation to convert U.S. currency into gold on demand, and forbade any contractual clause requiring final payment in gold (U.S. Senate 1934: 63–64). In addition, the Glass–Steagal Act of 1932 ended the Real Bills Doctrine by allowing any economic unit access to the Discount Window, and by allowing the latter to accept any type of collateral (Section 13.3 of the Federal Reserve Act). The 1932 Act also allowed the Federal Reserve to provide uncollateralized advances of funds to banks if necessary (Section 10A of the Federal Reserve Act). By making the U.S. dollar an inconvertible currency domestically, and by broadening the powers of the Federal Reserve, the United States acquired more, but not full,[1] monetary sovereignty and so acquired more financial flexibility to promote economic and financial stability.

In addition to a big bank, a big government was also created through a large increase in federal expenditures and purchases. At first, this was first done reluctantly and as an emergency policy from 1933 to 1946 and, prior to World War Two, Roosevelt always tried to find means to reduce the size of the involvement of the federal government and ways to end New Deal programs:

> [Roosevelt] was embarrassed by Republican criticism of the budget deficits under the New Deal. He justified them by arguing that it was only extraordinary spending for humanitarian reasons that unbalanced the budget [...]. He looked for ways to show that deficits were being scaled down so that he could promise a balanced budget for fiscal 1938. [...] In 1936, an election year, he was even prepared to cut spending on the Civilian Conservation Corps.
>
> (Badger 1989: 111)

Thus, while Managerial Capitalism in the United States has its roots in the New Deal macroeconomic and regulatory policies, Managerial Capitalism did not reach maturity until after World War Two. Afterwards, the size of federal government spending in the economy grew above 10 percent of GDP, and its macroeconomic stabilization mission was institutionalized through the passage of the Full Employment Act of 1946 and the establishment of the Council of Economic Affairs. In addition, the Social Security Act of 1935 and later amendments put the federal government in charge of helping individuals to deal with the unavailability of, and inability to, work. This involvement was, however, rather different from the New Deal, and had to do with fine-tuning the economy and providing income guarantee instead of job guarantee by directly and indirectly hiring persons willing to work but unable to do so.

The size of the federal government purchases increased quite dramatically from 2.5 percent of GDP in 1929 to about 12 percent of GDP from 1946 to 1970. The increase is even more dramatic if one includes transfers and other payments made by the federal government that averaged about 18 percent of GDP from 1946 to 1970. At the same time, the relative size of the federal government doubled relative to state and local governments. Prior to the Great Depression, only around 20 to 30 percent of government spending was done at the federal level; after World War Two around 50 to 60 percent of government spending was done at the federal level (Figures 2.2 and 2.3).

As explained in the previous chapter, this larger involvement was crucial to promote economic stability through the cash-flow and balance-sheet impacts of a big government and a big bank. In addition to larger involvement in the stabilization of the economy, federal authorities increased their regulatory and supervisory involvement. This was necessary not only to avoid the fraudulent and dangerous economic practices that occurred in the 1920s, but also to prevent the emergence of moral hazard. Indeed, a larger involvement of the federal government meant that the possibility of serious economic disasters of the size of the Great Depression became improbable. As a consequence, private economic units could take more risk on both sides of their balance sheet, because they knew that the federal authorities would intervene in case of macroeconomic problems. To prevent, or at least limit, the growth of moral hazard, the 1930s regulatory framework regulated financial markets and banking more tightly, and numerous federal regulatory agencies were created (the Securities and Exchange Commission and the Federal Deposit Insurance Corporation are among them).

Finally, the federal government became more involved in the development of the U.S. economy through government programs such as the Federal Housing Administration, the Federal National Mortgage Association ("Fannie Mae"), Veteran Affairs, the Small Business Administration, and many other government agencies. The federal government was also more involved in the development of the infrastructure of the United States, first via the New Deal programs and then through annual budget appropriations. These programs significantly contributed to the widespread improvement of the well-being of the

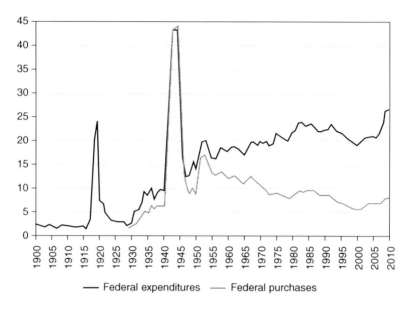

— Federal expenditures   — Federal purchases

Figure 2.2 Federal expenditures and purchases as a percentage of GDP, 1900–2010 (sources: BEA; Historical Statistics of the United States).

Note
Federal expenditures include federal purchases, interest payments, transfers and subsidies, and other miscellaneous items less consumption of fixed capital. Federal purchases are composed of purchases of goods and services for consumption and investment purposes.

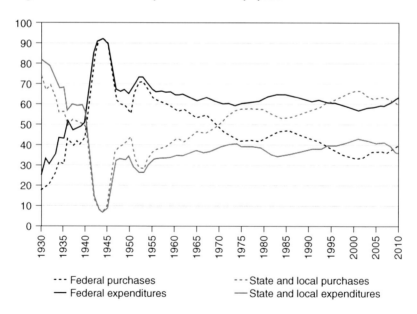

    - - - Federal purchases   - - - State and local purchases
    — Federal expenditures   — State and local expenditures

Figure 2.3 Relative size of federal and state and local governments purchases (%) (source: BEA).

U.S. population by promoting homeownership, electrification, water access, and access to credit at preferential conditions that were favorable to business creation and education, among others.

Commitment banking model

Besides big government and big bank, a major characteristic of Managerial Capitalism is the prevalence of a specific business model in banking that helped to reinforce the stability provided by macroeconomic policies, federal development programs, and federal regulation and supervision. This model is the product of the 1930s regulatory framework that considered the payments system a public utility. As such depository institutions were seen as too crucial to be involved in a highly competitive industry, and were protected on both their asset side and liability side by compartmentalization and access to stable and low-cost credit lines at the Federal Reserve. Given the regulatory framework and market structure, the incentive of banks was to develop long-term recurring relationships with existing customers, and to grow their customer base carefully by checking the creditworthiness of potential borrowers. Once they granted advances of funds, the promissory notes of the borrowers stayed on the balance sheet of banks until the advances were fully repaid.

This commitment business model—sometimes also called the 3-6-3 model (pay 3 percent on deposits, charge 6 percent on advances, and hit the golf course at 3 p.m.) or the originate-and-hold model—promoted economic stability in several ways. First, it promoted a careful underwriting of loans, which tremendously helped loan officers to improve their expertise in judging the reliability of a project and to tame the expectations of entrepreneurs. Second, the willingness to commit to business relations for an extended period of time, and on a recurring basis, meant that banks had an intimate knowledge of the projects they financed, and they developed a strong relationship with their customers. As a consequence, banks were aware of what their clients were doing and, through covenants and codicils, could make sure that the projects were implemented in the way described in contracts. Third, given that the profitability of banks rested on the success of their clients, banks were more than eager to find solutions in case of problems. Loan modifications were done in the most mutually beneficial way in order to make sure that the advances got repaid and that both parties were winners. This was all the more easy to do since banks retained the outstanding contracts, which made legal matters easier to work out for the best interests of both the banks and clients.

Given the limited competition, appropriate regulation, and careful business practices centered on performing as a going concern, depository institutions thrived. Table 2.2 shows that, relative to the period of MMC, during the Golden Age the gross saving of depository institutions grew at a slower but steadier pace. The number of failures and assistances was also dramatically smaller—around four failures and assistances per year versus 113 during MMC—and represented only 2.8 percent of all failures and assistances that occurred between 1945 and 2010.

Table 2.2 Gross saving and failures of depository institutions

	U.S. depository institutions (%)	Credit unions (%)	Commercial banks (%)
Gross saving, average growth rate			
1945–1971	8.2	15.1	9.1
1982–2010	24.0	14.1	11.7
Gross saving, std. deviation			
1945–1971	15.1	20.1	16.4
1982–2010	225.8	31.2	26.1
Insured bank failures and assistances	*Number (% of total)*		*Yearly average*
1945–1971	100 (2.8)		3.7
1982–2010	3,266 (93.5)		112.6

Sources: Board of Governors of the Federal Reserve System, Federal Deposit Insurance Corporation.

Note
Gross saving is defined as undistributed profit plus consumption of fixed capital.

Achievements of the Golden Age

Beyond the data already presented about stability, the Golden Age of Managerial Capitalism was a dynamic period of great economic achievements. Figure 2.4 shows that the U.S. economy recorded a high growth rate averaging 5 percent from the early 1950s. The growth of real GDP per capita was also at its highest level with an average growth rate of 0.91 percent from 1950 to 1973 during periods of expansion (Table 2.3). Government spending was one of the sources of economic growth, but most of the economic expansion came from a mix of domestic private investment and consumption. Between 55 and 60 percent of economic growth came from the growth of private domestic consumption.

Given the rapid and sustained expansion of economic activity and the limited financial instability, businesses were thriving. The number of business failures during the Golden Age was at historical lows averaging about 0.4 percent annually between 1946 and 1970, which is less than half as much as any other period of time—when the average is close to 1 percent. When companies did fail, the impact on creditors was probably limited because their inflation-adjusted indebtedness was low relative to historical standards, especially before 1965 (Figure 2.5). In addition, given the predominance of the originate-and-hold banking model, the quality of the leverage was strong.

The more stable business environment was accompanied by a rapid improvement in the standard of living of the population and a general decrease in

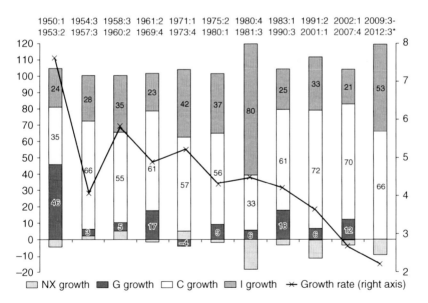

Figure 2.4 Real GDP growth and its sources over periods of expansion (%) (sources: BEA; NBER).

Note
* means that the expansion is ongoing.

Table 2.3 Average growth rate of real GDP per capita during periods of expansion (%)

1950:1 1953:2	1954:3 1957:3	1958:3 1960:2	1961:2 1969:4	1971:1 1973:4	1975:2 1980:1	1980:4 1981:3	1983:1 1990:3	1991:2 2001:1	2002:1 2007:4	2009:3 2012:3
1.28	0.47	1.07	0.91	0.83	0.72	0.48	0.80	0.58	0.42	0.48

Sources: see Figure 2.2.

poverty. Thanks to strong unions, limited international labor competition, and the geo-political set up, individuals were able to capture some of the benefits of higher labor productivity by demanding better working conditions, paid vacations, better benefits, on-the-job training, and many other elements that improved the quality of life of workers in and out of their job environment (Barkin 1974). A big government contributed significantly to this improvement through its commitment—albeit limited—to full employment and its involvement in the economic development of the country.

While existing datasets about average working hours do not give a consistent signal, the average weekly hours of work in non-agricultural occupations declined by about three hours—from forty hours to thirty-seven hours—from 1948 to the mid 1970s and stagnated until the end of the 1990s (Figure 2.6). Productivity in nonfarm businesses grew constantly allowing workers to perform the same tasks in less time. The real hourly compensation grew on average at the

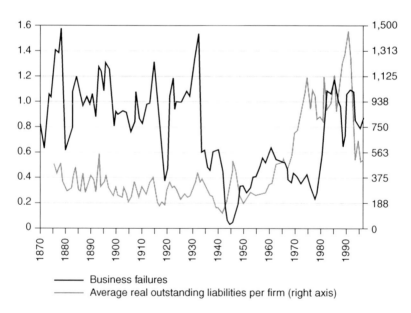

——— Business failures
——— Average real outstanding liabilities per firm (right axis)

Figure 2.5 Business failures (%) and their average outstanding real liability (thousands in 2005 dollars), 1870–1997 (source: Historical Statistics of the United States).

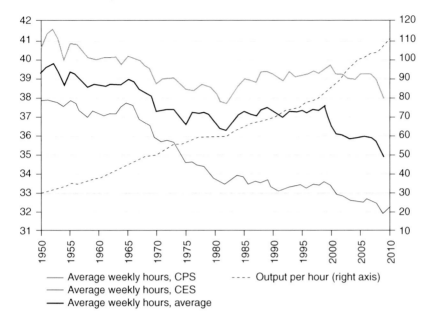

Figure 2.6 Average weekly hours and labor productivity, nonfarm occupations (index 2005 = 100) (source: BLS).

Note
There are two datasets at the Bureau of Labor Statistics (BLS) that compute the average weekly hours, the current population survey (CPS) for the non-agricultural sector and the current establishment survey (CES) for the nonfarm business sector. Levels and trends are different given the scope and definition of each survey (Frazis and Stewart 2010). Labor productivity comes from the CES.

same pace as the average productivity of labor from 1948 to 1970 (Table 2.4). All this gave individuals, the material and financial means to devote more time to their families, leisure, community involvement, and other desired activities.

The family median real income doubled for all families in the span of twenty years and went from $25,000 to $50,000 on average during the Golden Age (Figure 2.7). Even families with only one income earner saw their income double over that period of time from $20,000 to $40,000. Figure 4.4 (Chapter 4) shows that homeownership grew from 45 percent of the population after World War

Table 2.4 Average difference between the growth of real hourly compensation and the growth rate of labor productivity, nonfarm businesses (percentage points)

	Average	Std. dev.
1948Q1–1970Q4	0.003	3.614
1983Q1–2007Q4	−1.053	3.434

Source: Bureau of Labor Statistics.

Two to about 64 percent by 1968. Since that time improvements in homeowner-ship rates have only been marginal. Income inequalities decreased until the end of the 1960s and the poverty rate declined by ten percentage points from 19 to 9 percent of the U.S. population living in poverty (Figure 2.8). The reader may note that a significant decline in the poverty rate occurs before the implementa-tion of the "War on Poverty" policy by Johnson in 1964, so shared prosperity was a central source of improvement in the economic condition of the popula-tion. A central component of this shared prosperity was the expansion of Social Security benefits to the aged as well as black population moving to the northeast (Bell and Wray 2004).

Overall, the set up of Managerial Capitalism was designed to promote stability and shared prosperity. An essential element that contributed to the Golden Age was the presence of a big federal government in terms of the size and composition of spending, progressive tax structure, and regulation and supervision. Through regulation, it shaped the structure of the banking industry and transformed it into a routine business that was very effective at judging the creditworthiness of borrowers. Through spending and taxes, the government was able to sustain the aggregate income and net worth of households and businesses, and so to provide a more stable environment to make economic decisions. This created a virtuous circle that allowed private spending to sustain economic activ-ity without resorting to rising debt burdens; hedge finance prevailed. Labor

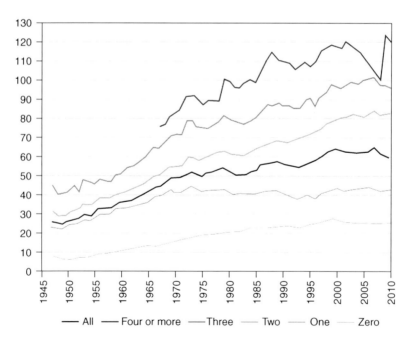

Figure 2.7 Family median real income by number of earners (thousands, 2010 dollars) (source: U.S. Census Bureau).

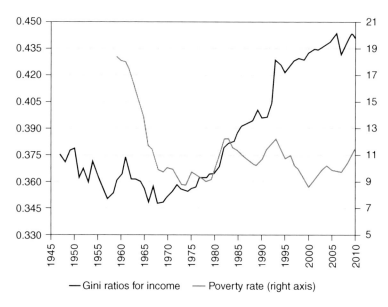

Figure 2.8 Income inequality and rate of poverty of families (source: U.S. Census Bureau).

unions were able to make sure that this virtuous circle benefited the greatest share of the population possible. Similar trends are observed in other developed countries during that period of time.

Transition to MMC: flaws and dynamics of Managerial Capitalism

While the Golden Age period of Managerial Capitalism was a time of great socio-economic achievements, it also set the stage for a rise in the financial fragility of the U.S. economy, and, from the late 1960s, the frequency and size of financial crises progressively increased. In addition, the characteristics that made the Golden Age stable were also prone to eventually generate economic instability in terms of inflationary pressures. The return of economic and financial instability marked the end of the Golden Age and a period of transition to MMC. In this subsection, some of the most important factors that led to the return of instability are analyzed.

Psychological and economic aspects

Thanks to government finance during World War Two, financial institutions started the Golden Age with highly liquid balance sheets containing mostly safe government securities. However, as the Golden Age proceeded, banks sought ways to make profits by gradually taking more risk on their asset and liability sides.

On the asset side, the Golden Age encouraged financial institutions to expand their market in order to maintain their profitability. Homeownership rate grew and the financing gap of business also increased; thereby creating an opportunity for banks to expand their business. As a consequence the proportion of default-free liquid assets (federal government debt) declined, and was progressively replaced by illiquid and default-prone assets from the private nonfinancial sector. Figure 2.9 shows the dramatic decline in the proportion of liquid assets from 65 percent in 1945 to 10 percent of financial assets by the 1970s. The decline in the proportion of liquid assets meant that the capacity of banks to absorb shocks induced by credit risk, interest-rate risk, and other types of risks declined while the size of these risks grew.

On the liability side, financial institutions had to innovate in order to be able to keep up with the expansion of their assets. Until the mid 1950s, the quantity of Treasuries on their asset side was large enough to serve as a refinancing source at the Discount Window. However, the supply of Treasuries did not keep up with the needs of banks because the federal government ran mostly a balanced budget during the Golden Age. Thus, the size of government securities in their balance sheet became too small to sustain their refinancing operations, and so banks innovated by reviving the Federal Funds market and, later on, by developing new instruments like negotiable certificates of deposit, repurchase agreements, and the Eurodollar market (Minsky 1957, 1983a). As a consequence, the proportion of borrowed funds (that is liabilities other than deposits) of FDIC-insured commercial banks grew constantly from the early 1960s from a

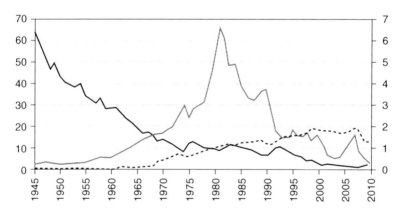

— Ratio of liquid assets to financial assets, %
--- Ratio of borrowed funds to liabilities, %
— Interest paid relative to pre-tax net operating income, ratio (right axis)

Figure 2.9 Financial situation of commercial banks (sources: Federal Deposit Insurance Corporation; Board of Governors of the Federal Reserve System).

Note
The proportion of liquid asset is for all U.S.-chartered commercial banks. The two other series are for FDIC-insured commercial banks.

negligible amount to about 10 percent of their liabilities by 1980 (Figure 2.9). These innovations made the profitability of banks more dependent on the prevailing market conditions and put them in direct competition for refinancing sources. In addition, money market mutual funds emerged in the 1970s and provided higher rewards than those offered on deposits. As a consequence, the stable funding sources provided by depositors were disrupted and banks had to respond by providing better remuneration on their deposits and securities; however, they were limited in their capacity to do so by Regulation Q that set maximum interest rates on deposits and certificates of deposit. Regulators responded by raising the maximum rate that could be paid on deposits and securities, but this was only a temporary solution to deal with continuously rising short-term rates (Minsky 1969; Cargill and Garcia 1982; Wojnilower 1980).

The growth in the financial fragility of depository institutions was accompanied by rising financial fragility among nonfinancial businesses. From the mid 1960s, the financing gap of nonfinancial corporations was positive and grew almost continuously to reach $75 billion by 1980, which implies that they had to draw down their hoards and increasingly use external funds (Figure 2.10). Nonfinancial corporations became more dependent on the good functioning of capital markets, and their capacity to solve liquidity problems on their own declined with the decline in the amount of liquid safe assets and safe liabilities relative to

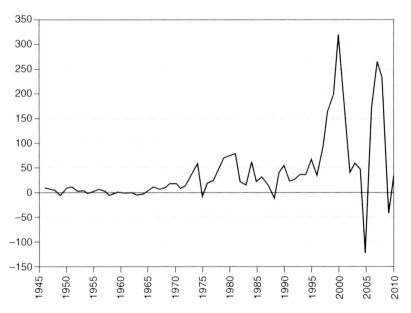

Figure 2.10 Financing gap of nonfarm nonfinancial corporate business (billions of dollars) (source: Board of Governors of the Federal Reserve System).

Note
The financing gap is the difference between capital expenditures less the sum of U.S. internal funds and IVA.

outstanding debts (Figure 2.11). The debt-to-income ratio of nonfinancial corporations was constant around ten from the mid 1950s to the mid 1960s. From
1965, the ratio rose to reach fifteen by the 1970s and 25 by 1980. The proportion
of short-term debts rose from 30 percent of outstanding debts in the early 1960s
to 35 to 40 percent by the 1970s. The ratio of interest payments to net operating
surplus grew dramatically from 15 percent in the 1960s to over 35 percent in the
1970s. Finally, the proportion of liquid assets relative to liabilities declined dramatically from 55 percent in 1945 to 10 percent in the 1970s. These trends can
be explained by the long period of economic stability that promoted a growth of
investment and increased the willingness to use external funds and to draw down
cash on hand to fund the growth of productive capacities.

Figure 2.12 illustrates that similar trends can be observed in the household
sector with a greater reliance on debt, an increase in the proportion of short-term
debts until the early 1970s, a decline in the proportion of liquid assets relative to
the amount of liabilities from the early 1950s until the mid 1960s. These trends
toward greater fragility can be explained largely by the growth of homeownership
after World War Two. Homeownership was promoted by long-term stability, rising
income, and government help via the creation of government institutions like the
Federal Housing Administration, the Veteran Administration, and the Federal
National Mortgage Administration. However, the quantity of liquid assets was still
greater than the amount of outstanding debts so the overall financial fragility of

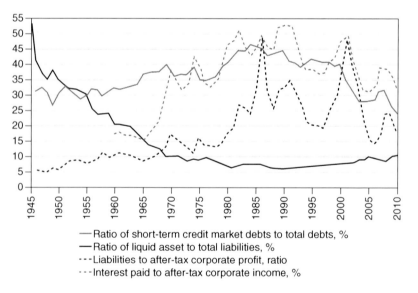

—— Ratio of short-term credit market debts to total debts, %
—— Ratio of liquid asset to total liabilities, %
--- Liabilities to after-tax corporate profit, ratio
--- Interest paid to after-tax corporate income, %

Figure 2.11 Financial situation of nonfinancial corporations (source: Board of Governors
of the Federal Reserve System).

Note
After-tax corporate income is equal to net operating surplus with IVA and CCadj plus property
income.

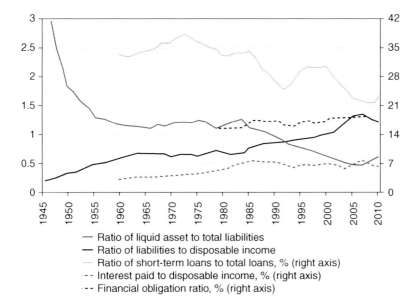

Figure 2.12 Financial situation of household sector (source: Board of Governors of the Federal Reserve System).

households was rather limited and hedge finance prevailed. A more important trend among households was the growing amount of savings induced by the period of prosperity. This generated large amounts of funds that needed to be managed and is a direct cause of the rise of money managers.

Overall, the major private sectors of the U.S. economy became more dependent on the continuous availability of external funding at a stable cost, and growingly dependent on the availability of short-term sources of funds. In a later chapter, the growing financial fragility of the U.S. economy will be measured more carefully, but the point here is that it did grow overtime during the Golden Age. That growth was reflected partly by the decline in the capacity to absorb shocks induced by risks on the asset and liability sides, while the size of those risks grew.

Beyond the changes in financing and funding methods that increased financial fragility, economic stability was threatened by the growth of inflation from the 1960s. The latter was generated by several factors. First, the unit labor cost grew rapidly as nominal hourly compensation started to grow much faster than average labor productivity (Figure 2.13). From the late 1960s through the 1970s, nominal hourly compensation grew annually in the 5 to 10 percent range while average labor productivity grew mostly in the 0 to 5 percent range. The rise in unit labor cost can be partly attributed to the growing demands by unions during the Golden Age. A long period of stability gave union leaders the belief that they were in a strong position to demand increases in nominal hourly compensation that outpaced the rise of labor productivity, which led to a rapid increase in the unit labor cost by the mid 1960s.

Second, inflation also had an external component with the double oil shocks of the 1970s that dramatically affected the cost of living of an oil-dependent economy like the United States (Figure 2.13). The growth rate of the personal consumption expenditure price index (PCE) was much higher than the growth rate of PCE less energy and food in 1974, 1979, and 1980. Figure 2.13 also shows that inflation and the growth rate of unit labor cost were closely correlated during the 1970s, which suggests that workers tried to get raises that could match inflationary pressures that were driven by energy, food, and shelter costs during the 1970s. This external source of inflation fueled the demands of workers in terms of nominal wage growth thereby creating a reinforcing feedback loop between unit cost of labor and inflation.

Finally, the federal government's purchases of goods and services was high but mostly focused on unproductive economic activities, which tends to promote inflation (Han and Mulligan 2008) (Figure 2.14). Thus, while the government did participate in the development of the economy, the government has mostly oriented its spending toward consuming economic resources since World War Two. The main government spending on goods and services since World War Two has been defense spending that represented around 80 percent of purchases by the government during the Golden Age. Beyond purchases of goods and services, transfers and entitlements are other types of government expenditures that tend to promote inflationary pressures by raising aggregate demand without adding to the productive capacity of the economy.

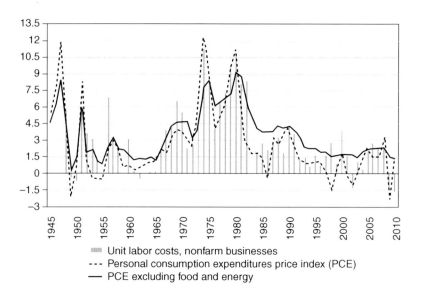

Figure 2.13 Growth rate of inflation, energy cost, and unit labor cost (%) (sources: BEA; BLS).

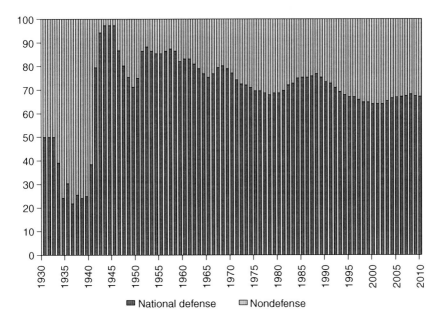

Figure 2.14 Composition of federal purchases of goods and services (%) (source: BEA, Table 2.9.5).

Rising inflation promoted financial instability in two ways. First, expectations of future inflation became engrained in the minds of economic agents and so made expected cash inflows (profit, salary, interest) more dependent on the realization of growing output prices rather than growing markets and productivity gains. This increased the volatility of cash inflows because it is well known that higher inflation is accompanied by a higher volatility of inflation. At the same time, debt contracts progressively included expectations of future inflation; thereby raising the expected size of cash outflows. Thus, while the growth of cash inflows became more volatile, debt commitments grew in size due to rising interest rates. Second, rapidly growing output prices refocused the policy agenda away from full employment toward inflation, and so made the central bank more prone to change its interest rates in response to inflation (Tymoigne 2009). This was especially damaging for financial institutions, like thrifts, that relied on a stable refinancing source to fund their positions in illiquid long-term debts (mostly mortgages).

Policy factors

Prolonged expansion promoted the use of leverage in the funding of economic activity. In addition, some government policies contributed to the growth of financial fragility during the Golden Age and set the stage for further instability during the Great Moderation. These policy elements can be divided into three categories; fine-tuning, inflation fighting, and the return of free-market ideology.

The big government that emerged out of World War Two was very different from the one initiated during the Great Depression. In the 1930s, the federal government was mostly involved in decentralized planning through institutions like the National Resources Planning Board. The Board was terminated in 1943 by Congress, but concerns about the need to plan the economy were still strong because of worries that the unemployment rate would go back to levels similar to the 1930s after the war. The 1945 Full Employment Bill tried to reinstate some form of planning by proposing to put in place a structural "last resort [...] program of federal spending and investment" (Bailey 1950: 13–14) in order to make sure that "all Americans able to work and seeking work have the right to useful, remunerative, regular, and full-time employment" (Section 2b of the Full Employment Bill of 1945, in Bailey 1950: 243). However, the Bill did not pass the House of Representatives and it was replaced by the Employment Act of 1946 that was substantially different from the 1945 Bill (Santoni 1986). Rather than guaranteeing the right to employment, the 1946 Act transformed the U.S. government into a full-fledged fine-tuner in order to make employment consistent with business interests:

> All that was assimilated from Keynes by the policy establishment and its clients was the analysis of an economy in deep depression and a policy tool of deficit financing. [...] Keynesian economics, even in the mind of the economics profession, but particularly in the view of politicians and the public, became a series of simple-minded guidelines to monetary and fiscal policy. [...] The institutional structure has not been adapted to reflect the knowledge that the collapse of aggregate demand and profits, such as occasionally occurred and often threatened to occur in pre-1933 small government capitalism, is never a clear and present danger in Big Government capitalism such as has ruled since World War II.
>
> (Minsky 1986a: 291, 295)

The Federal Reserve became more active in fine-tuning the economy from the early 1950s, even though the Federal Reserve was not created to fine-tune the economy but to promote financial stability via the provision of a stable refinancing source and banking supervision. The Treasury Accord of 1951 set the stage for a change in the mission of the Federal Reserve away from providing interest-rate stability toward fine-tuning the economy. The move toward fine-tuning paved the way for incoherent, discretionary programs, time inconsistency problems, and credibility problems, which ultimately led to the incapacity to manage both price stability and employment in the 1970s. There were no structural core policies put in place to deal with employment and price stability.

With the move toward fine-tuning, preoccupations about inflation progressively gained ground among policy makers and became a central concern in the

1970s. The volatility and level of the federal funds rate progressively increased from the mid 1950s to culminate during the Volcker experiment with an average federal funds rate well above 12 percent (Figure 2.15). This level and volatility were transferred to the rest of the interest rate structure; however, the regulatory reforms put in place in the 1930s required that a stable low-cost source of refinancing be available for depository institutions.

Combined with the growth of competition in the banking industry, the aggressive monetary policy was extremely adverse to the savings and loan industry and the rest of the depository institutions. The ratio of interest paid to operating income rose dramatically for commercial banks (Figure 2.9). At the beginning of the 1950s interest paid was about a quarter of operating income, but by 1980 interest paid was seven times bigger than operating income. The high and volatile policy rates of the Federal Reserve were directly responsible for this state of affairs and Federal Open Market Committee members were aware of the strains they put on the thrifts but decided to continue, which led to the first stage of the savings and loan crisis (Tymoigne 2009).

Finally, policy aspects contributed to instability through a progressive return of the free market thinking among policy makers. At the core of the culture of the United States is the idea that self-reliance and freedom of choice are to be promoted whenever possible. This idea was crushed during the Great Depression but a long period of economic stability progressively erased the memory of the past, and a new generation was brought up within the cultural environment of

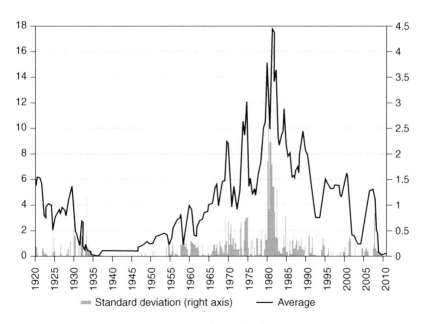

Figure 2.15 Federal funds rate, level, and volatility (%) (sources: Board of Governors of the Federal Reserve System; Federal Reserve Bank of New York).

the U.S. society. Combined with economic stability and the creation of political and institutional organization to promote free market thinking (Crockett 1995), the dismantling of the regulations put in place during the 1930s became a central theme of academic and political life from the 1970s. There was a growing push for deregulation in the financial industry, the labor market, health care, transportation, and many other areas of socio-economic life. This also led to a call for lesser involvement of the federal government in the economy and federal government purchases relative to GDP continuously declined from 12.6 percent in 1967 to 8.2 percent in 1979.

Money Manager Capitalism

The impact of all the previous changes was a progressive return of instability and a transition to a new form of capitalism. The first relevant financial crisis of the postwar period occurred in 1966 in the municipal bond market when thrifts had to sell their muni-bond positions following their incapacity to roll over their certificates of deposit because of the uncompetitive return they were allowed to provide under Regulation Q. This was followed by a rapidly growing list of crises in the 1970s and 1980s (Greider 1987; Wolfson 1994). The first clear expression of the failure of Managerial Capitalism was the savings and loans crisis, which showed that the old banking model was not adapted to the new economic environment characterized by volatile cost of funding, strong competition from shadow banks, and a large increase in retirement savings looking for high rates of returns.

In order to cope with growing volatility, depository institutions progressively changed their business model and demanded a leveled playing field with nonbank financial institutions. They demanded that their operations be deregulated and this demand fitted squarely with the change in the political atmosphere promoting a return of laissez-faire. Their demand was satisfied by the passage of the Depository Institution Deregulation and Monetary Control Act of 1980 and the Garn-St. Germain Depository Institutions Act of 1982. This set the second stage of the savings and loan crisis as their liability and asset structure changed dramatically, and deregulation led to massive frauds by Charles Keating and the like (Black 2005). The share of home mortgages in the assets held by savings institutions dropped from 60 percent in the late 1970s to 35 percent in 1987 and was replaced by riskier assets like mortgage-backed securities, commercial and multifamily residential mortgages, business loans, and corporate securities. On the liability side of savings and loan institutions, the share of small time deposits dropped from 90 percent in the late 1970s to 55 percent in 1987, and savings institutions relied more heavily on volatile sources of funds like large time deposits and repurchase agreements.

The emergence of neoliberalism, the change in banking structure, and the return of instability led to the emergence of a new form of capitalism characterized by securitization, globalization, financialization, deregulation, and desupervision. Minsky called this form of capitalism Money Manager Capitalism.

The characteristics of MMC

Neoliberalism: pro-business mentality, deregulation, and desupervision

The rise of neoliberalism impacted the economic system through several chan-nels. One was the decline in union membership and labor's influence, a second was the decline in the involvement of the government in economic activity, and a third was a return of the free-market ideology among regulators. A central implication of these trends has been a decline in the size and quality of govern-ment involvement, which has made the government less effective at stabilizing the economy. As explained in Chapter 1, big government and big bank are needed to promote the economic stability of capitalism so a return of laissez-faire meant a progressive return of instability. In addition, economic gains have been weaker and have not been shared by a majority of the population.

LABOR MARKET AND REAL WAGES

The return of free-market ideology and pro-business mentality, as well as the increase in the unemployment rate, led to a decline in the bargaining power of labor and stagnation in real wages. In the United States, labor union membership declined as unions came to be seen as selfish, racist, pro-war, and as a force destroying jobs rather than improving the quality of life of workers. The move to a service-based economy also played an important role in the decline in unioni-zation as those jobs are not unionized except for government jobs in state and local governments. Finally, globalization promoted an increase in competition among workers, pushed down the growth of wages, and promoted off-shoring to the countries with relatively lower labor costs.

As a consequence of the stagnation of real wages, the trend toward shared prosperity was destroyed, and poverty and inequality rose. Income inequality grew rapidly from the mid 1970s, and the poverty rate also rose and was higher throughout the 1980s and 1990s compared to the late 1960s and early 1970s (Figure 2.8). Western and Rosenfeld (2011) find that one-fifth to one-third of the increase in inequalities is due to the decline in union membership.

The rise in inequalities was accompanied by a stagnation of real income. On average, families had a stagnant income throughout the 1970s and real income grew only slightly from $50,000 to $60,000 from the early 1980s to the late 1990s before stagnating again throughout the 2000s (Figure 2.7). Families with only one income earner did not record any gain in real income since 1970 with a real income stuck at $40,000 for the past forty years. Table 2.4 confirms this trend by showing that real hourly compensation did not keep up with labor pro-ductivity and the annual growth of the former was on average one percentage point lower than the growth of the latter from the 1980s. The gains in labor pro-ductivity were passed instead to non-labor income like profit and interest.

Thus, compared to the Golden Age, the Great Moderation was a period of limited economic gains for the majority of the population and the prosperity that occurred during the Great Moderation was not a shared prosperity. This was all the more problematic that, over the course of MMC, economic growth slowed considerably with the annual growth rate of the real GDP declining from 4.5 to 2.5 percent. The same is true with real GDP per capita that only grew by around half a percent since 1980. One may argue that the slower growth rates recorded during the Great Moderation were due to the absence of significant recessions but the Great Recession did not result in a boost in economic growth; on the contrary, economic growth is still on a declining trend (Figure 2.4). In addition, the trend toward declining economic growth started in the 1970s and it was not reversed by the relatively severe recessions of the mid 1970s and early 1980s.

GOVERNMENT DISENGAGEMENT IN ECONOMIC ACTIVITY AND DEVELOPMENT

MMC is characterized by a marked decline of the involvement of the government in the economy. The purchase of goods and services by the federal government has declined dramatically since the mid 1980s and reached its lowest size relative to GDP in 2000 when it equaled 6 percent of GDP (Figure 2.2). Most of the burden of spending on goods and services has been transferred to state and local governments that are now responsible for 60 percent of this type of expenditure (Figure 2.3). In addition, the amount of investment in nondefense activities by all levels of government has declined significantly compared to the 1950s and 1960s (Figure 2.16).

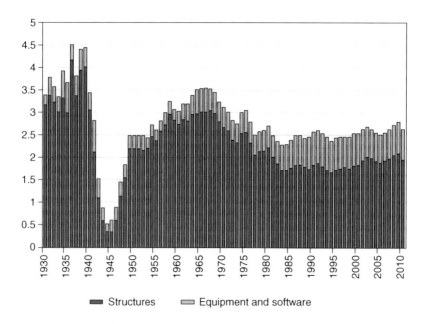

Figure 2.16 Gross investment in nondefense activities by government sector relative to GDP (%) (source: BEA).

While this type of expenditure was never very high relative to the size of the economy, investment on nondefense structures has represented only between 1.5 and 2 percent of GDP since 1980, compared to close to 2.5 to 3 percent during the Golden Age. The difference is even more staggering if one looks at the New Deal period when the same type of expenditure represented 3 to 4 percent of GDP.

Given the lack of commitment to the development of infrastructure during the MMC, and the unwillingness to provide enough funding to maintain the existing infrastructure, U.S. public infrastructure has degraded rapidly. The American Society of Civil Engineers has rated the state of infrastructures in the United States since 1988 and a notable decline in its adequacy has been recorded. Table 2.5 shows that since 1998, infrastructure has been graded D+ or below and the funds needed to restore existing infrastructure and to respond to the needs of the population have grown from $1.3 trillion in 2001 to $2.2 trillion in 2009. The consequence of this lack of commitment to infrastructures has been catastrophic, and numerous examples of bridge failures, water contamination, and airport congestion and near plane accidents have been reported. In addition, this lack of commitment negatively impacted the competitiveness of the United States and decreased access to reliable public infrastructure for the general population.

The government has also dropped the ball in terms of tax structure (steep decline in progressiveness), education (preference for loans over grants), welfare (preference for workfare), and many other aspects of economic life. It would take too long to go through them in detail; the essential point is that the U.S. government has been willing to become less involved in economic affairs and the improvement of the economic welfare of its population. As a consequence a larger share of the burden of improvement and maintenance of the standard of living has been put on the private sector, especially households.

PRO-MARKET REGULATORY PHILOSOPHY

The return of the free-market narrative has had a profound impact on the regulatory and supervisory system. Not only did the deregulatory wave that started in the financial industry at the beginning of the 1980s continue during the Great Moderation, but the philosophy of policy makers also changed dramatically and altered what regulators and supervisors could do given the political climate. Regulators and supervisors became more and more skeptical about the usefulness of their role in promoting a safe and sound financial system. The change in

Table 2.5 Grades of U.S. infrastructures and funding needs

	1988	1998	2001	2003	2005	2009
Average grade	C	D	D+	D+	D	D
5 year needs (trillions)	N.A.	N.A.	1.3	1.6	1.6	2.2
5 year needs (2005 dollars, trillions)	N.A.	N.A.	1.74	2.05	1.6	1.96

Source: American Society of Civil Engineers.

the philosophy of regulation and supervision involved three main aspects: the primacy of profitability as a measure of soundness, the sacrosanct role of innovation, and the promotion of self-regulation via risk-management techniques.

Profitability became a central regulatory criterion to judge the sustainability of a business so much so that profitability became equated with soundness, and highly profitable companies were set as an example for their industry. This was the case during the savings and loan crisis with highly fraudulent businesses held out as good examples to follow precisely because of the high (fake) profits recorded (Black 2005), and recently Senator Christopher Dodd stated: "Banks' regulators were so focused on banks' profitability, they failed to recognize that loans so clearly unsafe for consumers were also a threat to the banks' bottom line" (U.S. Senate 2009: 2). Indeed, if one follows the market logic, if a business is profitable it must mean that it responds to preferences of its customers and so it must provide some benefits to society. The belief is that profitable businesses should be subject only to routine regulation and supervision, and there is no need for government to make sure that the underlying source of profitability is sound. Indeed, market forces will do most of the job of weeding out unsustainable businesses.

It was also believed that financial innovations should be left alone and the more innovations there are, the more efficient the financial system becomes, and the better the economy performs. A 1999 speech on derivatives by Chairman Greenspan is a perfect example of this view:

> The reason that [the growth of derivatives] has continued despite adversity, or perhaps because of it, is that these new financial instruments are an increasingly important vehicle for unbundling risks. These instruments enhance the ability to differentiate risk and allocate it to those investors most able and willing to take it. This unbundling improves the ability of the market to engender a set of product and asset prices far more calibrated to the value preferences of consumers than was possible before derivative markets were developed. The product and asset price signals enable entrepreneurs to finely allocate real capital facilities to produce those goods and services most valued by consumers, a process that has undoubtedly improved national productivity growth and standards of living.
>
> (Greenspan 1999)

No constraint or oversight should be put on the innovation process in the financial industry because this would delay the welfare benefits that come from innovations, and because market mechanisms will weed out innovations that do not fulfill the needs of customers and so do not contribute to the improvement in economic welfare.

Not everybody among regulators shared this view—for example Brooksley Born at the Commodity Futures Trading Commission (CFTC) pushed for better government oversight of derivatives at the end of the 1990s—but a majority of regulators did. Born came to the conclusion that it would be impossible for her to make any significant improvement to the regulation of derivatives and so resigned from her position as Chairman of the CFTC. We will see in Chapter 3 that other regulators have raised concerns about the need for better regulation but they too were ignored or even ridiculed.

In addition to the central role given to profitability and the promotion of financial innovations, the regulatory framework that has prevailed under MMC involves the promotion of self-regulation and risk management. This belief in the capacity of financial companies to self-regulate is still strong, even after the 2008 crisis. The following quote from a Treasury report is an example of that state of mind: "Treasury believes market participants will be reluctant to self-certify rules harmful to the market place" (Department of the Treasury 2008: 116). Participants in the financial system have been viewed as sophisticated individuals who are the best able to understand what they are doing, and so are the most able to promote their long-term economic well-being. On the contrary, the government has no, or limited, expertise in banking and finance and so should not impose any restriction on what people can do with their money. This belief is all the more strong when the economy has been performing well for a long time.

This regulatory approach may recognize that financial crises and instability are possible but argues that they are rare events that are unpredictable and random. The best that can be done is to protect against random shocks through appropriate buffers like capital and liquidity ratios. At the same time, however, having too much capital and liquidity is costly and so the point becomes to find the optimal level of both. The move toward risk management is the ultimate expression of this belief. It uses complex mathematical algorithms to determine what the appropriate level of buffer is given existing risks on- and off-balance sheet. The goal has been to refine the measure of the different risks as well as the methods used to calculate the appropriate buffer. The government has a limited role in determining those appropriate buffers, especially for "sophisticated" financial institutions.

Top regulators and supervisors appointed by Congress have been screened through hearings to make sure that they shared this philosophy. They, then, set the tone in their respective agencies regardless of the eagerness of lower-level staff members to enforce regulations and to promote effective supervision. This made it very difficult for in-field supervisors to issue cease and desist orders, to bring criminal charges rather than civil charges, and to close unsustainable businesses without strong resistance from policy makers and top regulators. Black (2005) provides a very detailed insider's account of this state of affairs in the 1980s. The most experienced staff members were passed over for promotion or "asked" to leave, legal barriers were put on staff to prevent them from closing down profitable but unsound businesses, and regulators were highly influenced by businesses and voted to remove themselves from the power to supervise. In addition, federal regulators competed to regulate and supervise existing financial institutions, which allowed financial institutions to shop for the most lenient regulator and to switch regulators when they considered their current regulator too intrusive (Black 2005; Financial Crisis Inquiry Commission 2011). As a consequence, even though the amount of regulation in place is high, rules have not been applied or they have been applied leniently in order to promote the needs of businesses and market mechanisms.

Financialization

The financialization of the economy means that finance has become central to the daily operations of the economic system. More precisely, the private non-financial sectors of the economy have become more dependent on the smooth functioning of the financial sector in order to maintain the liquidity and solvency of their balance sheet, and to improve and maintain their economic welfare. Households have become more reliant on financial assets to obtain an income (interest, dividends, and capital gains) and have increased their use of debt to fund education, health care, housing, transportation, leisure, and, more broadly, to maintain and grow their standard of living (Figures 2.17 and 2.18). Businesses also have recorded a very rapid increase in financial assets in their portfolio and a growth of debt.

In the late 1940s, noncorporate and corporate nonfinancial business respectively held 10 and 20 percent of their assets in financial assets and this was mostly unchanged until the end of the 1980s. By the late 2000s, their proportion of financial assets had more than doubled with respectively 30 and 50 percent of the asset portfolio of noncorporate and corporate nonfinancial business composed of financial assets. While the proportion of financial assets held by households stayed approximately constant at 65 percent for the past sixty years, the proportion of their personal income that has come from holding financial assets has increased dramatically with the growing number of retirees and mutual fund shareholders, and the growing reliance on stock options as a means of remuneration. The rise of inequalities has reinforced this trend as top income earners mostly get these types of income.

In addition to the reliance on the financial sector for their portfolio choices, nonfinancial sectors have also increased their use of debt instruments to fund the holding of their assets. The increase is especially dramatic for households and noncorporate nonfinancial businesses with a ratio of credit market instruments to total assets of 5 percent around the late 1940s compared to 20 and 35 percent respectively in 2010 (Figure 2.18). This increase in indebtedness occurred in two waves; one in the Golden Age, one in the Great Moderation.

The counterpart of these trends has been a growing share of outstanding financial assets held by private finance (Figure 2.19). From the late 1960s, the share of financial assets held directly by households dropped significantly from about 52 to 30 percent. Instead, a growing share of assets has been held by private financial institutions, which went from 25 percent in the late 1940s to 40 percent right before the crisis. The rest of the world recorded most of the rest of the gains from 2 to 10 percent of U.S. financial assets. This growing importance of finance can be attributed to at least three main elements: the growth of private pension funds and mutual funds during the Golden Age, the better rate of return on equity that could be obtained on financial activities relative to nonfinancial activities, and the growing need to recourse to external funding as real income stagnated and as the funding gap for businesses grew.

As explained earlier, the Golden Age was a period of prosperity for households and they accumulated a lot of savings. Part of this financial wealth was used to acquire a home; another part was used to acquire corporate equities and to put money into pension funds and mutual funds. Corporate equities, mutual funds shares, pension funds, and life insurance reserves have become central elements of the balance sheet of households (Figure 2.20). In 1945, pension funds and life insurance reserves represented less than 10 percent of the total assets of households and mutual fund shares were a negligible asset. This state of affairs prevailed until the end of the 1970s but from 1980 their share grew rapidly to reach 25 percent of the assets held by households. Together with corporate

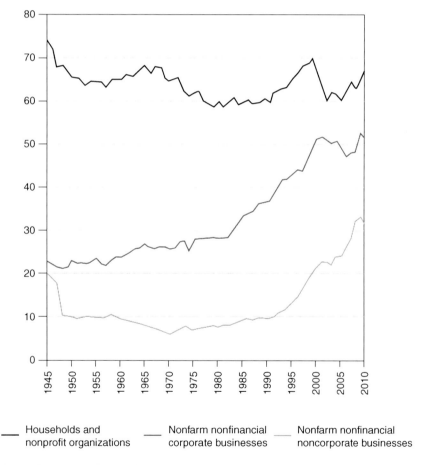

——— Households and
       nonprofit organizations

——— Nonfarm nonfinancial
       corporate businesses

___ Nonfarm nonfinancial
       noncorporate businesses

Figure 2.17 Proportion of financial assets in nonfinancial private balance sheets (%) (source: BEA).

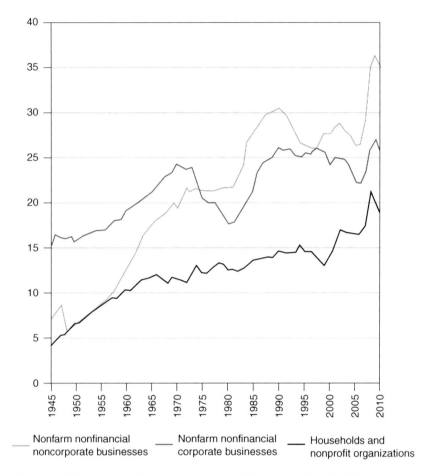

Figure 2.18 Debt outstanding relative to assets (%) (source: Board of Governors of the Federal Reserve System).

equities, mutual funds shares and pension funds reserves have represented around 40 percent of assets held by households since the mid 1990s.

With the growth of pension funds and mutual funds, households became more dependent for their standard of living on the smooth functioning of financial markets, because institutional investors are heavily reliant on corporate equities and corporate bonds to generate income for households from interest, dividend, and capital gains.

While financialization grew out of the prosperity of the Golden Age, financialization was further promoted among households by the stagnation of real income that occurred from the 1970s. The earnings of a single individual could no longer help to improve the standard of living of a family. As shown in Figures 2.6 and 2.7, households responded to the stagnating real income by working longer hours, by

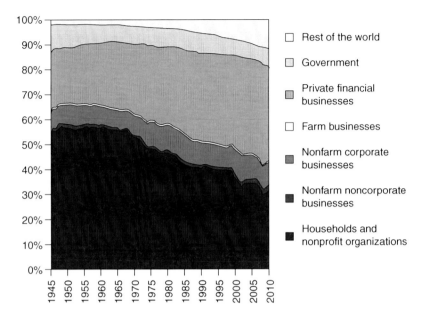

Figure 2.19 Distribution of U.S. financial assets among the different macroeconomic sectors (source: Board of Governors of the Federal Reserve System).

Note
Government includes monetary authorities and public retirement funds.

having at least a second person working in the family, and/or by working multiple jobs. They also responded by going massively into debt to consume and invest (Figure 2.12). The debt-to-income ratio rose from about 60 percent in the mid 1980s to 100 percent in 2000, and 140 percent following the housing boom.

The same occurred in the nonfinancial business sector but partly for different reasons. On the asset side, businesses have had to increase the amount of financial assets they held for two main reasons. First, with the growth of pension funds, corporations have been required to hold more financial assets in order to meet the pensions of their workers. Second, businesses became more involved in the financial industry because the rate of return on net worth was much higher than in nonfinancial economic activities. The average rate of return for nonfinancial corporations was about 5 percent during the Golden Age, and declined to around 3.5 percent during the Great Moderation (Figure 2.21). The rate of return of financial businesses has been much higher but also much more volatile, especially before the mid 1990s. The 2000s trend seemed to be about to repeat the trends observed in the early 1970s and 1980s but was struck down by the Great Recession. Thus, major nonfinancial corporations such as Ford and General Electric have made at least half of the net operating income from financial services since the early 1990s, and their outstanding cash balance from financial operations went from 30 percent in 1991 to over 50 percent by 1993 for General

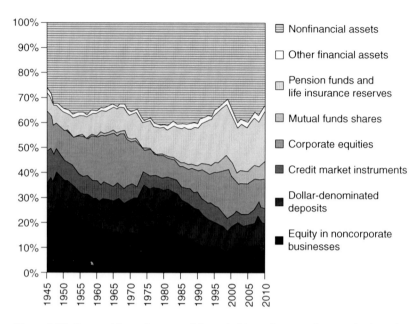

Figure 2.20 Composition of assets of households and nonprofit organizations (source: Board of Governors of the Federal Reserve System).

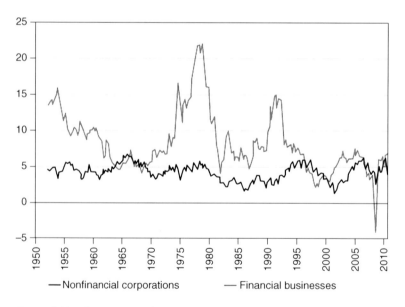

Figure 2.21 After-tax rate of return on net worth (%) (source: Board of Governors of the Federal Reserve System).

Electric and 2003 for Ford. The capacity to arbitrage between financial and non-financial activities was greatly improved by the deregulations of the 1980s (Froud *et al.* 2006).

Businesses, like households, have become more dependent on the financial sector to finance and refinance their asset positions, and the financing gap of investment has grown continuously since the mid 1960s and reached historical highs in the 2000s (Figure 2.10). Businesses also have used derivative markets not only to hedge but also, and mostly, to speculate with the size of the derivative market growing from $70 trillion in 1998 (twice the world GDP) to almost $700 trillion by 2008 (ten times the world GDP). As shown later, major banks were the main driver behind the rapid growth of derivatives. While a standard response to the speculative nature of derivatives is that speculation is the other side of hedging, most derivative contracts have involved two speculators—a bull and a bear with no economic interest in the underlying assets or an economic interest that is more than offset by the speculative interest (Hu and Black 2008; Hu in U.S. House of Representatives 2008c).

Banking under Money Manager Capitalism: securitization, globalization, and market concentration

Partly because of the growth of instability and partly because of globalization, the financial sector recorded dramatic changes in its structure in the transformation to MMC. Not only did finance change its methods of operations by relying heavily on securitization and derivatives, but it also became much more concentrated. The modus operandi and the scale of operation of financial institutions went from the dominance of mostly small-to-medium local specialized companies keeping their loans on their balance sheet, to the dominance of a few large international companies involved in many aspects of finance and making a profit from multiple sources aside from interest payments by borrowers.

The banking structure of the post 1930s required a stable refinancing source in order to function properly. With the Federal Reserve unwilling to continue to be in this role, it became too dangerous for banks to keep on their balance sheets long-term illiquid promissory notes, like mortgages, and so they developed securitization partly to deal with the interest-rate and liquidity risks. Private-label securitization of mortgages started at the end of the 1970s when the volatility of the short-term rate was increasing rapidly. In addition, in 1981, minimum capital requirements were imposed on banks supervised by federal regulators so they had an incentive to off-load credit risk by selling their promissory notes. The 1988 Basel Accords reinforced this trend and by the mid 1980s the securitization of non-mortgage illiquid financial claims grew rapidly.

BASIC PRINCIPLES OF SECURITIZATION

Since the early 1970s, the pace of securitization has grown exponentially and has been extended to a wider and wider range of activities. Taken in a broad sense, the concept of securitization is not new, for example the issuance of shares is a form of securitization of capital equipment; similarly, when someone exchanges her promissory note for a demand deposit she is securitizing her promissory note. However, since 1970 securitization is understood as a form of off-balance sheet operation to transfer financial risks (especially, credit risk, interest-rate risk, and liquidity risk) embedded in illiquid financial claims held by financial institutions. Even though the only direct implication of securitization is to transfer financial risk, this may help indirectly to fund economic activity. However, securitization may occur without any transfer of funds to originators or anybody else, and, recently, it has mostly concerned financial claims in secondary markets instead of primary markets.

A simplified example presents the original intent of securitization; it involves many parties that can be put in four groups: obligor, originators/transferor/servicer, SPE/transferee/trustee, and security buyers. Say that Joe the plumber wants to invest in a new car for his company. Unfortunately, he does not have any money so he goes to his local Bank of America (BoA). After a review of Joe's finances, BoA agrees to provide funds to Joe in exchange for his promissory note that takes the form of an auto loan on BoA's balance sheet. All this allows Joe to buy a car from his local car dealer who happens to have its account at BoA. Figure 2.22 illustrates the state of affairs.

Joe's promissory note exposes BoA to several risks and costs. First, the promissory note contains a high credit risk and so has a 100 percent weight attached to it when calculating required capital. Second, the promissory note is illiquid which limits the flexibility of BoA in case it needs cash fast and may lead to the use of costly refinancing methods. In order to restore the original liquidity of its balance sheet and to decrease capital requirements, BoA decides to try to sell Joe's promissory note. Unfortunately, nobody else is willing to acquire it because of its high credit risk (otherwise Joe would not have needed to go to BoA). In order to solve this problem, BoA creates a special purpose entity (SPE) (also called special purpose vehicle (SPV) or special purpose company (SPC)) and sells Joe's promissory note to the SPE.

In order to fund the purchase of the auto loan, the SPE borrows funds by issuing its own promissory note for cash to individuals or companies willing to acquire them. Security buyers are sometimes called "savers" but security buyers may not have any savings but rather may buy securities by using leverage (either through *ex-nihilo* bank advances or through partially funded or unfunded positions). Contrary to Joe's note, the SPE promissory note is supposed to be

Joe (obligor)		BoA (originator/transferor/servicer)	
Δ Assets	Δ Liabilities	Δ Assets	Δ Liabilities
Car +$X	Auto loan +$X	Auto loan +$X	Car dealer's acc. +$X

Figure 2.22 Accounting record of Joe's loan contract and car purchase.

tradable, it is a security; this auto-loan-backed security is called a certificate for automobile receivables (CAR). The proceeds of the issuance are passed to BoA in exchange for the auto loan. After all interbank clearing is done, one gets Figure 2.23 (it is assumed that none of the security buyers have an account at BoA).

As explained more carefully below, the auto loan (Joe's promissory note) has been securitized into several CARs, and has been transferred to the SPE who holds it in trust for the sole benefit of CAR holders. BoA will act as a servicer for a fee[2] by collecting the monthly debt payments from Joe and transferring them to the SPE manager who will use the proceeds to service the CARs. This very simple example shows the basic tenets of securitization. In the real world, there are many different versions of this principle that take more or less complex forms.

First, the servicer, the transferor, and the originator can be different entities, and this is also true for the SPE and the trust. In addition, there may be different types of servicers operating at different levels of the securitization process (primary servicer vs. master servicer) and under different circumstances (specialized servicers who work out loans in case of defaults, and back-up servicers who replace a servicer who cannot make payments to the SPE). Furthermore, credit rating agencies are an important element of securitization because they are supposed to provide security buyers with a clue about the credit quality of the securities issued by the SPE. Finally, within a single securitization procedure, there may be several SPEs involved at different levels of securitization.

Second, asset-backed securities (ABS), a general term for securities created through a securitization process,[3] are backed by a pool of relatively homogeneous (in terms of loan-to-value, credit risk, servicing method, etc.) financial claims rather than just one loan; in fact that is an essential reason why the SPE exists. Indeed, the SPE allows many economic agents to participate in a pool of risky financial claims without having to break down the pool into individual portions. SPE security buyers are the collective owners of the pool of reference (in the case of CARs the pool contains many auto loans with relatively homogeneous characteristics). The SPE is similar to a mutual fund with the main

BoA (originator/transferor/servicer)		SPE (trustee/transferee/security issuer)	
Δ Assets	Δ Liabilities	Δ Assets	Δ Liabilities
Auto loan −$X Reserve +$X		Auto loan +$X	CARs +$X

Security buyers	
Δ Assets	Δ Liabilities
CARs +$X Bank acc. −$X	

Figure 2.23 Accounting record of the securitization of Joe's auto loan.

difference that rewards and risks are not proportional to the stake in the fund; indeed, as explained below, SPE securities usually have different classes of credit risk and maturity (Bond Market Association 2007: 711).

Third, instead of selling the securities to financial market participants, the SPE may just give its promissory notes (CARs) to BoA in exchange for the illiquid financial claims (auto loans), and BoA may decide to keep or to sell the CARs. If it decides to keep the CARs, BoA may still be able to lower the amount of capital required relative to Joe's promissory notes because CARs with a high credit rating do not require 100 percent capital equity against them. If BoA decides to sell, not all securities are liquid and some of them may involve a buy-and-hold strategy on the part of the security holders and the originator. In this case, the originator (and security buyers) may try to securitize the ABSs they hold (leading to resecuritization). Fourth, there is usually a private or federal insurance mechanism that comes into the deal to enhance the creditworthiness of all, or some, of the securities issued by the SPE. Fifth, securitization may proceed without the occurrence of a sale and even if financial claims do not currently exist; indeed, synthetic securitization involves no sale and securitization may concern future flows of income from currently inexistent assets (Kothari 2006: 93–97, 764). Sixth, an SPE can be used in several securitization procedures simultaneously. The master servicer, however, must make sure that each pool of assets is clearly assigned to a specific issuance of securities and so a specific group of beneficiaries (Kothari 2006: 640–641).

Seventh, the servicer usually pays the SPE in advance of the collection of each periodic debt service on the pool and then keeps them, which may lead to financial difficulties for the servicer if obligors (Joe) become delinquent and then default. The strength of this risk depends on the requirements of the deal in terms of advance payment by the servicer: mandatory advancing requires that the servicer continues to pay the SPE even if obligors default,[4] while optional advancing does not legally bind the servicer to continue to advance payments to the SPE (Fabozzi and Dunlevy 2002: 373–374).

Eighth, over time, the intent of securitization has changed and the main reason for securitizing no longer is to remove newly originated illiquid financial claims from the banks' balance sheets but, rather, to make portfolio arbitrages based on existing financial claims. More precisely, a collateral manager may be hired to buy existing financial claims in the secondary market (including the securities of other SPEs) and to create an SPE. This SPE will be able to enter into complex management strategies involving buying and reselling financial claims to maximize return on equity. Thus, the initiative for the securitization process, and so the creation of the SPE, may come from the side of security buyers rather than from the loan originators (Kothari 2006: 423ff.). In this case, there is no originator but rather a "sponsor" of an SPE, and the cash flow generated by the use of the underlying assets may be of no concern because payments to the holders of SPE securities may be based on capital gains obtained through active asset management (Boultwood and Meissner 2008). The rise of synthetic deals has been extremely beneficial for setting up arbitrage securitization (Kothari 2006: 538).

THE HEART OF SECURITIZATION: SPECIAL PURPOSE ENTITY AND STRUCTURED FINANCE

The SPE has different names, like "special investment vehicle" or "conduit," depending on the structure of its balance sheet and the intent of its creation (International Monetary Fund 2008a: 71; Polizu 2007). Sometimes, it takes the name of the securities it issues (SPEs that issue collateralized debt obligations (CDOs) are called "CDOs"). The operational aspects of SPE vary but, at least in their original intent, one essential characteristic of all SPEs is that the management of their assets and liabilities entails absolutely no discretion. This implies that specific triggers are set to define what should happen if, for example, cumulative losses increase above x percent, or if the value of the pool declines by x percent, or if the loan originator defaults. In the first case, some SPE securities may not receive any servicing at all, or the method of reimbursement of liabilities may change (e.g., proportional to sequential repayment); in the second case the SPE is allowed to sell some assets in a pre-programmed fashion. In addition, in the original intent of securitization, the asset selection for the SPE is made by the originator (rather than the SPE manager) and assets are purely passive. The perfect example of a passive asset is a saving deposit, for which interest is accumulated automatically from the initial amount deposited. Swaps are other passive assets. Non-passive financial assets are shares (involve voting rights) and options (involve a decision to exercise or not exercise the option).

With innovations in the securitization process (from generic to synthetic) and change in purpose of securitization (from balance sheet purpose to arbitrage purpose), the SPE progressively went from a role "limited to the collections of principal and interest on passive assets and distribution of the cash flows to the beneficial interest holders in the entity based on a predefined formula" (Counterparty Risk Management Policy Group III 2008: 45)—a "brain-dead" entity, a pure conduit—to a more active role where assets and liabilities are managed more or less fully, to obtain the highest return possible on equity. For example, in 2000, none of the European synthetic CDOs were managed, but this changed rapidly from 2001, and in 2003 22 percent were managed (Moore 2004: 16).

The SPE is an essential device in the securitization process because it allows the isolation process necessary in the transfer of risk out of the balance sheet of the originator. Security buyers can only look at the assets bought, not the overall financial health of the originator, and, in case of bankruptcy of the originator, the security buyers' claim is limited strictly (at least in theory) to the securitized assets (Joe's auto loan) without any additional recourse on the originator.

In order to achieve isolation, the capacity to prove that the sale of illiquid claims is true ("truth in sale") is key in the generic securitization process. Indeed, it aims at showing that the originator and the SPE are completely independent legally and financially, even though the latter was created by the former (Kothari 2006: 531–532). If the SPE was not independent from the originator, there would be a threat that the SPE could be involved in a bankruptcy by the originator, and that other creditors besides SPE security holders could have a claim on the securitized assets. In addition, a sale is essential for generic securitization; otherwise the transaction is just a collateralized loan between the originator (BoA) and the security buyers, in which case BoA cannot legally remove Joe's promissory note from its balance sheet (Kothari 2006: 576ff.).

While securitization can be used for pure capital requirement arbitrage (that is, transforming loans into securities and holding securities allows the bank to reduce required capital), a central aim of the originator when creating an SPE is to make sure that as many of the SPE securities are sold to financial-market participants rather than stay on the originator's book, who is the buyer of last resort, because this is how the embedded risks are transferred. In order to achieve this aim, the SPE must accommodate as closely as possible the preferences of security buyers in terms of credit risk, maturity, and other factors. In order to deal with those issues, the SPE first establishes a specific organizational structure and then issues several classes of securities, which is where structured finance plays a crucial role.

Leaving aside the benefits of structured finance and assuming that all SPE securities are the same, an SPE can accommodate the preferences of some security buyers through its balance-sheet structure. That structure determines how SPE securities are amortized relative to the financial claims on the asset side (Kothari 2006: 79ff.). The first and simplest is a pass-through structure where the maturity of assets and liabilities of the SPE are matched. As a consequence, payments collected from assets (minus fees to pay for overall management) are directly passed to security holders without any alteration, which leads to erratic principal payments because of usual prepayments or delinquencies (i.e., late payments) by borrowers. Most security buyers do not like that and prefer a standard type of security that has a fixed maturity date at which all the principal is paid at once.

In order to smooth principal payments to security holders, the SPE can be structured in a second way—a pay-through structure. Any excess principal collected on the pool of reference assets relative to the principal to be paid to security buyers is used to buy new assets. Stated another way, assuming that no principal is due on SPE liabilities, the outstanding amount of assets and liabilities of an SPE stay constant, but the pool of reference declines and is replaced progressively by new assets. One of the main disadvantages of the pay-through structure is that assets that can be bought with the excess principal are limited to very safe passive securities, which leads to lower return than the interest rate on SPE securities, creating a negative carry (Kothari 2006: 87). This negative carry intensifies as the pool of reference is amortized and the asset side of the balance sheet is progressively transformed into safe assets.

A third SPE structure is the revolving structure (used for credit card receivables, consumer finance, home-equity lines of credit, and CDOs). Thus, it funds short-term financial claims with long-term securities, which allows security buyers to be involved in short-term financial deals for the long term. Contrary to a pay-through structure, the SPE uses the principal payment collected to buy the same financial claims (short-term receivables) until its SPE securities need to be repaid (Kothari 2006: 79ff., 388). A fourth structure, the direct opposite of the revolving structure and the closest to the traditional bank, is the asset-backed commercial paper conduit (ABCP) that buys long-term financial claims and issues commercial papers (Kothari 2006: 461).

Structured finance aims at correcting some of the flaws of each SPE structure and further accommodating the preferences of security buyers. It does so by creating different classes of securities with specific credit rating, maturity, sources of coupon payment (stripping of debt services collected to create interest-only and principal-only bonds), types of coupon payment (variable or fixed), and protection against risk of unscheduled amortization (prepayment and/or delinquency) (Kothari 2006: 344–345). Thus, within a pay-through structure some unscheduled principal payment may be passed to some SPE securities, and within a pass-through structure some specific classes of assets may have a highly protected amortization schedule that fully smoothes amortization (Kothari 2006: 82ff.). Structured finance blurs the differences between SPE structures.

The process of carving the initial outstanding principal of the pool of reference to create SPE securities with different amortization procedures is called (time) "tranching." The SPE creates securities with a different maturity from the maturity of the underlying pool by allocating more of the principal payment collected on reference assets to some SPE securities. The SPE may choose to have a sequential amortization, which means that all classes of securities receive some interest payment but some securities do not receive any of the principal service collected until other securities have been completely repaid. The SPE may also choose to have a proportional amortization scheme (where each security class is repaid in proportion to its outstanding amount), or it may choose to mix both repayment methods. In addition, the SPE can create special classes that either take none of the unscheduled repayment risk (planned amortization class (PAC) within a class of bonds), or all of the risk (support bond class or companion bond class), or some of the risk (targeted amortization class (TAC) protects against prepayment risk but not delinquency risk) (Adelson 2006; Kothari 2006).

SPE structure and tranching deal with maturity issues; however, not only do potential buyers have different placement horizons but they also have a different credit-risk tolerance. Some of them, like pension funds, may have bylaws or federal regulations that prohibit them from buying securities below a certain credit rating. In order to deal with this issue, the SPE can create a capital structure with securities that have a credit rating unrelated to the credit quality of the underlying pool of reference (Figure 2.24). This process is called "subordination." It involves credit tranching rather than time tranching and is implemented by creating classes of security with different degrees of seniority. The seniority of a security determines how quickly it will be affected by losses on the underlying pool. SPE securities with the same seniority may have different amortization procedures with some repaid fully before others start to be reimbursed.

Some classes are subordinated to more senior classes in the sense that they are wiped out first (and so security buyers lose the funds they initially provided to the SPE) if default occurs on the underlying financial claims.

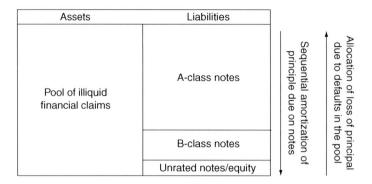

Figure 2.24 Balance sheet of a special purpose entity with sequential amortization and tranching.

A common capital structure is the six-pack structure with sequential amortization. It contains six classes of SPE securities; each class has a specific credit risk and is repaid in a sequence determined by its seniority. The class A, called senior tranche, contains the SPE securities with the lowest credit risk of all classes because all other classes (called subordinated tranches) have to be wiped out in function of their seniority before the A-class securities have their principal affected. The A-class may be divided into subclasses like senior-A class (AAA rating) and junior-A class (AA and A ratings). While all classes receive a portion of the interest payment collected, the entire principal collected on the pool of reference is used first to amortize A-class bonds until all of them are repaid, after which all the principal collected is used to amortize B-class bonds, and so on. The first-loss notes are usually not rated, they are the last one to be repaid and are the first to take a hit in case of default if there is no equity; therefore, a higher coupon rate is attached to them.

Because of the credit support (i.e., number of subordinated classes) it requires, the A-class is always the overwhelming class of the SPE structure and the pure equity is extremely limited and created by overcollateralization (the SPE buys the pool at a discount, which creates some equity in the liability structure of the SPE), initial cash retention, and/or temporary accumulation of excess spreads (which ultimately are paid to the originator or whoever is the equity holder in the SPE). There may be no equity but the first-loss/unrated note is considered equity for regulatory purpose because, even though it is an SPE security that the creator of the SPE would like to sell, the creator is forced to keep it on his balance sheet given that there is usually a limited or no demand for it.

The SPE uses several credit enhancement techniques in order to protect some security holders against defaults in the pool of reference. The enhancements are provided by the originator (or the sponsor), third parties, and the SPE capital structure (Kothari 2006: 210ff.). First, credit enhancement is provided by the SPE capital structure itself through subordination. The amount of credit support to provide to a class depends on the credit rating that the SPE wants to achieve for a certain class of securities.[5] Assuming that to get an AAA rating a class of bonds must have an 8 percent credit support—credit losses have to generate an 8 percent deduction in the outstanding principal of the reference pool before the principal of AAA notes is affected—92 percent of the capital structure will be composed of senior securities (AAA) while the rest will be composed of mezzanine tranches (AA to BBB) and junior tranches (BB to unrated).

Second, the originator provides credit enhancement through excess spread/ profit (the difference between the interest income collected on the reference pool, and the sum of servicing fees, management expenses, and interest payments to SPE securities), overcollateralization, cash infusion and retention (either the originator provides a loan to the SPE, or allows the SPE to hoard some of the initial cash proceeds and/or some of the excess spread), and the holding of the unrated SPE securities. Overall, the originator's enhancement is lower than the 8 percent capital requirement of banks imposed by Basel I (Kothari 2006: 422). In a typical cash CDO, the equity size represents 7 percent of the capital structure; typically this number is as low as 3.75 percent on a synthetic CDO (Moore 2004).

Finally, a third party (private company or government) can also provide credit protection in the form of a derivative contract or a traditional insurance contract, which protects some securities (it is common that an AAA rating can only be obtained if an insurance mechanism exists). Monoline insurers (insurers that specialize in protecting against default on securities, especially municipal bonds) and credit derivative product companies (CDPC) (that sell credit protection through credit default swaps) take positions mostly on the super-senior credit exposure, while hedge funds take positions mostly on junior exposures. Banks hold mostly senior tranches (about 60 percent of their holdings) while mutual funds, pension funds, and life insurance companies hold mostly junior bonds and mezzanine bonds (Bond Market Association 2007: 768). Even though hedge funds are the most involved in junior tranches, the previous money managers are not far behind (International Monetary Fund 2008a: 80).

OTHER ASPECTS OF THE STRUCTURE OF BANKING

With the financialization of the economy, and the deregulation and securitization of the financial industry came a change in the organizational and managerial structures of banks toward a business more focused on growth and shareholder value. Minsky analyzed two alternative arrangements to the commercial bank plus investment bank model. The first is the universal bank model that was adopted in Germany and Japan; the second is the Public Holding Company model (PHC). A universal bank model combines commercial banking and investment banking functions in a bank that provides both the short-term lending and the long-term funding of the operations of firms. It issues liabilities, including demand deposits, to households and buys the stocks and bonds of firms. A universal bank might also provide a variety of other financial services, including mortgage lending, retail brokering, and insurance. The alternative is the PHC model in which the holding company owns various types of financial firms with some degree of separation provided by firewalls. The PHC holds stocks and bonds of firms and finances positions by borrowing from banks, the market, and the Treasury. Minsky argued that the development of Money Manager Capitalism has led to a convergence of these two models. This prescient recognition in 1992 helps to explain the current crisis, in which problems with mortgages first brought down investment banks and then the short-term lending market (such as commercial paper) that bank holding companies had relied upon for financing their positions in assets—including collateralized debt obligations held by SPV subsidiaries.

Since at least 1999, with the Financial Modernization Act, the U.S. no longer has had any sharp distinction between investment banking and commercial banking. Banking has been largely organized into holding companies with subsidiaries that can engage across the spectrum of financial activities. Some activities have been farmed-out to independent or quasi-independent specialists (independent mortgage brokers, SPVs). Many financial services have been supposedly taken out of financial institutions to be performed by "markets." However, this has been more apparent than real because the dominant financial institutions controlled those markets (they created the SPE that bought their assets) and set prices of financial assets (often using complex and proprietary models, also known as level-3 valuation). For our purposes, there are a handful of behemoth financial institutions that provide the four main financial services: commercial banking (short-term finance for business and government), payments services (for households, firms, and government), investment banking (long-term finance for firms and government), and mortgages (residential and commercial real estate). A lot of the debts have been securitized and ultimately held in pension, university endowment, and sovereign wealth funds.

The convergence of the various types of banks within the umbrella bank holding company and shadow banks was fueled by the emergence of MMC, and the expansion of government guarantees to a wider segment of the financial industry. In terms of the rise of MMC, in the 1970s, investment banks innovated to provide financial market substitutes (money market mutual funds, commercial paper market, repo market, and securitization) that were not subject to the regulatory requirements of the time; especially regulation Q (interest rate ceiling on savings deposits), regulation D (reserve requirements), and capital requirements. Commercial banks were given a monopoly position in deposit taking but were constrained by these regulations, and so were unable to provide these substitute instruments that were more attractive to financial market participants. As a consequence, commercial banks pushed for a deregulation of their industry to be able to enter financial markets. Regulators and the courts progressively ruled that these financial-market activities were related to the regulated activities of the commercial banks, allowing them to reclaim securities market activities that had been precluded in the New Deal legislation (Kregel 1998a; Financial Crisis Inquiry Commission 2011; Cargill and Garcia 1982;

D'Arista and Schlesinger 1993). This, in turn, further promoted the growth of money managers. Thus, while the financial sector gained control over a growing share of outstanding assets, within the financial sector money managers have captured a bigger share of the assets held by the financial sector. Since the mid 1990s, money managers have held 40 percent of the financial assets of the financial sector, compared to 5 percent in 1945 and less than 20 percent in the late 1970s (Figure 2.25).

Besides the growth of money managers, changes in the banking structure were also encouraged by the expansion of the government safety net, as Minsky remarked: "This convergence is also reflected in the United States by a proliferation of government endorsements of private obligations" (1993c: 47). Indeed, it is impossible to tell the story of the current crisis without reference to the implicit guarantee given by the Treasury to the mortgage market through its GSEs (Fannie and Freddie), through the student loan market (Sallie), and even through the "Greenspan Put" and the Bernanke "Great Moderation"—that gave the impression to financial-market participants that the government would never let markets fail. As explained more carefully in Chapter 3, their expectation was validated in the aftermath of the crisis, when the government's guarantee of liabilities went far beyond FDIC-insured deposits to cover larger denomination deposits as well as money market funds, and the Fed extended lender of last resort facilities to virtually all financial institutions. This really was a foregone conclusion once Glass–Steagall was gutted and investment banking, commercial

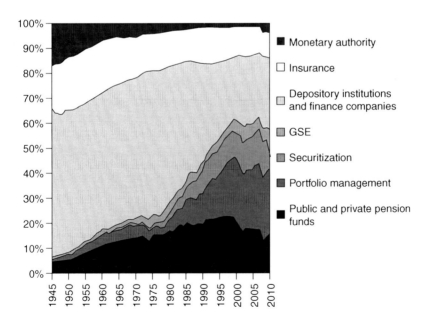

Figure 2.25 Distribution of financial assets held by the financial sector (source: Board of Governors of the Federal Reserve System).

banking, and all manner of financial services were consolidated in a single financial "big box" superstore with explicit government guarantees over a portion of
the liabilities. Government could no longer limit its safety net to deposit
banking.

In addition to the change in the banking structure, the rise of money managers
also has led to changes in the managerial structures of financial institutions. The
growing dominance of money managers has meant a more systematic management of the funds they collect because money managers are under extreme competition to perform on a short-term basis. They set a specific rate of return to
meet in order to attract customers, and compare their result to their target and to
how the rest of the competition did. While this focus on short-term performance
is understandable for hedge funds, it also prevails in pension funds and mutual
funds with a long-term maturity. Given the large sum of funds they control,
money managers have been able to influence the decisions of the boards of directors of the companies in which they had a significant stake. Given that money
managers are heavily focused on short-term capital gains, companies had to
more carefully watch changes in the value of their stocks and short-term business performances. Money managers also have pushed for more involvement in
financial activities by nonfinancial companies because of the higher rates of
return. This move toward shareholder value also led to a change in the incentive
structure of management with more emphasis on stock options, which is believed
to help align the incentives of managers and money managers. Prior to the
1990s, the compensation of chief executive officers (CEOs) was based over-
whelmingly on salary. By 1992 the proportion of salary in CEO compensation
had declined to 42 percent and by 2008 it represented only 17 percent of CEO
compensation. Instead, stocks, stock options, and bonuses became dominant
means to remunerate CEOs, and the first two means exploded in the 1990s
(Frydman and Jenter 2010).

As explained in Chapter 3, this change in remuneration strategy led to the
same pump-and-dump strategies that drove the 1929 stock market boom. Investment greatly increased leverage, and financial institutions moved increasingly to
ever shorter short-term finance. In addition, the mentality of the top management
was drastically changed. Traders like Robert Rubin at Citibank (who would
become Treasury secretary) and Lloyd Blankfein at Goldman Sachs rapidly
climbed the echelons of banking. Traders necessarily take a short view—you are
only as good as your last trade. More importantly, traders take a zero-sum view
of deals: there will be a winner and a loser, with the investment bank pocketing
fees for bringing the two sides together. Better yet, the investment bank would
take one of the two sides—the winning side, preferably—and pocket the fees
and collect the winnings. Why would anyone voluntarily become the client,
knowing that the deal was ultimately zero-sum and that the investment bank
would have the winning hand? No doubt there were some clients with an out-
sized view of their own competence or luck; but most customers were wrongly
swayed by investment banks' good reputation. But from the perspective of hired
management, the purpose of a good reputation is to exploit it—what William

Black, calls control fraud (i.e., top managers use the company they run in a fraudulent manner to benefit themselves).

The refocus of the financial structure toward securitization, short-term gains, and stock market valuation led to a trend toward the concentration and globalization of the financial industry, as well as a change in the source of profitability of banks. In terms of concentration, the number of FDIC-insured commercial banks has declined dramatically from a peak of 14,483 institutions in 1984 to 7,401 in 2006 right before the beginning of the financial crisis. In addition, the share of assets held by large depository institutions increased dramatically from the early 1990s from about 30 to 80 percent, and, since the mid 2000s, the five biggest banks have held over 95 percent of the derivatives held by depository institutions (Figure 2.26). In terms of globalization, the share of assets held by foreign banks grew rapidly from the 1970s to reach 16 percent of assets held by commercial banks operating in the United States (Figure 2.27). This trend is much more pronounced outside the United States.

The share of interest income in overall gross income declined among FDIC-insured commercial banks from 90 percent in the late 1970s to 70 percent in 2010 (Figure 2.28). Fees on late payments, overdrafts, and, among others, servicing business have become more important sources of profitability. In addition, large financial holding companies have been much more involved in trading

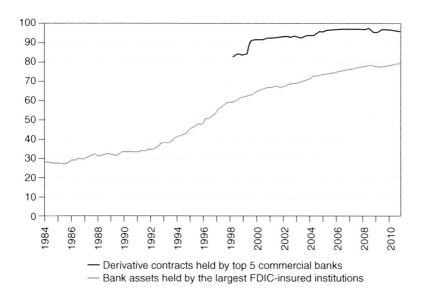

— Derivative contracts held by top 5 commercial banks
— Bank assets held by the largest FDIC-insured institutions

Figure 2.26 Asset and derivative concentration among depository institutions (%) (sources: Federal Depository Institution Corporation (Quarterly Bank Profile Time Series), Office of the Comptroller of the Currency (Quarterly Reports on Bank Derivatives Activities).

Note
The largest financial institutions have more than $10 billion in assets.

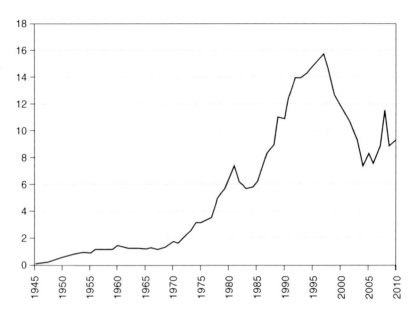

Figure 2.27 Share of assets of U.S. commercial banks held by foreign banks in the U.S. (%) (source: Board of Governors of the Federal Reserve System).

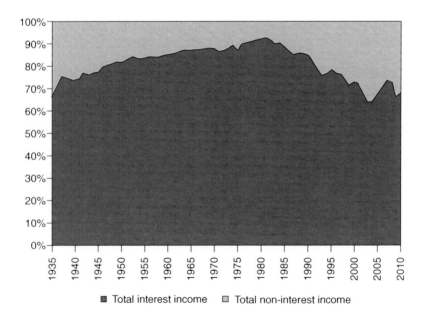

■ Total interest income   □ Total non-interest income

Figure 2.28 Source of income of FDIC-insured commercial banks (source: Federal Deposit Insurance Corporation).

activities, which have provided profitability not only via fees from portfolio management but also via capital gains from trading for their own account. Top banks (Citibank, Bank of America, JP Morgan Chase, Goldman Sachs since it got a bank charter, and others that vary over the years) depend much more on trading revenues than other banks do, with around 6 percent of gross revenues determined by trading activities until 2007 (Figure 2.29).

Similarities between the Great Moderation and the Roaring Twenties

MMC prior to the Great Recession has some important similarities with Finance Capitalism prior to the Great Depression. In addition to globalization, one can point at income inequalities, indebtedness, source of bank income, the share of financial income, and financial instability as similar elements. While the size of the government is much bigger than in the 1920s, as noted earlier, there has been a trend toward decline of the involvement the federal government in economic affairs over the transformation to MMC.

In terms of inequalities, the share of national income captured by top income earners is similar to the 1920s with the top decile capturing almost 50 percent of national income, and the top centile getting almost 20 percent of national income (Figure 2.30). If one includes capital gains into the measure of national income, the share of the top income earners is even higher than in the 1920s. Similar to the end of the 1920s, capital gains make a significant difference by increasing

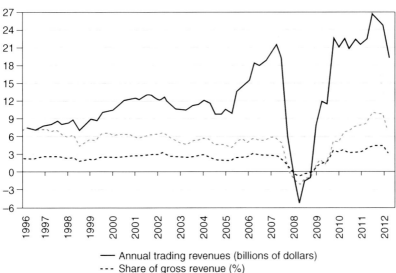

— Annual trading revenues (billions of dollars)
--- Share of gross revenue (%)
--- Share of gross revenue (%), top banks

Figure 2.29 Trading revenues from cash instruments and derivatives for commercial banks holding derivatives (source: Office of the Comptroller of the Currency (Quarterly Reports on Bank Derivatives Activities)).

the share of national income distributed to top income earners by about four or five percentage points. This dependence on capital gains is actually larger today than in the 1920s. Figure 3.8 (Chapter 3) provides data for the wealthiest individuals who live in the United States. The 1920s was a period of increasing dependence on capital gains as a source of income. The share of capital gains grew from 3 percent of their income source in 1920 to 15 percent for the top decile in 1928. Since the mid 1950s, with the growth of managed money and stock options, this source of income has grown again and has represented on average around 15 percent of their income since the early 1990s.

The return of a high level of inequalities was also accompanied by the return of high levels of indebtedness. The indebtedness can be captured through several datasets, and Figure 2.31 provides several measures of nominal indebtedness relative to nominal GDP from 1916 to 2010. Regardless of the data used, indebtedness today is at a historical high relative to GDP. The previous peak was reached in 1933 with a debt level three times as big as GDP but in 2008 the ratio was between 3.5 and 4.7. A marked difference between the two periods is the fact that indebtedness relative to GDP grew for an extended period of time for about thirty years from the late 1970s (and did so at an accelerating rate except in the second part of the 1980s), whereas in the 1920s overall indebtedness was growing in sync with GDP except for the Great Depression. A more stable economy induced by big government has allowed a given level of income to support a greater amount of debt by preventing income from falling too much during recessions.

If one decomposes the debt of the economy among major economic sectors, further similarities emerge between Finance Capitalism prior to the Great

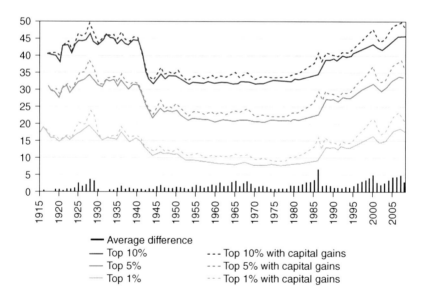

Figure 2.30 Share of national income earned by top income earners in the United States with and without capital gains (%) (source: World Top Incomes Database).

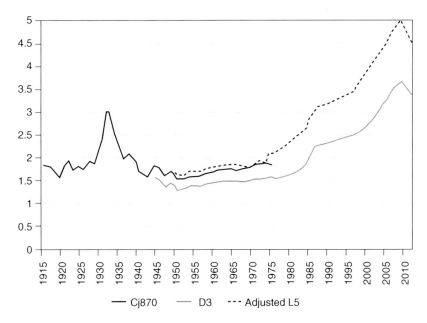

Figure 2.31 Indebtedness in the United States relative to GDP, 1916–2012 (sources: Historical Statistics of the United States; Board of Governors of the Federal Reserve System; BEA).

Note
Cj870 is titled "Net Public and Private Debt" and was compiled by the Census Bureau until 1976. D3 is a flow of funds dataset titled "Credit Market Debt Outstanding by Sector." L5 is a dataset that includes all liabilities (except capital equity) and it was adjusted to fit with the definition of debt given by the Census Bureau (see Appendix).

Depression and MMC prior to the Great Recession. The household sector was also highly indebted with a debt-to-GDP ratio of 0.5, which was a historical high for the early twentieth century (Figures 2.32 and 2.33). This can also be seen in Figure 2.34 that shows households' indebtedness relative to disposable income grew rapidly during the 1920s from 10 percent of disposable income to 50 percent. However, the current level of indebtedness is much higher and peaked at almost 140 percent of disposable income in 2008. The late 1970s marked the beginning of a long period of rising indebtedness that was interrupted only by the two recessions of the early 1980s. The indebtedness grew at an accelerated rate in the early 2000s. This high indebtedness was accompanied by a marked decline in the liquidity of households' balance sheets as well as a continuous increase in the debt-service ratios (Figure 2.12). For example, the ratio of liquid assets to liabilities declined from 120 percent in 1980 to 50 percent in 2006. The same trend applies to the personal sector in terms of indebtedness with a level that peaked at 190 percent of disposable personal income in 2007.

A notable difference from the 1920s is the level of indebtedness of private financial companies. Compared to the late period of Finance Capitalism, the use of debt has exploded to reach a peak of 100 to 125 percent of GDP prior to the Great Recession; this ratio was insignificant in the 1920s (Figures 2.32 and 2.33). The growing use of leverage through derivative, securitization, and other financial innovations also explains the massive growth of debt in the private financial sector relative to the size of the economy.

In addition to indebtedness and income inequalities, two other similarities are the source of income of banks and the share of financial income in the nonfinancial sectors. The share of interest, rent, and dividend in personal income was at a similar percentage of 15 to 20 percent in the 1920s and from 1980 to the Great Recession. The share of corporate profits captured by financial corporations averaged 13 percent from 1950 to 1980 but climbed rapidly from the early 1980s to average 28 percent from 1990 to 2007. The share rose above 30 percent from 2001 to 2005 and peaked at 40 percent in 2003 (Figure 2.35). Data about the share of financial profit among corporations is not available prior to 1929, but the downward trend that occurred after 1929 seems to indicate a greater importance of finance as a source of profit for corporations in the 1920s. Data about the share of income captured by the financial sector confirm the larger role played by the financial sector prior to the Great Depression and today. The share of the finance, insurance, and real estate sector in national income has grown rapidly

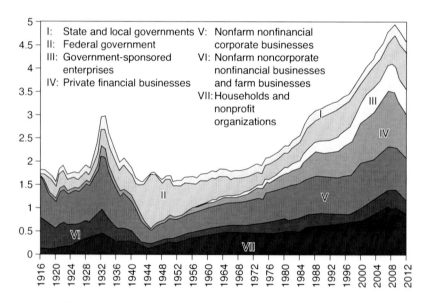

Figure 2.32 Liabilities (excluding equity) relative to GDP by major economic sector (adjusted 15 series) (ratio) (sources: Historical Statistics of the United States; Board of Governors of the Federal Reserve System; BEA).

Note
Private financial businesses exclude government-sponsored enterprises and monetary authorities.

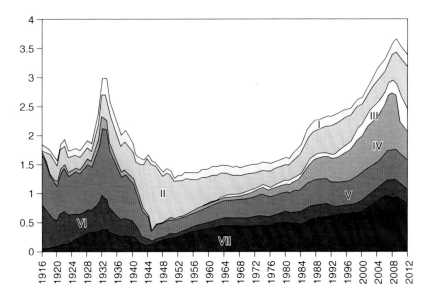

Figure 2.33 Credit market debt relative to GDP (D3 series) (ratio) (sources and legend: see Figure 2.32).

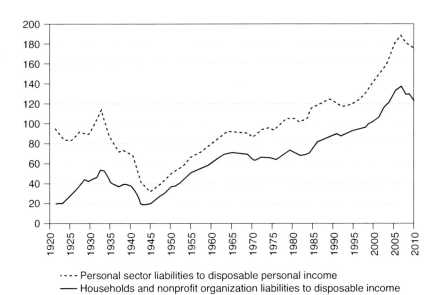

---- Personal sector liabilities to disposable personal income
—— Households and nonprofit organization liabilities to disposable income

Figure 2.34 Liabilities of households and nonprofit organizations relative to disposable and personal income (%) (sources: Creamer and Bernstein 1956; BEA; Historical Statistics of the United States; NBER).

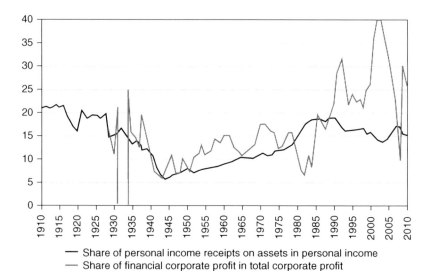

— Share of personal income receipts on assets in personal income
— Share of financial corporate profit in total corporate profit

Figure 2.35 Share of financial income for households and corporations (%) (sources: BEA; Creamer and Bernstein 1956).

Note
Financial corporate profit excludes the profit of Federal Reserve banks. Capital gains are not included.

from 1980 from 13 to 18 percent by the 1990s, reaching levels unseen since the 1920s when the share of the finance, insurance, and real estate sector in national income reached 15 percent (Figure 2.36).

As a consequence, the share of individuals employed in the financial sector increased rapidly in the postwar period and reached a similar level as in the early 1930s (Figure 2.36). This share grew from 1945 until 1987 after which it stayed constant at 6 percent. Although it is a largely unsavory world (see, for example, Das 2006), large numbers of young and talented individuals have been lured toward the financial sector by the extremely high pay. Individuals with high skills have had less incentive to be involved in innovative entrepreneurship (Kedrosky and Stangler 2011) or in solving existing social problems.

Beyond inequality, indebtedness, source of banks' income, and greater dependence on finance as a source of income, one may note two other similarities. One is the role of the federal government in the economy and the other is the return of financial instability. As already noted earlier, federal government purchases of goods and services have declined dramatically to 6 percent of GDP in 2000. This level of federal government spending relative to the size of the economy had not been recorded since the 1930s. The main difference is the size of entitlement and other transfers that brings the size of

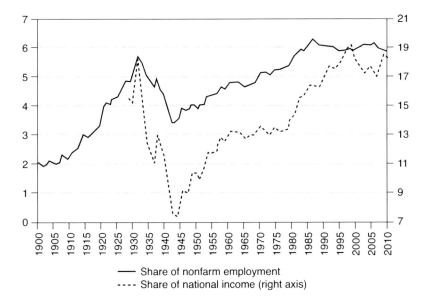

Figure 2.36 Share of financial sector in the economy (%) (sources: Historical Statistics of the United States; BLS; BEA).

the government to 26 percent of GDP versus 3 percent in 1929. However, a larger proportion of this financial burden has been carried by the state and local government compared to the Golden Age. While far more regulations are in place compared to the 1920s, the unwillingness to apply them in meaningful ways, or to introduce new regulation to constrain the growth of unsustainable economic activities, has been a central characteristic of both periods of time.

Given all these similarities, it is not surprising to see that financial instability has been high in the two time periods. As noted earlier, these two periods have been far more unstable than the Golden Age. The culmination of the instability of Finance Capitalism was the Great Depression and the peak of the instability of MMC was, for the moment, the Great Recession. Bordo *et al.* (2001) note that the average duration of a financial crisis is about the same pre- and postwar, the main difference is its average effect on the economy with an average cumulative decline of 11.3 percent between 1880 and 1939 and 8 percent from 1973 to 1997.

Implications for financial stability and the Minskian framework

Because of its characteristics, Money Manager Capitalism is prone to financial instability. It is heavily dependent on debt as well as capital gains in order to sustain economic activity. Minsky noted this from the late 1980s:

The independence of operating corporations from the money and financial markets that characterized managerial capitalism was thus a transitory stage. The emergence of return and capital-gains-oriented blocks of managed money resulted in financial markets once again being a major influence in determining the performance of the economy. However, unlike the earlier epoch of finance capitalism, the emphasis was not upon the capital development of the economy but rather upon the quick turn of the speculator, upon trading profits. [...] A peculiar regime emerged in which the main business in the financial markets became far removed from the financing of the capital development of the country. Furthermore, the main purpose of those who controlled corporations was no longer making profits from production and trade but rather to assure that the liabilities of the corporations were fully priced in the financial market, to give value to stockholders. The giving of value to, stockholders took the form of pledging a very high proportion of prospective cash flows to satisfy debt liabilities.

(1993a: 111–112)

Managed money capitalism has diminished the financial independence of corporate management. Managed money capitalism is part of the trend toward an increase in the proportion of financing that takes place through markets rather than through intermediaries. The large money market banks are important in financing the positions of block traders and in bridge financing takeovers and leveraged buyouts (financing the deal in the interval between the accepted offer and the issuance of junk bonds). [...] The capitalism of managed money emphasizes cash flows in the near near-term to support stock prices and heavily indebted liability structures. Whereas the diminished role of institutions may have decreased the likelihood of debt deflation, the growth of heavy indebtedness may well restrain the overall propensity to innovate or to take chances [...] MMC may be more vulnerable to shortfalls of gross profits than the lightly indebted managerial capitalism.

(1990c: 70–71)

Households and nonfinancial businesses and financial institutions like pension funds and mutual funds have come to expect that rising asset prices will occur and will be a means to complement their income and repay existing debts. This is all the more so that money managers usually target rates of return that are above the growth rate of national income, which imply that dividends and interest cannot, by themselves, provide the targeted returns. Thus, Ponzi finance has become more frequent and so the risk of debt-deflation has also increased because the risk of massive liquidation in order to meet debt commitments has increased.

The changes in the structure of banking also have made the emergence of Ponzi finance even more likely because now banks have less of an incentive to check carefully the creditworthiness of their customers because the credit risks and other risks are transferred to money managers via securitization. Thus, the underwriting of loans and the underwriting of securities have become less strict and more prone to involve bets about the future direction of asset prices rather than the future direction of national income. Stated alternatively, under the new banking structure collateral-based lending is prone to grow relative to income-based lending.

Not only have households, nonfinancial firms, and financial companies been more engaged in Ponzi finance, but the government has promoted the growth of Ponzi finance through deregulation and desupervision. The latter trend came at the same time as the size and cost of financial rescue by the federal government grew. As shown in Table 2.2, FDIC assistances have been much larger during MMC, but the same is true for other official institutions like the Federal Reserve. The 1966 municipal crisis was small and easily managed but over time larger banks failed and the Federal Reserve also started to help rescue financial institutions that it did not regulate, like Long-Term Capital Management in 1998. The growth of rescues together with the decline in regulation and supervision have meant that moral hazard have grown tremendously in the financial industry. The "Greenspan Put" was the ultimate expression of this moral hazard.

Given the current economic set up, a long period of stability may no longer be necessary to promote the growth of financial instability; instead rising asset prices may be the only thing really necessary to allow Ponzi finance to emerge. Commercial real estate in the 1980s, stock market in the 1990s, housing in the early 2000s, commodities in the late 2000s.

Conclusion

The Minskian framework does not merely help to explain the Great Recession; it helps to explain macroeconomic dynamics over the past century. It can explain why Finance Capitalism was unstable, why Managerial Capitalism was more stable, and how financial instability returned from the late 1960s. At the core of the explanation of the stability of Managerial Capitalism is the big government and big bank that emerged as a response to the Great Depression. The greater involvement of the federal government and the central bank in the economy through spending, taxing, discounting, and regulation provided a more stable economic and financial environment for the private sector. Together with strong labor unions, the international political environment, and limited globalization, big government and big bank provided a set up that was prone to shared prosperity. The Golden Age of the 1950s and 1960s is the ultimate expression of the virtuous circle created by this socio-politico-economic set up. It was a period of decline in the poverty rate and inequalities combined with rapid economic growth that involved an increase of spending on infrastructure and social welfare. This allowed businesses and households to improve their economic position without having to use debt in a way that was unsustainable. The private sector used hedge finance to acquire and hold assets on its balance sheet. Depository institutions and thrifts, given their balance sheet structure, have always been involved in speculative finance, but they were protected by limited competition and a guaranteed access to a smooth refinancing channel via the central bank.

However, long-term prosperity also led to changes in economic, psychological, institutional, and political elements that promoted instability. Businesses became more daring in their funding practices in order to maintain their rate of return on equity, households became more willing to take on debt to fund consumption and investment, and banks innovated to find new cheap sources of funds as the Federal Reserve changed its policy and as the Treasury mostly ran a balanced budget. In addition, the confidence in the capacity of market mechanisms to manage the economy returned.

From the late 1960s, the regulations put in place in the 1930s started to be challenged by financial innovations, by the Federal Reserve, and by politicians who promoted free-market ideas. By the late 1970s, the banking structure and regulations put in place during the 1930s were no longer adequate to deal with the new economic and political environment that promoted fine-tuning and limited government intervention. As a consequence, the banking structure of the 1930s collapsed, and depository institutions demanded a leveled playing field with investment banks. Financial institutions were deregulated and they innovated to deal with the new instability. The growth of securitization and derivatives is a direct response to the return of instability. The 1999 Act simply made official the de facto repeal of the 1930s protections.

Money Manager Capitalism is the latest stage of capitalism. It represents a hybrid between Finance Capitalism and Managerial Capitalism, in which market mechanisms are promoted as much as possible but big government is still present. However, the quality of the government involvement has declined dramatically because the federal government is much less involved in the productive development of the economy, because the regulatory framework has become much more lenient and less effective, and because the fine-tuning of inflation has become a major goal of government. Coupled with other similar characteristics of Finance Capitalism—high indebtedness, reliance on financial markets as a source of income, income inequalities, and others—Money Manager Capitalism has recorded a return of financial instability.

In order to cope with this instability, bigger and bigger government financial rescues have been necessary but the long-term effectiveness of these government interventions has declined because, given the absence of effective regulation and supervision, they have promoted moral hazard.

3 The Great Moderation and the growth of Ponzi finance

Prior to 2007, several economists noted that the volatility of output growth and output inflation had declined dramatically since the mid 1980s and that only two minor recessions had occurred in the U.S. A debate started to explain the causes of the long period of stability. Some authors argued that structural changes had occurred in the economy while others emphasized the role of improved monetary policy. Stock and Watson (2002, 2005) provide a summary of the debate and named the period the "Great Moderation," a name later endorsed in a speech by then Vice-Chairman Bernanke (2004). Stock and Watson concluded that most of the stability of the Great Moderation was attributable to unexplained factors instead of improvements in the structure of the economy or in monetary policy; luck was the main cause of the Great Moderation.

While economists debated over the causes of the Great Moderation, the growing financial fragility of the economy was completely overlooked except by a minority of economists. Beyond the changes analyzed in the previous chapter, several institutional and policy changes occurred that further increased the financial fragility of capitalism in developed countries. The latter became more and more dependent on the use of debt and capital gains as a means to sustain an economic growth highly focused on household spending on consumption goods and housing.

Economic expansion and growing private debt: the 1990s

The 1990s were a long period of prosperity in Europe and the United States that was accompanied by a retrenchment of government intervention in economic affairs that expressed itself at the macroeconomic level by a reduction in the fiscal deficit and, in some countries, a return to a fiscal surplus. This implies that a larger share of the burden of sustaining economic growth was shifted toward the non-government sector and it turned out that the domestic private sector was the main sector that carried this burden. As a consequence, the move toward a surplus budget by the federal government was accompanied by a move toward deficit in the domestic private sector.

In less than ten years the U.S. domestic private sector turned from net lender to net borrower (Figure 3.1). From the early 1990s, there is a downward trend in net lending by the domestic private sector from about 5 percent of GDP in 1993, 0 percent in 1997, and –5 percent in 2000. After a brief respite during the 2001 recession, when private spending retrenched, the sector was once again a large net borrower by 2004. Similar trends were followed in some major countries of Europe, like France, Germany, and the United Kingdom in the 1990s and early 2000s (Figure 3.2). Spain, Ireland, and Portugal also recorded a massive increase in the net borrowing by the domestic sector, which was partly offset by a decreasing deficit or rising surplus by the government sector in Spain and Ireland. Sweden recorded similar changes in government finances from a deficit over 10 percent of GDP in 1993 to a fiscal surplus of about 5 percent of GDP in 2000. This led to a rapid decline in the domestic sector net lending from 10 to 0 percent of GDP by the end of the 1990s. In the first decade of the new millennium, Sweden was able to have both a domestic private sector surplus and a government surplus by recording large current account surplus as foreigners were willing to go into deficit vis-à-vis Sweden.

Outside Europe and the United States, Australia and New Zealand also experienced similar trends. The Australian domestic private sector was a net borrower from 1994 and, by the early 2000s, net borrowing reached an unprecedented 7 percent of GDP. One may note that Japan also had recorded a sharp decline in net saving by the domestic private sector right before the massive crisis that was followed by two lost decades.

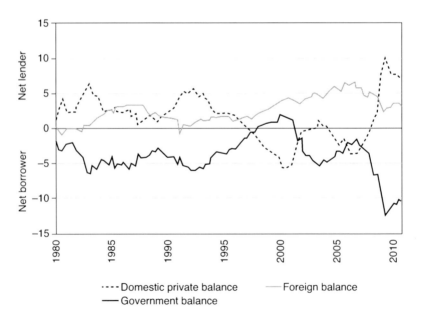

Figure 3.1 Net lending/borrowing in the United States (% of GDP) (source: Board of Governors of the Federal Reserve System).

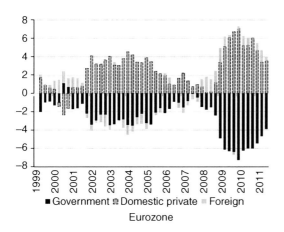

Eurozone

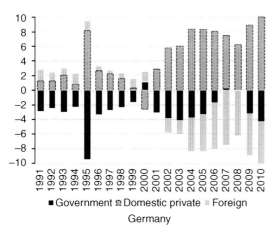

Germany

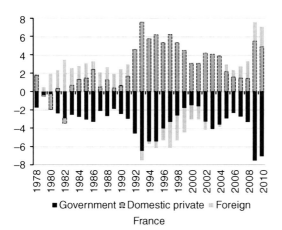

France

Figure 3.2 Net lending/borrowing around the world (% of GDP) (sources: National Statistical Institutes; National Central Banks; Eurostats; OECD).

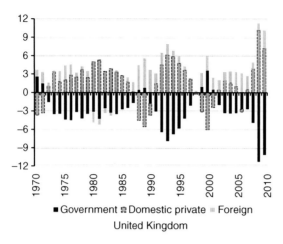

■ Government ▣ Domestic private ▩ Foreign

United Kingdom

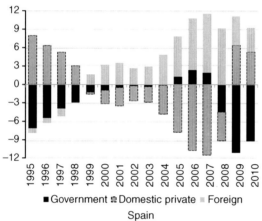

■ Government ▣ Domestic private ▩ Foreign

Spain

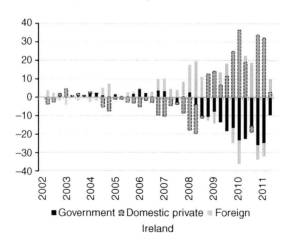

■ Government ▣ Domestic private ▩ Foreign

Ireland

Figure 3.2 continued

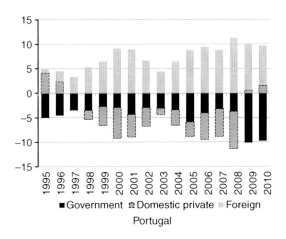

Portugal

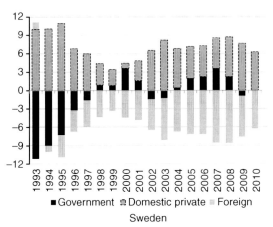

Sweden

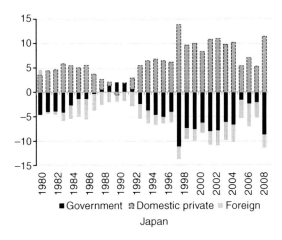

Japan

Figure 3.2 continued

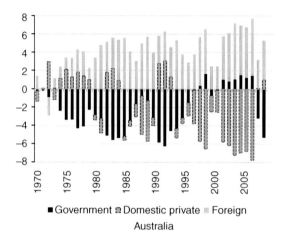

Figure 3.2 continued

The fact that economic growth was not affected significantly by fiscal retrenchments meant that the domestic private sector was willing and able to become a net borrower on a massive scale, which led to the debt trends presented in Chapter 2. This net borrowing trend was made possible by changes in regulation and banking structure and was further reinforced by growing inequalities and poverty that made it difficult for households to maintain their standard of living without going into debt. A long period of economic stability also changed mentalities about the use of debt to finance economic activities.

Government policies and the growth of Ponzi finance

The deregulatory trend of the early 1980s that contributed to the breakdown of Managerial Capitalism continued during the Great Moderation. Two major changes in regulation occurred in the United States, one was the Financial Modernization Act of 1999, the other was the Commodity Futures Modernization Act of 2000. They were complemented by additional incremental changes to the regulation of pension funds and housing finance that reinforced the trends that the two previous changes promoted.

After intense lobbying by the biggest commercial banks, the Financial Modernization Act of 1999 effectively removed any barriers to the creation of financial holding companies that combine commercial and investment banking. As explained in Chapter 2, this was in fact a post-facto legalization of the banking trends that had been growing since the 1970s. These profound changes in banking structure were, however, not accompanied by any significant changes in the regulatory structure to supervise financial holding companies. Instead, another patch was added to an already intricate regulatory framework; the

Federal Reserve became the umbrella supervisor of all other federal agencies in charge of regulating each component of financial holding companies. This lack of broad and comprehensive regulatory overhaul was due partly to the free-market thinking of the day but also the sheer complexity of financial holding companies that regroup many entities that are incoherently related to each other in a loose fashion and so extremely difficult, if not impossible, to regulate and supervise.

The Commodity Futures Modernization Act of 2000 was passed after an intense fight between the Commodity Futures Trade Commission (CFTC)—led by Brooksley Born—and Alan Greenspan (Federal Reserve), Larry Summers (U.S. Treasury), and Arthur Levitt (Securities and Exchange Commission). The CFTC wanted to be able to gather information about OTC derivatives and potentially regulate them but ultimately lost. The Act aimed at clearly defining regulatory responsibilities of the Securities and Exchange Commission (SEC) and the CFTC, but in the process ended up removing the regulation of some swap transactions from both Commissions. Regarding the former, the Act amended the Securities Act of 1933 and Securities Exchange Act of 1934 in the following way:

> The [Securities and Exchange] Commission is prohibited from registering, or requiring, recommending, or suggesting, the registration under this title of any security-based swap agreement [...] The Commission is prohibited from (A) promulgating, interpreting, or enforcing rules; or (B) issuing orders of general applicability; under this title in a manner that imposes or specifies reporting or recordkeeping requirements, procedures, or standards as prophylactic measures against fraud, manipulation, or insider trading with respect to any security-based swap agreement.
>
> (Commodity Futures Modernization Act of 2000, Section 302(a), Section 303(a))

Regarding the CFTC, the Act excludes from its regulatory responsibilities non-agricultural "commodities" (defined broadly to include financial instruments (section 101(4)(13))) involved in OTC swap transactions entered into by eligible participants (like financial institutions).

> No provision of this Act shall apply to or govern any agreement, contract, or transaction in a commodity other than an agricultural commodity if the agreement, contract, or transaction is (1) entered into only between persons that are eligible contract participants at the time they enter into the agreement, contract, or transaction; (2) subject to individual negotiation by the parties; and (3) not executed or traded on a trading facility.
>
> (Commodity Futures Modernization Act of 2000, Section 105(b))

Credit default swaps (CDS) and equity default swaps (EDS) are covered by this section and so cannot be regulated by the CFTC. This left CDSs and EDSs completely unregulated by federal agencies, which, as shown later, created a favorable environment for the growth of OTC transactions and led to a huge boom in the CDS market. In turn, the growth of CDSs allowed synthetic securitization for arbitrage purposes to grow very rapidly.

In August 2000, the following amendment to the Employee Retirement Income Security Act was proposed, following a request by Morgan Stanley sent to the Department of Labor in October 1999:

> The proposed amendment to the Underwriter Exemptions (the Proposed Amendment) is requested in order to permit plans to invest in investment grade mortgage-backed securities (MBS) and asset-backed securities (ABS) (collectively, Securities) involving categories of transactions which are either senior or subordinated, and/or in certain cases, permit the entity issuing such Securities (Issuer) to hold receivables with loan-to-value property ratios (HLTV ratios) in excess of 100 percent. Specifically, the requested amendment would exempt transactions involving senior or subordinated Securities rated "AAA," "AA," "A" or "BBB" issued by Issuers whose assets are comprised of the following categories of receivables: (1) Automobile and other motor vehicle loans, (2) residential and home equity loans which may have HLTV ratios in excess of 100 percent, (3) manufactured housing loans and (4) commercial mortgages (the Designated Transactions).
>
> (Department of Labor 2000a: 51455–51456)

This amendment (as well as others that have facilitated the involvement of pension funds in securitization activities) was approved in November 2000 (Department of Labor 2000b), which allowed pension funds to buy SPE securities with an investment grade. Note that this means that pension funds could buy a tranche of CDO-squared with an investment grade, even though the underlying assets are partly based on non-investment grade security classes. Note also that from that time, pension funds could participate in securitization procedures involving risky mortgages and home equity loans, including those with loan-to-value ratio above 100 percent. All this was essential to boost the demand for investment-grade SPE securities and to sustain the growth of mortgage lending, which, in turn, was essential to allow the housing boom to proceed. As explained later, the high investment grade on some SPE securities was really a mirage because of the existing embedded leverage and the inappropriate rating methods.

Finally, Blundell-Wignall *et al.* (2008: 3) note that, in 2004, four regulatory changes combined to create ideal arbitrage conditions in favor of subprime mortgages:

> (1) the Bush Administration "American Dream" zero equity mortgage proposals became operative, helping low-income families to obtain mortgages; (2) the then regulator of Fannie Mae and Freddie Mac, the Office of Federal Housing Enterprise Oversight (OFHEO), imposed greater capital requirements

and balance sheet controls on those two government-sponsored mortgage securitisation monoliths, opening the way for banks to move in on their "patch" with plenty of low income mortgages coming on stream; (3) the Basel II accord on international bank regulation was published and opened an arbitrage opportunity for banks that caused them to accelerate off-balance-sheet activity; and (4) the SEC agreed to allow investment banks (IB's) voluntarily to benefit from regulation changes to manage their risk using capital calculations under the "consolidated supervised entities program."

The American Dream Downpayment Act of 2003 provides downpayment assistance to low income households, while other changes complemented this initiative by working on the lenders' side. These changes accelerated the growth of non-prime mortgage lending.

Beyond deregulation and desupervision, there was also a deliberate choice not to enforce existing laws. For example, while Bernanke has argued that he did not have the authority to regulate mortgage brokers, the latter are heavily regulated at the federal and state level by a host of laws:

> Mortgage brokers are governed by a host of federal laws and regulations. For example, mortgage brokers must comply with: the Real Estate Settlement Procedures Act (RESPA), the Truth in Lending Act (TILA), the Home Ownership and Equity Protection Act (HOEPA), the Fair Credit Reporting Act (FCRA), the Equal Credit Opportunity Act (ECOA), the Gramm–Leach–Bliley Act (GLBA), and the Federal Trade Commission Act (FTC Act), as well as fair lending and fair housing laws. Many of these statutes, coupled with their implementing regulations, provide substantive protection to borrowers who seek mortgage financing. These laws impose disclosure requirements on brokers, define high-cost loans, and contain anti-discrimination provisions. Additionally, mortgage brokers are under the oversight of the Department of Housing and Urban Development (HUD) and the Federal Trade Commission (FTC); and to the extent their promulgated laws apply to mortgage brokers, the Federal Reserve Board, the Internal Revenue Service, and the Department of Labor.
>
> (National Association of Mortgage Brokers 2006)

However, regulators like the Federal Reserve deliberately loosely implemented existing regulations or chose "to not conduct consumer compliance examinations of, nor to investigate consumer complaints regarding, nonbank subsidiaries of bank holding companies" (Appelbaum 2009). In addition, the Federal Reserve and the Office of the Comptroller of the Currency (OCC) blocked efforts of federal regulators (Brooksley Born was one of their victims), and states like Georgia and North Carolina were prohibited by OCC and the Office of Thrift Supervision from investigating local subsidiaries of national chartered banks (Forrester 2006; Center for Responsible Lending 2003). Chairman Bair at the

FDIC worked with Federal Reserve Governor Gramlich to raise concerns about abusive lending practices from 2001 but their effort did not lead anywhere.

Finally, in 1994, the Government Accountability Office (GAO) strongly criticized the existing derivatives legislation. It noted that "no comprehensive industry or federal regulatory requirements existed to ensure that U.S. OTC derivatives dealers followed good risk-management practices" and that "regulatory gaps and weaknesses that presently exist must be addressed, especially considering the rapid growth in derivatives activity" (Government Accountability Office 1994: 7–8). None of the recommendations was implemented and instead large cuts were made by Congress to the budget of the GAO. These cuts were estimated to reduce the staff of the GAO by 850 persons (20 percent of its employees); thereby limiting its capacity to write another critical report (Chittum 2009; Government Accountability Office 1997).

Other regulators also suffered large cuts in their staff. The FDIC staff was cut drastically and constantly from 20,000 in the early 1990s to 5,000 employees right before the Great Recession (Figure 3.3). This occurred at the same time as the financial industry became more concentrated and more complex. In addition, the cut in staff was much more rapid than the decline in the number of FDIC-insured institutions to be supervised, thereby increasing the burden of supervision on each employee. This double trend of increasing complexity and increasing burden on supervisors drastically decreased the capacity to perform effective supervision and regulation.

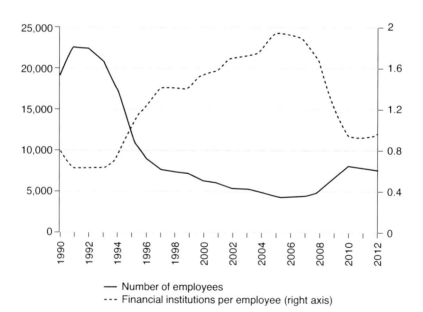

— Number of employees
- - - Financial institutions per employee (right axis)

Figure 3.3 Number of employees at the Federal Deposit Insurance Corporation (source: Federal Deposit Insurance Corporation).

The SEC, under Christopher Cox (who, like Alan Greenspan, is a follower of Ayn Rand's economic thinking) also decreased its staff and, by 2009, the Securities and Exchange Commission had 400 people to examine 11,000 investment advisers, which led it to contract with private auditors and other external reviewers. In addition, the SEC did not develop the necessary tools it needed to be able to deal with the new responsibility that came with the new capital rules it passed and the consolidated supervised entities program. More precisely, from 2004, the SEC allowed brokers-dealers to use their own models to calculate their required capital, and it also became the regulator of holding companies. However, Cox decreased the size of its risk-management staff and did not develop the necessary models to perform proper supervision. It also did not perform a single supervision of consolidated entities (Barth *et al.* 2012).

Similar trends occurred in Europe from the 1980s (Baltensperger and Dermine 1987). For example, the Spanish mortgage market was deregulated throughout the 1980s and 1990s in order to improve competition and to allow securitization (Ferrer *et al.* 2006). As shown later, Spain, Italy, and the Netherlands became key players in European securitization. This deregulatory trend continued up to the beginning of the crisis with France passing the 2005 Confidence and Economic Modernization Act (*Loi pour la Confiance et la Modernisation de l'Economie*) that reformed mortgage lending in order to introduce revolving home equity lending and reverse mortgages (Lamoussière-Pouvreau and Masset-Denèvre 2007).

Beyond the deregulation, desupervision, and deenforcement that allowed the private sector to fulfill its desire to deficit spend, a major contributor to the growth of financial fragility was the change in the stand of fiscal policy that forced the private sector to deficit spend. Fiscal retrenchments were the result both of deliberate policies to reduce deficits and of the automatic stabilizers. In the United States, President Clinton was celebrated for bringing the federal finances back into a surplus. While the recession of 2001 did lead to a return of a deficit, President Bush vowed to bring back the fiscal position of the federal government to a surplus by 2012 and, with the help of the return of economic expansion, the deficit position of the government sector slowly declined. In Europe, the convergence criteria of the Maastricht Treaty and the Growth and Stability Pact committed countries to reduce the size of their deficit drastically and to keep it as low as possible. The economic expansion of the 1990s greatly helped European countries to achieve this result.

Decline in the quality of debts: the growth of Ponzi finance through underwriting

Loan underwriting

As the domestic private sector became a net borrower, its indebtedness grew rapidly. Chapter 2 showed that the growth of indebtedness was particularly rapid in two sub-sectors of the domestic private sector—households and the financial industry. However, the trend toward greater financial fragility was greatly increased by the decline in the quality of this indebtedness. This decline in the quality of loan underwriting was broad from consumer finance to mortgage finance, and from subprime borrowers to prime borrowers. It took the form of a decline in the amount of required loan documentation, a decline in the quality of the documentation provided, a decline in the quality of the loans provided, and a decline in the required amount of collateral. During the Great Moderation, loan officers grew more and more daring in ignoring information essential to evaluate the capacity of borrowers to service loans, and in providing loans that involved expectations of refinancing and/or sale of assets.

Decline in loan underwriting

If one focuses on the amount of information, Figure 3.4 illustrates well the decline in underwriting among mortgages originated to purchase a house. From 2001 to 2006, the proportion of so-called "liar loans" origination almost tripled with 50 percent of the securitized purchase mortgages originated in 2006 having limited or no documentation to determine income, employment, and/or assets owned by the borrowers. Lower documentation was not limited to subprime lending as prime purchase mortgages recorded the highest growth of low-doc loans between 2001 and 2006.

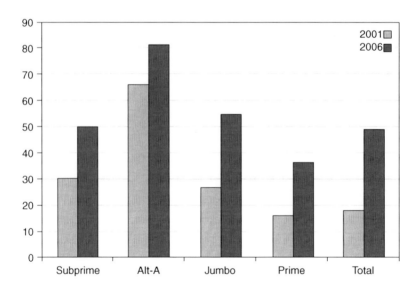

Figure 3.4 Distribution of low/no-doc share of purchase origination (% of origination dollars of securitized loans) (source: Zelman 2007).

Note
Prime mortgages have 0 percent of no-doc mortgages.

Two of the main innovations that promoted the decline in loan documentation in mortgages were the invention of credit scoring and underwriting software. The use of credit scoring (like the FICO score) was first limited but progressively became a central element in the determination of creditworthiness.

> Until a few years ago, FICO was just one factor in the underwriting process. But as Wall Street grew hungrier for mortgages it could stuff into securities and sell to investors, it came to value FICO as an easily understood risk measure. Lenders were all too happy to use it as a substitute for laborious underwriting. "There were investors around the world demanding more and more deals, with investment bankers happily supplying the business," says Ron Chicaferro, a mortgage consultant in Scottsdale, Ariz. "It trickled down to the lender, who told their sales force, The faster you can get me a score and close a loan, the better. We'll forgo the documentation."
>
> (Foust and Pressman 2008)

Instead of laborious underwriting that took weeks to perform, one could get a loan in seconds and mortgage companies used this as a selling point. For example, New Century boasted that FastQual, its automated underwriting system, could give a loan answer in just twelve seconds. According to Zelman (2007), in 2005 and 2006 at least 50 percent of all mortgages backing new private-label mortgage-backed securities (PL MBS) had a low documentation; and this proportion climbed to 77 percent in 2006 for PL MBSs backed by alt-A mortgages. Among the PL MBSs issued in 2006, 5.8 percent of the jumbo mortgages backing them did not have any documentation, 3.3 percent for alt-A mortgages and 0.2 percent for subprime mortgages. The lenders compounded these problems by not verifying information that was provided even though it was very easy to do so. Morgenson (2008) notes that income could be verified quickly and cheaply by making a request to the Internal Revenue Service but this was not done; as shown later, fraud was the main reason why no verification was undertaken.

In addition to loosening underwriting criteria by decreasing documentation requirements, financial institutions further pushed back limits to market growth by lowering the quality of the mortgages provided and the amount of protection. In terms of loan quality, the proportion of purchase mortgages with large payment shocks rose dramatically. The rise of non-traditional mortgages took several forms. One form was an increase in interest-only mortgages (IOs) and payment-option mortgages that reduce for a while the size of mortgage service— typically two or three years after, payment jumps when the initial "teaser rate" expires and/or principal payment comes due (Figure 3.5). Another form has been an increase in the proportion of adjustable-rate mortgages (ARM) because of their lower monthly cost relative to fixed-rate mortgages, at least until the end of 2006 (Figure 3.6). The proportion of ARMs almost doubled from 2002 to 2006 and represented about 26 percent of outstanding mortgages before the Great Recession.

Originally exotic mortgages, like ARM-IO and option-ARM, were created for wealthy home buyers with large fluctuations in monthly income who could pay a large part of principal at once (Chui 2006: 3; Lui 2005). However, over time, these mortgages were progressively provided to all households. Interest-only mortgages were highly popular and their proportion in new mortgages grew from almost nothing to 30 percent of all originations to non-prime borrowers by 2004. By the later part of 2003, non-prime mortgagors moved to pay-option mortgages and this shift accelerated as the Federal Reserve increased its policy rates. These mortgages allowed borrowers to pay only part of the interest due on their mortgages and none of the principal. One of the main characteristics of these exotic mortgages is that the interest rate can rise sharply and the amortization rate can decline very suddenly; moreover, any unpaid interest is added to the outstanding principal. As a consequence, mortgage service may increase very rapidly and may prevent even prime mortgagors from servicing their mortgage.

All these dangerous payment characteristics were compounded by a decline in the protection required by bankers. They granted simultaneous second mortgages to cover all or part of the difference between home price and the first mortgage (piggyback lending), granted mortgages with high loan-to-value ratios that not uncommonly were over 100 percent, and increased rapidly their provision of home-equity loans. They also qualified mortgagors on the basis of the teaser rate instead of the full debt service due.

As a consequence of the simultaneous increase in the level of indebtedness and decline in the quality of indebtedness, the financial fragility of households

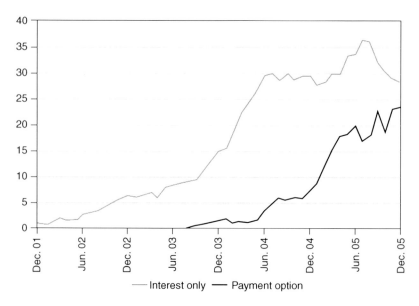

Figure 3.5 Share of exotic mortgages in non-prime mortgage originations (%) (source: Federal Deposit Insurance Corporation (*FDIC Outlook*, Summer 2006)).

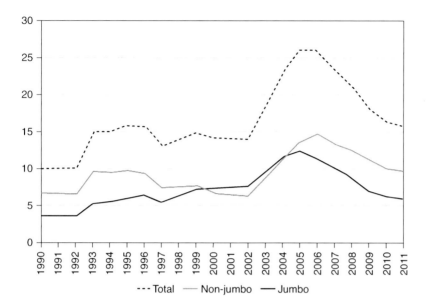

Figure 3.6 Share of adjustable-rate mortgages in outstanding conventional mortgages (%) (source: Federal Housing Finance Agency).

increased tremendously. More precisely, the capacity of households to pay their debts depended more and more on the continuation of rising home prices; the latter was necessary for the maintenance of low-cost refinancing and the capacity to sell a home at a high enough price, which were both growingly needed to meet debt services. An employee at Barclays Capital summarized all these points neatly: "A lot of the loans were not designed to be repaid, they were designed to be refinanced. That works only when housing prices are going up" (Levy 2009). Stated alternatively, households were growingly involved in speculative and Ponzi finance; thereby raising the interdependence between debt and asset prices.

This growth of Ponzi finance was made possible by a very rapid increase in capital gains as a source of wealth and income. This reliance on capital gains has been unusually large in the U.S. and other developed countries (Figures 3.7 to 3.9). This has been especially the case for the top deciles, even more so for the top 1 percent. Households in the United States recorded a rapid increase in unrealized capital gains from the middle of the 1990s. The burst of the dot-com bubble led to a large drop in unrealized capital gains from $5 trillion to almost –$2 trillion, but they rose back up with the housing boom. One may note again the similarities with the Roaring Twenties when the share of capital in income grew from 5 percent to almost 30 percent in just ten years for the top 1 percent. It took almost forty years for the share of capital gains to return to 30 percent of their income and the early 1980s recorded another rapid increase in this share following the deregulation of banking and the rapid growth of financial markets.

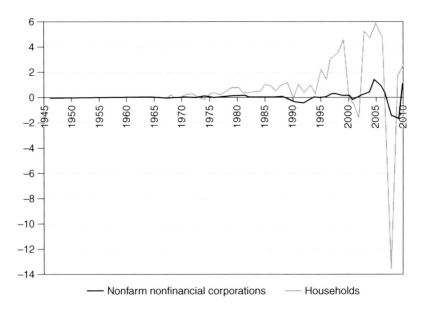

Figure 3.7 Unrealized capital gains on assets, United States (trillions of dollars) (source: Board of Governors of the Federal Reserve System).

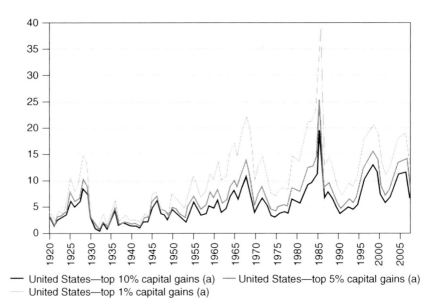

Figure 3.8 Share of capital gains in total income including capital gains, top income earners in the United States (%) (source: World Top Incomes Database).

A similar rapid increase, followed by a rapid decline, occurred in the late 1990s and early 2000. Figure 3.9 suggests a similar trend abroad with capital gains having a significant impact on the share of income received by the top income earners. For example, in Sweden, the share of income of the top decile was not affected by capital gains before 1985 but, by 2007, it added around 4 percent to that decile's share of income.

Causes and consequences of the worsening of loan underwriting

Behind this decline in underwriting are three central causes: competitive pressures amid a declining pool of high quality borrowers, changes in the banking structure induced by securitization and deregulation, and a continuous amount of reassuring information about the safety of external funding.

As the Great Moderation proceeded, it became more and more difficult for bankers to find borrowers with high quality creditworthiness, i.e., a capacity to pay based on stable income and a good cushion of liquid assets and collateral. The lack of shared prosperity over the Great Moderation, combined with the growth of speculative activities in financial and nonfinancial markets, meant that real income was stagnant, liquid savings were declining, and capital gains became an important source of income and wealth. The low interest rate of early 2000 provided an opportunity to incentivize creditworthy borrowers with stable income to refinance, but by 2003 the mortgage market was completely saturated in the prime business.

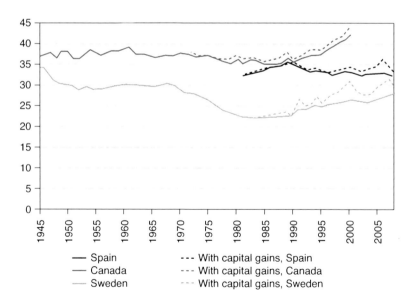

Figure 3.9 Share of top 10 percent with and without capital gains (%) (source: World Top Incomes Database).

In order to keep their business profitable, mortgage companies turned toward the non-prime side of the business. They developed that side of the business by first taking the most creditworthy non-prime borrowers and then went further by qualifying people on the basis of teaser rates and without consideration for amortization, by not verifying documentation and by requiring less collateral:

> According to our contacts, homebuyers were primarily qualified at the introductory teaser rate rather than the fully amortizing rate, which for many buyers was the main reason they were even qualified in the first place. We believe that much of the subprime surge and easing of lending standards came in the aftermath of the refinancing boom from 2001–2003. Mortgage lenders had staffed up in order to handle the flood of refinance business and then were suddenly hit with a drop in business. In order to maintain production volume, originators began chasing the purchase market by easing underwriting standards and taking share from the GSEs.
>
> (Zelman 2007: 24)

The decline in the quality of underwriting actually ended up affecting the entire market as mortgage companies were able to incentivize prime borrowers to refinance into toxic mortgages.

The decline in lending standard was observed both in consumer and commercial credit in the 1990s and after the 2001 recession (Figure 3.10). Mortgages recorded an average net tightening of –1.8 percent from 1992 to 2001 and –1.5

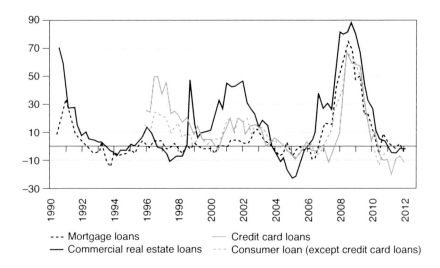

Figure 3.10 Net percentage of banks tightening standards (source: Board of Governors of the Federal Reserve System (Senior Loan Officer Survey on Bank Lending Practices)).

percent from 2003 to 2007. Commercial real estate lending also recorded a loosening in credit standards during the 1990s and after 2002. Consumer loans recorded a significant decline in net tightening from the mid 1990s, when 50 percent of banks in net terms tightened their standards, to 2000 when no bank was tightening in net terms. After 2001 the lending standards on consumer credit loosened, and from 2004 there was a net loosening of the standards by 3.1 percent on average until 2007.

As expected, the loosening of underwriting standards led to a massive increase in the share of non-prime outstanding mortgages. This share grew from about 2 percent of outstanding mortgages in 2000 to about 14 percent of the total mortgage market by 2007 (Figure 3.11). However, most of the rapid growth in subprime mortgage lending was over by 2004 and instead the industry turned toward alt-A mortgages. Indeed, the origination of securitized products based on alt-A mortgages grew much more rapidly than subprime-based securitization from 2004 (Figure 3.12). The share of subprime stagnated at 20 percent after 2004 while alt-A grew from 3 percent in 2003 to about 15 percent of new mortgage securitization in 2006.

Beyond loosening lending standards, financial institutions innovated to incentivize existing good borrowers to either take on more debt, or to refinance based on the rising value of their home. The growth of home equity lending, together with cash-out refinance mortgages, played a major role in maintaining the profitability of banks. The 1990s saw two major waves of mortgage refinancing

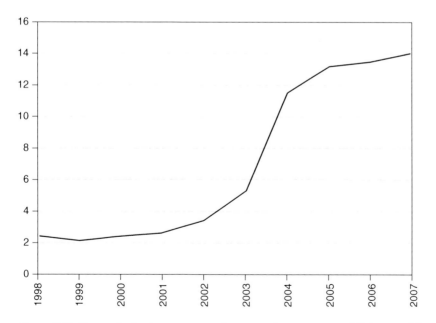

Figure 3.11 Share of subprime mortgages in outstanding mortgages (%) (source: Mortgage Bankers Association).

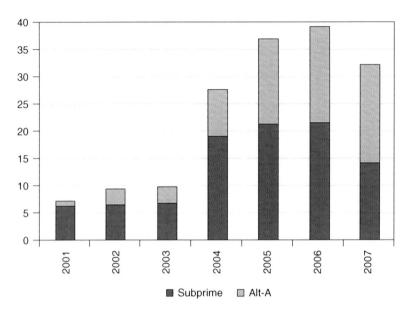

Figure 3.12 Share of non-prime mortgages in securitized mortgage originations (%) (source: Loan Performance and Credit Suisse in Rosen 2007).

reaching about 70 percent of all originations (Figure 3.13). A second wave of term-rate refinance occurred in the prime market mostly after the recession of 2001 when the Federal Reserve dramatically lowered its interest rate. After that cash-out refinance was the main driver of refinancing activities until the crisis, with over half of the refinancing done for that purpose between 2004 and 2008. This is the so-called practice of using homes as "ATM machines" to obtain cash to finance purchases of goods and services or repay other debts.

While the search for new business opportunities was a key element behind the decline in loan underwriting, it was reinforced by a change in the banking structure and the emergence of the originate-to-distribute model, of which securitization is a crucial element. The evolution of securitization and its move toward Ponzi finance will be discussed below, but the main impact was to change the incentive structure in banking. Major banks, so they thought, no longer had to care about the quality of underwriting because most of their income from loans would come from the servicing and packaging fees on the loans and securitized products.

A crucial implication of this evolution was the change in the remuneration structure of loan officers. Instead of being paid a fixed salary and basing promotion on their capacity to provide quality underwriting, commissions became a larger portion of their remuneration and the commissions would be larger for granting non-prime loans. For example, New Century Financial workers spoke out about the pressures and incentive to generate bad loans:

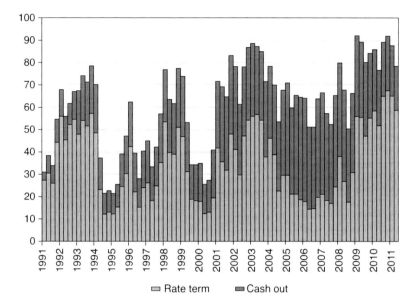

Figure 3.13 Proportion of refinance mortgage in all mortgages (%) (source: Financial Housing Finance Agency).

We were constantly told, "If you look the other way and let an additional three to four loans in a day that would mean millions more in revenue for New Century over the course of the week," [...] no one, from the top levels down to the lower levels of the office, didn't want those loans to go through.

(Cho 2007)

The same occurred in many large institutions such as WaMu and other top sub-prime lenders (U.S. Senate 2011). This incentive strategy was all the more rewarded where accounting practices allowed lenders to record profit on an accrual basis; thus profits obtained on pay-option mortgages were recorded in advance of actual mortgage payment. By 2006, with the rapid promotion of pay-option mortgages as an "affordability" product, it was not infrequent for deferred interest income—so called "phantom profit"—to represent the majority of pretax profit for some lenders from which bonuses were calculated. For example, Countrywide reported $295 million in deferred interest revenues for the twelve months ending June 2006, vs. $5.9 million in the previous twelve months. For other lenders, deferred interest represented up to 67 percent of their pre-tax profit (Der Hovanesian 2006; *Bloomberg Businessweek* 2006).

Subprime lending became a vertically integrated business in which the same company would do the origination, servicing, and securitization (Center for Public Integrity 2009). For example, Merrill Lynch owned First Franklin Corp., the fourth largest subprime lender. Countrywide Financial, the largest subprime lender, also owned Countrywide Securities Corp. Wells Fargo, Lehman Brothers, JP Morgan, Citigroup, and Bear Stearns also owned major subprime lenders. Finally, New Century Financial Corp., the third biggest subprime lender, had financial backing from major commercial and investment banks. Its main creditors when it filed for bankruptcy were Goldman Sachs, Bank of America, Morgan Stanley, Citigroup, Barclays, Bear Stearns, Credit Suisse First Boston, Deutsche Bank, IXIS Real Estate Capital, and UBS. This is partly how a problem that seemed small, and that Bernanke did not think would cause much of problem for the U.S. economy, created massive losses for the entire financial system.

Finally, beyond change in the banking structure and profitability concerns, the long period of stability induced by the Great Moderation provided data that fed lending decisions. Two central datasets in mortgage lending are home prices and delinquency rates because they are crucial to determine expected losses on mortgages. Both moved in a way that lowered expected losses and promoted the growth of financial fragility.

For Ponzi finance to emerge, there needs to be some assets that have recorded a long-term upward trend so that individuals come to consider this upward trend as normal and so start to make lending and borrowing decisions on that basis. During the Great Moderation the stock market and the housing market provided such foundations. House prices have grown almost constantly in the U.S. and Europe from the early 1990s (Figure 3.14). The UK recorded a decline in the first half of the 1990s and the United States also recorded a small decline in

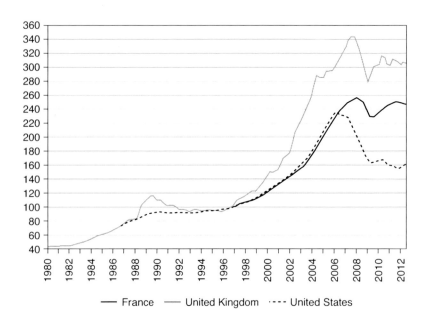

Figure 3.14 Home price index, base year 1996 (sources: Standard and Poor's; Nationwide; INSEE).

the early 1990s but this was followed by a constant upward trend. This upward trend was central in creating a state of credit that became more reliant on rising home prices as a justification to provide loans to households and businesses. It was expected that the recovery rate would be over 100 percent in case of default, allowing banks to recover not only their principal but also unearned interest and fees in case of default.

Beyond a continuous upward trend of asset prices, the views of bankers about the future were heavily influenced by the relatively stable economic growth and low unemployment rate. These favorable economic conditions led to an almost continuous decline in delinquency rates from the mid 1990s despite the growth of leverage among households and businesses. The 2001 recession did not lead to any significant increase in delinquency, except for business loans; and even there the increase was mild compared to the early 1980s (Figure 3.15).

Commercial real estate recorded very high delinquency rates in the late 1980s and early 1990s due to the Savings and Loan crisis, but it declined continuously to record-low levels by 2006. Residential mortgages also recorded an almost continuous decline in delinquency barely interrupted by the 2001 recession. Similar trends can be observed in other developed countries (Figure 3.16). It is noteworthy that Australia and Canada had very low and stable delinquency rate through the twenty years preceding the Great Recession.

This lasting decline in the delinquency rate, combined with rising home prices, meant that bankers were constantly provided with information that seemed to suggest that home prices always go up and mortgage lending is safe and getting safer. Even if a recession occurred, bankers believed that there would not be much of an impact on creditworthiness because home prices and

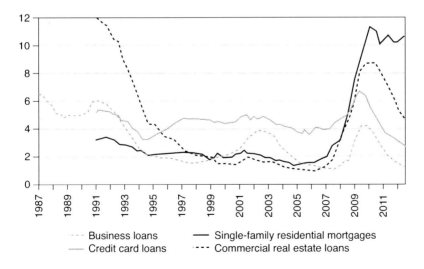

Figure 3.15 Delinquency rates in the United States (%) (source: Board of Governors of the Federal Reserve System).

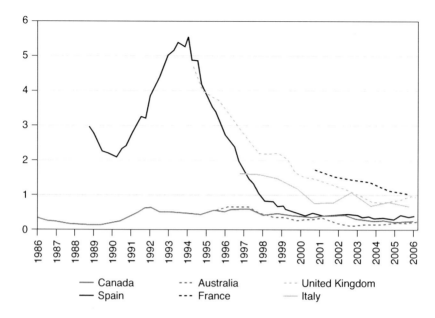

Figure 3.16 Mortgage delinquency rates (%) (source: OECD *Economic Outlook No. 80*).

delinquency rates were insensitive to the state of the economy. This state of credit was all the more prevalent that the information inputted in business decisions only includes recent information. Combined with deregulation and restructuration of banking, and search for new areas of business growth, this positive information provided the necessary ground for Ponzi finance to emerge. It also led bankers to lower their guard in terms of protections against loan and trading losses by increasing loan-to-value ratios (and so decreasing the amount of equity in the funding of housing and other economic activities), and by decreasing the proportion of loan-loss reserves that reached a historical low of 1.16 percent of total loans in the middle of 2006 when loan underwriting was at its worst (Figure 3.17). The fact that protection against loan losses was so low even though risk was mounting also suggests that control frauds were successful at managing their banks for their benefits. As Black (2005) noted, the best way to increase profit in the short run is to grow like crazy, to make bad loans at a premium yield, to push for more leverage, and not to reserve properly against losses. This guarantees short-term high profit (and so high reward for the control frauds) but also massive losses in the near future. As explained later, fraud was an important component that contributed to the crisis.

However, securitization was also extremely important and so it needs to be discussed in detail. Indeed, the decline in the underwriting of loans could not have occurred without a decline in the quality of the underwriting of securities that was centrally caused by a move in the securitization business toward Ponzi finance.

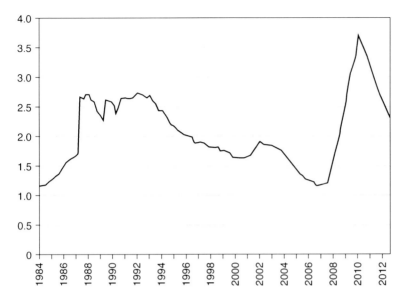

Figure 3.17 Loan-loss reserves as a percentage of total loans (source: Federal Financial Institutions Examination Council).

Security underwriting

Over the course of the Great Moderation, the quality of the underwriting of securities degraded tremendously, which helped to sustain the decline in loan underwriting. That deterioration was used to spur the growth of securitization and sustain its profitability. Over time, a giant Ponzi game was created in securitization via the creation of financial instruments that increasingly relied on asset-price movements and leverage in order to maintain the profitability of securitization. The initial purpose of securitization—moving risks off balance sheets—was progressively replaced by another purpose—highly leveraged speculation.

Evolution of securitization: engineering Ponzi finance

Since the 1970s, there has been a number of innovations on the two sides of the balance sheet of special purpose entities (SPEs) in terms of funding deals (funded vs. unfunded), motive for creating them (balance sheet vs. arbitrage), management style (unmanaged vs. managed), source of profitability (cash flow vs. market value), and method of transferring financial risks (generic vs. synthetic). For example, early SPEs that issued collateralized debt obligations (CDOs) were fully funded, i.e., they issued enough securities to be able to buy a pool of illiquid financial claims, they involved the transfer of ownership of the illiquid financial claims through sale ("generic CDO"), the CDOs were serviced from collecting debt services on the pool of claims ("cash-flow CDO"), they were created to remove illiquid claims from the balance sheet of the originator ("balance-sheet CDO"), and were pass-through structures ("unmanaged CDO"). Today, CDO SPEs are only partially funded (or unfunded), risks are transferred without transferring the illiquid financial claims embedding the risks (synthetic CDO), many CDOs make money from actively trading their assets (managed CDO) and making capital gains (market-value CDO), and they were created to allow the holders of the equity in the SPE to make money on the difference between the sum of cash inflows from income and capital gains and cash out-flows from payments to the creditors of the SPE (arbitrage CDO). The asset and liability management frequently described for banks from the 1950s to the 1980s has been frenetic for SPEs since the end of the 1980s.

Financial innovations have created more and more complex financial instruments relying on higher and higher leverage and backed by ever more artificial assets. Everything started in the mortgage sector but other classes of financial claims were progressively included. Given that in principle asset-backed securities (ABSs) can be created from any stream of cash flows, the Securities Industry and Financial Markets Association (SIFMA) concludes on its websites that "issuers and investment banks will continue to search for—and find—new types of assets to securitize to meet the growing [financial] investor demand for ABS."

EVOLUTION OF BASIC SECURITIZATION: FROM MORTGAGES TO
RESECURITIZATION

In 1970, the Government National Mortgage Association ("Ginnie Mae") sponsored the issuance of a new type of bond by insuring it—mortgage-backed security (MBS). The Federal Home Loan Mortgage Corporation ("Freddie Mac") started to issue MBSs in 1971 and Federal National Mortgage Association ("Fannie Mae") did the same from 1983. Private-label MBSs (i.e., those backed by non-conforming mortgages) were first issued in 1977 by Bank of America in collaboration with Salomon Brothers. PL MBSs include prime mortgages that are non-conforming either because they are jumbo mortgages (i.e., their outstanding amount is too high to meet the conforming loan limit) or because they do not comply with other criteria set by Ginnie, Fannie, and Freddie.

The first, and still most common, MBS is the participation certificate (PC) most commonly known as "pass-through certificates." PCs are securities issued by special purpose entities (SPEs) that are fully amortized instead of having the whole principal paid at maturity. Given the risk involved in pass-through structures, PC can only accommodate the preferences of some security buyers. To widen the demand for their securities, SPEs progressively moved toward a pay-through structure. Freddie Mac issued the first collateralized mortgage obligation (CMO) in 1983 and stripped mortgage-back securities (SMBSs) were created in 1986 by Fannie Mae (Obay 2000; Mohebbi *et al.* 2005). CMO can have as many as fifty different classes of bonds (arranged by maturity and seniority), while extreme income stripping allows for full accommodation of the preferences of financial market participants who do not have the same views about the future direction of interest rates (and so prepayment risk) (Adelson 2006).

Given the implicit government insurance, agency MBSs are free of credit risk so they do not need to have any additional credit enhancement. On contrary, PL MBSs do not have a government guarantee and have to deal with non-conforming mortgages that are riskier. As a consequence, PL MBSs cannot reach an AAA rating without providing some credit enhancement in the forms presented in Chapter 2. The outstanding volume of agency PC far outweighs any other MBSs even though the amount of PL MBSs grew rapidly from 2003 to 2007 because of the trend in loan underwriting explained earlier (Figure 3.18). While Fannie and Freddie did buy some non-conforming mortgages, they represented a small amount of their overall portfolio and they were not used to meet the lending goals set by HUD (Financial Crisis Inquiry Commission 2011). Thus, most of the growth of PL MBSs reflects the growth of non-conforming lending.

Once the securitization techniques for mortgages were fully understood, they were rapidly extended to all kinds of economic activities. It started with equipment leases in 1985 with computers (Kothari 2006: 402, 410), followed by auto loans (certificate for automobile receivables, CAR). Credit cards (certificates for amortizing revolving debts, CARD) were securitized in 1986 by Bank One with the help of Salomon Brothers (Obay 2000: 74ff.; Kothari 2006); students loans and home equity loans followed. "First-level" securitization now has been

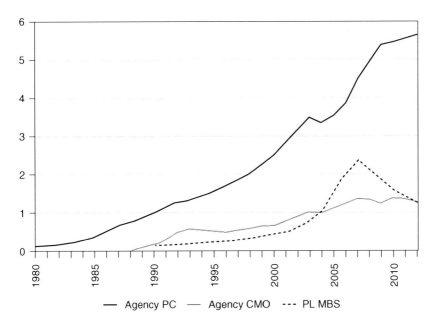

Figure 3.18 Outstanding volume of mortgage backed securities, United States (trillions of dollars) (source: Securities Industry and Financial Markets Association).

extended to intellectual property rights (royalties on music (Bowie Bonds), movies (Bond Bonds), perfumes (Calvin Klein Bonds)), as well as future flows (i.e., securities backed by the expected cash inflows from assets not yet produced) and many other sources of cash flows (Kothari 2006: 65, 501ff.; Hurst 2001). In 2007, frontier collateral in first-level securitization was in carbon emission allowances, infrastructure loans, non-performing loans, among others (de Vries Robbé and Ali 2007).

From the middle of the 1990s, the outstanding amount of ABSs grew sixfold and reached about $3 trillion in 2007 (Figure 3.19). Car loans and credit card receivables were the dominant underlying assets at the beginning, but home equity loans and collateralized debt obligations are currently the main underlying assets, while credit card receivables and student loans are also a sizeable portion of the securitization process.

However, there is a finite amount of illiquid receivables that can be transformed into securities, simply because there are a limited number of economic activities or their number grows too slowly to meet the demands of financial institutions in terms of market expansion. In order to counter this barrier to financial business growth, "second-level" securitization (resecuritization), "third level" securitization (re-resecuritization), and "fourth-level" securitization (re-re-resecuritization) have been developed progressively on the basis of CDOs; they

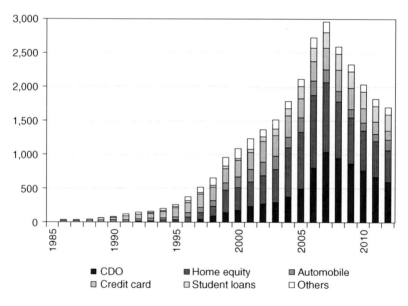

Figure 3.19 Outstanding asset-backed securities in the United States by underlying assets (billions of dollars) (source: SIFMA).

Note

Other underlying assets include: equipment, manufacturing housing, auto leases, small business loans, trade receivables, claims on intangibles, nonperforming loans, and other miscellaneous financial claims.

consist of securitizing securities. The CMO was the first case of resecuritization when an SPE used a pool of MBSs as collateral (CMOs can also be directly backed by mortgages). The CDO is an extension of the CMO that was first applied to high-yield bonds (collateralized bond obligations, CBO) by Drexel Burnham Lambert in 1987, followed by high-yield corporate loans (collateralized loan obligations, CLO) in 1989 as well distressed bonds (Lucas *et al.* 2006: 5; Goodman 2001: 141; Kothari 2006: 443). CDOs backed by emerging market bonds (EMCDO) were created in 1994. From 1995, the pool of assets bought by CDO SPEs began to contain some asset-backed securities (starting with residential MBSs) in addition to corporate loans and bonds (Lucas *et al.* 2006: 5). Today, CDOs are backed by all sorts of ABSs, derivatives, and other financial claims. In 2007, the frontier of second-level securitization was in commodity options (commodity option obligation, COO) (Jobst 2007; de Vries Robbé 2006).

The next step (third-level securitization) was to create CDOs-squared; that is, CDOs backed by other CDOs, which occurred around 1998 (Watterson 2005). The fourth level of securitization was reached with the issuance of CDOs partly backed by CDOs-squared–CDOs-cubed (Boultwood and Meissner 2008). Second- through fourth-level CDOs are called structured-finance CDOs (SFCDO) or asset-backed (security) CDOs (ABSCDO or ABCDO) and after 2001 they have been mainly backed by residential and commercial MBSs:

> Also, certain types of ABSs present in SF CDOs from 1999 through 2001 disappeared from later vintages: manufactured housing loans, aircraft leases, franchise business loans, and 12b-1 mutual fund fees. All of these assets had horrible performance in older SF CDOs. In their place, SF CDOs have recently focused more on RMBSs and CMBSs.
>
> (Lucas *et al.* 2006: 7)

Table 3.1 shows that SFCDO have been collateralized mainly by subprime mortgage products in recent years. A total of 50 percent of underlying assets in high grade ABS CDOs were subprime residential mortgage backed securities (RMBS). Thus, a majority of investment grade securities were created on the basis of non-investment grade assets that, by 2004, were increasingly of questionable value.

Table 3.1 Typical collateral composition of ABS CDOs (%)

	High grade ABS CDO	*Mezzanine ABS CDO*
Subprime RMBS	50	77
Other RMBS	25	12
CDO	19	6
Other	6	5

Source: Bank for International Settlements (2008: 5).

From 1995 to 2003, the outstanding amount of CDOs grew from virtually zero to $400 billion (Figure 3.20). This was followed by a four-year period during which the market size more than tripled. While CDOs were first used to move financial claims off balance sheet, by 2002 and until the Great Recession the main purpose of issuance of CDOs was to profit from the differential in rate of returns through the use of leverage on leverage (i.e., collateralization of debt). Indeed, the share of arbitrage CDOs rapidly climbed after 1995 and, by 2002, the amount of arbitrage CDOs represented over 50 percent of outstanding CDOs and climbed rapidly to 70 percent by 2006; after that the share of arbitrage CDOs declined but they still represent over 50 percent of outstanding CDOs as of 2012. At the same time as arbitrage became the main driver of CDO issuances, the quality of the underlying pool of assets declined. During the boom phase of the Great Moderation, the proportion of investment-grade bonds declined dramatically and was replaced by structured-finance products and high yield loans (Figure 3.21). From 2003 to 2008, SFCDOs were a major collateral and CDOs-squared comprised up to 20 percent of the total CDO market in 2005 and 2006 (Boultwood and Meissner 2008).

Similar trends can be observed in Europe with a rapid growth of securitized products from the late 1990s with outstanding amounts rising tenfold in ten years from $300 billion to $3 trillion (Figure 3.22). The UK financial sector

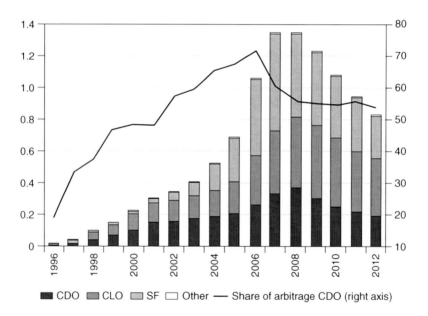

Figure 3.20 Global outstanding amount of CDOs (trillions of dollars) and relative size of arbitrage CDOs (%) (source: SIFMA).

Note
A substantial amount of CDOs has unknown purpose (arbitrage or balance sheet).

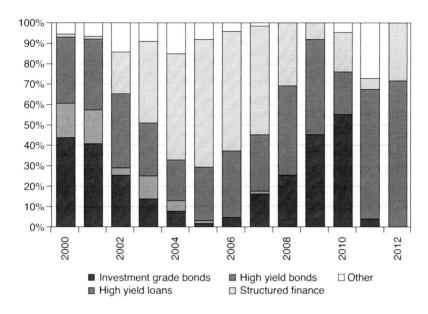

Figure 3.21 Type of collateral underlying CDO issuance, proportion (source: SIFMA).

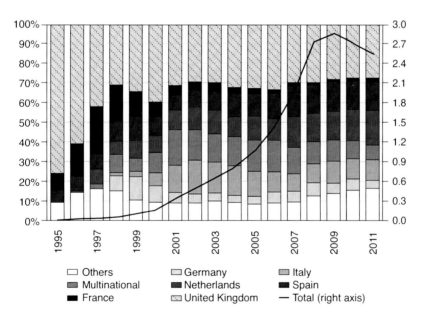

Figure 3.22 Outstanding amount of securitized products in Europe (trillions of dollars) and main countries that are the sources of underlying assets (source: SIFMA).

Note
Data includes ABSs, MBSs, CDOs, and others.

was the leader in securitization in the second part of the 1990s and, together with France, accounted for at least half of all outstanding securitized products. After 2000 Spain, Italy, and the Netherlands became key players in the securitization industry with about 30 percent of securitized products coming from these countries.

SYNTHETIC SECURITIZATION

The process of piling up levels of securitization has limits because modeling becomes extremely complex, and data to evaluate the viability and credit quality of the products is very limited. Securitization can also work by stretching a given level of securitization (intensive securitization rather than extensive securitization). Synthetic securitization achieved this goal by eliminating the need to transfer the ownership of a financial claim through sale. Further developments have limited the use of the SPE to a small portion of the deal. All these innovations make it easier to create an SPE by eliminating the need to establish truth in sale (which can be legally quite challenging), and by eliminating the need to raise cash to fund the entire asset position which can be costly and complex to set up (Goodman 2001: 143).

In order for synthetic securitization to happen, innovations had first to appear in the derivative markets. The creation of credit default swaps (CDS) in 1993 by Bankers Trust (Nelken 1999) allowed a boom in cash-flow synthetic CDOs. The creation of equity default swaps (EDS) in 2003 allowed market-value synthetic CDOs to boom (Logie and Castagnino 2006). CDSs and EDSs are over-the-counter (OTC) insurance contracts that are triggered respectively by default on underlying financial claims, and by a decline in the price of the share of a company by a given percentage. Focusing on CDSs, the CDS seller acts like an insurance company by providing protection in case a contingency occurs (default). If the bond issuer defaults, the buyer of the CDS receives the difference between the face value and the market value of the bond. More precisely the payment will equal $(1-R)E$ with R the recovery rate and E the exposure.

As in the case of most derivatives, one of the main characteristics of CDSs (and EDSs) is that there is no need to be a bondholder (or shareholder) of a company to buy or to sell a swap protecting against the default (or decline in the price of the shares) of a company. This capacity to have "naked" positions in CDS has led progressively to a change in their purpose of issuance:

> Credit Default Swaps (CDS) were originally created in the mid-1990s as a means to transfer credit exposure for commercial loans and to free up regulatory capital in commercial banks. By entering into CDS, a commercial bank shifted the risk of default to a third-party and this shifted risk did not count against their regulatory capital requirements. [...] However, in the early 2000s, the CDS market changed in three substantive manners: Numerous new parties became involved in the CDS market through the development of a secondary market for both the sellers of protection and the buyers

of protection [...] and speculation became rampant in the market such that sellers and buyer of CDS were no longer owners of the underlying asset (bond or loan), but were just "betting" on the possibility of a credit event of a specific asset.

(Zabel 2008: 548)

The date of 2000 used by Zabel to note the change in purpose of issuance of CDSs is related to a change in their regulation under the Commodity Futures Modernization Act of 2000, which has enhanced greatly the speculative use of CDSs by removing any regulatory oversight on this market. As a consequence, the CDS market has boomed tremendously since 2001 (Figure 3.23).

From less than $1 billion, the market reached $62 trillion in 2007, before crashing rapidly in 2008. The first CDSs were corporate CDSs, i.e., they provide protection against default of one or several corporation(s). Following developments in the synthetic-CDOs business, ABS CDSs (or ABCDS) were developed in 2005 to provide protection against default on ABSs, especially those referencing mortgages and home equity loans (Clark 2007; Flanagan *et al.* 2005).

The first synthetic SPE was created in Europe by Swiss Bank in August 1997 (Goodman 2001: 145). It was a fully funded deal, which means that the SPE issued credit-linked notes (CLN) for cash that is used to buy high-grade assets such as Treasuries or AAA ABSs. The SPE then issues some CDSs to the originator for the same amount as the notional value of CLNs and in exchange the originator pays a premium to the SPE that helps to remunerate the CLNs. In case

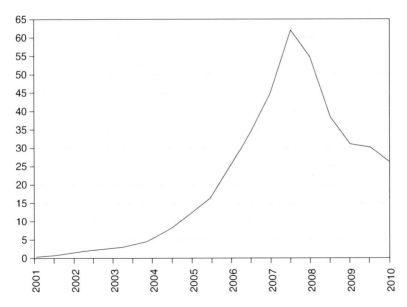

Figure 3.23 Notional amount of credit default swaps (trillions of dollars) (source: International Swaps and Derivatives Association).

of default, the SPE liquidates the needed amount of high-grade assets and CLNs take a loss according to seniority.

In December 1997, JP Morgan launched the first partially funded synthetic CDOs, called BISTRO (Broad Index Secured Trust Offering) (Goodman 2001: 149; Boultwood and Meissner 2008; JP Morgan 2000: 74ff.). In this case, the SPE only participates partially in the protection provided to the originator and the rest is left unfunded by the issuer (O'Kane 2001: 58–59). Usually only 5 to 15 percent of the notional value of the reference portfolio is funded through the use of an SPE which then buys safe assets with the cash collected (Goodman 2001: 149). The unfunded part above the A-class CLNs is called the "super-senior tranche" because its seniority is above the A-class and the assets backing the CLNs are supposed to be very safe so the chance that the super-senior tranche will be affected by losses is considered to be extremely low:

> It is broadly accepted that the risk embedded in the super-senior tranche of a synthetic CLO referencing a pool of investment-grade assets is remote in the extreme. This is because even if a super-senior swap accounts for as much as 90 percent of a CDOs's capital structure (which is not uncommon), more than 10 percent of the assets within the reference pool would have to default for losses to be sustained by the most senior tranche – an improbably high default rate for investment-grade bonds when the historical norm has been for a default rate of about 0.3 percent. Because the perceived risk associated with the super-senior swap is so low, the investor in this tranche is typically paid a premium that is no more than 8 basis points to 10bp of the CDOs's notional size.
>
> (Moore 2004: 14)

The super-senior exposure is not securitized so it does not have an explicit rating (implicitly it is above AAA, sometimes noted AAAA or AAA+). The originator assumes the super-senior exposure and the first-loss exposure. Most of the time, the originator seeks protection on the super-senior credit exposure by buying CDSs from a counterparty (usually a bank from an OECD country which is considered financially strong) in order to reduce the capital weight. The unfunded structure (super-senior exposure and equity) leaves the originator with some credit risk, or with some counterparty risk if the originator buys a CDS. In 2004, the first synthetic ABS CDOs were issued "with home equity loan and residential mortgage backed securities markets as the underlying reference obligations" (Clark 2007: 32). As explained below, the belief in the safety of super-senior tranches was unfounded, not only because of the improper rating but also because of the embedded leverage involved in securitizing securities.

Since 2000, the rapid growth of the CDS market has been a main driver of the CDO market; especially in Europe where "in 2003, 92 percent of all European CDOs rated by Moody's were accounted for by synthetic structures, up from 88 percent in 2002" (Moore 2004: 7). Until 2001 most synthetic securitization was driven by balance-sheet motives but since 2001 worldwide issuance of synthetic arbitrage CDOs has become the main driver of the CDO market (Moore 2004). Hybrid securitization (that mixes generic and synthetic aspects) has also developed tremendously.

In May 2005, with the downgrade of Ford and GM, some tranches recorded losses much larger than predicted, which led to a reconsideration of the reliability of models to value CDO tranches. Consequently, the demand for CDOs-squared declined, the demand for protection against mark-to-market volatility rose, and financial-market participants decided to return toward more funded structures (Renault 2007: 391ff.; Jobst 2007: 536). Regarding the latter, SPE sponsors wanted to fund the super-senior tranche by issuing super-senior securities. A complete funding of the super-senior tranche is impossible, however, because the return on the super-senior risk is extremely low (0.08 to 0.1 percent) so there is not much demand for this credit exposure. To boost the demand for super-senior tranches beyond monolines (Carter and Osako 2006: 3), the leveraged super-senior note (LSS) was introduced, which is a CLN with a seniority above the A-class CLN. The buyer of an LSS takes position on the entire super-senior exposure (and so receives a return based on the notional value of the super-senior exposure) while providing only a small amount of funds upfront, thus creating a leverage (typically ten to twenty-five times the notional value insured (Boultwood and Meissner 2008)) that boosts the return obtained by the LSS buyer:

> For example, take a senior exposure covering the 10 percent to 100 percent portion of a portfolio with a notional equal to €100 million, and a swap that pays a premium of 5 bps per year. If the funded portion of the resultant €90 million exposure is €6 million, the tranche is thus 15 times leveraged, i.e., €90 million/€6 million. The 5 bps per year on the €90 million is thus the equivalent of 75 bps per year on the notional of the funded portion (5 bps*15).
>
> (Chandler and Jobst 2005: 3)

This additional reward is justified by widening the scope of protection that an LSS provides. Contrary to other CLNs, a LLS must provide protections not only against credit risk but also market risk. Developing reliable mark-to-market triggers in LSS notes is still in its infancy and is based on proxies given by the libor-spread (or losses) on corporate bonds. A specific widening of the spread would cause an unwinding of the contract (Chandler and Jobst 2005; Jobst 2007: 509).

Causes and consequences of the worsening of security underwriting

The main motives for these innovations in security underwriting have been to avoid the high weight set by Basel I on loan products and to increase return on equity by leveraging asset positions in order to counter limitation of market growth (Moore 2004). These preoccupations were central among all key players of the securitization process, from loan originators to investment banks to credit rating agencies and monolines, and to pension funds and hedge funds.

In order for all the previous innovations to take place, major innovations had to occur in the credit rating methods because asset-backed bonds cannot be issued without ratings. This was all the more an issue because little reliable data was available to determine the expected losses on many of these securities. For example, the expected loss on SFCDO depends not only on the expected loss on backing financial claims, but also on the potential interdependence among these claims—default on one of the claims may trigger default on one or several other claims in the pool. This is especially true during a period of economic recession and even more so during a debt deflation. However, Adelson (2005: 21) noted "we just don't know about the correlation among the assets that go into real estate CDOs." As a consequence, assumptions about default correlations among the financial claims in the reference pool can be set quite arbitrarily, can affect dramatically the expected loss on the pool, and can be quite unstable over time. It is well known that assets that have uncorrelated, or inversely correlated, returns in periods of tranquility usually end up having similar correlations in periods of crisis (International Monetary Fund 2008a).

Credit rating agencies found several ways to get around the estimation of expected losses. One way was to just set arbitrary default correlations and default rates based on the data available for proxy securities. For example, the observed cumulative default rate over five years on AAA corporate bonds is 0.03 percent; credit rating agencies used this point of reference and adjusted it upward to compute the expected losses on the asset pools of SPEs. However, the five-year cumulative losses on AAA SPE securities turned out to be much higher than expected. Similarly, the probability of single and multiple downgrades on AAA corporate bonds is much lower than on AAA SPE securities (International Monetary Fund 2008a: 61). As explained in the section on loan underwriting, the possibility of rating error was reinforced by the long period of economic stability recorded during the Great Moderation, especially so in the housing market that came to be the main driver of securitization after 2000.

A second way to get around the problem of measuring default correlation was provided by mathematical advancements such as the Copula formula. Under specific conditions, the formula shows that default correlations could be captured by one number; thereby eliminating the need to spend time trying to estimate correlations among the thousands of financial claims in the pool. Instead, one just needs to look at the prices of CDSs and assume that financial market participants can price default risk correctly. If the price of a CDS goes up then default risk on an underlying asset has gone up and if the premium of the CDSs insuring the securities in the pool move together then one can conclude that default correlation has increased. The Copula formula was added to the credit rating system on August 10, 2004 (Jones 2009), which contributed to a rapid increase in synthetic securitization.

A third way credit rating agencies got around the problem of rating all the new types of bonds was to loosen the rating procedure. Mark Froeba, a former employee of Moody's, provides an insider's view of the changes that occurred in his company and how they promoted financial fragility:

In conclusion, I have tried to show that Moody's managers deliberately engin-eered a change to its culture intended to ensure that rating analysis never jeop-ardized market share and revenue. They accomplished this both by rewarding those who collaborated and punishing those who resisted. In addition to intim-idating analysts who did not embrace the new values, they also emboldened bankers to resist Moody's analysts if doing so was good for Moody's business. Finally, I have tried to provide you with an example of the extent to which the new culture corrupted the rating process. The adjusted European CLO Rating Factor Table appears to have been adopted for the sole purpose of preserving Moody's European CLO market share despite the fact that it might have resulted in Moody's assigning ratings that were wrong by as much as one and a half to two notches. As I indicated to Moody's outside counsel in the summer of 2008, every single investor in a Moody's rated European CLO may have a claim against Moody's for damages associated with the fact that their CLO investments were not priced correctly.

(Froeba 2010)

Other former Moody's employees like Eric Kolchinsky (2010) describe the same dynamics at play. Further investigations by Congress, uncovered that investment bankers knew that ratings were inflated and that the structured products they were underwriting were "toxic waste" and "crap" (U.S. Senate 2011). A UBS AG employee refers, in an email, of investment-grade CDOs as "vomit" (Kolker and Voreacos 2009).

The major driver behind all these changes in the rating methods was profit-ability concerns and a long period of stability that provided a stream of data that seemed to indicate that leverage was safe. Competition among the three main rating agencies was ferocious and, as the quote above suggests, over time the incentive structure was changed to promote volume over quality of rating. Credit risk analysts were asked to use inadequate models, were given little time to analyze a proposed issuance, did not have the chance to look at the underlying assets, and were pushed to get the deal through. S&P and Moody's managers forced analysts to grade MBSs they had never reviewed. Pressures on analysts were even worse in CDO business that provided three times more revenues to rating agencies. Frank Raiter, Managing Director and Head of residential mortgage backed securities ratings at Standard and Poor's, received the following email from his superior after asking for a sample of loans to be able to provide a rating for a CDO:

Any request for loan level tapes is TOTALLY UNREASONABLE!!! Most investors don't have it and can't provide it. Nevertheless we MUST produce a credit estimate. [...] It is your responsibility to provide those credit estim-ates and your responsibility to devise some method for doing so.

(U.S. House of Representatives 2008a)

Not only did risk analysts avoid looking at the underlying assets and borrowers' capacity to pay, but "there was no model—there was nothing—that could work for modeling interest-only, adjustable, non-payment liar's loans" according to Stephen Berger chairman of Odyssey Investment Partner LLC (Blair Smith 2008).

Thus, as in loan underwriting, the entity that is supposed to play the role of designated skeptic and to provide a careful analysis of a financial deal did not perform its duty. This was all the more difficult to do for rating agencies because they were paid by the companies that submitted a security for rating. This kind of dynamic was compounded by the fact that credit rating agencies provided their rating models to their customers so they could structure a bond in such a way that it would meet their desired rating. This is important because most private-label securitized products would not have been sold if an AAA rating had not been obtained.

Once the gatekeepers in the securitization process were no longer doing their job properly, things got out of hand very quickly. Not only did participants abuse the system but regulation based on credit ratings fell apart. As shown previously, investment banks were able to push through securitized products with worse and worse asset pools and by the 2000s most of the assets in the underlying pool were non-investment grade financial claims and subprime mortgages. We know why non-prime mortgages grew and non-investment grade loans grew for similar reasons:

> Banks are motivated to securitize investment-grade commercial loans because by doing so they effectively subject themselves to the market's capital requirements for such loans instead of their regulator's. Tight competition has compressed the margin that banks earn on investment-grade loans to the point that more institutions are considering investment-grade lending to be an inefficient use of capital.
>
> (Kalser and Puwalski 1998)

The main financial claims underlying CDOs were high-yield claims and structured products, and the latter relied heavily on subprime mortgages in the 2000s. The same profitability concerns were at the core of the boom in EDSs:

> By 2004, it was becoming increasingly difficult in many countries to structure investment-grade credit portfolios that had significant returns. In response to this, new derivatives were developed that had a similar structure to existing credit derivatives but whose value depended on the equity value of the reference firm.
>
> (Medova and Smith 2006: 84)

By relying on capital gains and leverage, investment banks hoped to maintain their profitability and to find new markets for securitized products.

The whole securitization process could not have gone on without the existence of a demand for securitization products. One of the main reasons such a demand existed was because securitized financial claims provided a greater return given credit risk:

Many fixed-income investors have strict rating constraints for their investments while also facing yield targets. The tightness of spreads prevailing over the last few years has made it hard for these investors to achieve their return targets while maintaining the risk of their portfolios within their risk limits. In order to achieve it, many have turned to CDOs that are typically higher yielding than cash assets. For example, in December 2005, AAA corporate bonds were trading at a spread of 5 basis points over Libor, whereas CDOs with comparable maturities were offering spreads between 25 basis points (AAA CLOs—Collateral Loan Obligations) and 50 basis points (AAA synthetic investment-grade CDOs).

(Renault 2007: 376–377)

This impetus to earn higher rates of return on a limited range of financial claims was strong among pension funds; especially so in the 2000s because interest rates were low and the stock market was not performing as well as in the 1990s:

"What we were looking for was a higher return with some additional risk, but not too much risk, to help us meet our 7.5 percent earnings assumption," says Einhorn, who until this year had his fund's assets split 60–40 between publicly traded stocks and bonds. [...] As administrator of the Teamsters Pension Trust Fund of Philadelphia and Vicinity, a multiemployer plan that covers more than 27,600 active and retired union members, Einhorn had begun evaluating private real estate as an investment option in the first quarter of 2002. [...] Whatever his timing, Einhorn is clearly not the only plan sponsor confronting a funding crisis, nor the only one casting around for fresh ways to invest pension monies. Thanks to slumping equity markets, companies in the S&P 500 saw their aggregate pension assets shrink by $173 billion from 1999 through 2002, estimates Credit Suisse First Boston. The average S&P 500 corporate pension plan lost 8.65 percent in 2002 and 7.37 percent in 2001, according to CSFB. At the same time, declining interest rates drove up the present value of the S&P 500's collective pension obligations by $289 billion, leaving those plans underfunded to the tune of $216 billion. Further declines in interest rates since then have exacerbated the problem. Now, many corporations that enjoyed a pension funding "holiday" in the 1990s are confronted with having to make sizable contributions to their plans. Fearing that neither equities nor fixed-income investments will generate the returns they produced in the past two decades, many plan sponsors are looking at alternative investments—a term generally applied to hedge funds, real estate, and private equity—to juice up their portfolios.

(Mayer 2003)

Pension funds were enticed by investment banks like Bear Stearns to buy unrated equity tranches of CDOs and, in 2008, 7 percent of all equity tranches in the U.S. were held by pension funds, endowments, and religious organizations. The

California Public Employees' Retirement System invested $140 million in unrated CDO tranches (Evans 2007). Some pension funds were forbidden to buy non-investment grade portions of CDOs but Wall Street banks got around this legal barrier by creating financial instruments that promoted principal protection. For example, constant proportion portfolio insurance (CPPI) helped to increase the demand for rated equity tranches by creating a principal-protected CLN (Renault 2007; Whetten 2005). Thus, pressures to meet profitability targets on the demand side of securitization were also a major factor making the decline in the underwriting of securities possible.

In each of the sectors of securitization, some individuals did try to warn that there was a strong degradation of the quality of securitization and even fraud. Mark Froeba and Eric Kolchinsky did so at Moody's, and Matthew Lee at Lehman Brothers did the same (Lee in U.S. House of Representatives 2010). But all of them ended up being ignored, demoted, or fired. There was a strong incentive to ignore the accumulating problems given the dependence of profit and bonuses on the continuation of business as usual. Some top bank managers also thought that "the whole system was based on raping the public" (Stefanski in Schwartz 2007) and refused to lower their underwriting standards; but, this came at the cost of accepting a massive loss of market share. Most bankers, especially on Wall Street, cannot accept such a decline; in fact they cannot even accept stable market shares, as Mr. Blankfein noted:

> It should be clear that self-regulation has its limits. We rationalised and justified the downward pricing of risk on the grounds that it was different. We did so because our self-interest in preserving and expending our market share, as competitors, sometimes blinds us—especially when exuberance is at its peak.
>
> (Blankfein 2009)

Wall Street financial institutions are growth-oriented businesses and so must find ways to constantly expand their business.

One of the main consequences of the change in the rating method of agencies was the creation of a circularity in the rating process. Credit rating agencies entered unfamiliar territory when they had to rate exotic securities with limited data about default and recovery rates. As a consequence they looked for help in the financial market by taking signals provided by CDS and EDS premium; the Copula formula was the latest way to do this. However, the CDS and EDS premia were themselves dependent on the rating of underlying securities. Thus, the rating upon which securitization was based was not only unreliable but also was highly procyclical, making it even more probable that Ponzi finance could emerge through waves of optimism and positive reinforcement among financial market participants.

Another major consequence of previous developments was that a large portion of the banking business became a black box that no regulator had the authority to check. Not only the quality of the assets declined but shadow banking was highly dependent on short-term refinancing sources—namely the repurchase and commercial paper markets—to maintain positions in long-term assets. The growth of use of special purpose entities was "encouraged by the implicit belief that ready access to [short-term] financing would always be there" (Counterparty Risk Management Policy Group III 2008: 38) in order to fund positions in long-term assets. Thus, the originate-and-hold banking model was now transferred to the shadow banking sector. However, a crucial difference between the two banking models is that shadow banking does not have easy access to the central bank's refinancing channels, which means that if short-term markets close the only solution left is to liquidate assets. Further, while banks rely largely on stable insured deposits to refinance position, shadow banks rely on uninsured liabilities that can be volatile.

Finally, a central consequence of the building up of leverage and the use of short-term funding to sustain asset positions was a very high sensitivity to changes in home prices. So much so that even not unusual fluctuations in home prices would lead to the collapse of some securitization structures (Table 3.2). This is all the more so because the equity available in subprime housing finance is very thin or inexistent. A typical CDO-squared has a senior AAA tranche with 40 percent credit support; however the collateral of a CDO-squared is the mezzanine tranche of a CDO that is itself collateralized on the lowest tranches of RMBSs, usually the bottom 5 percent. Thus, assuming no equity is present in subprime housing finance, a 5 percent write-down wipes out low-rate MBSs (5 percent of the capital structure of SPE1), the CDOs based on them (SPE2), and the CDO-squared based on the CDOs of SPE2 (SPE3). Even worse, given the size of the embedded leverage in a CDO-squared, it is completely wiped out after a 1.2 percent write-down in mortgages ($5\% \times 24\%$). The senior AAA tranche of CDOs-squared starts to be affected if losses on subprime mortgages are greater than 0.78 percent. Thus, the 40 percent credit support in a CDO-squared is highly misleading because it excludes the embedded leverage (or collateralization of debt) that is present in that structured product.

Boom, MMC, and fraud

Overall, the financial fragility of the financial system increased by deepening the layering of debts and by putting a lot of emphasis on expected capital gains and refinancing to service the accumulated debts. This was done primarily by shifting the traditional banking model out of regulatory oversight through securitization, and by growing the securitization business based on unsound underwriting practices in both loan and security markets.

While all the previous trends developed over the so-called "Great Moderation," they rapidly accelerated through the late 1990s and early 2000s. The mild 2001 recession in the United States briefly limited the emergence of a lending boom in the housing market, but, by 2003, through the combinations of all the previously discussed factors, the conditions were ideal for a lending boom during which Ponzi finance grew tremendously not only in housing finance but also in leverage buyout and corporate funding.

Table 3.2 Financial layering, or embedded leverage, or leverage on leverage

Households	*SPE1*	*SPE2*	*SPE3*	
Houses	Subprime mortgages			
	Subprime mortgages	High-rate MBSs	Low-rate MBSs	High rate CDOs	Mezzanine CDOs
				Mezzanine CDOs (14%)	Senior-AAA CDO²'s (60%)
	Equity (very thin or none)	Low-rate MBSs (5%)		Low-rate CDOs (10%)	Other CDO²'s (40%)

Source: International Monetary Fund (2008a).

Housing was seen as a "sure thing" in terms of portfolio decisions. A 2003 flier sent to brokers from a mortgage company tells it all: "Did You Know NovaStar Offers to Completely Ignore Consumer Credit!" (NovaStar was a large pioneering mortgage company that blew up) (Morgenson 2007). In 2006 mortgage brokers at Strategic Mortgages promoted complex mortgages and advertized them as family friendly loan products: "An OPTION ARM loan is a very conservative loan in today's market. Its payment cap assures that your loan will always be affordable." Mortgage brokers were granting large highly toxic mortgages to people with little or no income. A household making $30,000 received a mortgage of $500,000; even prisoners could obtain mortgages (Klein and Goldfarb 2008). Make-belief was high and entire neighborhoods were caught in the frenzy and borrowed on the basis of the current and expected future equity in their home (Steinhauer 2009). By 2006, however, the housing market showed considerable slowdown and builders had to provide incentives through price cuts and upgrades in order to maintain the demand for housing.

In the bond market, signs of boom were also present. A 2006 newspaper article clearly shows the mood of the moment:

> With Wall Street caught up in a wave of acquisitions, normally cautious bond investors are living like Las Vegas high rollers [...]. And for some companies, the more they borrow, the safer they are deemed. [...] The wave of recent purchases by private equity groups has pushed issuance of high-risk debt to record levels. [...] But instead of worrying that defaults will increase, debt prices are signaling that bondholders believe that companies will have few problems paying off new loans. [...] For many acquirers, debt has never been easier to get. Global issuance of risky high-yield, or junk, bonds has reached record levels. [...] Many of those issuances offer surprisingly low yields, suggesting that despite the glut of new debt, demand is still outpacing supply and [financial] investors are betting companies will not default on their new, risky loans. A further sign that borrowers, rather than [financial] investors, are calling the shots is the growth of pay-in-kind notes, which allow a company to pay a bond's interest with more debt rather than with cash.
>
> (Duhigg 2006)

This is a textbook example of boom period. By the end of the housing boom, financial institutions used unorthodox measures to keep the Ponzi process alive. The issuance of pay-in-kind (PIK) bonds—the coupon is paid by means other than cash: borrowing, issuance of shares, or other means—grew rapidly from 2006 and reached $20 billion (Figure 3.24). In addition, level-3 valuation of securities—in which an internal model is used instead of a market price—grew very rapidly from 2007 (International Monetary Fund 2008b). This also allowed financial institutions to avoid recognizing losses that were mounting by late 2006 based on market price. Of course, level-3 valuation can lead to large abuses and, sometimes, financial firms used different pricing models to value financial assets for their customers and internally (Counterparty Risk Management Policy Group III 2008: 88).

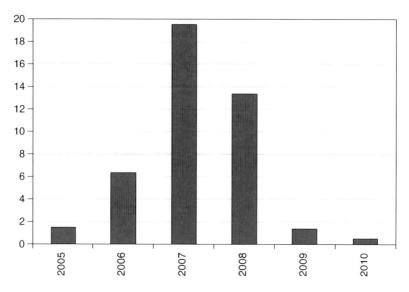

Figure 3.24 Volume of issuance of PIK toggle bonds (billions of dollars) (source: Standard & Poor's LCD).

In addition, the securitization business was running out of steam as the demand for such products started to dry up, especially for the AAA tranches. To counter that problem, additional special purpose entities were created for the sole purpose of creating a demand for the unwanted tranches. A senior European securitization banker noted:

> We created a lot more triple A product than there are now buyers for it. We manufactured buyers in the form of off-balance sheet SIVs and conduits and that's the adjustment we're now going through, trying to find where to place all this stuff.
>
> (Davies 2008)

Citigroup created twelve SPEs that issued CDOs for the sole purpose of creating a strawbuyer. Merrill Lynch issued twenty-two of such SPEs (Bernstein and Eisinger 2010). In addition, SPEs sold CDOs to each other:

> Some CDOs now purchase mezzanine or subordinate tranches of similar CDOs from other managers who have similar investment styles. This somewhat undermines diversification (amplifies correlation) while boosting leverage. Another possible area of concern is the going trend of including unrated assets in CDOs.
>
> (Adelson 2005: 6)

By 2005, it became clear to some members of the financial community that the preservation of a satisfactory level of profitability relied more and more on a pyramid scheme, which was a concern among some members of the financial community. However, a "long" period of steadily declining default rates and rising home prices, combined with the optimism of the day, pushed those worries aside for two more years.

Beyond the euphoria, the boom was also characterized by a massive increase in fraudulent activities. The decline in the quantity of required information was compounded by the decline in the quality of the information provided. The Financial Crimes Enforcement Network found that mortgage brokers, appraisers, and borrowers were at the center of the fraudulent schemes that consisted mainly in misrepresentation of income/assets/debts and forged/fraudulent documents (accounting for over 70 percent of all frauds in the mortgage industry) (Financial Crimes Enforcement Network 2008). Fraud became a quasi-institutionalized way of operating for all eyes to see, with websites advertising software that allowed printing of fake pay stubs and fraudulent methods used to raise credit scores (Creswell 2007). Companies such as TradeLineSolutions promised their customers to improve FICO scores by adding a person with an excellent credit history to their own without her consent or knowledge. In addition, companies such as Washington Mutual and Countrywide fabricated documents in order to qualify more households (U.S. Senate 2011). As a consequence, since the end of 2006, FICO's predictive power declined because of tricks (many illegal) used to improve FICO scores. Moreover, beyond the fabrication of documentation, a lack of information, and the rigging of information, companies like Washington Mutual also maintained a black list of honest appraisers. As a consequence, many appraisers had an incentive to look the other way when they found a major problem in a house in order to hit the appraisal value required in a mortgage contract (Streitfeld 2009).

Predatory lending grew tremendously and households were provided mortgages that they would never be able to repay. A lawsuit against Countrywide notes that the lender used discriminatory lending practices, inflated earnings, and abusive bankruptcy or foreclosure processes. Almost 60 percent of its borrowers in subprime adjustable rate mortgages could only qualify on the basis of the minimum mortgage payment (Morgenson 2008; Graybow and Keating 2008).

In 2007, credit rating agencies finally analyzed the underlying assets of residential mortgage-backed securities and found numerous instances of fraud. Fitch found it "disconcerting" and noted that Ponzi finance was central in the propagation of fraud and its sustainability:

> Fitch believes that much of the poor underwriting and fraud associated with the increases in affordability products was masked by the ability of the borrower to refinance or quickly re-sell the property prior to the loan defaulting, due to rapidly rising home prices.
>
> (Pendley *et al.* 2007: 1)

One may note that credit rating agencies previously claimed that they were not qualified to judge the underlying assets in the pool. Moody's MBS analysts stated: "We aren't loan officers. Our expertise is as statisticians on aggregate basis. We want to know, of 1000 individuals, based on historical performance, what percent will pay their loans?" Moody's CDO analyst stated: "We're structure experts. We're not underlying asset experts" (Lowenstein 2008). Even though they did not feel qualified to perform an analysis of the underlying assets, the fraud was so obvious that it would have been easy to stop. Unfortunately, rating agencies did not bother to even look until it was too late, at which point no additional business could be obtained by looking the other way. As shown earlier, some employees of the agencies did try to look but were pressured to reconsider.

Besides fraud in underwriting, there was also fraud in the allocation of securities. After the crisis, institutional investors noted that their funds were improperly placed in subprime securities and derivatives instead of Treasuries and corporate bonds. The mortgage electronic registration system (MERS) is another clear example of the abuses—improper transfer, or outright destruction, of mortgage notes, improper recording of payments, and other fraudulent activities (Wray 2010a, 2010b, 2010c; Porter 2007; Congressional Oversight Panel 2010a).

The Federal Bureau of Investigation warned from 2004 about the rising trend in fraud but nothing was done about it. Earlier, Federal Reserve Governor Gramlich was also concerned about predatory lending but nothing was done. Other members of the Federal Reserve staff also raised concerns but they were ignored or dismissed. Notably, the staff of the Fed after the second hearings on Home Ownership and Equity Protection Act (HOEPA) in 2000 recommended that loans based solely on collateral value without consideration for borrower's ability to repay should be banned. The Fed rejected the proposal and only slightly tightened the HOEPA rules hoping to cover more subprime loans (previously it covered only 1 percent of them). However, banks reacted and changed the terms of the loans so that again only a very limited amount of mortgages were covered (Financial Crisis Inquiry Commission 2011: 93).

Finally, in December 2005, the five federal regulatory agencies became concerned about innovations in the subprime mortgage industry and proposed to issue a guidance. A guidance is not law but it shows the expectations of regulators by guiding the priorities of in-field supervisors. It also provides financial institutions with an idea of what to expect when supervisors come. The guidance stated that financial institutions should carefully underwrite subprime mortgages by qualifying people on the basis of the full debt service payment (instead of the initial teaser interest payments) and by verifying income, assets, and job. All these are reasonable demands that deal with practices that have proven toxic since the beginnings of banking. The guidance was submitted for comments to the industry and received a barrage of criticisms; a long back-and-forth followed. It was argued that the guidance would exclude "good people" from access to the "American dream" and reduce the competitiveness and flexibility of the U.S. financial system. Here is a typical statement taken from a Senate hearing on this issue:

Many innovative loans products, such as the interest-only ARM or the 40-year mortgage, have contributed to the greater availability of diverse loan products and enhanced consumer choice, which has directly resulted in increased competition and more affordable credit. Second, NAMB believes that innovation and technological advancement in the mortgage marketplace has occurred because the market has been free to identify market needs and develop loan products to satisfy that need. Government regulation of this innovative spirit, whether in the area of pricing, compensation, or in product development, will only result in firm boundaries that will prevent the marketplace from adequately responding to consumer needs in the future. [...] The bottom line is that unwarranted tightening of underwriting guidelines could hurt the robust housing industry and deny deserving consumers the chance at homeownership.

(Hanzimanolis in U.S. Senate 2006)

Mr. Hanzimanolis was the President-Elect of the National Association of Mortgage Brokers. During the hearing, another argument against the guidance was that low default rates on mortgages proved the reliability of the mortgage practices and so the non-necessity to constrain them; stability "proves" that markets are stable and regulation is a burden.

Conclusion

The Great Recession was partly the result of a long process of deregulation and unchecked financial innovations that ultimately led to a decline in underwriting standards and consumer protection. These changes were driven by a long period of economic stability (which pushes institutions to find new ways to make money as markets saturate, and which increased the confidence to use leverage in financial innovations and existing economic activities), cutthroat competition (which pushes financial institutions to innovate frenetically and promotes sloppy underwriting and rating standards), and beliefs that market mechanisms and the profit motive always lead to socially optimal outcomes and that government should get out of the way (which lead to great political and social pressures on regulators and supervisors). This period of time was a classical example of the transition from hedge to Ponzi financing that Minsky analyzed in detail: from cash-flow cash CDO to market-value unfunded CDO; from MBS to CMO to CDO-cubed and LSS; from fixed-rate mortgages to adjustable-rate mortgages, interest-only mortgages and, finally, payment-options mortgages; from transaction-determined prices to model-determined prices; from reliable credit rating to sloppy rating procedures; from credit protection to market-value protection. All these changes in financial products and structures represent a progressive shift away from an income-related activity with low/moderate leverage requiring little refinancing, to a capital-related activity requiring large leveraging and constant refinancing at low interest rate.

The originate-to-distribute model virtually eliminated underwriting, to be replaced by a combination of property valuation by assessors who were paid to overvalue real estate, by credit ratings agencies who were paid to overrate securities, by accountants who were paid to ignore problems, and by monoline insurers whose promises were not backed by sufficient loss reserves. Some mortgages were Ponzi from the very beginning—they required rising real estate prices as well as continual access to refinance because borrowers did not have the capacity to service the loans. Much of the activity was actually off the balance sheets of banks and thrifts, with mortgage brokers arranging for finance, with investment banks packaging the securities, and with the "shadow banks" or "managed money" holding the securities. While Fannie and Freddie have been subjected to much ridicule, in truth neither of them made or arranged for any of the mortgages, and they only began to purchase the toxic securities because that was all that markets were selling.

Once established, the Ponzi process has required ever more daring (legal and illegal) financial practices, which ultimately have consisted in letting borrowers choose what income to state and how much debt to service, and letting financial companies use esoteric methods to price and to rate SPE securities. This Ponzi process was sustained by all sectors involved in the securitization process, bankers and appraisers (for all the fees they earn: servicing fee, brokering fee, late fee from delinquency, and fee from foreclosing on home with rising prices), homebuyers (for access to a home and speculation), and security holders (pension funds, hedge funds, etc. for capacity to earn higher returns on securities). As a consequence there were strong socio-political pressures to let it go unchecked.

Most analysts have pointed at subprime lending, speculation, and greed to explain the crisis. While these are contributing factors, they are not the main factors. Not only was subprime lending only half of the story in terms of non-prime lending (alt-A was as bad if not worse), but non-prime lending is not synonymous with "bad" lending or Ponzi lending. On the contrary, non-prime lending may be a perfectly normal way to do business, as long as the financial terms are adapted to the needs of the borrowers and are related to their core income so that borrowers have chance to repay. Of course default rates are much higher on non-prime loans but that is a given, and lenders who decide to enter into this business should be able to protect themselves against this higher default rate. In addition, prime delinquencies have also risen dramatically to historically high levels, which shows that non-prime lending (even more so subprime lending) is only part of the story.

Speculation also is not the main cause of the current crisis because some people entered Ponzi-inducing mortgages even though they did not plan to speculate with their house, and because mortgage companies were forced to enter in the Ponzi process for reasons as simple as justifying their staffing. Most of the lending was to refinance ownership or for cash-out equity, thus, this was not to finance speculative home flipping. In terms of consumer finance, the Ponzi process was the result of growing income inequality together with growing consumerism. This led people to use willingly a growing amount of revolving funds to a point where they could not afford payments, and also created a large increase in economic insecurity.

Finally, greed also is not a main cause because greed needs to be nurtured for it to flourish and the current crisis could have occurred without greed. We would not deny that greed is important, it is; but it is only part of a grander mechanism that provides incentives and forces one to behave in a greedy way. Market mechanisms pushed economic entities to behave in a greedy way in all good conscience even if they are of high morality, because greed is necessary for their own economic survival. In addition, individuals may find comfort in following the majority. Overall, it is not a question of morality and "bad" behavior but one of systemic failure. Financial institutions have been supervised on an individual basis to uncover "bad behaviors" without recognizing that the system itself encourages (legal and illegal) dangerous financial practices, and that everybody may be behaving "properly/wisely/cleverly" according to the social norms of behavior but still may generate great systemic instability.

Chapter 2 examined the similarities in terms of leverage, dependence on financial income, and inequalities between MMC and Finance Capitalism. Now one may note that there is another similarity in terms of the way investment banks were involved in the boom. Indeed, the 1929 crash resulted from excesses promoted by investment trust subsidiaries of Wall Street's banks. As Galbraith (1961) makes clear, stocks could be manipulated by insiders—Wall Street's financial institutions—through a variety of "pump and dump" schemes. Since the famous firms like Goldman Sachs were partnerships, they did not issue stock; hence, to profit from the stock market boom, they put together investment trusts that would purport to hold valuable equities in other firms (often in other affiliates, which sometimes held no stocks other than those in Wall Street trusts) and then sell shares in these trusts to a gullible public.

Effectively, trusts were an early form of mutual fund, with the "mother" investment house investing a small amount of capital in their offspring, highly leveraged using other people's money. Goldman and others would then whip up a speculative fever in shares, reaping capital gains. However, trust investments amounted to little more than pyramid schemes—there was very little in the way of real production or income associated with all this trading in paper. Indeed, as Galbraith showed, the "real" economy was long past its peak—there were no "fundamentals" to drive the Wall Street boom. Inevitably, it collapsed and a debt deflation began as everyone tried to sell out of their positions in stocks—causing prices to collapse. Spending on the "real economy" suffered and we were off to the Great Depression. The banking crisis had been made very much worse because banks were caught holding stocks with little or no value, many of them issued by these investment trusts. Ironically, even the investment banks that had created the trusts got burned because they also held the worthless stocks in other investment trust subsidiaries in order to help create an artificial market for garbage. In some cases, this was because they got caught holding stocks they were trying to sell when the market crashed. However, many had invested in the pyramid schemes they created.

Note how similar this is to the recent practice of SPEs buying CDOs from each other; thereby helping to create an artificial market for garbage. Traders adopted the "greater fool" theory: they were sure the whole thing would inevitably collapse, but each trader thought he could sell out his position at the peak, shunting toxic assets off to the greater fools. Just as in 1929, traders found that selling into a collapsing market meant losses, and falling asset prices meant collateral calls with no access to finance. Like in 1928–1929, the banks that originated the toxic waste for sale to customers got caught holding it for precisely the same reasons.

In some ways, things were even worse than they had been in 1929 because the investment banks went public in the 1990s—issuing equities directly into the portfolios of households and indirectly to households through the portfolios of managed money. Indeed, by the 1990s the big investment banks were still partnerships so they found it impossible to directly benefit from a run-up of the stock market, which is similar to their situation in the 1920s. An investment bank could earn fees by arranging initial public offerings for start-ups, and it could trade stocks for others or for its own account. This offered the opportunity to exploit inside information, or to manipulate the timing of trades, or to push the underperforming stocks onto clients. But in the euphoric irrational exuberance of the late 1990s, the traditional investment banking business paled by comparison with speculation in stocks. How could an investment bank's management get a bigger share of the action? In the late 1990s, the largest partnerships went public to enjoy the advantages of stock issue in a boom. As a consequence they moved from a business that used partner's money, with low leverage, to a new business model: maximize share prices. Before this transformation, trading profits were a small part of investment bank revenues—for example, before it went public, only 28 percent of Goldman Sach's revenues came from trading and investing activities. That rose to 80 percent of revenue. Top management was rewarded with bonuses for doing so, and, to align interests, part of their compensation was in the form of stock options.

With investment banks going public, it was not a simple matter of having Goldman or Citibank jettison one of its unwanted offspring as they could do after the 1929 crash when they closed their investment trusts—problems with the stock or other liabilities of the behemoth financial institutions rattled Wall Street and threatened the solvency of pension funds and other invested funds. This finally became clear to the authorities after the problems with Bear Stearns and Lehman Brothers. The layering and linkages among firms—made opaque by over-the-counter derivatives such as credit default swaps—made it impossible to let them fail one-by-one, as failure of one would bring down the whole house of cards.

The crisis and response

The possibility of a crisis was generated by the previous trends. Until the very beginning of the crisis in 2007, these trends in the loan and security markets were praised by Greenspan and Bernanke. In a 2002 speech, Greenspan summarized well the consensus of the moment regarding the capacity of the economic system to absorb shocks like the dot-com bubble:

> If risk is properly dispersed, shocks to the overall economic system will be better absorbed and less likely to create cascading failures that could threaten financial stability. The broad success of that paradigm seemed to be most evident in the United States over the past two and one-half years. [...] These episodes suggest a marked increase over the past two or three decades in the ability of modern economies to absorb unanticipated shocks.
>
> (Greenspan 2002)

From the capacity of credit scoring to improve access to credit, to the benefits of securitization and derivatives in allocating risks toward the entity the most able to bear, the financial system was seen as highly unlikely to record any major crisis.

Several economists who work within the Post Keynesian framework recognized almost ten years before the Great Recession that some of the previous trends were not sustainable (Galbraith 2009; Bezemer 2010). Wynne Godley was the first to really focus on the accounting balances presented in the first section and to note that the trends were unsustainable. Dimitri Papadimitriou, Gennaro Zezza, and many others at the Levy Economics Institute embraced his analysis (Papadimitriou *et al.* 2002; Papadimitriou *et al.* 2006). Other authors like Steve Keen, Michael Hudson, and Nouriel Roubini also saw it coming. Outside academia there were also some people who knew that things were not going well (Fishbein and Woodall 2006; McCulley 2007a, 2007b; Baker 2002).

The crisis: immediate causes and unfolding of the disaster

The immediate causes of the crisis involved financial events as well as two policy events. On the financial side, principal payments started to kick in for interest-only mortgages and teaser interest rates began to be reset upward. People who had been qualified on the basis of the teaser rate or interest rate only could no longer service their mortgage, which led to an increase in delinquency from the third quarter of 2006. On the policy side, first, the Federal Reserve started to raise its target interest rate rapidly from early 2004, which affected ARMs very rapidly and led to a significant slowdown in ARM originations from 2006. Second, from the end of 2003, the Treasury decided to reduce its deficit and planned to reach a surplus by 2012.

The Bush Administration succeeded in reducing the deficit not because of policies to contain spending or raise taxes but because of the automatic stabilizers. The growth rate of taxes outpaced the growth rate of outlays from 2004, and so the deficit declined (Figure 3.25). Tax revenues were hitting a growth rate of 15 percent per year by 2005—far above GDP growth hence, reducing non-government sector after-tax income, and faster than government spending, which

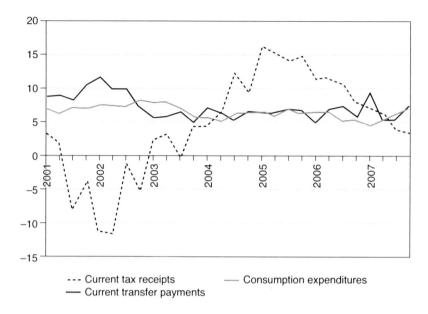

Figure 3.25 Growth rate of tax, expenditures, and transfer payments (%) (source: BEA).

grew just above 5 percent. Such fiscal tightening often is followed by a down-turn (Wray 1999) and the downturn that accompanied the global financial crisis (GFC) was no exception.

These monetary and fiscal policy trends progressively squeezed the income of the private sector while raising its debt burden. Given the growing financial fragility of the private sector induced by the previous tendencies, only a relatively small decline in income and/or increase in interest rate were necessary to unwind the Ponzi process in the mortgage industry.

As a consequence of the rise in delinquency, defaults on mortgages started to rise sharply. This was fine for banks who expected that homeowners would be able to make a profit from selling houses at a high enough price. However, the number of potential home buyers had been exhausted so it was not possible to sell the houses at a high enough price to cover the fees, interest, and principal due on mortgages. Instead, home prices started to decline by late 2006. Thus, loan originators and other SPE sponsors did not receive their scheduled debt service payments and so could not service the securities issued by SPEs, which greatly affected the profitability of financial institutions involved in securitization. Loan originators no longer received servicing fees, SPE no longer received loan services, and SPE liability holders no longer received payments. This led to a decline in lending activities which, given that the growth of home prices was based on Ponzi finance, led to a sharp decline in house prices; thereby reinforcing losses in the securitization chain. The decline in home prices was so steep that originators could not recover the outstanding principal of mortgages, let alone cover liabilities entailed in MBSs or CDOs.

Home prices declined by over 30 percent on average in the U.S. from 2006 to 2009 and delinquency rates on mortgages soared on all mortgages, especially so for adjustable rate mortgages regardless of the credit risk of the borrower (Figures 3.15 and 3.26). By 2010, serious delinquency peaked at 5 percent on prime FRM (compared to 0.64 percent on average prior to 2007), 17 percent on prime ARM (compared to 1.16 percent on average prior to 2007), 20 percent on subprime FRM (compared to 8 percent on average prior to 2007), 42 percent on subprime ARM (compared to 7.6 percent on average prior to 2007). Thus the combination of high default rates and falling of home prices (and so low recovery rate) created actual losses on foreclosures far higher than what many securitization structures could sustain. As explained earlier, some securitization products could only sustain marginal declines in home prices. In addition, banks did not protect themselves enough against credit risk by increasing loan-to-value ratio and decreasing their loan loss reserves that reached a historical low in 2006 even as the size of expected losses was growing rapidly. Even if adequate protection was available (say 20 percent of equity in house funding), this was not always enough to protect against the sharp drop of home prices.

The combination of high leverage and high losses led to a large decline in the value of all tranches of SPE securities—senior or subordinated. By July 2008, BBB rated CDSs on ABSs traded on average at a 90 percent discount and AAA ABCDS did so at a 60 percent discount (International Monetary Fund 2008b: 13).

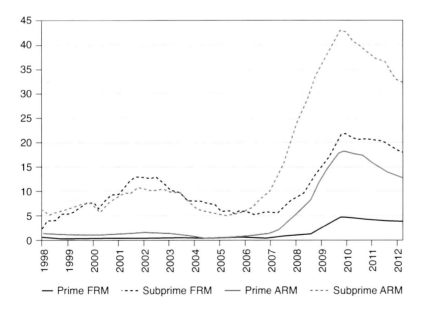

Figure 3.26 Percentage of single-family mortgage in serious delinquency (source: Mortgage Bankers Association).

In addition, credit rating agencies changed the rating of structured products to account for new estimation of expected losses, which led to further declines in the value of structured products. The sharp decline in the value of structured production was reinforced by the lack of liquidity of this market, but ultimately it was a solvency crisis that caused the sharp decline in the value of home and securitized products.

Defaults and large declines in the value of securities triggered the unwinding of swap contracts and other securities affected by them like leveraged super-senior notes. The unwinding was so large that super-senior tranches were affected. Given the losses, net sellers of credit protection (mostly insurance companies like American International Group), could not meet payments on CDSs and other securities, and their financial problems were transmitted rapidly to others. Indeed, net buyers of CDSs (mostly banks), who thought they had hedged their short CDS positions by buying CDSs, found that the counterparty could not pay; therefore, net buyers could not make good on the contingent payments required by the CDSs they sold.

All these developments in the CDS and other markets were compounded by additional factors, which, all together, led to massive liquidations and spectacular failures in the financial sector. First, problems in the mortgage sector made it very difficult for SPEs to refinance their positions once the value of the assets in SPEs was seen as questionable, sparking a run on the SPEs. Given that SPEs could not refinance, they had to make position by selling positions. This pressure to make position by selling assets was reinforced by the automatic unwinding triggers of SPEs. Unfortunately, the assets they held were mostly illiquid and facing large losses so they could only be sold at large discount. This initiated a debt deflation as asset prices were pushed further down.

The financial difficulties of SPEs led to a return to the originators' balance sheet of the credit risk and liquidity risk that they wanted to avoid because of credit lines granted to SPEs, or because of other forms of guarantees provided to SPEs like liquidity provision and buy-back guarantees. As a consequence, originators' equity capital and cash reserves were rapidly depleted, which reinforced the refinancing and liquidation pressures on the financial system. Second, monolines (especially Ambac and MBIA) were downgraded in the middle of 2008, which contributed to massive liquidations and write-downs of structured products. Indeed, their downgrading affected the strength of the third-party insurance they provided, and so affected the credit rating of securities relying on this insurance; therefore, pension funds and others that were required to buy only investment-grade securities had to sell some of their positions.

Finally, a panic was set off and the amount of margin requirements on security at least doubled or tripled. From January 2007 to April 2008, initial margins rose from around 3 to 15 percent on AAA ABS CDOs, from 15 percent to at least 40 percent on BBB ABS CDOs, from 4 percent to at least 20 percent on alt-A MBSs, and from 3 to 15 percent on average on AAA MBSs. Even the initial margin on Treasuries rose (International Monetary Fund 2008b). The same phenomenon occurred in mortgage lending with loan-to-value ratios declining sharply after they went up to 100 percent or more. This sudden drastic tightening in lending standards reinforced the deflationary tendencies induced by the large amount of defensive liquidations, and so asset prices declined dramatically as credit was cut off.

All in all, the crisis was rather typical. It was just one more example of a simplification of the layering of debts through a debt deflation. It was dubbed the "Minsky moment" but it should really be called the "Fisher moment," for Irving Fisher who laid out the mechanisms at play in the early 1930s, or even the "Veblen moment" for Thorstein Veblen whose *Theory of the Business Enterprise* published in 1904 already includes many of the elements that explain a debt deflation. In this instance, the layering was due to the securitization, resecuritization, and synthetic securitization that developed from the late 1990s in Europe and the United States. Models used to create these layers were inadequate at capturing the size of expected losses because they underestimated the potential size of decline in housing prices and the size of cross-correlation among assets, and because the financial engineering backing the securitization deals was unsound. As a consequence, realized credit losses were much higher than expected losses, which meant that insufficient margins of safety had been kept and so creditors could not be paid.

Response to the crisis: a critical view

All these events brought the U.S. financial system (and with it the whole U.S. economy) to the brink of complete destruction. As a consequence, in addition to trillions of dollars of advances provided by the Federal Reserve to meet short-term liquidity needs, the federal government had to intervene in an unprecedented manner through massive lending programs, capital injections, and purchases of toxic securities. While the total amount of funds actually disbursed by federal financial agencies never reached more than $6.3 trillion, they pledged up to $23.9 trillion as of July 21, 2010 according to the Troubled Asset Relief Program Special Inspector General (SIGTARP 2010).

Through 2008, Bernanke reassured Congress that the crisis was just a subprime crisis and so would be contained given how small that market was relative to the mortgage market and given how well markets allocate risk. This position, of course, did not account for the amount of debt layering based on subprime lending presented above. It also did not account for the difficulties in the prime mortgage market and how concentrated the risk was among very few institutions. Finally, this position did not account for the fact that, even with securitization, bankers were still exposed to credit risk through buy-back clauses and liquidity guarantees to SPEs, and through the high reliance on monolines as the ultimate guarantors of securitization. Of course, two central reasons why regulators did not account for all this was, one, that they could not because they passed laws that limited their capacity to look at what was going on in exotic markets at the core of securitization, and, two, because they would not use existing regulations to stop dangerous financial practices in the mortgage industry.

When the full blown crisis occurred in the September 2008, Greenspan, Bernanke, and others conceded that they went too far in believing in the efficiency of markets—it was the time for a public *mea culpa*. Donald Kohn, former Vice Chairman of the Federal Reserve, stated: "I placed too much confidence in the ability of the private market participants to police themselves" (Kohn in House of Commons 2011: Ev3). A humble Greenspan was asked to testify to Congress and created some stir by stating: "I made a mistake in presuming that the self-interest of organizations, specifically banks and others, were such is [*sic*] that they were best capable of protecting their own shareholders and their equity in the firms" (Greenspan in U.S. House of Representatives 2008b: 34). Similar remarks were made in the United Kingdom by Adair Turner, chair of the UK Financial Services Authority (FSA):

> In the past, in the years running up to the crisis, it was the strong mindset of the FSA—shared with securities and prudential regulators and central banks across the world, it was almost part of our DNA—that we assumed that financial innovation was always beneficial, that more trading and more liquidity creation was always valuable, that ever more complex products were by definition beneficial because they completed more markets, allowing a more precise matching of instruments to investor demand for liquidity, risk and return combinations. And that mindset did affect our approach— and the approach of the whole world regulatory community—to the setting of capital requirements on trading activity; it affected our willingness to demand risk reduction in the CDS market; and it influenced the degree to which we could even consider short-selling bans in conditions of exceptional market volatility.[...] [Stepping out of that mindset] poses for regulators the challenge of complexity, because it involves rejecting an intellectually elegant but also profoundly mistaken faith in ever perfect and self-equilibrating markets, ever rational human behaviors.
>
> (Turner 2009)

This period of *mea culpa* did not last long and already in 2008, in the middle of the financial crisis, the U.S. Department of Treasury stated: "Treasury believes market participants will be reluctant to self-certify rules harmful to the marketplace" (Department of the Treasury 2008: 116). Thus, while Turner hints at a change in the mindset among regulators and Greenspan admits to a flaw in his laissez-faire philosophy, one has reason to doubt that there has been a real shift in thinking among business leaders, bankers, and policy makers.

Instead a patchwork approach has been used that mostly protected, and even rewarded the behaviors of, large financial institutions at the heart of the growth of financial fragility. Indeed, while most of the problems stem from borrowers having difficulties in repaying their mortgages due to poor underwriting, most of the response has been to help financial institutions through emergency policies to contain liquidity problems without tackling the underlying problems of underwriting based on dubious creditworthiness and rising unemployment.

In truth, the global financial crisis was not simply a liquidity crisis but rather a solvency crisis brought on by risky and often fraudulent practices. After the crisis hit, not only did all "finance" disappear, but there was also no market for the risky assets—so there was no way that banks could sell assets to cover "withdrawals" (these were not normal withdrawals by depositors but rather a demand by creditors to be paid). As markets turned against one institution after another, the stock prices of financial institutions collapsed, margin calls were made, and credit ratings agencies downgraded securities and other assets. The big banks began to fail.

It is important to note that most of the solvency problems were initially limited to a handful of financial institutions—the biggest ones, including the top half-dozen banks, the big investment banks, a few big mortgage lenders, and the money-market mutual funds. All but the money-market mutual funds (MMMFs) had been heavily involved in the risky activities; the MMMFs got in trouble only because they held the commercial paper of these (likely) insolvent institutions. The vast majority of U.S. banks were not holding the most troubled assets, although some had made what would turn out to be risky home equity loans and commercial loans after the economy sank into recession. In most cases, for all but the biggest financial institutions, it was the global financial crisis and then the deep recession that created problems with their loans. Eventually, they suffered because of the crisis caused, mostly, by the behavior of the biggest institutions.

Government's response to a failing, insolvent bank is supposed to be much different from its response to a liquidity crisis. In short, the government is supposed to step in, seize the institution, fire the management, and begin a resolution. There are alternative approaches to resolution but in the case of the United States there is a mandate to minimize costs to the Treasury (the FDIC maintains a fund to cover some of the losses so that insured depositors are paid dollar for dollar). Normally, stockholders lose, as do the uninsured creditors—which would have included other financial institutions. It is the Treasury (through the FDIC) that is responsible for resolution. In the midst of the crisis, Treasury Secretary Paulson did ask Congress for funds to deal with the crisis and was provided with roughly $800 billion under the Troubled Asset Relief Program (TARP). However, rather than resolving institutions that were probably insolvent, he first tried to buy troubled assets from them; apparently after realizing that he would need much more funding to take all the bad assets off their books, he switched to an attempt at recapitalizing them—buying stock in the troubled banks. Yet the crisis continued to escalate, with problems spilling over to insurers of securities and then to AIG, all of the investment banks, and, finally, the biggest commercial banks.

Deal making and special-purpose vehicles

With Congress reluctant to provide any more funding, the Fed and Treasury gradually worked out an alternative approach. In addition to injecting capital into troubled institutions, the Treasury conducted a stress test to identify institutions likely to fail. However, many analysts believed these tests set thresholds that were far too lax. When an institution did face failure, the Treasury and the Fed— usually represented by the Federal Reserve Bank of New York—would try to make a deal to merge the failing institution into another. Often it would be necessary for the Fed to lend to the failing institution for some period while the deal was negotiated. In addition, the Fed created a number of special facilities to provide funding for institutions and also to take troubled assets off their books. By purchasing bad assets, the Fed could conceivably turn a failing bank into a solvent bank.

It must be emphasized that the U.S. Treasury and, indeed, the economic team of the Obama Administration was heavily represented by individuals with experience in investment banking. Davidoff and Zaring (2009) argue that the "bailout" can be characterized as "deal making through contracts," as the Treasury and Fed stretched the boundaries of law with behind-closed-doors hard-headed negotiations. It appears that the government did negotiate with a view to keeping its own risk exposure limited; at the same time, it insisted on large "haircuts" to stockholders' equity but minimal losses to bondholders. It also avoided penalties on bank directors and officers—rarely investigating possible fraud or dereliction of duty. Finally, it avoided "market solutions" in favor of "orderly solutions." In other words, where markets would shut down an insolvent financial institution, the government would instead find a way to keep the institution operating by merger. The one major exception was Lehman Brothers, as the government allowed the investment bank to fail. Davidoff and Zaring attribute this to an attempt to demonstrate government's willingness to negotiate tough terms.

Further, through the crisis government relied on the two institutions that are least constrained by the law: the Fed and the Treasury. Throughout the crisis, the government would stretch and flex its authoritative muscles but would not boldly violate the law. Davidoff and Zaring argue that the federal government was allowed substantial leeway in its interpretation as state courts were not likely to interfere. Further, the Fed has in the past interpreted its activities as exempt from "sunshine" laws. In sum, the Fed and the Treasury acted largely independently, without congressional oversight on appropriations of funding to "bail out" troubled institutions. In many ways, this deal-making approach that was favored over a resolution-by-authority approach is troubling from the perspectives of transparency and accountability, as well as the likely creation of moral hazard problems.

The other element of this approach was the unprecedented assistance through the Fed's special facilities that were created to provide loans as well as to purchase troubled assets (and to lend to institutions and even individuals that would purchase troubled assets). To be sure, in a crisis the central bank must act as a lender of last resort, but the Fed's actions went far beyond "normal" lending. First, it is probable that the biggest recipients of funds were insolvent. We cannot be sure of this because the Treasury's stress tests were weak, and while the FDIC is responsible for declaring depository institutions insolvent, it had a strong incentive to avoid doing so: its reserves were far too small to handle failures of large banks and it could not risk going to a skeptical Congress to ask for more funding. Second, the Fed provided funding to financial institutions (and to financial markets in an attempt to support particular financial instruments) that went far beyond the member banks that it is supposed to support. To do so, the Fed had to make use of special sections of the Federal Reserve Act (FRA), some of which had not been used since the Great Depression. And, as in the case of the deal making, the Fed appears to have stretched its interpretation of those sections beyond the boundaries of the law.

Note that it would not be accurate to call every intervention by the Fed a "bailout." Lending reserves by the Fed to a bank that is short of "liquidity" (reserves needed to meet withdrawals or clearing against other banks) is expected to increase sharply in a crisis. Further, the Fed decided to engage in massive Quantitative Easing that saw its balance sheet grow from well under $1 trillion before the crisis to nearly $3 trillion; bank reserves increase by a similar amount as the Fed's balance sheet grows when it buys assets. Such actions do not necessarily indicate a bailout, as they could be consistent with liquidity provision to solvent banks. Still, Quantitative Easing (QE) included asset purchases by the Fed that went well beyond Treasuries—the usual asset bought by the Fed when it wants to inject reserves into banks.

The Fed bought around $1 trillion of MBSs in its QE (Figure 3.27), and while some of these were backed by Fannie and Freddie (hence, ultimately were government liabilities in the sense that Uncle Sam would cover losses), the Fed also bought "private label" MBSs. The Fed, through its "Maiden Lane III" SPE, also indirectly holds CDOs-squared. To the extent the Fed paid more than market price to buy "trashy" assets from financial institutions, that could be construed as a bailout. In any case, the Fed's actions went far beyond this—to include highly unusual actions that are reasonably characterized as a "bailout" of institutions that were probably insolvent. And the volume of such intervention is truly unprecedented—even the Great Crash saw nothing on this scale.

There are two main measures of the total Fed intervention that could qualify as unusual. The first measure is "peak outstanding" Fed lending summed across each special facility (at a point in time). Several researchers have provided such a calculation—including the Government Accountability Office (GAO), Bloomberg, and the Fed itself—and all reached a number around $1.5 trillion. This occurred in December 2008—and represents the maximum outstanding loans made through the Fed's special facilities on any day since the crisis began. This peak measure gives an idea of the maximum effort to save the financial system at a point in time, and also some indication of the Fed's total exposure to risk of loss. To be sure, the Fed demands collateral against its loans, and it is highly improbable that the Fed would lose anything close to that even in a worst case scenario. Indeed, many of the special facilities were successfully wound down with no losses; the only facilities that are likely to incur substantial losses are those associated with the rescue of AIG.

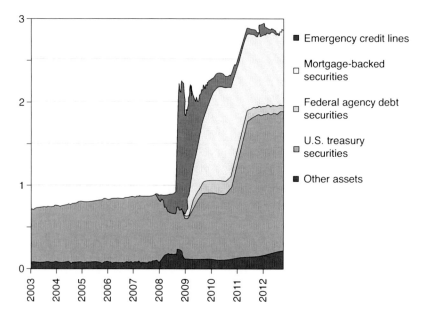

Figure 3.27 Factors affecting reserve balances, assets of the Federal Reserve banks (trillions of dollars) (source: Board of Governors of the Federal Reserve System).

Note
The category "Other assets" includes the traditional credit lines at the Discount Window, repurchase agreements, and other miscellaneous assets.

The second method is to add up Fed lending and asset purchases through these special facilities over time to obtain a cumulative measure of the Fed's response. To be clear, if the Fed lent $1 billion each day, and that was repaid each evening only to be renewed the next morning with another $1 billion, that would total $30 billion of Fed response over a month. The cumulative measure counts every new loan and every asset purchase made over the course of the life of each special facility. Some of the facilities lasted only a short period, others lasted for two years or more. In some cases, a financial institution borrowed a large amount of funds for a very short period; in other cases, an institution repeatedly borrowed, returning to the Fed many times and remaining in debt for periods up to nearly two years. The cumulative measure would capture such repeated borrowing as continued Fed assistance to the troubled institution. Thus, even if the second institution borrowed less on any given day, the Fed's response to help it could sum to a number as large as a short period of assistance through a large loan to an institution that recovered quickly and needed no further help. Another reason to provide a cumulative measure is to indicate just how unprecedented the Fed's intervention was in terms of time. The crisis began in early 2007 (although most of the facilities were created in 2008) and major Fed interventions continued until 2010 (Fed support for Eurobanks was ramped up again in 2012).

The cumulative lending and asset purchases made through the special facilities totals more than $29 trillion for the period to November 2011 (Felkerson 2011). For comparison, after the crash of 1929, the Fed lent to 123 institutions a total of $23 million (in today's dollars) between 1932 and 1936. The word "unprecedented" really does not adequately describe the Fed's intervention to rescue financial institutions. At the beginning of 2008, the Fed's balance sheet was $926 billion, of which 80 percent of its assets were U.S. Treasury bonds; in November 2010, its balance sheet had reached $2.3 trillion, of which almost half of its assets were MBSs. Over the next year, it ramped up its purchases of Treasuries (and reduced its use of the special facilities) so that its balance sheet was close to $3 trillion—three times larger than it was on the eve of the crisis.

Finally, many of the Fed's "bail-out" facilities used SPVs created to buy assets or to make loans. In an ironic twist the Fed followed the example set by banks as it created SPVs to subvert constraints written into the FRA (Maiden Lane I, II, III). As discussed above, there is no problem with Fed lending to member banks to stop a run. It is a bit more problematic to lend to *insolvent* member banks, but still legal. In "unusual and exigent" circumstances, the Fed is free to go much farther under Section 13(3) of the FRA. In such circumstances the Fed can lend to individuals, partnerships, and corporations at a discount, but only if they are unable to secure adequate credit from other banks. Further, according to FRA, the Fed must lend against indorsed or secured assets. However, the Fed's invocation of Section 13(3) to justify its intervention is problematic: it created SPVs and then lent to them so that they could buy troubled assets. In other words it financed the purchase of an asset rather than making a loan. In most cases, the Fed's loan was to its own SPV and not to the party that needed assistance. In some cases the loans were not technically "discounts" and were not against endorsed assets (the SPVs owned no assets until they got the loans that allowed them to buy troubled assets); and in most cases the beneficiaries could have obtained loans from other banks, albeit at higher interest rates. In all these respects, the law was "stretched" if not subverted. In all these respects, this looks like "bailout" and not "liquidity provision."

The volume of Fed assistance of questionable legality under 13(3) was very large. Its four SPVs lent approximately $1.75 trillion (about 6 percent of the total Fed cumulative intervention). In addition, it implemented questionable loan programs that either lent against ineligible assets or lent to parties that were not troubled a total of $9.2 trillion (30 percent of the total intervention). In sum, of the cumulative $29 trillion lent and spent by Fall 2011, over a third was perhaps improperly justified under section 13(3) (Felkerson 2011).

Further help to the financial sector and a lack of commitment to help
the nonfinancial sector

Beyond the intervention of the Federal Reserve, the government did provide assistances to the financial sector at preferential conditions through other means.

In 2009, the financial industry pushed for a relaxation of accounting rules in order to avoid reporting major losses on securitized products. Major financial institutions wanted to be allowed to use level-3 valuation (in-house model) instead of level-1 (market value) or level-2 (proxy market) valuation of their assets. They argued that the prevailing large discounts on securitized products were the result of a liquidity crisis instead of a solvency crisis so mark-to-market valuation should be relaxed for a while. Both the SEC and the Financial Accounting Standards Board (FASB) resisted the push to modify the reporting of financial information and instead argued that government policies should be used to help the economy. Mr. Hertz, Chairman of FASB, made the following statement:

> We also agree with the SEC that suspending or eliminating existing fair value requirements would not be advisable for the role of accounting and reporting standards is to help the investing public in the capital markets with sound, unbiased financial information on companies. Its purpose is not to determine regulatory capital or capital adequacy. [...] Thus, to the extent there are valid concerns relating to procyclicality, I believe these are more appropriately and more effectively addressed through regulatory mechanisms and via fiscal and monetary policy than by trying to alter the financial information reported to investors.
>
> (Herz in U.S. House of Representative 2009b)

But in a congressional hearing legislators from both sides, lobbied by the American Bankers Association, demanded the FASB to act. As a consequence, banks could record higher profits by assuming that securities were worth more than what people were willing to pay for them. This allowed them to hide losses and so helped to sustain their stock price.

Beyond massive effort by the Fed, FDIC, and others to stabilize financial institutions, the Obama Administration continued the Bush–Paulson TARP under a cloud of secrecy that allowed the Treasury to pick winners for government funding (Morgenson and Van Natta 2009). After weeks of outcry about slow progress to improve oversight, the TARP Special Inspector General (SIGTARP) and the Congressional Oversight Panel (COP) were finally made operational in December 2008. SIGTARP and COP have been very worried about fraud, especially with the extension of TARP programs toward so-called "legacy/troubled" assets. Both have been complaining about the lack of transparency of TARP and have noted that the Treasury "has repeatedly failed to adopt recommendations" that SIGTARP made in terms of uses of funds, valuation and performance of TARP assets, TALF borrowers, and other matters (SIGTARP 2009: 7).

The Capital Purchase Program (CPP) of TARP was followed by eleven additional sub-programs in which some of the $700 billion allocated to TARP was used as seed money; seven of those plans have been directed toward restoring the profitability and solvency of financial institutions, and, with CPP, they account for 77 percent of the $441 billion already used in 2009 (SIGTARP 2009: 37ff.).

Within TARP, three core plans were the Capital Assistance Program (CAP), the Public–Private Investment Program (PPIP), and Term Asset-Backed Securities Loan Facility (TALF), which aimed at showing to the public that banks were solvent and only needed temporary assistance because of malfunctioning financial markets. For example, the PPIP was promoted to create a market for "legacy" assets. The program was highly generous for potential buyers, with the Treasury and FDIC taking most of the risk and receiving very few of the gains; however, the program failed because of the unwillingness of banks to sell at a huge discount (sometimes as low as 10 cents on the dollar) that would reveal the deep insolvency of the biggest banks. Above all, banks do not want these legacy assets to be valued properly.

PIMCO flirted with the idea of creating a fund that would allow investors to take positions in toxic waste, but apparently decided this could create a public relations nightmare. If PIMCO were seen to be making profits at taxpayer expense, there could be a backlash. Worse, if the public bought into the fund which then collapsed because the troubled assets never recovered, PIMCO would be blamed for bilking investors. BlackRock rushed into the void, announcing it would create a cash for trash fund to be capitalized by the federal government. BlackRock would earn fee income, while investors in the fund as well as taxpayers would earn returns if the bets pay off. This would let the general public share in recovery. Of course, if the assets continue to depreciate, Uncle Sam and the investors assume the losses. Previously, BlackRock, with the support of the Treasury and three big U.S. banks, proposed to do the same thing under the Single Master Liquidity Enhancement Conduit (M-LEC), a.k.a. "superfund," scheme. The main difference was that banks were supposed to take most of the risk. The superfund never took off because its sponsors never found enough willing banks to participate in its funding. Financial insiders knew that M-LEC was too small (only $75 billion when trillions were needed) and only a temporary means to park trash to avoid a massive unloading of toxic assets by SPEs. Having failed to find any other financial professional willing to hold the hot potatoes, financial institutions holding toxic assets turned to Uncle Sam for more cash to burn.

All those programs have failed to deal with the core issue at stake: many financial institutions are probably insolvent and need to be closed; assets must be analyzed carefully to figure out their profit potential and the true financial state of financial institutions; and an investigation must be open to determine responsibility among top managers. Even though financial markets have stabilized, they are still under heavy assistance by the government and we have not dealt with the solvency problems. In addition, big banks have been taking massive risks again through speculative trading in derivatives and commodities, and trading revenues have risen dramatically from −$6 billion in 2008 to over $21 billion after 2010, which is about 9 to 10 percent of revenues for top banks, an unprecedented amount since data are available (Figure 2.29, Chapter 2). In May 2012, a $3 billion dollar loss made by a trader at JP Morgan on a single bet showed how aggressive top banks have been in the derivatives markets; a behavior much more akin to a hedge fund than a bank.

The COP clearly illustrates the problem with the approach used by the Obama Administration:

> The recently announced Public–Private Investment Fund focuses directly on the problem of impaired assets; that initiative reflects the working premise that it is possible through government-subsidized, highly leveraged asset purchase vehicles to obtain valuations for non-performing or otherwise troubled assets, sell those assets at those values to willing buyers, and perhaps avoid the need for the reorganization or even the break-up of systemically significant financial institutions. Treasury has not explained its assumption that the proper values for these assets are their book values—in the case, for example, of land or whole mortgages—and more than their "mark-to-market" value in the case of ABSs, CDOs, and like securities; if values fall below those floors, the banks involved may be insolvent in any event. Treasury has also failed to explain its assumptions about the economic events that would cause investors to default or how long it believes assets will have to be held to produce a reasonable return for private investors.
>
> (Congressional Oversight Panel 2009a: 75)

> TALF cannot address the creditworthiness issue. It can provide more funds to the lenders for lending, but asset-backed securities have never been the source of significant funding for small businesses. This report raises the question of whether TALF will have a meaningful impact on small business credit.
>
> (Congressional Oversight Panel 2009b: 4)

In short, the entire array of programs will work only if we have a temporary illiquidity problem, not a problem of excessive leverage, excessive debt, and a legacy of assets that were vastly overvalued based on economic scenarios that had no chance of coming to fruition. Given the inappropriate premises under which the Administration has dealt with the leverage of financial institutions, we may expect that problems will continue to languish if the Administration does not change its course of actions. This will constrain heavily the capacity of the U.S. economy to recover and may lead to a Japanese-style lost decade because all efforts to save insolvent banks do nothing to resolve economic growth and stimulate the nonfinancial business sector. The end result is that the current approach to tackle the leverage problem may not succeed in saving insolvent banks.

In addition to eight TARP programs and other policies oriented toward the financial system, several programs have dealt with nonfinancial sector debt. However, the total committed support for the nonfinancial sector is only about $903.6 billion (including, in addition to expenses directly committed to help nonfinancial entities, the $700 billion of potential guarantees by FDIC, the $75 billion allocated to servicers to help to modify mortgages, and the $43.8 billion used to help credit unions to modify mortgages). All this represents about 3.8 percent of the $23.9 trillion pledged to rescue the economy.

Among the programs helping households, the Making Home Affordable Program (MHA), which expanded the Hope for Homeowners program put in place during the Bush Administration, was allocated $50 billion through TARP (for a total funding allocation of $75 billion). MHA aims at providing financial assistance to servicers to modify private-label mortgages and to refinance conforming mortgages. This program was expanded by the Helping Families Save Their Homes Act in May 2009. HOPE NOW, a private initiative supported by the Treasury, HUD, and Freddie Mac has been in place since 2008. However, none of these programs has been able to keep pace with the size of the problem as foreclosures have been growing rapidly (Figure 3.28). The percentage of loans in foreclosures quadrupled during the crisis and has stayed around its historical high of 4.5 percent since 2009 even though there have been some improvements from late 2011.

This has created frustration among households that have been unable, despite months of trying, to reach their servicers. This problem is not even close to going away because interest-rate resettings continued until at least the end of 2011 and the number of residences that are underwater is extremely large (International Monetary Fund 2007: 8). Depending on the survey used, the size of the problem varies. In the first quarter of 2012, almost 24 percent of all residences with mortgages are underwater according to Corelogic (2012). According to the U.S. Census Bureau, the amount of mortgagors underwater or near underwater is also unusually high with 14 percent of mortgages having a loan-to-value ratio of

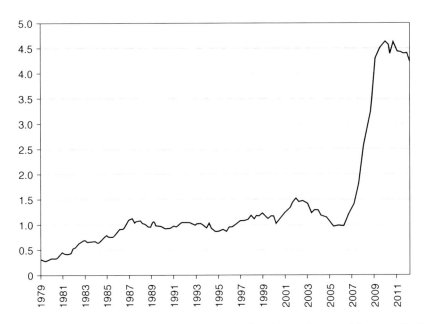

Figure 3.28 Percentage of mortgage loans in foreclosure (source: Mortgage Bankers Association).

100 percent or more in 2011, and 22 percent having a LTV above 90 percent (Figure 3.29). Thus, marginal and temporary loan modifications will not suffice; we need a significant and permanent reduction of debt payments in order to deal with the large decline in home equity and the fraudulent, or poor, underwriting that put households in toxic mortgages with large payment shocks. This is even truer if one considers that second-lien mortgages are even more likely to default again once modified. A permanent reduction in principal due and a permanent reduction in interest should be such that debt servicing becomes possible through the normal source of funding of homeowners—income—for the length of the loan (meaning no balloon payment, no teaser payment, and no refinance based on home price appreciation).

Beyond the fact that the decline in mortgage service may not be large enough, there have been several other major issues that relate to the cost, lack of permanency, and the limited and slow volume of modifications.

Most of the modifications that have occurred have been focused on temporarily modifying the monthly mortgage service without dealing with the problem of negative equity. Table 3.3 shows that the preferred means used to modify mortgages have been to capitalize amounts past due and interest-rate reduction; which have been done in 80 percent of the modifications. Raising the maturity of the mortgages has also been done in about half of the modifications especially so

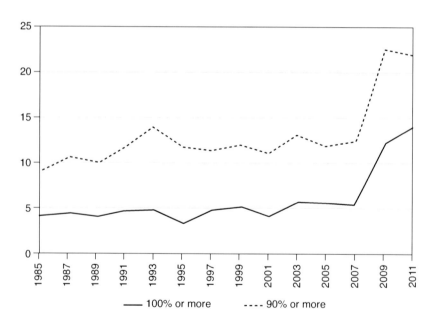

Figure 3.29 Distribution of loan-to-value ratios (%) (source: U.S. Census Bureau (American Housing Survey)).

Note
About 26 percent of mortgages had an unreported value in 2011.

Table 3.3 Changes in loan terms made by modifications made, percentage of modifications

	Capitalization	Rate reduction	Term extension	Principal deferral	Principal reduction	Rate freeze	Not reported
Q1 2009	70.2	63.2	25.1	1.1	1.8	12.6	7
Q2 2009	65.8	72.2	45.8	2.5	10	8	5.8
Q3 2009	68.2	81.1	47.4	3.1	13	2.7	1.9
Q4 2009	82.8	84.5	45.3	5.8	6.8	1.9	1.2
Q1 2010	91.4	82.6	45.8	10.2	1.9	1.3	1
Q2 2010	94.1	87	51.4	11	2.1	4.2	0.5
Q3 2010	87.6	86.5	57.6	10.1	5.7	1.9	0.7
Q4 2010	91.6	84.2	56.1	9	2.7	2.4	1.1
Q1 2011	86.9	82.6	58.1	11.2	2.8	2	2.9
Q2 2011	90.8	79.5	61.1	18.6	5.8	2.1	1.7
Q3 2011	88.5	77.5	57.8	20.5	7.8	4.6	1
Q4 2011	93.3	78.2	55.5	24.5	8.5	6.4	1.5
Q1 2012	91.6	80.6	73.7	24.6	10.2	6.2	1.2
Average	84.8	80.0	52.4	11.7	6.1	4.3	2.1

Source: Office of the Comptroller of the Currency (Mortgage Metrics Reports).

Note
Most changes in loan terms involve a combination of modifications.

Table 3.4 Redefault rates of loans modified by change in payment, average for 2008–2011 (sixty or more days delinquent, %)

Months after modification	3 months	6 months	9 months	12 months
Decreased by 20% or more	10.0	16.7	21.8	25.5
Decreased by 10% to less than 20%	13.7	24.8	32.4	37.3
Decreased by less than 10%	16.5	30.8	39.0	42.9
Unchanged	29.3	34.4	38.5	40.6
Increased	24.5	41.6	50.4	54.4
Average	17.6	27.5	33.9	37.7

Source: Office of the Comptroller of the Currency (Mortgage Metrics Reports).

after the second quarter of 2010. Principal deferral—modifications that temporarily remove a portion of the principal from the amount used to calculate monthly principal and interest payments—also picked up in 2011 in a moderate way. Table 3.3 shows that principal reduction has been among the least favorite means used to modify mortgages with only about 6 percent of mortgages receiving a reduction. In addition, this reduction was probably limited.

Most modifications have led to a decline in mortgages service costs, and in over 60 percent of the modifications the decline allowed the monthly mortgage service to be lowered by 20 percent or more (Office of the Comptroller of the Currency 2012: Table 22). This is important because the success of a mortgage is directly tied to the size of the modification. Redefault on mortgages with at least a 20 percent reduction in the monthly service has a sixty-day delinquency rate of 25.5 percent after twelve months, which is significantly lower than the average of 37.7 percent (Table 3.4).

However, permanent modifications are really not permanent as terms can be changed after five years (Congressional Oversight Panel 2011: 91, n. 286). This presupposes that the state of the economy will have improved enough to grant a progressive return to the original mortgage contract, which brings forward several issues. First, given how weak the economic recovery has been and given how large the decline in home prices has been, it is doubtful that economic results will be strong enough to allow an increase in mortgage service. Chapter 5 shows that the peak level of employment prior to the Great Recession will not be recovered before 2015 at least. Second, households are drowning in debt and are probably unwilling to go back to the financial ways of the pre-recession boom, when a growing debt ratio was at the basis of the growth of house prices. As a consequence, it will take far more than five years for home prices to return to their peak value, which means that widespread negative equity will persist. Finally, it goes without saying that the exotic mortgages contracts should not return. Thus, if the changes of terms consist of putting households back into ARMs with (or even without) exotic characteristics, redefault will rise rapidly.

While the government has put in place quite a few programs to deal with mortgage delinquency, their implementation has been very slow and their effectiveness has been very limited. Less than half of the positions at the MHA program had been filled after the first eight months of its existence, and the Government Accountability Office (2011) noted that servicers have not hired enough staff, or trained them properly, to make the program work. As of March 2012 only 999,552 mortgages had started to be permanently modified and the pace of permanent modification has slowed considerably after the middle of 2010 with around 30,000 modifications started every month (Figure 3.30). Similarly, as of March 2012 only 973,583 permanent modifications have been done through the HOPE NOW program. The GAO also noted that: "affidavits used in foreclosures frequently were signed by persons who did not satisfy personal knowledge requirements and were not properly notarized" (Government Accountability Office 2011: 26). These so-called "robo-signers" (ranging from teens, to Walmart employees, and others who had no idea what a mortgage was) signed hundreds of affidavits everyday and, of course, could not check if a foreclosure was done correctly.

Loan modifications may entail large fees and penalties that households cannot afford to pay; and, depending on circumstances and state laws, mortgage modifications might lead to a change from a non-recourse loan to a recourse loan, which makes households who redefault much worse off than they were before the modification. In addition, loan modifications usually have occurred far too

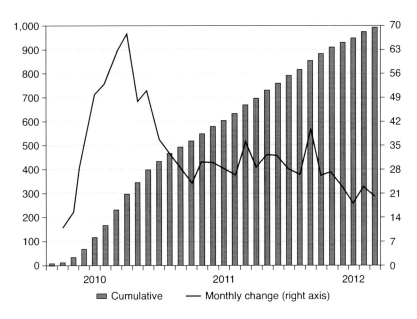

Figure 3.30 Home affordable modification program, number of permanent modification started (thousands) (source: U.S. Department of the Treasury (Making Home Affordable Reports)).

Note
September 2009 data includes the months of May through September.

late—after the borrower has long been delinquent. In fact, past policy initiatives like Project Lifeline gave a strong incentive to become ninety-day delinquent because a loan modification would not be considered until a borrower reached that stage. This state of affairs contributes to higher redefault rates because data show that "the more serious the delinquency, the less likely the borrower will remain current after modification" (Office of the Comptroller of the Currency 2009: 31).

A major obstacle to significant modification is securitization, which prevents modifications because the financial interests in outstanding mortgages have been spread among many different parties through securitization and resecuritization. This is especially true for non-conforming mortgages that were packaged into private-label MBSs, which prevents servicers from providing significant loan modifications. These limits to substantial modifications are compounded by the fact that servicers have a fiduciary duty toward the holders of SPE securities. As a consequence, the redefault rate is much higher on securitized mortgages:

> Loans held on the books of servicing banks and thrifts had the lowest re-default rates at 35.06 percent after three months, and 50.86 percent after six months, compared to loans serviced on behalf of third parties. The lower re-default rate for loans held by servicers may suggest that there is greater flexibility to modify loans in more sustainable ways when loans are held on a servicers' own books than when loans have been sold to third parties.
> (Office of the Comptroller of the Currency 2008: 21)

In addition, nobody seems to know where the mortgage deed is or who holds it, often leaving judges with little means to bring financial troubles to a close. The practice of foreclosing without the deed, even though illegal, apparently had become very common during the boom (Porter 2007).

Servicers have contributed to this problem by providing dubious or marginal modifications, charging dubious fees, prematurely foreclosing, destroying checks made by homeowners to service their mortgages, and other illegal actions that mostly went unpunished. Porter (2007) found unsubstantiated fees and missing documentation in about half of the loans examined, and a report by the Associated Press shows that these types of problems are quite common among servicers helped by the MHA program (Associated Press 2009). In fact, servicers have an incentive not to renegotiate but rather to hold out for a foreclosure. Indeed, perhaps the real problem is that those same financial institutions that created this mess are preventing resolution because it is far more profitable for them to ride out the collapse as there is a lot of money to be made squeezing debtors with fees and penalties (Goodman 2009; UBS 2007). Servicers have a financial incentive to impose additional fees on consumers:

> Mortgage servicers earn revenue in three major ways. First, they receive a fixed fee for each loan. Typical arrangements pay servicers between .25 percent and 1.375 percent of the note principal for each loan. Second,

servicers earn "float" income from accrued interest between when consumers pay and when those funds are remitted to investors. Third, servicers often are permitted to retain all, or part, of any default fees, such as late charges, that consumers pay. In this way, a borrower's default can boost a servicer's profits. A significant fraction of servicers' total revenue comes from retained fee income. Because of this structure, servicers' incentives upon default may not align with investors' incentives. Servicers have incentives to make it difficult for consumers to cure defaults. [...] Mortgage servicers can exploit consumers' difficulty in recognizing errors or overcharges by failing to provide comprehensible or complete information. In fact, poor service to consumers can actually maximize servicers' profits.

(Porter 2007: 5–6)

When a house is finally foreclosed, the mortgage servicer has first claim to the revenue from sale of the house. According to a UBS study, foreclosure can take up to two years and total costs—including paying off the servicer—can absorb 90 percent of the revenue from the home sale. This is why the total losses on home mortgages (borne mostly by the securities holders) are so huge even if home values fall by "only" 30 percent. Mortgage companies actively interfere to ensure that homeowners are not able to renegotiate terms of mortgages instead of going into foreclosure. When the foreclosure proceeds, the mortgage companies not only accumulate late fees, but also pay for many other services—often to their own subsidiaries that are paid for title searches, insurance policies, appraisals, and legal findings. That is all recouped with the property sale. This explains why none of the government policies to date has been able to keep many people in their homes by negotiating better mortgages. Indeed, even though the government is offering mortgage companies up to $4,000 to modify a loan, they make more money if they drive the owner out of the home. Ideally, they will accumulate claims on the house up to the total market value, recovered with the sale of the foreclosed house.

Overall, the policy strategy that has been followed by the Bush and Obama Administrations has been to help as much as possible the lenders directly while having limited direct involvement on the borrowers' side. This strategy has failed. One of the main beliefs has been that by helping banks directly through the purchase of their bad assets and the injection of reserves, and through the limitation of loss recognition, banks would be encouraged to lend. However, it takes two to tango in a lending agreement. Not only does the finance of borrowers need to be strong enough relative to the standards of banks, but also customers themselves have to be willing to borrow funds. In an anemic economy burdened with large amount of debt, stagnant income, and high unemployment, bank lending has been slow. A more effective course would be to help borrowers directly to sustain their income (mostly by sustaining employment) and to restructure their debt in a way that brings them back into hedge finance.

Conclusion

In an ideal world, we could recover from this crisis without major reform to eliminate Money Manager Capitalism. We could even recover without our high debt ratios as a lot of the debts will cancel, the homeowner will not lose her job, and the finance, insurance, and real estate sector can continue to force 25 to 30 percent of all corporate profits in its direction. But that is not the world in which we live. In our actual world, the homeowner missed some payments, the MBSs issued against her mortgage got downgraded, the monoline insurers went bust, the credit default swaps went bad, the economy slowed and the homeowner lost her job and then her house, real estate prices collapsed, and in spite of its best efforts to save Money Manager Capitalism, the federal government has not yet found a way out of the morass as the biggest banks remain insolvent and sustainable recovery remains out of reach.

In his *General Theory*, Keynes argued that the fetish for liquidity causes substandard growth, financial instability, and unemployment. The desire for a liquid position is antisocial because there is no such thing as liquidity in the aggregate. The stock market makes ownership liquid for the individual "investor," but since all equities must be held by someone, my ability to sell out depends on your willingness to buy in.

Over the past several decades, the financial sector taken as a whole moved into very short-term finance of positions in assets with very high leverage. This is related to the transformation of investment banking partnerships that had a long-term interest in the well-being of their clients to publicly held "pump-and-dump" enterprises whose main interest appears to be the well-being of top management. It is also related to the rise of shadow banks that offered deposit-like liabilities but without the protection of FDIC, to the "Greenspan Put" and the Bernanke "Great Moderation" that appeared to guarantee that all financial practices—no matter how crazily risky—would be backstopped by Uncle Sam, and to very low overnight interest rate targets by the Fed (through to 2004) that made shorter-term finance cheap relative to longer-term finance.

Together with deregulation and desupervision, all of these trends encouraged financial institutions to rely on extremely short-term finance and to use as much of it as possible. Typically, financial institutions were financing their positions in assets by issuing IOUs with a maturity measured in days or hours. Overnight finance was common—through repos, asset-backed commercial paper, and deposit-like liabilities.

On the other hand, the assets were increasingly esoteric positions in mark-to-myth structured assets with indeterminate market values—indeed, often with no real markets into which they could be sold. (A lot of this was "bespoke" business, with the assets never entering any market.) Further, many of these assets had no clearly defined income flows—virtually by definition, a NINJA loan (no income, no job, no asset) has no plausible source of income to service the debt. That is just the most outlandish example, but much of the asset-backed commercial papers had no reliable source of sufficient income to service the liabilities issued. To a significant extent, disaster could be avoided only by asset price appreciation so that positions could be refinanced. That included many of the exotic prime and non-prime mortgages. Default was assured unless the borrower could refinance into better terms.

Meanwhile, the U.S. debt-to-GDP ratios reached almost 500 percent—that is, a dollar of income was needed to service $5 of debt. Inevitably, the short-term liabilities of financial institutions could not be serviced, and they could be rolled over only so long as the myths were maintained. As soon as some holders of these risky assets wondered whether they would be repaid, the whole house of cards collapsed. And that largely took the form of one financial institution refusing to "roll over" another financial institution's short-term IOUs. Half a decade later and trillions of lost dollars of wealth later, we are still in crisis.

The Fed's bailouts of Wall Street certainly stretched and might have violated both the law as established in the FRA (and its amendments) and also well-established procedure. There is a long tradition in the Fed of making a distinction between continuous versus emergency borrowing at the Fed. The Fed is permitted to lend (freely, as Bagehot recommended) to resolve a liquidity crisis, but it has long refused to provide "continuous" lending. Here the idea is that the Fed should stop a liquidity crisis but then solvent financial institutions should quickly return to market funding of their positions in assets. And yet, the crisis started in 2008. Five years later, the Fed is still lending and at "subsidized" (below market) interest rates. This creates a tremendous moral hazard problem.

The Fed is also generally prohibited from lending to "nonbank" financial institutions—what we now call shadow banks that are not members of the Federal Reserve System and that do not issue FDIC-insured deposits. However, there is an exception granted in the Fed's "13(3)" provisions that allow the Fed to lend in "unusual and exigent" conditions. Certainly the crisis in 2008 qualifies as unusual and exigent. However, the 13(3) restrictions are tight and the Fed seems to have stretched the law. Some might object that while there was some questionable, possibly illegal activity by our nation's central bank, was it not justified by the circumstances?

The problem is that this "bailout" validated the questionable, risky, and in some cases illegal activities of top management on Wall Street, those running the "control frauds." The effect of the bailout has been to continue if not increase the distribution of income and wealth flowing to the top one-tenth of 1 percent. It has kept the same management in control of the worst serial abusers as they paid record bonuses to top management. Some of their fraudulent activity has been exposed, and the top banks have paid numerous fines for bad behaviors. There have been a lot of settlements and civil cases, indicating that fraud was rampant. Yet, Washington has been seemingly paralyzed—the U.S. Attorney General has not begun a single investigation of criminal behavior by top management.

With the deal-making and bailout approaches of the Fed and Treasury, it is unlikely that financial institutions have learned much from the crisis—except that risky behaviors will lead to a bailout. In the savings-and-loan crisis of the

1980s, many institutions were shut down and resolved, and more than 1,000 officers in top management served jail time. In the current crisis, no top officer has been prosecuted, much less jailed. Banks have been slapped on the wrists with some fines—usually without being forced to admit wrongdoing.

Critics have long argued that continued expansion of government's safety net to protect institutions deemed too big to fail not only runs afoul of established legal tradition but also produces perverse incentives and competitive advantages. The largest institutions enjoy "subsidized" interest rates—their uninsured liabilities have de facto protection because of the way the government (the Fed, FDIC, OCC, and Treasury) props them up, eliminating risk of default on their liabilities (usually only stockholders lose). The deal-making approach extended the principle of lender of last resort activities to entirely novel areas—protecting creditors of even shadow banks and, as discussed, favoring bond holders while forcing stockholders and securities holders (and defrauded homeowners) to take losses.

With all the government support most of the financial institutions have so far survived the crisis. While they are reluctant to quickly resume the practices that caused the crisis, they did not suffer much from them. It is probable that if the economy and financial sector were to recover, risky practices would come back. Further, and more alarmingly, the financial sector bounced right back to taking 25 to 30 percent of corporate profits, to pay-outs of huge bonuses to top management and traders, and to accounting for 20 percent of value added toward national GDP.

All of this is in sharp contrast to the 1930s New Deal reform. The Hoover and Roosevelt Administrations first followed the Bush and Obama strategy, but ultimately recognized that the main way to help the economy was through a thorough investigation of the crisis and a punishment of fraudsters, a recognition of losses, a cleansing of debts, and a promotion of hedge finance. The Pecora Commission was given relatively free rein to investigate the causes of the crisis and to go after the fraud. The deleveraging was done by helping borrowers as much as possible and closing insolvent banking institutions. Thousands of banks were closed after a bank holiday, large employment programs were created, and modifications of mortgages were done on a large scale through programs like the Home Owners' Loan Corporation (HOLC):

> The HOLC operated on a significantly larger scale in relation to the U.S. housing market than HAMP has operated to date. The HOLC provided refinancing for about 10 percent of all non-farm, owner-occupied homes in the country, and for about 20 percent of all mortgaged homes. For HAMP to achieve a comparable scale, it would have to yield between 7.6 million–10.1 million permanent modifications.
>
> (Congressional Oversight Panel 2010b: 119)

As shown earlier, HAMP only yielded one million permanent modifications as of March 2012. While the scale of the Great Recession is not as large as the

Great Depression because of massive government involvement to prevent a full-blown debt deflation, the size of the problem is actually much larger given how large indebtedness is and how badly the quality of underwriting was allowed to deteriorate.

The New Deal policies were implemented swiftly despite the massive size and complexity of the problems. After years of depression, there was a political will to commit the time, effort, and money to get to the bottom of the problems as quickly as possible. Thousands of banks were examined in about a week and millions of unemployed were put to work in a matter of weeks. Similar resolve in terms of bank resolution was shown during the S&L crisis. In contrast, after the Great Recession, there was no real systematic analysis of banks:

> In the context of the FDIC, Secretary Geithner testified today that this event pushed the financial system to the brink of collapse. But Chairman Bernanke testified we sent two people to be on site at Lehman. We sent 50 credit people to the largest savings and loan in America. It had $30 billion in assets. We had a whole lot less staff than the Fed does. We forced out the CEO. We replaced the CEO. And we did that not through regulation, but because of our leverage as creditors. Now, I ask you, who had more leverage as creditors in 2008; the Fed, compared to the Federal Home Loan Bank of San Francisco 19 years earlier? Incomprehensibly, greater leverage in the Fed, and it simply was not used.
>
> (Black in U.S. House of Representatives 2010)

Similarly, the macroeconomic response has been very limited. As shown in Figure 2.4, the current contribution of the government sector to economic growth is zero. Even though the federal government did provide a $700 billion fiscal stimulus, it was too small to offset decline in spending at the state and local levels and was implemented very slowly. The composition of the stimulus was also not appropriate to deal with the employment problem. Concerns about the size of the deficit almost immediately put constraints on an appropriate response by the federal government.

What should have been done? As William Black argues, these too-big-to-fail institutions are also "systemically dangerous institutions" (SDIs). It could be argued that they actually destroy economic value—not just the capital value of the firm, but also the financial and real wealth of the economy as a whole. Total financial losses that can be attributed to the global financial crisis already exceed $10 trillion, and will eventually sum to much more. And, of course, that does not include the real economic losses—nearly ten million jobs in the United States alone. Bagehot's recommendations are sound but must be amended. Any of the "too big to fail" financial institutions that needed funding should have been required to submit to Fed oversight. Top management should have been required to proffer resignations as a condition of lending (with the Fed or Treasury holding the letters until they could decide which should be accepted—this is how Jessie Jones resolved the bank crisis in the 1930s). Short-term lending against the best collateral should have been provided at penalty rates. A comprehensive "cease and desist" order should have been enforced to stop all trading, all lending, all asset sales, and all bonus payments until an assessment of bank solvency could have been completed. The FDIC should have been called in (in the case of institutions with insured deposits), but in any case, the critically undercapitalized institutions should have been dissolved according to existing law: at the least cost to the Treasury and to avoid increasing concentration in the financial sector.

This would have left the financial system healthier and smaller; it would have avoided the moral hazard problem that has grown over the past three decades as each risky innovation was validated by a government-engineered rescue; and it would have reduced the influence that a handful of huge banks have over policy makers in Washington. At the same time, much more effort should have been concentrated on the borrowers' side by sustaining macroeconomic income and by modifying debt contracts. The first is clearly within the purview of Congress—to adopt fiscal policies to restore jobs and rising income. The second requires actions by the regulators at the Fed, Fannie and Freddie, banks, FDIC, SEC, Treasury, and Congress to force creditors to come to the table to negotiate real debt relief and promote hedge finance. In the next two chapters we turn to such policies.

4   Policy implications for finance

The previous chapters have argued that financial instability is a core element of modern capitalism. Over periods of prolonged economic growth, capitalist economies increasingly rely on Ponzi finance to continue to grow. In addition, over the past half century, the structure of capitalism has moved to a stage that is highly dependent on Ponzi finance to generate economic growth. This greater reliance on Ponzi finance has made the economic system more prone to destructive debt deflations that have required larger and larger government emergency interventions to avoid them.

This chapter focuses on the financial policy implications drawn from the analysis developed in the previous chapters. The chapter argues that the regulation and supervision of financial institutions should be based on the notion of position-making operations. This leads to specific policies in terms of the structure of the financial industry, the supervision of banks, central banking, and the measurement of financial fragility. However, the authors of this book also recognize that a given set of policies ends up generating counter-reactions by economic units to avoid the constraints imposed by these policies so a given set of rules may be effective only for a certain period of time. Thus, rather than providing narrow policies, this chapter focuses on the broad points that should guide policies.

At the core of the policy recommendations for the financial industry is the conception of financial fragility developed in Chapter 1. In this book, financial fragility points attention to the means indebted economic units use to repay debts rather than on the ability to repay per se. It is not because the ability to pay is high (low credit risk) that financial fragility is low; indeed, low credit risk may be possible only if refinancing sources stay open and asset prices continuously rise. In this case, it may appear that ability to pay is high but it is actually fragile. Similarly, limited ability to pay (high credit risk) may not be a major source of instability if this high credit risk is mainly based on income instead of refinancing and asset sales. For example, subprime mortgages have a much higher probability of default than prime mortgages but they are not a major concern in terms of risk of debt deflation if underwriting is done properly to verify income, cash reserves, and jobs, and if enough collateral is sought by banks. In this case, collateral plays its proper role of protecting banks and all their creditors against an unexpected credit event, instead of being the expected source of debt servicing.

Financial fragility is defined by a high reliance on position-making operations. The incapacity to make positions as expected leads to liquidity and solvency problems. In order to account for position-making risk effectively, one needs to do more than just impose capital and liquidity buffers on banks, develop deposit insurance, and have a central bank acting as lender of last resort. These elements of banking regulations and supervision are important but cannot replace a more proactive and flexible approach that accounts for financial innovations: "Anticipatory vigilance upon the part of the regulators is required to prevent increased risk exposure. But such vigilance, combined with intelligence, could contain particular unit risk exposure without the imposition of risk-related premiums or capital requirements" (Campbell and Minsky 1987: 258). A flexible regulatory framework allows regulators to be aware of changes in refinancing channels, loan and security underwriting methods, and other crucial elements that are essential to determine the financial fragility of an overall economy.

This way of approaching financial policy leads to very specific recommendations in terms of the organization of the financial industry, in terms of the crucial variables to focus on as regulators and, among others, in terms of the role of the central bank in the financial system. It also leads to a reconsideration of economic priorities away from economic growth toward a more holistic approach to economic improvement centered on full employment and sustainability. This entails changing the view point of regulators away from profitability and growth, which are currently the overarching concerns and means of judging health.

Moreover, currently regulators follow a "bad-bank" approach to regulation that is focused on one or several specific bank risks (credit risk, interest risk, fraud risk, and others) in order to regulate and supervise financial institutions. Minsky recognized a long time ago the need from a more holistic approach focused on systemic risk:

> When conceived in terms of bank runs and defaults, a particular bank fails because of its own, idiosyncratic attributes. Its management has been incompetent or committed fraud. Such a failure may have repercussions on other banking institutions, in that for a time financial markets fail to work normally. [...] A more complete description of the instability of an "economy with banking" needs to look behind the runs and analyze the structure of balance sheets payment commitments and position-making activities. [...] In the position-making view, bank failures do not arise simply because of incompetent or corrupt management. They occur mainly because of the interdependence of payment commitments and position-making transactions across institutions and units.
>
> (Campbell and Minsky 1987: 255–256)

Defaults and runs do not mostly happen by accidents/shocks, lack of luck, and imperfections; their probability of occurrence increases over a period of economic expansion because position-making rises and so does financial interdependence. Moreover, the impact of a shock (default, decline in income, rising policy rates, etc.) on the economy will depend on the financial fragility of this economy. Therefore, in addition to having a bank specific approach to regulation, a systemic approach to regulation is necessary. Minsky proposed to do this through the lenses of the hedge/speculative/Ponzi categories by determining how position-making risk emerges and grows and by figuring out ways to prevent, or at least to constrain, its growth.

Detecting financial fragility: definition and measurement

Financial fragility, financial instability, and financial crisis

As Schroeder (2009), Hume and Sentence (2009), and Tymoigne (2007b, 2009) note, the conceptualization of financial fragility depends heavily on the underlying theoretical framework. There are two conceptions of financial fragility; one that relies on a state and conflates financial fragility with financial crisis, versus one that rests on a process and makes a clear difference between financial fragility and financial crisis. The way one conceives financial fragility has a large impact on the conduct of financial regulation so it is necessary to spend a bit of time explaining the difference between the two conceptions.

In the standard economic models, money and finance are neutral and financial markets are efficient, so, until the 1990s, there was very little interest in the study of financial crises (Gertler 1988). This progressively changed and Mishkin (1991), Bernanke and Gertler (1990), and Kiyotaki and Moore (1997) have provided a theoretical foundation based on asymmetry of information to understand what happens during a financial crisis. Suarez and Sussman (1997, 2007) have completed this imperfection view of financial crises by focusing on the reversion mechanisms instead of the propagation mechanisms. The imperfection view can be complemented by the Monetarist view of financial crises (Schwartz 1988, 1998) and by the irrational approach developed by behavioral economics (Shiller 1999; De Bondt and Thaler 1985, 1995). The former states that financial crises are due to the incompetence of policy makers, and the latter states that behavioral imperfections of individuals contribute to the emergence of crises. As a result of individual imperfections, market imperfections, and poor discretionary policy making, the financial system amplifies, rather than corrects, the effects of shocks on the optimal saving-investment equilibrium, which leads to bubbles and financial crises. The cause of the shock is left unexplained and considered to be a random event; "nature decides which of the [economic state] occurs" (Goodhart *et al.* 2004: 5). Sometimes a large shock occurs that ripples through the economic system, and the point is to predict its occurrence. Thus, Aspachs *et al.* (2007) use rising probability of default of households and lower bank profit to measure financial fragility and use decline in real GDP to measure financial instability. Gonzalez-Hermosillo (1999) and Demirgüç-Kunt and Detragiache (1998) note that rising non-performing loans are a sign of crisis or near bank failure. Davis (1995) defines financial fragility as rising default rate and foreclosures.

In addition, economists following this static approach to financial fragility have developed "early warning systems" (EWS) through many different methods. Some of them have relied on microeconomic data, others have relied on macroeconomic data, and some of them have combined both sets. Some of them have relied on regression techniques to determine the probability of a crisis while others have used indicators to signal a problem. EWS were first developed to complement on-site supervision of banks in order to help supervisors to eliminate "dishonest, incompetent, and inequitable elements of banking" (Sinkey 1977: 40), which is consistent with the bad-bank approach to regulation. Macro-oriented EWS were first developed to deal with currency crises in emerging economies in the mid 1990s, and were rapidly extended to the detection of banking crises, especially in emerging countries where traditional indicators of banking supervision have not been reliable (Rojas-Suarez 2002). A good review of the literature is provided by Gaytàn and Johnson (2002), the International Monetary Fund (2009), Schroeder (2008), Klein and Shabbir (2003), Grabel (2003), and Berg *et al.* (2005), Edison (2003), and Lestano and Kuper (2003). All these review papers conclude that EWS fail to perform better than an educated guess. Indeed, there are several issues with all these models and the goal they want to achieve.

First, it is not surprising to find a strong correlation between fragility and crisis given that the variables used to define fragility are a manifestation of a financial crisis. Thus, there is an endogeneity issue at stake in econometric models of EWS. Some authors do recognize this issue but it is hard to deal with this problem unless one clearly separates fragility and instability. A more relevant definition of financial fragility would be able to detect problems when everything is going well—default rates are stable or declining, non-performing loans are stable or declining, and GDP is growing, among others. Second, the capacity to provide a signal of a problem before a crisis is evident is very limited. Lestano and Kuper (2003) note that banking crisis models produce the best signals two or three quarters ahead. While Goldstein *et al.* (2000) claim that this is good enough (they find an average of eleven months' lead time for banking crises), this is quite short to be able to deal with problems. By the time a crisis is predicted, most of the damage has already been done and it is extremely difficult to implement policies that can change the course of the economy quickly enough to effectively overcome the fragility. Third, by associating economic success and financial stability with rising profits and declining default rates, one creates a strong intellectual barrier against preemptive regulatory and supervisory actions. Policy makers become highly reluctant to intervene to eliminate unsustainable financial practices of "successful" businesses. For example, Black (2005) notes that tremendous pressure was put on examiners not to close fraudulent S&Ls because their high profitability made them models for the industry. But in fact virtually all the "high fliers" collapsed into massive insolvency.

Fourth, the fact that some models use mostly security price data to extract risk perception and so to predict crises leads to a number of issues. For example,

Segoviano and Goodhart (2009) use CDS spreads and out-of-the-money option prices to measure the probability of default of banks, and note that CDS spreads slightly precede bank crises. While they recognize that the price of securities is volatile and may involve illiquid markets, they argue that the trend of prices gives a good signal of future crises. Indeed, in their framework, financial market participants are forward-looking and mostly driven by fundamental analysis, and financial markets allow participants to allocate efficiently their resources. Thus, "if markets are efficient," an adverse price signal for a specific sector of the economy provides a clear sign that some financial problems are upcoming (Fell and Schinasi 2005: 114; International Monetary Fund 2009). This, however, is a big "if." The 2007 crisis cast into doubt the whole efficient market ideology.

Finally, economists in this framework tend to put a lot of emphasis on government debt and to bypass the importance of private debt. Stated alternatively, a rise in government debt is seen as much more problematic than a rise in private debt and will draw concerns much earlier—in fact almost immediately. These analysts tend to see government deficits as a source of instability independently of the nature of the monetary system in place, and there is a strong bias toward the idea that the government deficit is a source of financial problems under virtually any condition. In their analysis of the crisis, Reinhart and Rogoff (2009) mostly looked at government debt while they noted in passing the importance of private debt. However, a typical result found by EWS is that government surpluses are a leading indicator of banking and currency crises, which leads to puzzled observations or intricate theories to try to explain this:

> The level of fiscal balance relative to GDP appears also to be statistically significantly related to the length of the contraction, but the relationship has an economically counter-intuitive sign: a higher surplus position at the beginning of the crisis is related to a longer contraction.
>
> (Cecchetti *et al.* 2009: 18, n. 23)

> This counter-intuitive result is now well documented in the literature: many of the countries hit by a crisis actually ran a fiscal surplus, noticeably Mexico in 1994 and the Asian countries in 1997. This fact led many authors to reject first generation models of currency crises for more elaborate models in which moral hazard plays a role (a country with a government surplus is more likely to bail out risky investment projects).
>
> (Bussière and Fratzscher 2002: 27)

The fact that surpluses are associated with crises is easily understandable if one accounts for national accounting relationships. Government surpluses drain financial resources out of the private sector, which leads to problems in meeting debt commitments and a need to refinance and liquidate in the private sector. When this involves foreign-currency-denominated transactions, any refinancing problems are prone to generate a currency crisis and a banking crisis (Kregel 1998b). Thus, a currency crisis may be led by the depressive effect of government surpluses on the finances of the private sector, rather than from a speculative attack against the government fiscal deficit.

Recently some mainstream economists (Bårdsen *et al.* 2008; Hume and Sentence 2009) have been critical of current mainstream macroeconomic models and their inability to account for financial fragility in an endogenous fashion. For example, they note that general equilibrium model is "a model of an exchange economy [so] we cannot analyse the relationship between financial instability and economic growth" (Bårdsen *et al.* 2008: 22). This is typical of canonical models like Kiyotaki and Moore (1997) that study the impacts of an exogenous productivity shock on the interaction between asset prices and credit constraints within the context of an elaborated peasant economy.

In the evolutionary view of financial instability, financial crises occur endogenously given existing market mechanisms and regulations. A consequence of this framework is that the focus is not on the prediction of financial crises. By focusing on the prediction of crises, much of the effort is spent on, first, getting variables with good predictive properties, and, second, looking for "all plausible sources of risk to financial stability" especially those "that could prove to be systematically relevant" (Fell and Shinasi 2005: 114). In fact, there is an obsession with the measurement of probability and sources of risk as well as the size of the expected downturn. However, this is a rather futile exercise that loses sight of the broader picture. When an economy is financially fragile there are many different sources of risks that can be very complex or impossible to measure because of lack of data. As Bell (2000) notes, most banking crises involve, at least in part, random triggers that are impossible to predict. More importantly, when an economy is fragile, even usual adverse fluctuations in income, asset prices, and other variables can lead to a crisis.

Thus, rather, than focusing on predicting financial crises, something probably impossible to do, the evolutionary approach focuses on detecting the conditions that make a financial crisis and debt deflation possible. In order to do that, this approach focuses on the funding practices used to sustain economic growth during periods of economic stability. In that case, there may not be any immediate source of risk but the funding practices involve future dependence on limited fluctuations in incomes and asset prices around their short-term trend. Thus, the goal is to capture early the worsening in the funding quality used to sustain economic activity when everything is going well, so as to take preemptive measures by determining the cause of the worsening.

As shown in the previous chapter, this is clearly illustrated by the last housing boom. From the first quarter of 2003 to the fourth quarter of 2006, the serious delinquency on all mortgages declined, interest-rate spreads declined, the wealth of households grew rapidly, and the profitability of banks was very high. Thus, it appeared that all indicators pointed to a robust expansion without financial fragility—the chances of financial crises appeared remote. However, as explained in the previous chapter, all this was made possible by a Ponzi process in the housing sector in both the prime and non-prime sectors. The expectation that home prices would rise forever led to an expectation that cheap refinancing would be always available. Combined with the low-doc and low-cost effects of mortgages, the previous states of expectations led to a decline in monthly mortgage payments and growing refinancing, which, in turn, led to lower default rates for a short period of time. However, this improvement was only temporary because it was based on unsustainable funding practices, that is, funding practices that required growing position-making operations to sustain a given level of indebtedness. By the time default rates grew, it was too late to do anything substantial that could avoid the crisis. Rising default rates and declining wealth and profit were an expression of the crisis rather than a predictor of the crisis. Thus, contrary to the static approach to financial fragility, one simply cannot use rising interest rate spreads, rising default rates, lower bank profits, and other indicators of lower economic growth or rising non-performing loans to detect financial fragility. By the time these indicators appear it is too late.

Several studies have been conducted using the evolutionary view of financial instability and they can be separated into two categories. The most straight-forward studies analyze the trend of several variables over time and check how they help to explain recessions. The second set of studies uses the hedge, specu-lative, and Ponzi categories and aims at detecting one or more of these cat-egories. In the first set of categories, authors usually find that leverage increases and liquidity decreases during periods of expansion (Minsky 1977a, 1984b, 1986a; Sinai 1976; Niggle 1989; Wolfson 1994; Grabel 2003; Estenson 1984). Leverage and liquidity are measured by looking at several balance sheet ratios, like the debt-to-income ratio, the proportion of short-term debts, the debt service-to-income ratio, and the proportion of cash and near-cash assets. Isenberg (1988, 1994) finds that, instead of applying to the whole economy, the fragilization of the economy can be localized in the most dynamic sectors of the economy. Minsky (1984b) notes that the household and government sectors were the main contributors to the 1929 crisis.

However, aggregate variables only give a first clue about what is going on within an economy or a sector. If some indicators behave suspiciously, it is necessary to look at sectoral level data more carefully. In that case, not all eco-nomic activities within a sector may lead to financial fragility. For example, Minsky notes that within the household sector, usually only speculation in the stock market is financed routinely in a Ponzi way. However, mortgage finance and consumption finance can also be funded by the recourse to Ponzi and specu-lative finance. Thus a solid analysis of financial fragility cannot be based only on macro data but also must look more in detail at which activities contribute to growing the fragility of a sector.

The second set of authors has developed a more elaborate strategy that aims at detecting the different stages of financial fragility. Some of them develop methods to detect all three stages (Schroeder 2009; Foley 2003; De Paula and Alves 2000). Other authors focus their attention on detecting a specific stage of fragility like Ponzi finance (Seccareccia 1988) or an overall index of fragility that shows overall position-making risk (Arza and Español 2008).

Financial fragility index

In this book, financial fragility is not merely a measure of the size of the leverage but also a measure of its quality defined by the expected reliance on refinancing and liquidation of illiquid assets in order to service debts. As a consequence, financial variables play a heavy role in determining financial fragility, but several points should be understood before engaging in such analysis.

First, monetarily sovereign governments are not subject to any effective budget constraint; in case of problems they can always bypass the self-imposed constraints they put on their budgetary procedures and use the central bank as their fiscal agent. Thus, monetarily sovereign governments are always hedge finance and there is no point in measuring financial fragility for them. The federal government of countries like the UK, the U.S., Japan can never go broke regardless of the size of its public debt or deficit relative to gross domestic product. If a government borrows in foreign currency or if it promises to convert its currency into something else, then a measure of financial fragility is warranted; otherwise, sovereign currency-issuing governments face no involuntary solvency risk.

Second, it is best to look at how financial variables behave simultaneously rather than in isolation. For example, a rising debt-to-income ratio does not necessarily mean that an economic unit is more fragile. Indeed, if the average maturity of debts increases, principal payments are stretched and so debt service may not be going up even though outstanding debt is rising. The creation of the thirty-year fixed-rate mortgage by the Federal Housing Administration has increased the capacity of households to sustain higher levels of debt relative to their income. Thus, if possible, one should look at the debt-service-to-income ratio and the amount of refinancing operations used to repay existing debts.

Third, the on-balance accounting documents of economic units may only tell part of the story because some economic units may have major off-balance positions. Hadley and Touhey (2006, 2007) noted that traditional liquidity ratios for commercial banks can be misleading because loans are no longer illiquid and core deposits are no longer the only stable source of funding. As a consequence, asset quality may no longer play a role in liquidity problems, and much more emphasis should be put on cash-flow analysis in order to assess funding structures, liquidity needs, and alternative sources of funds in relation to different economic and financial risks, and to determine contingency funding planning. As shown below, this view is similar to the one taken in this book.

Some preliminary considerations

Given that financial fragility is based on the notion of hedge, speculative, and Ponzi finance it may be good to start by reminding the reader of the implications of this categorization to show why the following focuses on cash flow, debt refinancing, and asset prices.

Hedge finance means that an economic unit is expected to be able to pay its liability commitments (CC) with the net cash flow it generates from its routine economic operations (work for most individuals, going concern for companies) (NCF_O). Thus at time zero, when a debt contract is signed, the following state of expectation in terms of cash flows from routine operations prevails:

$$E_0(NCF_{Ot}) > E_0(CC_t) \ \forall t$$

In addition, the available cash balance (M) is large enough to meet unforeseen deficiencies in realized net cash inflows from routine operations (there are cases where that might not be the case but they can be ignored for the sake of generalization):

$$NCF_{Ot} + M_t > CC_t \ \forall t$$

This implies that net cash flow from what Minsky calls defensive position-making (NCF_{PM})—refinancing (ΔL_R) and forced sales of non-liquid assets ($\Delta(P_A Q_A)$) in order to service debts—are not expected, and are not needed when cash flow expectations from routine operations are not met:

$$E_0(NCF_{PMt}) = NCF_{PMt} = \Delta L_{Rt} + \Delta(P_{At} Q_{At}) = 0 \ \forall t$$

Thus, even though indebtedness may be high (even relative to income), an economy in which most economic units rely on hedge finance is not prone to a debt deflation.

Speculative finance means that routine net cash flows are expected to be large enough to meet the income component of liabilities contracts (iL) but not the capital component of liabilities (aL). Thus, at the time a debt contract is signed, the following state of expectation prevails for routine cash flows:

$$E_0(NCF_{Ot}) < E_0(CC_t) \ \forall t$$

$$E_0(NCF_{Ot}) \geq E_0(iL_t) \ \forall t$$

$$E_0(NCF_{Ot}) < E_0(aL_t) \ \forall t$$

In addition, the available cash balance is not large enough to meet foreseen deficiencies in realized net cash inflows from routine operations. As a consequence, it is expected that position-making will be needed to meet part, or all, the capital servicing on liabilities, and usually that means that it is expected that debts will be rolled over. However, while position-making is needed, the size of cash flow from position-making relative to outstanding debts (L) should stay constant or decline:

$$E_0(NCF_{PMt}) = NCF_{PMt} > 0 \text{ and } d(E(NCF_{PM})/L)/dt \leq 0$$

The ratio will stay constant if position-making is needed to meet all capital servicing. The length of time during which routine cash flows are expected to fall short of capital repayment depends on the economic unit. The business model of banks is such that position-making is usually needed to meet the capital component of liabilities, and as such banks need a reliable and cheap refinancing source. Other businesses may only have a temporary need for position-making.

Ponzi finance means that an economic unit is not expected to generate enough net cash flow from its routine economic operations, or to have enough monetary assets to meet the capital and income services due on outstanding financial contracts. At time zero, it is expected that the following applies until a date n in terms of cash flow from routine operations:

$$E_0(NCF_{Ot}) < E_0(CC_t) \; \forall t < n$$

$$E_0(NCF_{Ot}) < E_0(iL_t) \; \forall t < n$$

$$E_0(NCF_{Ot}) < E_0(aL_t) \; \forall t < n$$

This implies that Ponzi finance relies on an expected growth of refinancing loans, and/or an expected full liquidation of asset positions at growing asset prices (P_A) in order to meet debt commitments on a given level of outstanding debts:

$$E(NCF_{PM}) = \Delta L_{Rt} + \Delta(P_{At}Q_{At}) > 0 \text{ and } d(E(NCF_{PM})/L)/dt > 0$$

This financial situation creates a high interdependence between asset prices and debt, and increases the interconnectedness between lenders and borrowers.

Leaving aside fraud, all of the previous financial schemes must have a positive expected present value to be implemented; otherwise an honest banker would not even consider lending. The main difference between the schemes is based on the degree to which refinancing and liquidation of non-monetary assets are needed to meet debt commitments to create a positive net worth. Hedge finance does not require any position-making operation; Ponzi finance requires growing position-making operations. Moreover, whereas at the individual level the choice between refinancing and liquidation is a matter of relative cost, at the aggregate level liquidation is impossible and so it is an abnormal source of cash inflows (Minsky 1962):

> As an empirical generalization, almost all financial commitments are met from two normal sources of cash: income flows and refinancing of positions. For most units—especially those that have real capital goods as their assets—the selling out of their position is not feasible (no market exists for a quick sale); for others, aside from marginal adjustments by way of special money markets, it is an unusual source of cash. [...] Financial instability occurs whenever a large number of units resort to extraordinary sources for cash.
>
> (Minsky 1972: 105)

Given that the index constructed below is an aggregate index concerned with the risk of debt deflation, the liquidation of non-liquid assets is considered an abnormal source of funds, so reliance on this source of cash to meet debt services increases financial fragility.

Another way to understand the classification is in terms of the underwriting characteristics underlying each scheme:

> Loans based on the value of pledged collateral are different in kind from loans based on the value of the cash flows that are expected from income-earning operations. True, in structuring a loan that is mainly based on prospective cash flows the loan officers may insist on a margin of safety in the form of pledged collateral. But this would not be the primary consideration [...]. The viability of loans mainly made because of collateral, however, depends upon the expected market value of the assets that are pledged. [...] Thus, the overall fragility-robustness of the financial structure, upon which the cyclical stability of the economy depends, emerges out of loans made by bankers. [...] An emphasis by bankers on the collateral value and the expected values of assets is conducive to the emergence of a fragile financial structure.
>
> (Minsky 1986a: 234)

Hedge finance involves income-based lending, that is, lending in which the creditworthiness of a borrower is heavily reliant on an analysis of its operational income. Collateral may still be used to determine the profitability of a loan but its role is to protect a bank against an unexpected credit event instead of being the expected source of debt servicing.

Ponzi finance involves, partially or fully, asset-based lending, that is, lending based on the expected price of assets. More precisely, income-based Ponzi finance involves financial contracts that contain a period of time during which rising refinancing is needed to cover debt services until operational income is high enough to cover debt service. Minsky always emphasized that capital equipment with a long period of maturation may involve such Ponzi financing. Such lending involves a decline in net worth while Ponzi finance exists, followed by an increase in net worth as assets generate an income greater than debt services. Asset-based Ponzi finance, also called a pyramid scheme, contains underwriting expectations such that operational income will never be high enough to service debts. More formally, income-based Ponzi finance involves $E(NCF_{Ot}) < E(CC_t)$ for $t < n$ but $E(NCF_{Ot}) > E(CC_t)$ after that period in such a way that the net worth is positive. Asset-based Ponzi finance is a case where n tends toward infinity, and the only means to generate a positive net worth is to sell assets at a price high enough to cover debt payments and generate a profit. Thus, in the case of sustained asset-based Ponzi finance, net worth will grow only if asset prices increase fast enough to more than compensate for the increase in debt.

According to the Financial Instability Hypothesis (FIH), the more Ponzi finance is used the more the economic system becomes fragile. That is, the more it is susceptible to a debt deflation from an initial disturbance: "The robustness or fragility of the financial system depends upon the size and strength of the margins of safety and the likelihood that initial disturbances are amplified" (Minsky 1986a: 209).

> The overall fragility-robustness of the financial structure, upon which the cyclical stability of the economy depends, emerges out of loans made by bankers. [...] An emphasis by bankers on the collateral value and the expected values of assets is conducive to the emergence of a fragile financial structure. [...] One measure of the riskiness of financial instruments is the expected source of the funds that are needed to fulfill financial contracts.
>
> (Minsky 1986a: 234–236)

Without this reliance on position-making, the impact of disturbances will be contained, and limited government involvement will be needed to promote financial stability. The source of the disturbance can be default, rising interest rate, disruption in refinancing sources, a natural disaster, or any other "shocks" that affect either the cash inflow or cash outflow of an economic unit. While a lot of work has been done to identify the sources of disturbance (especially credit risk and liquidity risk), the goal in this book is to focus on the risk of amplification of the shock induced by underwriting practices. In the Minskian framework, this amplification goes through a snowball effect between asset prices and debt that, if left unchecked, leads to a debt deflation. Thus, one of the main goals of the index is to capture this interdependence by focusing on how burdening debt and change in underwriting lead economic units to expect to sell their assets to service debts. In order to do so, one needs data about debt burden, refinancing needs, liquidity ratios, trends in asset prices, and any data that can proxy the growth of asset-based lending (such as cash-out refinance in the mortgage industry).

The important point for the index is that Ponzi finance can be detected even though defensive position-making operations have not yet occurred. As long as asset-based lending occurs, underwriting includes expectations of position-making operations and so the interdependence between debt and asset prices increases on the upside; thereby creating the condition for a debt-deflation on the downside.

One can conclude from this brief discussion of Minsky's theoretical framework that, as an economic unit (be it an individual, an economic sector, or an economy) transfers from hedge to Ponzi finance, one should observe that debt burden rises (the ratio of debt service to routine income rises), defensive refinancing needs and/or asset-based lending rise, asset prices rise, and the amount of liquid assets relative to liabilities declines. This should happen simultaneously if financial fragility is rising.

Financial fragility index in residential housing finance

By combining datasets about refinancing needs, asset-based lending debt burden, asset prices, and liquidity ratios, and by using the theoretical framework developed in this book together with the methodology presented in Tymoigne (2012a), it is possible to construct an index of financial fragility for residential housing finance in the United States, the United Kingdom, and France. In line with Minsky's framework, the goal is to capture unsustainable interactions between asset prices and debt on the upside. Figure 4.1 shows how the index changed over time.

All countries experienced a rapid increase in home prices in the first part of the first decade of the new millennium; however, financial fragility grew less rapidly in France compared to the U.S. and the UK. A tighter mortgage regulation until 2005 limited the capacity of French banks to underwrite mortgages on the basis of rising home prices instead of income. However, the financial fragility of France did rise by about 25 percent from 2005 to 2008, from the combination of a decline in liquidity buffers, rising outstanding mortgages, rising home prices, and rising debt services relative to disposable income. Households owning a property in France did experience a brief decline in financial fragility from 2008 and 2009, but fragility seems to be about to rise. Given that home equity lending has been authorized, unless underwriting standards stay strong, one may expect a rapid increase in the financial fragility of French households if the economic conditions become favorable.

In the United Kingdom, financial fragility in housing finance declined during the first half of the 1990s but started to go back up again from the last quarter of the 1990s. Home prices grew very rapidly, as did mortgage lending, home equity lending, and debt service relative to disposable income. At the same time, the

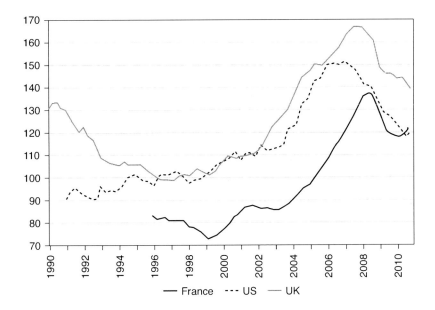

Figure 4.1 Index of financial fragility, base 1996.

liquidity buffer of households declined and the combination of all these trends made households more vulnerable to financial difficulties induced by unemployment, declines in home prices, rising interest rates, rising amortization rates, and decline in the availability of refinancing loans. As a consequence, financial fragility grew by almost 70 percent from 1996 to 2008 and by about 50 percent from early 2000 until 2008. The UK did not record any recession from the early 1990s to 2008, so financial fragility continuously grew during that period of time, and it did so at an accelerated rate (Figure 4.2). Since 2008, financial fragility has declined dramatically as housing finance is simplified through foreclosure, house sales, and the issuance of term-rate refinance and purchase mortgages at more affordable terms and with tighter underwriting standards.

Similar trends are observed in the United States. Like in the UK, financial fragility in housing funding grew from the late 1990s. Some members of the Federal Open Market Committee (FOMC), namely Gramlich and Jordan, became worried about the deterioration of households' finances: "There are people making real estate investments for residential and other purposes in the expectation that prices can only go up and go up at accelerating rates. Those expectations ultimately become destabilizing to the economic system" (Jordan in Federal Open Market Committee 1999: 123). Gramlich was worried about predatory lending and made his views known to Greenspan who did not consider it to be a significant problem. Greenspan seemed to be vindicated by the pause in the growth of fragility that occurred in the early 2000s because of a burst of the dot-com bubble in 2000 and a minor recession in 2001. However, from 2003, financial fragility grew very rapidly for the same reason as in the United

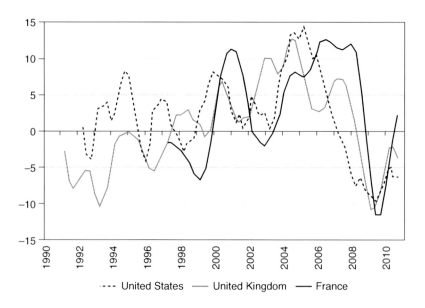

Figure 4.2 Four-quarter moving average of the annualized growth rate in the index.

Kingdom. Households in the United States were the first to experience a decline in financial fragility from 2007, followed by the United Kingdom and France. The decline in fragility has been the most dramatic in the U.S. and household fragility is almost back to its level of 2003, when most of the Ponzi financing in housing had not occurred.

Overall, this index provides some insights into the funding methods used by households to purchase and hold a house. It shows that the decline in housing underwriting standards started at least at the end of the 1990s in the U.S. and the UK and lasted until the second half of the 2000s. Some FOMC members in the United States were right to worry about the dangerous, albeit early, trends occurring in the housing market.

Note that the index is not comparable across countries. This would require a normalization procedure presented in Tymoigne (2012a), which can be done at the cost of loss of information. Another extension of the index would be to use it to create a heat map similar to the one the IMF constructed for different markets in its *Financial Stability Report* (Figure 4.3). The color changes depending on the deviation from the means. If the index value is below one standard deviation from the means of the index, the color is light grey. If the index value is between one and 1.5 standard deviation from the means, the color is grey. If the index value is greater than 1.5 standard deviation from the means of the index, the color is black. This heat map shows that financial fragility grew first in the U.S. in mid 2004, followed by the UK in 2005, and France in 2007. Financial fragility was really high from mid 2005 in the U.S., mid 2006 in the UK, and early 2008 in France. Since 2009, the financial fragility index has declined back to its means in the UK and the U.S. but is still relatively high in France.

In principle, the method underlying this index can be extended to all economic activities that require external funding. Instead of focusing on a specific activity, the index can also be constructed for an entire economic sector. In practice, as for any other economic problem, the construction of the index is impaired by the availability of data and its quality. Even the United States only provides partial data. A major research agenda is to develop reliable data about refinancing needs, underwriting methods, and debt-service ratio for different sectors and activities of the economy. For mortgage finance, one would need data about cash-out refinancing for all borrowers, outstanding home equity lending, use of

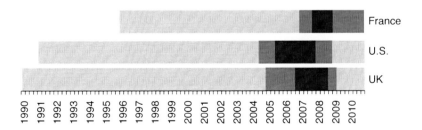

Figure 4.3 Heat map of residential mortgage.

external funds, the mortgage-debt service ratio, and the proportion of interest-only and payment-options mortgages, and this should be available for prime, alt-A, and prime borrowers. Most importantly, the expected refinancing needs induced by the previous data should be computed.

Given the central role of financial fragility in the Minskian framework, it is a core element to include in regulation. Beyond the need to develop indexes of financial fragility to detect problems in an economic sector or in a specific financial institution, one must put in place a much more proactive and flexible regulatory framework that promotes hedge finance.

Financial fragility and financial reform

Cash flow supervision of financial institutions and regulation of underwriting

In order to get a better understanding of financial fragility, regulators need to develop a cash-flow-oriented analysis of financial institutions by looking at the types of assets and liabilities that financial institutions have, deducing the core net cash inflows from operations and cash outflows from liabilities, and determining if, and to what extent, defensive position-making operations could become necessary, and under what economic and financial conditions the capacity to make position would be threatened:

> The crux of the report is the form on which the position-making accounts are identified. From the cash needs as derived from the liability structure and business operations and the cash position as derived from activity in the various accounts, a need to acquire or place cash by position-making activity emerges. The final steps in the examination procedure are to develop feasible position-making operations and to evaluate the liquidity of the bank under the hypothesized economic and financial conditions.
>
> (Minsky 1975c: 161)

This "conditional analysis," as Minsky called it, would greatly improve the capacity of regulators to judge the financial soundness of financial companies and the risk of debt deflation.

Concerns about financial stability should be continued through every phase of the business cycle, especially when the economy is doing well. "Normal/wise" growth of credit, and "normal/wise" use of leverage, relative to an arbitrary ratio, should be of great concern because stability leads to instability. What matters is not the normality relative to a trend but the types of funding practices used.

Beyond a cash-flow supervision of banks, regulations and supervision must also focus on the underwriting of loans and securities in order to detect Ponzi finance, especially collateral-based lending. Indeed, no matter how much thought is put into the determination of the appropriate size and composition of the capital and liquidity buffer, major banking crises will still occur if the underwriting of bank advances and securities is not done properly. Stated alternatively, there must be a proper verification of the ability to pay creditors because, no matter how high required buffers are for banks' balance sheet, if the quality of the loans is questionable financial crises will impact the economy. They will do so through a debt deflation and/or through the impact on expectations. Instead of judging the quality of loans purely from their probability of default, or loss given default, for financial stability purposes one must look at the underwriting.

This brings forward important considerations about the meaning of credit-worthiness and ability to pay. Currently, these concepts are analyzed from the point of view of a banker who is mostly interested in the question "will you pay on time?" Bankers verify the answer by estimating probability of default and other relevant elements of credit risk in order to assess risks of loss and so potential impact on profitability. The expected dynamic of asset prices is crucial for the estimation of credit risk because it affects the recovery rate and so expected losses. In addition, some borrowers may default even if they still can repay because, as the current crisis has shown, if home values decline steeply and generate large negative net worth it may make economic sense to default (Elul 2006; Congressional Budget Office 2008).

Thus, rising asset prices tend to lower the probability of default and to raise the recovery rate if default occurs, which reduces credit risk and so has a strong positive impact on ratings and FICO scores (Kothari 2006: 61). As a consequence, some people will qualify for a loan not because it is expected that they can meet payments with their income but because it is expected that collateral prices will go up. Thus, the credit rating and underwriting process may encourage a Ponzi process: the faster the house price growth, the higher the recovery rate and the lower the default rate, the lower the expected loss, the higher credit ratings and the more people qualify, which sustains the growth of house prices ... until not enough people can be qualified to overcompensate for foreclosures. Thus, a Ponzi process may contribute to a decline in default probability and an increase in credit ratings, while creditworthiness would actually worsen from the point of view of quality of the underwriting.

If one takes the viewpoint of managing financial stability instead of the banker's viewpoint, repayment based on reselling assets and refinancing is less credit-worthy than repayment based on routine income from business operations (or employment) generated by holding assets (or working). The main question becomes: "*How* will you repay on time?" As Minsky noted, beyond the probability of repayment: "One measure of the riskiness of financial instruments is the expected source of the funds that are needed to fulfill financial contracts" (Minsky 1986a: 237). Indeed, at the aggregate level asset liquidation is an abnormal source of funds because asset liquidation to service debt leads to a debt deflation. As shown in Chapter 3, this is exactly what happened recently.

From the point of view of systemic stability and long-term economic growth, both types of Ponzi finance—pyramid/asset-based and production/income-based—are a source of concern because, as long as they exist, the economy is exposed to the risk of debt deflation. At the same time, banning income-based

Ponzi finance may put too heavy a burden on economic growth; therefore, income-based Ponzi finance may be tolerated in government-insured activities, but should be strictly regulated and carefully monitored. Indeed, investment is a component of aggregate demand that may require Ponzi finance while the investment goods are produced, installed, and ready to generate enough income from their operation so forbidding income-based lending may be counterproductive for economic growth. Asset-based Ponzi finance should be forbidden in all activities that have an implicit or explicit government guarantee. It might be tolerated in other economic activities, but even then regulators should check for potential spillover effects.

Title 14 of Dodd–Frank actually goes in the direction of focusing on operating cash flows by forcing lenders to determine the capacity to pay off mortgagors on the basis of other means than the expected refinancing sources and expected equity in the house:

> A determination under this subsection of a consumer's ability to repay a residential mortgage loan shall include consideration of the consumer's credit history, current income, expected income the consumer is reasonably assured of receiving, current obligations, debt-to-income ratio or the residual income the consumer will have after paying non-mortgage debt and mortgage-related obligations, employment status, and other financial resources other than the consumer's equity in the dwelling or real property that secures repayment of the loan. A creditor shall determine the ability of the consumer to repay using a payment schedule that fully amortizes the loan over the term of the loan.
>
> (U.S. Congress 2010: 768)

While Title 14 is limited to residential mortgages (commercial mortgages were a big problem during the S&L speculative boom, and other loans should also follow the same underwriting methods), this Title is a potentially great contribution to financial stability, if enforced.

Managing financial innovations

In order to maintain a competitive profitability, financial institutions constantly innovate by creating new financial products and by using existing financial products in new ways. Over enduring periods of relative calm, financial innovations involve higher leverage, higher credit risk, higher liquidity risk, higher counterparty risk, and higher position-making risk and it is the duty of regulators to adapt regulation and supervision as quickly as possible. Regulators must discourage Ponzi-prone innovations even if financial institutions claim that it is the only way they can maintain their profitability and stay competitive. Regulators must discourage these developments because ultimately they lead to financial crises, destroy financial institutions, and threaten the viability of the entire economy. In addition, if competition is the only mechanism available to select innovations, the "good" innovations will be the ones that raise profitability irrespectively of the impact on systemic risk. What is good for Wall Street may not be good for Main Street, and the criterion for selecting a "good" innovation should neither be Wall Street's interest nor Main Street's interest but systemic stability. The latter should be the paramount criterion to judge financial innovations, because systemic stability is required to obtain permanent welfare gains. Stated alternatively, hedge financing should be promoted and Ponzi financing should be discouraged, especially asset-based Ponzi finance. Alternatives to income-based Ponzi finance should be found, even though it may be a common use in the production of investment goods that involve long delays before generating any income. In this case, developing financial instruments with a pay off that depends on the income generated by the investment projects may be preferable to the use of common debt. Equity financing is the most straightforward method but it is not available to all economic units so debt instruments with an amount of interest and principal due that changes with actual income may be an alternative. Beyond the purchase of investment goods, this financing technique could also be applied to households in the purchase of homes or for student loans.

Thus, instead of pushing for all kinds of financial innovation that provide short-term monetary gains and lead to long-term economic instability, the government should motivate financial firms to create innovations that make a country reputable for a sound and reliable financial system. This is where a good understanding of systemic risk based on a cash-flow analysis becomes very important.

Regulators could watch two things before allowing a financial product to enter the economy. First, if the cash-flow implications of a financial product cannot be determined with reasonable precision, probably this product should not be allowed to exist, or it should be restricted to the non-government-insured financial sector. Buyers and sellers of the product would be left on their own in case of problems while making sure that the payments system is protected by avoiding a disorderly liquidation of non-insured financial institutions. Second, a cash-flow analysis allows to determine if a financial product tends to promote a Ponzi process or not. For example, payment-option mortgages would be a type of financial product that should be restricted to customers with an income and cash reserves large enough to meet the demands of such a product, and the availability of position-making channels should not be used to measure the reliability of a product. Similarly, interest-only mortgages are Ponzi prone if they are granted to individuals who cannot pay the full debt service through their core sources of cash inflow and cash reserves (i.e., excluding refinancing and liquidation of the encumbered asset(s)).

It is also important to engage in regulatory follow-up after a financial innovation has been allowed. This is necessary because the use of an innovation often changes over time, especially as the return obtained from a product starts to decline and financial institutions feel pressed to find creative ways to keep their profitability on target. Thus, regulation should be flexible enough to deal with changes in business practices as they come along.

Structure of the financial industry: making finance work for the economy

Finance and economic development

In his proposal for development of the newly independent eastern European nations, Minsky argued that the critical problem is to "create a monetary and financial system which will facilitate economic development, the emergence of democracy and the integration with the capitalist world" (Minsky 1993c: 36). Except for the latter goal, this statement applies equally well to promotion of the capital development of the western nations.

The government itself has a definite role to play in that strategy as history shows in terms of housing, electrification, promoting small business, education, and many other areas where profitability is small or nil and the break even period is long, but socio-economic benefits are high. For example, in the U.S., most of the gains in the homeownership rate were achieved before 1968, through FHA, VA, and Fannie Mae government programs. After World War Two, the homeownership rate jumped from around 45 to 64 percent by 1968. Since that time, the rate has mostly stagnated except for the surge in the late 1990s and the 2000 boom due to the dynamics presented in Chapter 3. However, this gain was made possible by unsustainable funding practices and, in 2012, the homeownership rate had fallen back to 65.5 percent and is still on a declining trend (Figure 4.4). Fannie Mae used to be a pure government institution but, in 1968, it was split between Ginnie Mae (that remained a government institution) and Fannie Mae (that became a for-profit institution backed by government, i.e., a government-sponsored enterprise). The reason for the split was probably because Fannie Mae became a much more active player in the mortgage market after 1966 and the government did not want to take part in this effort directly.

Beyond promoting a healthy involvement of the government in the financial support of economic development, the private banking should be reformed to that end. Let us first enumerate the essential functions to be provided by the financial system:

1   a safe and sound payments system;
2   short-term loans to households and firms, and, possibly, to state and local government;
3   a safe and sound housing finance system;
4   a range of financial services including insurance, brokerage, and retirement services;
5   long-term funding of positions in expensive capital assets.

Obviously there is no reason why any single institution should provide all of these services, although the long-run trend has been to consolidate a wide range of services within the affiliates of a bank holding company. The New Deal

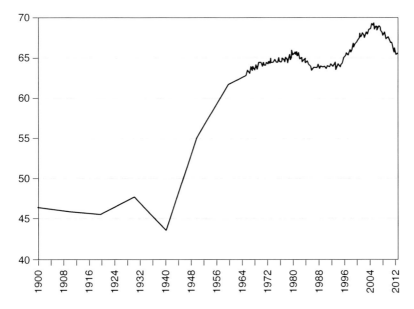

Figure 4.4 Homeownership rate in the U.S. (%) (source: U.S. Census Bureau).

reforms had separated institutions by function (and state laws against branching provided geographic constraints). The demise of commercial banking and the rise of shadow banking was mostly a consequence of the transition to Money Manager Capitalism.

In his draft book manuscript, Minsky dealt in detail with a Treasury proposal for "modernizing" the financial system. Briefly, this proposal made recommendations for "safer, more competitive banks," by "strengthening" deposit insurance, weakening Glass–Steagall, weakening state limits on branching, allowing corporations to own banks, and consolidating regulation and supervision in the Treasury at the expense of reduction of the role of the Fed. Minsky argued that the proposal was at best superficial because it ignored shadow banks. While he quibbled with the approach taken to rescue FDIC (recall that many thrifts had failed by the end of the 1980s and even the largest banks were in trouble in the early 1990s), he agreed that deposit insurance had to be strengthened.

He emphasized that weakening Glass–Steagall and state limits on branching were trying to "fix something that is not broke." He argued that small-to-medium sized banks are more profitable and relation oriented. In other words, there was no reason to allow or promote the rise of hegemonic financial institutions with national markets and broad scope. As many others have long argued, the economies of scale associated with banking are achieved at the size of relatively small banks. Minsky was not swayed by the Treasury's argument that banks were becoming uncompetitive because they could not branch across state lines or because certain practices were prohibited to them. He believed that repealing these constraints would simply reduce the profitability of the smaller, relation-oriented banks.

However, he did recognize that the smaller banks would lose market share, anyway, due to competition from shadow banks. Hence the solution would not be found in promoting bigger, less profitable banks that are not interested in relation-oriented banking. Rather, Minsky would allow greater scope to the activities of the small community banks. We might call this "intensifying" banking—allowing each small institution to provide a greater range of services—as opposed to promoting branching and concentration of power in the hands of a few large bank holding companies with a variety of subsidiaries.

Minsky argued that there are two main ways in which the capital development of the economy can be "ill done": the "Smithian" and the "Keynesian." The first refers to what might be called "misallocation": the wrong investments are financed. The second refers to an insufficiency of investment, which leads to a level of aggregate demand that is too low to promote high employment. The 1980s suffered from both, but most importantly from inappropriate investment—especially in commercial real estate investment. We could say that the 2000s again suffered from "Smithian" ill done capital development because far too much finance flowed into the residential real estate sector. In both cases, Minsky would point his finger to securitization. In the 1980s because the thrifts were not holding mortgages, they had funding capacity that flowed into commercial real estate; in the 2000s, the mania for risky (high return) asset-backed securities fueled subprime lending and exotic mortgages. In a prescient analysis, Minsky argued:

> Because of the way the mortgages were packaged it was possible to sell off a package of mortgages at a premium so that the originator and the investment banking firms walked away from the deal with a net income and no recourse from the holders. The instrument originators and the security underwriters did not hazard any of their wealth on the longer term viability of the underlying projects. Obviously in such packaged financing the selection and supervisory functions of lenders and underwriters are not as well done as they might be when the fortunes of the originators are at hazard over the longer term.
>
> (Minsky 1992b: 22–23)

The implication is rather obvious: good underwriting is promoted when the underwriter is exposed to the longer-term risks. This brings us back to Minsky's skeptical banker:

> When we go to the theater we enter into a conspiracy with the players to suspend disbelief. The financial developments of the 1980s [and 1990s and 2000s!] can be viewed as theater: promoters and portfolio managers suspended disbelief with respect to where the cash would come from that would [validate] the projects being financed. Bankers, the designated sceptic

in the financial structure placed their critical faculties on hold. As a result the capital development was not done well. Decentralization of finance may well be the way to reintroduce the necessary skepticism.

(Minsky 1992a: 37)

Decentralization plus maintaining exposure to risk could reorient institutions back toward relationship banking. Unfortunately most trends in recent years have favored concentration. The "too big to fail" doctrine that dates back to the problems of Continental Illinois gives an obvious advantage to the biggest banks. These are able to finance positions at the lowest cost because government stands behind them. Even in the case of FDIC-insured deposits (which have no default risk), smaller banks pay more simply because of the market perception that they are riskier because the government does not backstop them. Investment banks are now allowed to operate like a hedge fund, but now can obtain FDIC-insured deposits and rely on Fed and Treasury protection should risky trades go bad. It is very hard for a small bank to compete.

How can the system be reformed to favor relationship banking that seems to be more conducive to promoting the capital development of the economy? First it would be useful to reduce government protection for less desirable banking activities. There are two important kinds of protection government currently provides: liquidity and solvency. Liquidity is mostly provided by the Fed, which lends reserves at the Discount Window and buys assets. Minsky always advocated extension of the Discount Window operations to include a wide range of financial institutions. If the Fed had lent reserves without limit to all financial institutions when the crisis first hit, it is probable that the liquidity crisis could have been resolved more quickly. Hence, this kind of government protection should not be restrained in terms of financial institutions. As explained below, however, restrictions in terms of the assets that are accepted at the Discount Window are important.

It is the second kind, protection against default, that is more problematic. Deposit insurance guarantees there is no default risk on certain classes of deposits—now up to $250,000. This is essential for clearing at par and for maintaining a safe and secure payments system. There is no good reason to limit the insurance to $250,000, so the cap should be lifted. The question is about which types of institutions should be allowed to issue such deposits, or, which types of assets they could acquire by issuing such a financial instrument. Some considerations would include riskiness of assets, maturity of assets, and whether purchase of the assets fulfills the public purpose—the capital development of the economy. Risky assets put the FDIC on the hook since it must pay out dollar-for-dollar but if it resolves a failing institution it will receive only cents on the dollar of assets. In his discussion of the Treasury's proposal for rescuing the FDIC, Minsky made it clear that "cost to the Treasury" should not be a major concern (another reason for removing the cap—it is not important to limit Treasury's losses to the first $250,000 of a deposit). We can probably also conclude for the same reason that riskiness of assets financed by issuing insured deposits should not be the major concern. Maturity of the assets is no longer a concern if the Fed stands ready to lend reserves as needed—a bank could always meet deposit withdrawals by borrowing reserves, so would not need to sell longer-term assets. Hence, the major argument for limiting financial institutions' ability to finance positions in assets by issuing insured deposits is that government has a legitimate interest in promoting the public purpose. Banks should be prevented from issuing insured deposits to take position in assets in a manner that causes the capital development of the country to be "ill done."

Banks that receive government protection in the form of liquidity and (partial) solvency guarantees are essentially public–private partnerships. They promote the public purpose by specializing in activities that they can perform more competently than government can do. One of these is underwriting—assessing credit-worthiness and building relations with borrowers that enhance their willingness and ability to repay based on their income. Over the past decade a belief that underwriting is unnecessary flowered and then exploded. But in the global financial crisis, financial institutions discovered that credit rating and scoring cannot substitute for underwriting—in part because they can be manipulated, but also because elimination of relationship banking changes behavior of borrowers and lenders. This means that past default rates become irrelevant as credit raters have discovered. If banks are not doing underwriting, it is difficult to see why government needs them as partners: it would be much simpler to have government directly finance activities it perceives to be in the public interest—home mortgages, student loans, state and local government infrastructure, and even small business activities (commercial real estate and working capital expenses). Indeed, there has been a movement in that direction, with government taking back control over student loans. When government guarantees both the deposits as well as the loans it is difficult to see any role to be played by banks except underwriting.

The problem banks have faced over the past three or four decades is the "cream skimming" of their business by shadow banks (or, as Minsky called it, managed money). Uninsured checkable deposits in managed funds (such as money market mutual funds) offer a higher-earning but relatively convenient alternative to insured deposits, allowing much of the payments system to bypass banks. As Minsky argued, credit cards have also diverted the payments system out of banking (although the larger banks capture a lot of the credit card business). At the same time, banks were squeezed on the other side of their balance sheet by the development of the commercial paper market that allows firms to borrow short term at interest rates below those on bank loans (sometimes, firms could even borrow more cheaply than banks could). Again banks recaptured some of that business by earning fees for guaranteeing commercial paper. But these competitive pressures caused banks to jettison expensive underwriting and relationship banking, replaced by the originate-to-distribute model.

There is no simple solution to these competitive pressures, although Minsky offered some ideas. In several publications Minsky argued that policy should move to make the payments system a profit center for banks:

> One weakness of the banking system centers around the American scheme of paying for the payments system by the differential between the return on assets and the interest paid on deposits. In general the administration of the checking system costs some 3.5 percent of the amount of deposits subject to check. If the checking system were an independent profit center for banks then the banks would be in a better position to compete with the money funds.
>
> (Minsky 1992a: 36)

It is not desirable to try to return to the early postwar period in which banks and thrifts monopolized the payments system. However, in the 1800s, the federal government eliminated private bank notes by placing a tax on them. In a similar manner, preferential treatment of payments made through banks could restore a competitive edge. Transactions taxes could be placed on payments made through managed funds. In addition, banks could be offered lower, subsidized, fees for use of the Fed's clearing system. Minsky also held out some hope that by substituting debit cards for checks, banks could substantially lower their costs of operating the payments system—something that does seem to be happening (Minsky 1992a).

Part of the problem today is that the Fed requires that a portion of a bank's funding comes from retail deposits. Minsky argued this causes local banks to open more offices than necessary to compete for retail deposits. Recall that part of the reason for the New Deal's Regulation Q was precisely to eliminate competition for such deposits, on the belief that competition raised costs of such funds and induced banks to purchase riskier assets to cover those costs. The biggest "brand name" banks more easily attract retail deposits, and they also have the advantage that they are believed to be safer. For this reason, Warren Mosler has called for elimination of any requirement that banks maintain any specified proportion of their funding in the form of retail deposits. Combined with Minsky's argument that banks should be able to borrow reserves on demand at the Fed, this means bank's costs of funds would be the Fed's overnight interest rate—plus any "frown costs."

Some, including Minsky's Levy colleague Ronnie Phillips, have called for a return to the 100 percent money proposal of Irving Fisher and Milton Friedman. Deposit-issuing banks would be allowed to hold only Fed reserves and Treasury debt as assets. Minsky (1992a: 36–37) argued that this loses:

> sight of the main object: the capital development of the economy. The key role of banking is lending or, better, financing. The questions to be asked of any financial system are what do the assets of banks and other financial institutions represent, is the capital development of the economy better served if the proximate financiers are decentralized local institutions, and should the stricture lean towards compartmentalized or broad jurisdiction institutions.

To be sure, Minsky did not categorically reject the narrow bank proposal (indeed, he wrote a supportive note for the book by Ronnie Phillips, *The Chicago Plan & New Deal Banking Reform*)—he simply believed it addresses only a peripheral problem, safety and soundness of the payments and savings systems. It does not address promotion of the capital development of the economy.

Recall from above that there is the "Smithian" problem and the "Keynesian" problem: banks might finance the wrong projects, and might not finance the right amount. Opening the Discount Window to provide an elastic supply of reserve funding ensures that banks *can* finance positions in as many assets as they desire at the Fed's target rate. This does not ensure that we have solved the Keynesian problem, because banks might finance too much or too little activity to achieve full employment. Offering unlimited funding to them deals only with the liability side of banking, but leaves the asset side open. It is somewhat easier to resolve the "too much" part of the Keynesian problem because the Fed or other bank regulators can impose constraints on bank purchases of assets when it becomes apparent that they are financing too much activity. For example, in the past real estate boom it was obvious (except, apparently to mainstream economists and many at the Fed) that lending should have been curtailed.

The problem is that the usual response to too much lending is to raise the Fed's target rate. And because borrowing is not very interest sensitive, especially in a euphoric boom, rates must rise sharply to have much effect. Further, raising rates conflicts with the Fed's goal of maintaining financial stability because—as the Volcker experiment showed—interest rate hikes that are sufficiently large to kill a boom also are large enough to cause severe financial disruptions (something like three-quarters of all thrifts were driven to insolvency because rates earned on assets fell short of rates paid on liabilities). Indeed, this recognition is part of the reason that the Greenspan/Bernanke Fed turned to "gradualism"—a series of very small rate hikes that are well telegraphed. Unfortunately, this means that markets have plenty of time to prepare and to compensate for rate hikes (for example through floater rate loans plus derivatives to protect against interest rate risk), which means they have less impact. For these reasons, rate hikes are not an appropriate means of controlling bank lending. Instead the controls ought to be direct: raising downpayments and collateral requirements, regulating underwriting, and even issuing cease and desist orders to prevent further financing of some activities.

Currently, it is believed that capital requirements are a proper way to regulate bank lending: higher capital requirements not only make banks safer but they also constrain bank lending unless the banks can raise capital. Unfortunately, neither claim is correct. Higher capital requirements were imposed in the aftermath of the S&L fiasco, and codified in the Basel agreements. Rather than constraining bank purchases of assets, banks simply moved assets and liabilities off their balance sheets—putting them into SPV, for example. Basel also used risk-adjusted weightings for capital requirements, to encourage banks to hold less risky assets for which they were rewarded with lower capital requirements. Unfortunately, banks gamed the system in two ways: (a) since risk weightings were by class, banks would take the riskiest positions in each class, and (b) banks worked with credit ratings agencies to structure assets such as MBSs to achieve the risk weighting desired. For example, it was relatively easy to get triple-A rated tranches (almost as safe as sovereign government debt) out of packages of subprime and "liar loan" alt-A mortgages—with 85 to 90 percent of the risky mortgages underlying investment grade tranches.

Finally, all else equal, high capital ratios necessarily reduce return on equity (and, hence growth of net worth), so it is not necessarily true that higher capital ratios increase safety of banks because it means they are less profitable. Indeed, with higher capital ratios they need to choose a higher risk/return portfolio of assets to achieve a target return on equity. In addition, toward the end of the savings and loan crisis, James B. Thomson of the Federal Reserve Bank of Cleveland, concluded that "book solvency is positively related to failure" and he noted that: "One possible explanation is that banks beginning to experience difficulties improve their capital positions cosmetically by selling assets on which they have capital gains and by deferring sales of assets on which they have capital losses" (Thomson 1991: 13). This is typical of Ponzi finance. Again, if regulators want to constrain the growth rate of lending, it appears that direct credit controls are better.

The "too little" side of the Keynesian problem is more challenging; there is not much that can be done to encourage banks to lend when they do not want to. That is the old "you cannot push on a string" argument, and it describes the situation in the aftermath of the global financial crisis quite well. Nor should government policy try to get banks to make loans they do not want to make! After all if banks are our underwriters, and if their assessment is that there are no good loans to be made, then we should trust their judgment. In that case, private lending is not the way to stimulate aggregate demand to get the economy to move toward fuller employment. Instead, fiscal policy is the way to do it supplemented by direct government lending (e.g., student loans).

Solving the Smithian problem requires direct oversight of bank activity mostly on the asset side of their balance sheets. Financial activities that further the capital development of the economy need to be encouraged; those that cause it to be "ill done" need to be discouraged. One of the reasons that Minsky wanted the Fed to lend reserves to all comers was because he wanted private institutions to be "in the bank"—that is, to be debtors to the Fed. As a creditor, the Fed would be able to ask the banker question: "how will you repay me?":

> The Federal Reserve's powers to examine are inherent in its ability to lend to banks through the discount window [...]. As a lender to banks, either as the normal provider of the reserve base to commercial banks (the normal operation prior to the great depression) or as the potential lender of last resort, central banks have a right to knowledge about the balance sheet, income and competence of their clients, banks and bank managements. This is no more than any bank believes it has the right to know about its clients.
>
> (Minsky 1992c: 10)

The Fed would ask to see evidence for the cash flow that would generate ability of the bank to service loans. It is common practice for a central bank to lend against collateral, using a "haircut" to favor certain kinds of assets (for example, a bank might be able to borrow 100 cents on the dollar against government debt but only 75 cents against a dollar of mortgages). Collateral requirements and haircuts can be used to discipline banks—to influence the kinds of assets they purchase. Examination of the bank's books also allows the Fed to look for risky practices and to keep abreast of developments. It is clear that the Fed was caught with its pants down, so to speak, by the crisis that began in 2007 in part because it mostly supplied reserves in open market operations rather than at the Discount Window. Forcing private banks "into the bank" gives the Fed more leverage over their activities. For this reason Minsky opposed the Treasury's proposal to strip the Fed of some of its responsibilities for regulation and oversight of institutions. If anything, Minsky would have increased the Fed's role and would use the Discount Window as an important tool for oversight and to influence financial innovations on the asset side of banks (Kregel 1992).

His views are relevant to current discussions about the creation of the "super" systemic regulator, and he probably would have sided with those who want to increase the Fed's power. He also believed that because "a central bank needs to have business, supervisory and examination relations with banks and markets if it is to be knowledgeable about what is happening" reducing its responsibility for examining and supervising banks would also inhibit its "ability to perform its monetary policy function. This is so because monetary policy operations are constrained by the Federal Reserve's views of the effect such operations would have upon bank activities and market stability" (Minsky 1992a: 10). The Fed would be better informed to the extent that it supervised and examined banks.

Minsky worried that the trend to megabanks

> may well allow the weakest part of the system, the giant banks, to expand, not because they are efficient but because they can use the clout of their large asset base and cash flows to make life uncomfortable for local banks: predatory pricing and corners [of the market] cannot be ruled out in the American context.
>
> (Minsky 1992a: 12)

Further, since the size of loans depends on the capital base, big banks have a natural affinity for the "big deals," while small banks service smaller clients:

> A 1 billion dollar bank may well have 80 million dollars in capital. It therefore would have an 8 to 12 million dollar maximum line of credit [...] in the United States context this means the normal client for such banks is a community or smaller business: such banks are small business development corporations.
>
> (Minsky 1992a: 12)

Finally, promoting large banking institutions makes it difficult to cleanse bad debt because "if an economy is to be open to bankruptcy, no organization can be so large that its bankruptcy is politically unacceptable" (Minsky 1986a: 354). Too big to fail financial institutions subvert market mechanisms and behemoth banks use their size as an argument for government assistance regardless of the quality of their assets and management. This creates massive moral hazard.

For these reasons, Minsky advocated a proactive government policy to create and support small community development banks (CDBs) (Minsky *et al.* 1993). Very briefly, the argument advanced was that the capital development of the nation and of communities is fostered via the provision of a broad range of financial services. Unfortunately, many communities, lower income consumers, and smaller and start-up firms are inadequately provisioned with these services. For example, in many communities there are far more check cashing outlets and pawnshops than bank offices. Many households do not even have checking accounts. Small businesses often finance activities using credit card debt. Hence, the proposal would create a network of small community development banks to provide a full range of services (a sort of universal bank for underserved communities): (1) a payments system for check cashing and clearing, and credit and debit cards; (2) secure depositories for savings and transactions balances; (3) household financing for housing, consumer debts, and student loans; (4) commercial banking services for loans, payroll services, and advice; (5) investment banking services for determining the appropriate liability structure for the assets of a firm, and placing these liabilities; and (6) asset management and advice for households (Minsky *et al.* 1993: 10–11). The institutions would be kept small, local, and profitable. They would be public–private partnerships, with a new Federal Bank for Community Development Banks created to provide equity and to charter and supervise the CDBs. Each CDB could also be organized as a bank holding company. One example of its composition would be: (a) a narrow bank to provide payments services; (b) a commercial bank to provide loans to firms and mortgages to households; (c) an investment bank to intermediate equity issues and long-term debt of firms; and (d) a trust bank to act as a trustee and to provide financial advice.

Reform of the financial system does need to address the "shadow banks" of Money Manager Capitalism. Minsky believed that pension funds were largely responsible for the leverage buy-out boom (and bust) of the 1980s; similarly, as discussed in the next section, there is strong evidence that pension funds drove the commodities boom and bust of the mid 2000s. To be sure this is just a part of managed money, but it is a government protected and supported portion—both because it gets favorable tax treatment and because it has a quasi-government backing through the Pension Benefit Guarantee Corporation (Nersisyan and Wray 2010). Hence, it is yet another public–private partnership that ought to serve the public purpose. Minsky wondered "Should the power of pension funds be attenuated by having open ended IRA's? (No limit to contributions, withdrawals without penalty but all withdrawals taxed, interest and dividend accruals not taxed except as they are spent)" (Minsky 1992a: 35). The IRAs would compete with pension fund managers, reducing their influence.

Finally, returning to Minsky's views on the role that financial institutions play in forcing and allocating a surplus, he would certainly be appalled at recent trends. First, there has been an important shift away from the wage share and toward gross capital income. As explained in Chapter 2, stagnant wages played a role in promoting growth of household indebtedness over the past three decades, with rapid acceleration since the mid 1990s. As many followers of Wynne Godley have been arguing since 1996, the shift to a private sector deficit, that was unprecedently large and persistent, would prove to be unsustainable. The mountain of debt still crushing households after the global financial crisis is in part due to the shift of national income away from wages as households tried to maintain living standards. Equally problematic is the allocation of profits toward the financial sector—just before the crisis, the finance, insurance, and real estate sector got up to 40 percent of all corporate profits, and its share quickly returned close to that level after the rescue of Wall Street. This contrasts with a 10 to 15 percent share until the 1970s, and a 20 percent share until the 1990s. While value added by the sector also grew, from about 12 percent in the early postwar period to nearly 20 percent today, its share of profits was twice as high as its share of value added by the time of the 2000s bubble.

Hence there are three interrelated problems: the surplus forced by the financial sector is probably too large, the share of GDP coming from the financial sector is probably too large, and the share of the surplus allocated by the financial sector to itself is far too large. Downsizing finance is necessary to ensure that the capital development of the economy can be well done. With 40 percent of corporate profits going to finance, not only does this leave too little to other sectors but it encourages entrepreneurial effort and innovations to be directed to the financial sector, which has become too big in important respects to serve its role as promoter of the capital development of the economy.

Finance and retirement: pension funds vs. Social Security

Pension funds suffer when financial markets crash. It is important to understand, however, that this is a two way street: pension funds have become so large that they are capable of literally "moving markets." As they flow into a new class of assets, the sheer volume of funds under management will tend to cause prices to rise. Pension funds often follow a strategy through which they will allocate a percentage of funds to a particular asset class. This can occur on a "follow the leader" basis as the popularity of investing in a new asset class increases, pushing up prices and rewarding the decision. To increase portfolio returns, managers might decide to increase the allocation to well-performing classes of assets. This could contribute to a speculative bubble. Of course, trying to reverse flows—to move out of an asset class—will cause prices to fall, rapidly.

A good example is the commodities boom and bust between 2000 and 2008, and today's boomlet that began after the global financial crisis—which might be coming to an end. The deregulation at the end of the 1990s allowed pension managers to invest in commodities for the first time (Wray 2008b). Previously, pensions could not buy commodities because these are purely speculative bets. There is no return to holding commodities unless their prices rise—indeed, holding them is costly. However, Goldman Sachs (which created one of the two largest commodity indexes) and others promoted investment in commodities as a hedge, on the argument that commodity prices are uncorrelated with equities. In the aftermath of the dot-com collapse, that was appealing. In truth, when managed money flows into an asset class that had previously been uncorrelated with other assets, that asset will become correlated. Hence, by marketing commodity indexes as uncorrelated assets, a commodities bubble ensued that would collapse along with everything else. This is because when one asset class collapses—say, securitized mortgages—holders need to come up with cash and collateral to cover losses, which causes them to sell holdings in other asset classes. This is why silver and cattle became correlated when the Hunt brothers' attempt to corner the silver market failed: they had to sell their beef in order to cover their losses on silver.

Most of the positions taken were actually in commodity futures indexes, as pension funds decided to allocate, say, 5 percent of assets under management to commodities (Wray 2008b). However, there is a close link between index prices and spot prices. While pensions allocated only a small proportion of portfolios to these indexes, this amounted to a huge volume relative to the size of commodity markets. For example, Mike W. Masters showed that the allocation by pension funds (and other index speculators, with pensions accounting for about 85 percent of all index speculation) to oil was equivalent to the total growth of Chinese demand for oil for the half decade following 2004. Index and spot prices literally exploded, in what was probably the biggest commodity price bubble ever experienced (Masters in U.S. Senate 2008).

The bubble was also fueled by a policy change. As pension funds poured into commodities and commodity futures, driving up the price of energy, metals, and food, Congress mandated biofuels use—which added to pressures on food prices and contributed to starvation around the globe. When pensions started to move out of commodities in the late summer and fall of 2008 (pulling about one-third of their funds), prices collapsed; oil prices fell from about $150 a barrel to $40. Because other asset classes have performed poorly in recent months, pensions briefly moved back in, and commodity prices regained ground. While it is too early to tell, it looks like the commodities speculative bubble will eventually end—probably not because pensions will move out again but rather because demand for the actual commodities remains sluggish in the face of the global downturn. The point, however, is that pension funds are big enough to destabilize asset prices.

Pension funds are so large that they will bubble-up any financial market they are allowed to enter—and what goes up must come down. The problem really is that managed money, taken as a whole, is simply too large to be supported by the nation's ability to produce the output and income necessary to provide a foundation for the financial assets and debts that exist even in the aftermath of the financial crisis. Hence, returns cannot be obtained by making loans against production (or even income); rather, they can be generated only by "financialization," or layering and leveraging existing levels of production and income, as well as betting on asset-price directions.

In a sense, the entire pension industry can be justified only if through skill or luck fund management can beat the average risk-free return on Treasuries by enough that it can pay out all of those industry compensations plus add growth to the fund portfolio. Yet the expectation should be that fund managers are significantly less skilled and less "lucky" than, say, the highly compensated employees of the sophisticated financial institutions such as Goldman Sachs that they are dealing with. Hence, workers would be far better off if their employers were required to fully fund pensions with investments restricted to Treasury debt. At most, each pension plan would require a very small management staff that would log on to www.treasurydirect.gov to transfer funds out of the employing firm's bank deposit and into Treasuries, in an amount determined by actuarial tables plus nominal benefits promised. Unlike pricing packaged subprime loans and derivatives, this is not rocket science. This would eliminate the need for fund managers and Wall Street sales staff, lowering fund management costs, and increasing risk-free net return to the pensions.

Indeed, this raises the question, should the federal government promote and protect pensions at all? Surely, individuals should be free to place savings with fund managers of their choice, and each saver can try to find the above-average fund manager who can beat Treasury yields. But it makes no sense to promote a scheme that cannot succeed on average at the aggregate level—the typical fund manager probably cannot beat the average, so there is no strong reason to believe that managed funds will provide on average a net return that is above the return on U.S. Treasuries. It would be far better to remove the tax advantages and government guarantees provided to pension plans, and instead allow individuals to put their savings directly into Treasuries that are automatically government-backed and provide a risk-free return. Perhaps this sort of saving should still enjoy tax-advantaged status—but we remain ambivalent about tax-advantaged saving. It is not clear that there is a strong public purpose in promoting private saving—which, after all, is a deduction from aggregate demand and hence generates a bias toward demand gaps and slow economic growth.

Is there a better alternative that would allow us to provide a safe, secure, and decent living for our retirees? The U.S. retirement system is supposed to rest on a three-legged stool: pensions, individual savings, and Social Security. Pensions are mostly employer-related and are now seriously underfunded (and the general trend is toward defined-contribution plans, which make no promises about the level of retirement benefits or the living standard that will be provided). There are also huge and growing administrative problems posed by the transformation of the American workplace—with the typical worker switching jobs many times over the course of her career, and with the lifespan of the typical firm measured in years rather than decades. Firms also routinely game the bankruptcy laws to escape their pension liabilities. This makes the employer-based pension system less suited to current and future realities. And, finally, as discussed here, the most plausible long-term net return on managed money would be somewhat below the risk-free return on Treasuries.

The problem with private saving is that Americans do not save enough for their retirement. They never have. That is why government created Social Security, and why labor unions pushed for pensions. Even if individuals tried to do so, there is no reason to believe that they would achieve better returns than pension fund managers. Worse, they could be duped out of their savings by unscrupulous financial institutions selling risky investments.

Thus, the best solution would be to eliminate government support for pension plans and private saving, and instead boost Social Security benefits to ensure that anyone who works long enough to qualify will achieve a comfortable retirement. Certainly, individuals would be free to supplement this with private savings, according to ability and desires. And employers, unions, and employees can continue to negotiate pensions, as desired—but without public subsidies and guarantees.

We anticipate two main objections. First, such a scheme could put a lot of money managers and financial advisers out of business. True. But the U.S. financial system is still far too big even after the crisis. In our view, it makes no economic sense to send as much as 40 percent of corporate profits to the finance, insurance, and real estate sector—and we seem to be restoring the sector's share even now. Second, there is a concerted effort to convince Americans that Social Security is broke; hence, our proposal to ramp up benefits will be met with criticism and perhaps even fear. However, Social Security is a federal government program, and as such it cannot become insolvent. All payments can be made as they come due—even if benefits become more generous—if the U.S. government stands behind the promised benefits. That is exactly what stands behind U.S. Treasuries, so there is no reason for a ramped-up pension plan using funds to accumulate Treasuries. This takes care of the financial side of the provisioning for retirement (Bell and Wray 2000).

The more difficult issue to solve in terms of provisioning for retirement is the real side of the provisioning: how one can guarantee that the Social Security income will have enough purchasing power to meet the needs of retirees? Or, how can we make sure that goods and services will be available for the elderly? This brings up the issue of the dependency ratio (the ratio of non-workers to working-age population) and so problems such as tax rates, Social Security benefits, productivity of labor, immigrations, and retirement age. Given the amount of goods and services, higher payroll tax rates will reduce the real income of non-retirees relative to retirees and so redistribute purchasing power toward retirees (cutting benefits does the reverse). Higher productivity of labor and higher labor force will increase the production of goods and services of a given labor force. A larger labor force can be obtained through an immigration policy and, in the longer run, through a promotion of a higher fertility rate. Relatively minor and realistic adjustments to these variables solve the real side of the problem but there is a choice to make (Wray 1991, 2003, 2006; Eisner 1998). One thing that is certain is that none of the problems on the real side of provisioning are solved by putting money into a "locked box" and promoting fiscal surpluses. A monetarily sovereign government can credit bank accounts of domestic private economic units as needed, and fiscal surpluses drain financial resources out of the domestic private sector and so contribute to lower employment and economic activity.

Beyond economic growth as the main economic goal

The challenge of promoting financial stability extends beyond the matter of appropriate regulation; it also requires a critical examination of the goal and source of economic growth. The problem is not just that "growth for the sake of growth" is bad economics. It is also that the widespread emphasis on investment-led growth is highly prone to economic instability for economic and financial reasons.

One shortcoming of investment-led growth is the traditional Harrod-Domar issue: it is difficult for aggregate demand to keep up with the additional supply capacities created by previous investment. This is probably less of a problem in underdeveloped economies where improvements in standards of living are badly needed (provided, of course, that the capacities of production are used for internal markets rather than exports to developed countries). But it is definitely a concern for mature economies. As a result, in the latter case growth should be refocused on socio-ecologically durable domestic consumption. At the same time, it is important to avoid the financial dynamics that have been at play in the United States. The United States has been following a strategy of consumption-led growth for the past thirty years, but it has been based on unsound financial practices induced in part by growing income inequality and fiscal retrenchements.

Another shortcoming of investment-led growth is that it is prone to Ponzi finance. Minsky (1986a) explained in detail how investment was prone to income-based Ponzi finance. As we observed in the wave of mergers and acquisitions in the 1990s and more recently in the housing market, investment is also prone to collateral-based Ponzi finance. Indeed, it creates durable assets that may rise in value, thereby providing an incentive to underwrite loans on the basis of rising asset prices rather than income. While rising collateral-based lending might be fine in financial markets, especially when no government insurance is provided, it is more dangerous in the case of durable illiquid assets such as investment goods.

It is also important to reexamine the goal of growth regardless of its sources. While economic growth may help to improve standards of living and to meet the needs arising from population growth, it is not clear that there is a direct relationship between improved welfare and economic growth, especially for developed economies. Alternative measures to the GDP, such as the Genuine Progress Indicator, show no significant improvement in U.S. economic welfare since the mid 1970s (Figure 4.5). Rising socio-economic and environmental problems have outweighed the gains from increased final output.

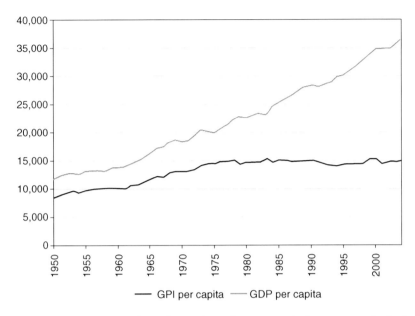

Figure 4.5 Gross domestic product and genuine progress indicator per capita in the U.S. (dollars, base 2000) (source: Talberth *et al.* 2007).

Although long-term economic growth may help improve standards of living up to a point, history shows that market mechanisms push economic units to focus on short-term results and to preserve short-term economic growth at all costs. As such, "more is always better" when it comes to quarterly economic growth—even though the underlying financial conditions may be deteriorating rapidly. Given the current view that places a positive value on any growth in economic output and profits, it is difficult for regulators or financial-market supervisors to find a reason for action when the economy is growing. In fact, they see an argument to withdraw and avoid putting "unnecessary barriers" on the pursuit of the American Dream.

The goal of long-term sustainable economic growth is laudable as a concept. But what often happens in practice is a complete disregard for sustainability, not only in financial terms but also in socio-ecological terms. There are other means to promote well-being that look beyond constantly rising production and finding new wants to fulfill. These warrant economists' increasing attention, not only because the aim of growth with sustainability is often ignored, but also because the risks to sustainability seem to be rising rapidly.

Financial policy: some final considerations

Even if a regulatory framework that promotes hedge financing is put in place at a point in time, pressures from market competition will lead to innovations either to bypass existing regulations or to open new market opportunities. In both cases, the new business practices may not be included in the previous regulatory framework and so the latter may become inadequate and promote instability. Thus, some changes to existing regulations must occur rapidly, especially if innovations occur in areas where a government safety net is available.

The regulatory framework put in place may be flexible and comprehensive but, for it to work well, the persons in charge of implementation should be competent and have a mindset that clearly values the benefits that regulation and supervision can provide. Unfortunately, for the past thirty years at least, priority has been given to economic growth over financial soundness, so regulatory and supervisory institutions have been understaffed, under-qualified, underfunded, and undermined. Individuals who do not believe in regulation were put in charge of regulatory institutions; people like Alan Greenspan (Federal Reserve), Darrel Dochow (Office of Thrift Supervision), Christopher Cox (Securities and Exchange Commission), or Henry Paulson and Robert Rubin (U.S. Department of Treasury). This has prevented an effective supervision despite the existence of a large body of regulations; and both supervision and regulation have declined over the past thirty years in the pursuit of "market efficiency."

Government institutions must be able to attract the best minds. At the hearings on the Madoff scandal, Markopolos, who exposed Madoff, noted: "To be effective, the SEC cannot afford to be less talented and educated than the industry, and I would argue it can't even strive to be as good as the industry, it needs to be better" (Markopolos in U.S. House of Representatives 2009a). This implies raising salaries significantly, increasing the information provided to regulatory institutions, and giving them broad powers. However, this also implies making regulators fully accountable to the public, something that has not been done for the past century (Barth *et al.* 2012).

Improving the disclosure of information provided to financial market participants will only help marginally to promote financial stability. Probably, improving the disclosure of information regarding the cash-flow pattern of a financial instrument under "normal" and extreme circumstances may help potential customers to make a better decision; however, regarding the recent financial products, the Counterparty Risk Management Policy Group also notes that: "There is almost universal agreement that, even with optimal disclosure in the underlying documentation, the characteristics of these instruments and the risk of loss associated with them were not fully understood by many market participants" (Counterparty Risk Management Policy Group III 2008: 53).

Financial products are so complex that it is impossible to comprehend fully the implications of the information provided. Moreover, information is constantly subject to interpretation by social norms regarding proper financial practices, and these norms loosen over time under competitive pressures and relatively stable economic conditions. Thus, a better and more frequent disclosure of information does not mean that this information will be included in the decision-making process, especially so if it is in the way of lucrative business opportunities. More importantly, disclosing more information about a Ponzi process is not improving its stability; instead Ponzi finance must be discouraged and if necessary growth on that basis must be stopped by regulators. This was done by some regulators, under tremendous opposition from the Reagan Administration and Congress, during the years preceding the savings and loan crisis, thereby greatly reducing the impact of that crisis on the economy (Black 2005).

Finally, improving risk management by introducing a countercyclical capital ratio, broadening the base of assets, or changing the calculation of the weight will only improve marginally financial stability because this type of regulation is highly reactive and permissive. Basically, financial institutions are allowed to do whatever they want as long as they meet the regulatory requirements defined by the norms:

> None of the reforms creates a mechanism to correct for disaster myopia. Disaster myopia is the tendency for the subjective probability of disaster to decline with the passage of time as the experience of the previous disaster recedes from memories. [...] The structure of deposit insurance and countercyclical monetary and fiscal policy that are used successfully to contain a crisis in one period are not likely to permanently stabilize a monetary economy in which financial innovations occur in response to profit opportunities. Recent innovations in the securitization of assets and the globalization of finance have introduced risks of financial dislocations that are only peripherally related to those the authorities are set up to handle.
>
> (Campbell and Minsky 1987: 259)

This notion of disaster myopia deals in part with the willingness to take more risk. Economic entities also are required to take more risk as the expansion persists because markets saturate, which leads to financial innovations requiring more leverage to compensate for declining returns, and to the courting of riskier borrowers to maintain lending volumes. Thus, regulators and supervisors must account not only for fraud and potential unexpected problems, but also for the fact that, in capitalist economies, businesses have to take more risk on their asset and liability sides as the economic expansion continues. The main challenge to regulators is to promote hedge financing while also letting entrepreneurs' creativeness express itself in such a way that long-term socio-economic benefits materialize.

Conclusion

The long-run U.S. trend has been to consolidate a wide range of services within the affiliates of a bank holding company. The New Deal reforms had separated institutions by functions (and state laws against branching provided geographic constraints). Natural evolution plus deregulation allowed the growth of a handful of dominant behemoths that play a key role in the provision of all of those services. Generally speaking, since economies of scale exhaust themselves fairly quickly in banking, as Minsky and others have argued, there ought to be a presumption in favor of limiting the size of banks. Larger institutions are much harder to regulate and supervise, creating incentives for the development of control frauds, in which owners are duped while managers are enriched. The supposed benefits and "synergies" that were to flow from bank consolidation and extension of scope have mostly been opportunities for institutions to bet against their own customers. Charles Keating's Lincoln Savings used its FDIC seal of approval to sell risky and ultimately worthless assets to its elderly widows who thought they were buying insured certificates of deposit (CDs). More recently, Goldman Sachs allowed hedge fund manager John Paulson to design sure-to-fail synthetic collateralized debt obligations (CDOs) that Goldman sold to its own customers, allowing both Goldman and Paulson to use credit default swaps (CDSs) to bet on failure (Eisinger and Bernstein 2010).

Financial institutions should be offered a stark choice between either holding a bank charter or engaging in speculative trading. In this scenario, investment banks would not be allowed to "play with house money" (FDIC-insured deposits) and chartered banks would be prohibited from securitizing. Chartered banks ought to be conceived of as public utilities, serving public purposes, and if as public utilities they are going to have access to government guarantees and Fed lending, then they should not be engaged in the kind of securitized lending that undermines solid underwriting. In this vein, banks ought to be required to hold loans to maturity. There is no legitimate reason why banks should move assets off their balance sheets. There is no need to make securitization itself illegal, but banks should not be allowed to do it.

In addition, one needs to make sure that securitization does not promote Ponzi finance. This implies making sure that underwriting of loans is done properly, that the assignation of the note and deed is done transparently and correctly, and that the securities created on the basis of the underlying loans are properly underwritten. The Great Recession showed that securitization failed at these three levels and progressively became a collateral-based Ponzi scheme. Underwriting of loans was poor, the Mortgage Electronic Registration Systems (MERS) did not properly assign mortgages, and securities were created without developing proper ratings to judge their reliability. If correct procedures are followed, probably most securitization would be unprofitable and would be restricted to its original purpose; the securitization of conforming mortgages by government-sponsored enterprises (GSE). In that case, the underlying loans have to meet strict credit standards, the assignation is clear given that mortgages stay on the balance sheet of GSEs, and the underwriting of asset-backed securities is done on the basis of loan with clear cash flows and well-established data about default and recovery rates. This means that the first way to make securitization safe is to have the proper underwriting upstream.

Banks should ultimately have a narrow focus and a limited set of operations. For instance, business functions not related to commercial and residential real estate mortgages and the making of short-term commercial loans should be excised from a bank's operations. Other financial institutions may engage in activities beyond this narrow scope, but if they do so they should not be provided with government backstops or guarantees.

For those institutions, including investment banks, that will engage in trading, we must change their incentive structures in order to promote better underwriting. It will be very difficult to reorient investment banking toward a long-term horizon with proper underwriting when debt is securitized and subject to lax oversight and when the average stock is held less than a year (and the stock market taken as a whole is a negative source of funding of capital assets, because firms are caught up in the casino, purchasing their own equity to share in the gains of a speculative bubble). Still, it is necessary to do so. Compensation for managers and traders at investment banks should be linked to long-term results. For instance, compensation could be tied to five-year income flows with "clawbacks" in the case of poor performance. Investment banks should ultimately be reoriented toward playing more of an intermediary role, through holding long-term debt and issuing their own debt to savers. Attempts to impose higher capital ratios, such as those mandated in Basel III, do not provide the necessary discipline—investment banks that "originate-to-distribute" do not hold the relevant assets on their books anyway.

More broadly, the compensation of bank employees should also be such that they have an incentive to perform proper underwriting of loans and securities. It is especially crucial that loan officers and other risk managers be able to operate in an environment that rewards a thorough evaluation of the creditworthiness of a borrower, and of the risk taken by a financial institution. A large portion, if not all, of their compensation should be based on a fixed salary instead of a commission and "old fashioned" credit analysis should be preferred over credit scoring. However, the rest of the company's employees should also have this long-term view. The emphasis on shareholder value over the past three decades does not promote these kinds of incentives because of the orientation toward rapid short-term growth.

While many point to the demise of Glass–Steagall as the source of all our troubles, the problem really was the demise of underwriting. In other words, the problem and solution are not really related to functional separation but rather to erosion of underwriting standards that is inevitable over a run of good times when a trader mentality triumphs. If a bank believes it can offload questionable assets before values are questioned, its incentive to do proper underwriting is reduced. And if asset prices are generally rising on trend, the bank will try to share in the gains by taking positions in the assets. This is why the current calls by some for a return to Glass–Steagall separation, or to force banks to "put skin in the game" by holding some fraction of the toxic waste they produce, are both wrong-headed.

While a traditional banker might feel safe with a capital leverage ratio of twelve or twenty—with careful underwriting to ensure that the borrower is able to make payments—for a mortgage originator or securitizer who has no plans to hold the mortgage what matters is the ability to place the security. Many considerations then come into play, including prospective asset price appreciation, credit ratings, monolines and credit default swap "insurance," and "overcollateralization" (markets for the lower tranches of securities).

What is important is that income flows take a back seat in such arrangements, and acceptable capital leverage ratios are much higher. For money managers, capital leverage ratios are typically at least thirty, and reach up to several hundred. But even these large numbers hide the reality that risk exposures can be very much higher because many commitments are not reported on balance sheets. There are unknown and essentially unquantifiable risks entailed in counterparties—for example in supposedly hedged credit default swaps in which one sells "insurance" on suspected toxic waste and then offsets risks by buying "insurance" that is only as good as the counterparty. Because balance sheets are linked in highly complex and unknown ways, failure of one counterparty can spread failures throughout the system. And all of these financial instruments linked to U.S. real estate markets (for example) ultimately rest on the shoulders of some homeowner trying to service her mortgage out of income flows—on average with several dollars of debts and only $1 of income to service them. As Minsky argued, "National income and its distribution is the 'rock' upon which the capitalist financial structure rests" (Minsky 1992c: 3). Unfortunately, that rock is holding up a huge financial structure, and the trend toward concentration of income and wealth at the top makes it ever more difficult to support the weight of the debt.

Since 2008, we have had a steady stream of recommendations concerning what to do to remedy the problem. Most of the "reforms" suggested misidentify the problem, or have no political viability. The Dodd–Frank legislation that finally was passed is toothless and will do little to remedy current problems or to prevent future crises. It does have one positive effect: many of the Fed's bailout actions last time around are now illegal—but where there is a will, there is a way to get around such restrictions. Still, so far as legislative reforms go, the best we can hope for is that the next crash will open the possibility for real reform.

Former Treasury adviser Morgan Ricks has offered a proposal that is thoughtful, coming down squarely in the middle of those who want to tweak with a few more regulations and those who want to close down the biggest institutions. Ricks (2011) quotes University of Chicago's Douglas Diamond that "financial crises are always and everywhere about short-term debt." Financial crises occur because of this conflict between the desire for liquidity by individuals, and the impossibility of liquidity for society as a whole. Think of it this way: all assets—financial or real—must find homes, so we cannot all get out of them simultaneously. In a crisis, that is precisely the problem: we all try to sell out, but cannot. In the global financial crisis, holders of the very short-term liabilities of financial institutions rationally decided to get out. A lot of the analyses of a run to liquidity rely on the supposition of irrationality, but there was nothing irrational about the run out of short-term financial institutions liabilities in 2008. And this was not merely a liquidity crisis—that is, short-term finance of illiquid positions in assets. Rather, these institutions were holding bad assets. The suspected insolvency led immediately to a liquidity crisis as creditors refused refinance.

So what is Ricks's solution? "Term out": force financial institutions that take risky bets to finance their positions in assets by issuing longer-term liabilities. In that case, there is no easy way to "run out." The creditors are locked into the crazy bets made by the debtors. Maybe they'll pay off; maybe they will not. His proposal is worth considering.

Following Ricks's suggestion, what should we do? One possibility is to segregate financial institutions into two mutually exclusive camps. One is subject to regulation and supervision of the asset side of its balance sheet. It is allowed to issue insured deposits. As these are payable on demand, they are by nature short term, and are the primary medium of exchange and means of payment that is necessary in any monetary economy. It is a safe and sound sector that restores the protection afforded by Glass–Steagall.

The other camp consists of all those who are not subject to such supervision and regulation. They are pretty much free to buy any assets, but they must "term out"—finance positions by using long-term liabilities. And they cannot issue anything that purports to be similar to a deposit. In short, they offer an experience that is not suitable for everyone. This will reduce the problem of short-termism with respect to financing positions in risky assets. It also mitigates the complaint about excessive regulation: any institution that hates regulation can avoid it almost completely by funding long-term. And it makes the payments system safe by keeping the risky operators out.

Will that long-term-funded and unregulated partition of the financial sector periodically crash and burn? Yes, it will, and those that take excessive risks will fail. While we do not necessarily advocate such approach, we find the proposal made by Ricks to be worth careful considerations.

5 Policy implications for employment

In a market economy, employment is the main source of income for most of the population.[1] It is through employment that people are able to fully participate in society both because employment itself is a social activity, and because the income earned allows one to enjoy the minimum economic and social benefits considered by many to be human rights. Without paying jobs, individuals are unable to partake in a large number of social activities. In capitalist, wage-labor societies, therefore, joblessness creates a long list of problems—both for the individuals and for society as a whole: self-pity, self-loathing, and rage at society (Harvey 2002); absolute and relative poverty, damage to social status and self respect, adverse psychological and physical health effects, stress, suicide, crime, and other anti-social behavior.

Even if the Great Recession is officially over, for the fourteen million Americans who were still unemployed in 2012 it certainly did not feel that way. The U.S. economy has performed especially poorly in terms of job growth even as economic growth has resumed. The current rate of job creation is not only insufficient to replace the jobs lost during the crisis but can barely keep up with labor force growth. At the recent pace of job creation, we only fall farther behind.

Surprisingly, however, the persistently high unemployment around 8 percent through 2012 and even worse underemployment situation (15 percent) has not generated the necessary amount of concern among politicians. This is all the more apparent if we consider that the employment–population ratio has reached a thirty-year low of about 58.5 percent and has stayed around that on average since 2009 despite a slowly declining unemployment rate. The lack of public debate about any serious jobs initiative has been conspicuous. Many commentators have claimed that unemployment is a lagging indicator and hence it takes a while for it to catch up to economic growth. The other popular argument is that a large number of people currently unemployed are structurally unemployed, i.e., many jobs lost in the construction sector will not come back even when the economy rebounds.

The conclusion that follows from these views is that public policy, particularly more government spending, will not help solve the problem of unemployment with some even claiming that it will worsen it. Instead, we are told, we must let the "free market" operate to create new kinds of jobs; at most, government might offer retraining for displaced workers with the wrong skill sets. The problem is claimed to be not so much one of Keynesian insufficient effective demand, but rather a supply side problem. The more neoliberal response is to increase labor market "flexibility" by removing "barriers to work" such as social safety nets, minimum wage laws, rigid union work rules, and safety regulations.

We start this chapter by a brief discussion of the causes of unemployment, both short term and long term. We argue that the conventional argument that unemployment is a job market issue is misguided and inapplicable to the real world. Rather, the currently high unemployment, and especially the long-term unemployment, is due to insufficient aggregate spending, i.e., total spending does not create enough jobs for everyone to be able to find employment. The private sector, while usually employing a large portion of the labor force, cannot be entrusted with the task of ensuring full employment. The public sector, on the other hand, can and should be charged with this task.

But what kind of policy is appropriate to solve not only the short-term unemployment problem but to make sure that everyone who wants a job can find one? While some have called for increased government spending, we disagree that blind "pump-priming" stimulus is the right solution. Rather, we propose a universal government Job Guarantee (JG) program which will hire anyone who is willing and ready to work. We discuss the design of this program as well as its implementation and affordability while answering the usual criticisms charged against such programs.

The lost commitment to full employment

One of the major deficiencies of market economies is the failure to provide full utilization of resources and particularly full employment of human resources. While the private sector plays an invaluable and dynamic role in providing employment, it cannot ensure enough jobs to keep up with population growth or to speed economic recovery—much less achieve the social goal of full employment for all. Even more importantly, private enterprises do not have employment as their goal: the purpose of private production is not job provision, but obtaining profits. If more profits can be obtained by downsizing employment, firms lay off workers. When sales fall, firms lay off workers. When more efficient production methods are found that permit firms to produce more with fewer workers, they lay off workers. In other words, firms hire more workers only when they have more customers than they can serve with the existing labor force. The fundamental drive is to create profits, not jobs. That should be obvious.

Firms hire the amount of workers they think they need to produce the amount of output they think they can profitably sell. There is no reason to believe that there are forces that push the for-profit sector to hire all the available resources, including labor, at any particular point in time, much less on a continuous basis through time. This is especially true in the current climate of financialization of the U.S. economy—in which the system of rewards has changed motivations. The goal of most large corporations is not even to achieve maximum profits but to increase shareholder value, i.e., their stock prices. There are a number of ways to do this and high employment is certainly not one of them. Quite the contrary, laying off workers is one of the main means to achieve "efficiency" the way the stock market understands it, which then translates into higher stock prices. In Chapter 2, we showed that there has been a long-term transformation of developed capitalist economies (especially that of the U.S.) toward a new version of Hilferding's "Finance Capitalism," where an ever larger share of corporate profits come from the realm of finance, which requires very little labor. As a result, the share of national income going to labor has fallen while even the most venerable industrial powerhouses like General Motors and General Electric seek more profits from their financial divisions and downsize their manufacturing business.

While one would expect that as the private sector has moved further away from attaining full employment, the public sector would have filled the void, the opposite has been true. In the 1950s and 1960s full, or at least high, employment was among the primary goals of economic policy. Governments across the developed world tried and achieved relatively high levels of employment through demand management as well as direct hiring and other active labor market policies. It was recognized that social policy is an invaluable instrument for attaining and maintaining full employment. In the U.S., the Employment Act of 1946 committed the federal government to the goal of high employment, and it was amended by the 1978 Humphrey-Hawkins Act that targeted a measured unemployment rate of 3 percent. While we rarely achieved that goal—at least for all Americans (we were tolerably close for the case of white men)—it was an oft-stated goal of policy.

In recent decades, however, full employment has been wrongly dismissed as not only impossible but economically counterproductive. Now, however, we act as if full employment would ruin us, destroying the value of our currency through inflation and depreciation, and weakening the labor discipline that high unemployment maintains through enforced destitution. This has been due to a number of factors such as the declining power of labor unions as well as the advent of neoliberal economic thinking. The capture of governments in most of the developed world by proponents of such thinking has pushed employment outside the domain of public policy and subjugated full employment to the whim of free markets.

Rather than viewing low unemployment as a goal of policy, unemployment came to be seen as a tool of policy. Indeed, public policy since the late 1970s has been biased against the creation of a sufficient supply of jobs on the belief that full employment is not consistent with price stability. Through the thick and thin of the business cycle, we leave tens of millions of Americans idle in the belief that this makes political, economic, and social sense (Wray 2011).

Cyclical, structural, and "Keynesian" causes of unemployment

There is a general consensus among most economists that cyclical, or short-term, unemployment—i.e., job loss due to the business cycle—is caused by declining aggregate demand. However, not much consensus exists about the kind of public policy that is appropriate to tackle cyclical unemployment. Economists who are characterized as "Keynesians" usually argue for government stimulus spending or tax cuts.

By contrast, those who can be characterized by the general term "neoclassical" argue that unemployment is a labor market problem, i.e., imperfections such as minimum wage legislation, unemployment benefits, or wage contracts make the labor market unable to adjust quickly to resolve recessions leaving a portion of the labor force unemployed. The logic is that if workers take a pay cut when the economy is slowing down "full employment," defined as the lack of involuntary unemployment *at the prevailing market clearing wage*, will be maintained. The appropriate action then is to make the labor market more flexible. This has been the policy direction in the U.S. and most developed countries in the last few decades. And while the labor market has become more and more flexible in downturns with employers laying off workers at the slightest sign of slowing business, it has been extremely "inflexible" in the upturn leaving a large number of the population unemployed even during "robust" recoveries and even as labor markets have been made more flexible.

There are a variety of approaches taken to explaining the problem of long-term joblessness, of which the most important views are behavioralist (problems with the individuals who are unemployed), structuralist (e.g., skills mismatch), and job shortage (Harvey 1999, 2000). In the U.S., the economic theory and the policy based on it emphasize behavioral and structural problems. It is argued that in the long run involuntary unemployment does not exist—the economy operates at what is called the natural rate of unemployment where everyone who is willing to work at the prevailing market wage can find a job. The natural rate of unemployment does not mean zero unemployment as there are always workers between jobs or who have just entered the economy. Additionally there are workers whose skills are no longer demanded because the structure of the economy has changed. Employers are looking for a skill set that the unemployed cannot provide. This is the so-called skill mismatch problem which can be solved by retraining and reeducating the unemployed to fit them to the available vacancies.

However, there is no fine line between short-term and long-term or structural unemployment. In the past twenty years, high unemployment has not been solely a phenomenon of recessions but even expansions occur without much job creation. Economic growth and employment have seemingly decoupled: the former no longer implies the latter. Jobless recovery is no longer an aberration but has rather become the new normal.

Figure 5.1 depicts the change in employment relative to the pre-recession level after the official start date of the recession. The figure only shows the data for periods in which it took at least two years to return to the pre-recession level of employment and one may note that, aside from the Great Depression, it is only since the 1981 recession that it took so long to recover. More troubling, it has taken longer and longer to recover from each recession since 1981. During the 1990–1991 recession, it took almost thirty-two months for employment to reach its pre-recession level; in the 2001 recession it took forty-eight months. Consequences of this trend have been an increase in the proportion of long-term unemployed since the 1970s, and an increase in the length of unemployment (Figure 5.2).

The current recession is an aberration from any historical norm both in terms of the speed and steepness of the decline in employment, and in terms of how persistent unemployment has been in terms of level and duration. The U.S. economy actually lost jobs at a faster rate than during the Great Depression, losing almost nine million jobs in two years compared to five million over the same period of time in the 1930s. The economy rebounded more quickly due to the intervention of the government through massive central bank intervention and a $700 billion stimulus package that helped to stop the bleeding. However, this intervention has been timid relative to the size of the problem and with the quick return of deficit hysteria and lack of commitment to any meaningful jobs program, it is unlikely that a jobs recovery is anywhere near. At the current trend of recovery, it would take around eighty to ninety months—around seven

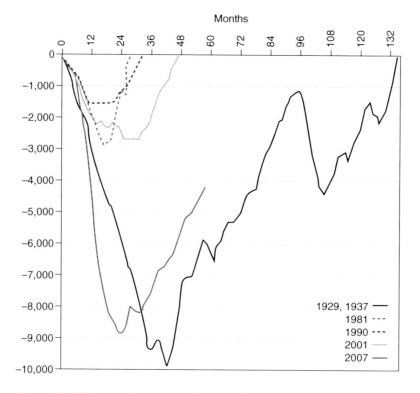

Figure 5.1 Difference between employment level and peak employment, nonfarm employment (thousands) (source: BLS).

Note
Data for the 2007 recession stops in November 2012.

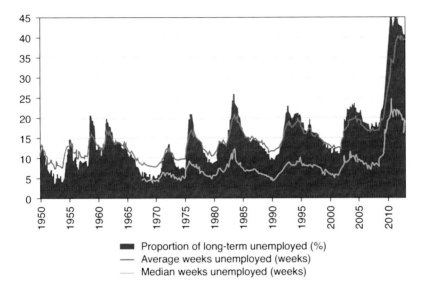

Figure 5.2 Duration and proportion of long-term unemployment (source: BLS).

Note
Long-term unemployed individuals are unemployed for more than 26 weeks.

years—to recover the jobs lost since January 2008 following the beginning of the recession in 2007. Given that the average frequency of recessions after World War Two is around six years, and given the state of the world economy, seven years is actually an optimistic estimate. It is likely that it will take much longer to regain all the jobs lost.

The reasons for the phenomenon of "jobless recovery" are numerous and beyond the scope of this chapter. A few of them such as the decline in the manufacturing sector, declining union power, as well as the government inaction in response to unemployment are worth mentioning. Additionally, it is natural to expect that as technology improves the private sector needs less and less labor to produce the same amount of output, the so-called "machine problem" highlighted by David Ricardo. Companies have used recessions to discard the "unnecessary" labor. While it may be unpopular to lay off a large number of people in good times, during recessions when everyone is laying off workers the firm will not face much opposition.

Still, many have claimed that persistent joblessness is no longer a cyclical issue but rather structural. The structure of the economy, they argue, has changed as the manufacturing sector shrank and other blue collar jobs disappeared. These jobs will not come back, therefore the workers need to be retrained if they are to find employment. A recent report from the Economic Policy Institute (EPI) casts doubt on many of the claims that the proponents of the "structural unemployment" argument make. First, if the currently high unemployment was primarily a structural problem, one would expect that it would be concentrated among those with lower educational attainment. The report demonstrates that the composition of unemployment by educational background has remained very stable over the recession with unemployment rates doubling for workers of almost all educational levels (Mishel and Shierholz 2011).

The EPI report provides further evidence which dispels the notion that the currently high unemployment is a structural issue. Rather it claims that persistent unemployment is the result of lack of demand for workers which stems from insufficient aggregate demand. In fact, in the past two to three decades the U.S. economy has operated with chronically deficient aggregate demand. As the government deficits got smaller and even turned to surpluses under Clinton, withdrawing demand from the economy, first the stock market bubble and later the housing bubble helped maintain the illusion of sustainable growth. However, neither of these bubbles could sustain aggregate demand at full employment level. Since the collapse of the housing market, consumers have cut back their spending and businesses facing sluggish sales have laid off workers. This creates a vicious cycle of low demand, low spending, and high unemployment which can only be stopped by an entity whose spending does not depend on its income, i.e., the government.

This problem is not restricted to the U.S. Before the global financial collapse, the International Labour Organization (ILO) released a major report on global unemployment. It concluded:

> Young people have more difficulties in labour markets than adults; women do not get the same opportunities as men, the lack of decent work is still high; and the potential a population has to offer is not always used because of a lack of human capital development or a mismatch between the supply and the demand side in labour markets.
>
> (2007: 9–10)

Moreover, the ILO reported that even at the peak of the global expansion, in 2007 200 million remained unemployed around the world in spite of strong growth. "Every region has to face major labour market challenges" because growth fuels productivity growth (up 26 percent in past decade) but does not create many new jobs (up only 16.6 percent). Again, jobless growth is now the norm in the U.S. and abroad. The Great Recession has caused even more joblessness (International Labour Organization 2012).

The conclusion that follows is that we need social policy to solve the problem of unemployment, both cyclical and long-term types. It is too important an issue both for economic and social reasons to leave it to the private markets. The question then is what kind of economic policy is appropriate to ensure full employment. If the problem is (mostly) a job shortage, which we argue it is, then retraining workers will only redistribute unemployment among the unfortunate, who are blamed for their joblessness.

Pump-priming vs. direct job creation as a solution to job shortage

Even those who understand that the problem is job shortage or demand shortage usually argue for more stimulus spending (or tax cuts), with little concern for how the stimulus is distributed throughout the economy. There are, however, a number of problems with this approach. First, it is highly possible that much of the government stimulus merely ends up in the pockets of firms as profits and there is no guarantee that those profits spur hiring of more workers. High profits might as well be used to engage in mergers and acquisitions and other financial investments rather than in job creation.

The current recession is an example of such a situation, where government spending has improved business profits and despite sitting on piles of cash (an estimated $2 trillion of it in 2012), U.S. corporations are not hiring. This is because they understand that U.S. households are loaded with debt and will not be spending, and in the current political climate there is no expectation that the government will step in to fill this gap. Merger and acquisition activities, on the other hand, have become even more intense than in the period of the boom prior to 2007.

Second, the "spend, spend, spend" policy may lead to inflation before full employment is achieved, which is clearly a problem that Keynes identified in 1937 when he argued for a rightly distributed aggregate demand over further increases in aggregate demand (Keynes 1937b; Tcherneva 2012). Inflation hurts those with fixed incomes, such as seniors, as well as creditors, therefore such policies will almost always face resistance from some voters and from the financial sector. Third, there is the problem of timing. Discretionary stimulus spending has to go through Congress and the whole political theater. Therefore before it is passed and put into action there will be job losses, which is an unnecessary and permanent loss socially and economically. Finally, while stimulus spending may attenuate short-term unemployment it does nothing to help those who have been displaced from the job market due to structural changes in the economy, or due to perceived "behavioral" problems or insufficient "moral character." There will always be some workers left behind even as fiscal stimulus becomes great enough to generate demand-pull inflation.

For all the above mentioned reasons we disagree with commentators who are merely calling for more stimulus spending. Instead, we propose a policy of direct employment creation by the public sector, a Job Guarantee (JG) program, which would offer to provide a job to anyone of legal working age who is ready and willing to work. The program would pay a uniform wage and provide a uniform benefit package. The legislated minimum wage is meaningless if there are unemployed individuals because their wage is zero. Only in combination with a job guarantee does a minimum wage become effective. Hence, the wage paid in the JG program would become the effective minimum wage; it would have to be matched by all other employers. Similarly, the package of benefits offered would set a standard that normally would be matched by other employers.

As we will explain below, by offering a uniform compensation, the JG program provides an anchor for labor costs. This is an important part of the proposal because it helps to provide macroeconomic stability even in the presence of full employment of labor resources. The compensation would not be indexed to a measure of the price level—it would be "fixed but adjustable," with periodic increases to catch up to inflation, much as the legislated minimum wage is occasionally increased.

Workers would do something useful, but with an ultimate goal of preparing them for work in non-JG jobs. Hence, training would be a part of every JG job. JG must take workers as they are, so there must be JG employment available for anyone "ready and willing" to work, regardless of level of education, training, or previous work experience. However, the JG experience should better equip workers for post-JG work.

A key justification for the JG is that no capitalist society has ever managed to operate at anything approaching true, full, employment on a consistent basis without direct job creation on a large scale by government. Further, the burden of joblessness is borne unequally, always concentrated among groups that already face other disadvantages.

Finally, only the government can offer an infinitely elastic demand for labor (offering to hire all who cannot otherwise find employment) because it does not need to heed narrow market efficiency concerns. Private firms can only hire the quantity of labor needed to produce the level of output expected to be sold at a profitable price. Government can take a broader view to include promotion of the public interest, including the right to work. Through a job guarantee it will not only provide employment for everyone who wants a job but will also provide goods and services that the society needs but which the private sector will not provide because they do not constitute a profit opportunity. For these reasons, government should and must play a role in providing jobs to achieve social justice.

The Job Guarantee: program design and benefits

The benefits of full employment include production of goods, services, and income; on-the-job training and skill development; poverty alleviation; community building and social networking; social, political, and economic stability; and social multipliers (positive feedbacks and reinforcing dynamics that create a virtuous cycle of socio-economic benefits). A JG program would restore the government's lost commitment to full employment in recognition of the fact that the total impact would exceed the sum of the benefits.

The program has no time limits or restrictions based on income, gender, education, or experience. It operates like a buffer stock: in a boom, employers will recruit workers out of the program; in a slump the JG safety net will allow those who lost their jobs to preserve good habits, keeping them work-ready. It will also help those unable to obtain work outside the program enhance their employability through training. Work records will be kept for all participants and made available to potential employers. Unemployment offices will be converted to employment offices, to match workers with jobs that suit them and to help employers recruit staff.

All state and local governments and registered non-profit organizations can propose projects; proposals will be submitted to a newly created office within the federal government's Labor Department for final approval and funding. The office will maintain a website providing details on all pending, approved, and ongoing projects, and final reports will be published after projects are complete. Participants will be subject to all federal work rules, and violations will lead to dismissal. Anyone who is dismissed three times in a twelve-month period will be ineligible to participate in the program for a year. Workers will be allowed to organize through labor unions.

The program will meet workers where they are and take them as they are: jobs will be available in local communities and will be tailored to suit employees' level of education and experience (though with the goal of improving skills). Proposals should include provisions for part-time work and other flexible arrangements for workers who need them, including but not restricted to flexible arrangements for parents of young children. While one may think that the JG program will be mostly composed of individuals with a lower level of education, a significant number of people with high levels of education will be in the pool on a long-term basis. Indeed, even in the best of times, educated individuals with significant skills are unemployed on a long-term basis. In the U.S., they represent on average 16 percent of the long-term unemployed and this proportion does not vary much overtime (Figure 5.3). This relatively permanent

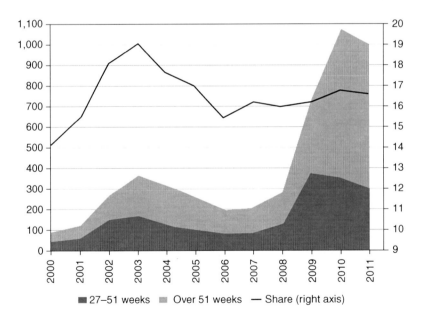

■ 27–51 weeks ■ Over 51 weeks — Share (right axis)

Figure 5.3 Number of individuals with a college degree (Bachelor's or more) who are long-term unemployed (thousands) and their proportion among all long-term unemployed (%) (source: BLS (Basic Current Population Survey, Table 39A, unpublished)).

pool of educated individuals would be a great source of help to train and supervise other members of the pool.

The package of benefits would be subject to congressional approval, but could include health care, child care, payment of Social Security taxes, and usual vacations and sick leave. The wage would be set by Congress and fixed until Congress approved a rate increase—much as the minimum wage is currently legislated.

The advantage of the uniform basic wage is that it would limit competition with other employers as workers could be attracted out of the JG program by paying a wage slightly above the program's wage. Obviously, higher skilled workers and those with higher educational attainment will be hired first. In an economic boom, employers will lower hiring standards to pull lower-skilled workers out of the program. The residual pool of workers in the program provides a buffer stock of employable labor, helping to reduce pressures on wages— and as wages for high-skilled workers are bid up, the buffer stock becomes ever more desirable as a source of cheaper labor.

All participants will obtain a Social Security number and maintain a bank account in an FDIC-insured bank. Weekly wages will be paid by the federal government directly to participants' accounts. The government will also provide funding for benefits as well as approved expenses up to a maximum of 10 to 25 percent of wages paid for a project (to cover the cost of administrative materials and equipment; the exact percent would be set centrally and could vary by type of project). Because the primary purpose of the program is to create jobs, the federal government should cover only a relatively small portion of non-wage costs.

Estimates of the gross cost of the JG programs vary from 1 to 2 percent of GDP, to 3 to 5 percent of GDP (Wray 1998; Tcherneva and Wray 2007; Harvey 1989; Tymoigne 2013; Kaboub 2013; Fullwiler 2007; Watts and Mitchell 2000). Net program costs will be lower, since spending on unemployment compensation and other relief will be reduced—this program will pay people for working, rather than paying them not to work. In addition, economic, social, and political benefits are several times larger than the cost (Wray 1998). The promise of increased national productivity and shared prosperity should far outweigh any fears about rising budget deficits.

We have seen time and again that no other means exist to ensure that everyone who wants to work will be able to obtain a job. Benefits include poverty reduction, amelioration of many social ills associated with chronic unemployment (health problems, spousal abuse, family break-up, drug abuse, crime), and enhanced skills due to training on the job. Forstater (1999) has emphasized how JG can be used to increase economic flexibility and to enhance the environment. More generally, JG can be used to provide goods and services that markets do not provide at all, or that are too expensive for low income households. Examples include social services (child and elder care, tutoring, public safety), small-scale public infrastructure provision or repair (clean water and sewage projects, roads), low income housing and repairs to owner-occupied housing (following the lead of Habitat for Humanity), and food preparation ("soup kitchens," local bakeries). Only community needs and imagination would limit the ability to provide adequate and useful jobs.

While today's neoliberals and their ancestors have managed to taint the memory of the New Deal's job creation programs, the truth is that these programs provided lasting benefits. The nay-sayers actually began to fabricate falsehoods about the New Deal and its participants from the very beginning. With corporate funding and ready access to the media, they painted a picture of lazy tramps leaning on shovels. But the contrary evidence is still plain to see, in the form of public buildings, dams, roads, national parks, and trails that still serve America. For example, workers in the WPA (Works Projects Administration)

> shouldered the tasks that began to transform the physical face of America. They built roads and schools and bridges and dams. The Cow Palace in San Francisco, La Guardia Airport in New York City and National (now Reagan) Airport in Washington, D.C., the Timberline Lodge in Oregon, the Outer Drive Bridge on Chicago's Lake Shore Drive, the River Walk in San Antonio [...]. Its workers sewed clothes and stuffed mattresses and repaired toys; served hot lunches to schoolchildren; ministered to the sick; delivered library books to remote hamlets by horseback; rescued flood victims; painted giant murals on the walls of hospitals, high schools, courthouses, and city halls; performed plays and played music before eager audiences; and wrote guides to the forty-eight states that even today remain models for what such books should be. And when the clouds of an oncoming world loomed over the United States, it was the WPA's workers who modernized the army and air bases and trained in vast numbers to supply the nation's military needs.
> (Taylor 2008: 2)

The New Deal federal jobs programs employed thirteen million different individuals; the WPA was its biggest job program, employing 8.5 million workers, lasting eight years, and spending about $10.5 billion (Taylor 2008). In the early part of the New Deal, millions more were employed through grants provided by the Federal Emergency Relief Administration to states and localities. Leaving aside the Civilian Works Administration that was implemented in the winter of 1933–1934, the peak level of non-administrative employees was reached in 1936 and 1938 with over four million people employed (Figure 5.4).

The New Deal job programs took a broken country and in many important respects helped to not only revive it, but to bring it into the twentieth century (Field 2011). The WPA built 650,000 miles of roads, 78,000 bridges, 125,000 civilian and military buildings, 700 miles of airport runways; it fed 900 million hot lunches to kids, operated 1,500 nursery schools, gave concerts before audiences of 150 million, and created 475,000 works of art. Quite simply, these programs transformed and modernized America (Taylor 2008: 523–524). In a massive report, the National Resource Planning Board notes the following accomplishment through June 30, 1940, for the CCC and NYA:

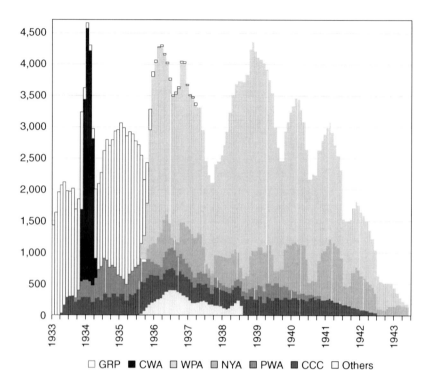

Figure 5.4 Monthly average of number of persons employed in the New Deal federal work programs and through the general relief programs, January 1933 to June 1943 (thousands) (sources: Bureau of Public Assistance 1943a, 1943b; Federal Works Agency 1941, 1942, 1947; Federal Security Agency 1944; Civilian Conservation Corps 1944; Emergency Conservation Work 1935; Works Progress Administration 1939.

Note
The data does not include administrative employees). CWA is the Civil Works Administration, WPA is the Work Projects Administration, NYA is the National Youth Administration, CCC is the Civilian Conservation Corps, PWA is the Public Works Administration, and GRP stands for the General Relief Work Programs implemented by the State Emergency Relief Administrations with the financial help of the Federal Emergency Relief Administration (FERA) from July 1933 (includes the Emergency Work Relief Program implemented by FERA from April 1934 to July 1935).

The accomplishments the CCC included: The construction of 37,203 vehicle bridges, 21,684,898 rods of fence, and 79,538 mileage of telephone lines; the development of almost 21,000 springs, waterhole, and small reservoirs; the building of more than 5 million permanent and temporary check dams in connection with treating gullies for erosion control; as well as the planting, seeding, or sodding of 114 million square yards of terraces for protection against erosion; the planting or seeding of almost 2,000,000 acres of forest land with an average of 1,000 trees to the acre; 5,741,000 man-days spent in

fighting forest fires and 5,392,000 man-days in fire presuppression and prevention work; forest-stand improvement on 3,694,930 acres; development
of about 55,000 acres of public camp and picnic grounds; stocking lakes,
ponds, and streams with 9.3 million fish.

(National Resources Planning Board 1942: 343, n. 8)

The accomplishments of youth workers [NYA] on the out-of-school
program had included the following: New construction or additions to more
than 6,000 public buildings, such as schools, libraries, gymnasiums, and
hospitals, and addition to or repair or improvement of about 18,300 others;
construction of almost 4,000 recreational structures, such as stadiums, band-
stands, and park shelters, and repair or improvement of nearly 6,000 others;
construction of 350 swimming or wading pools and 3,500 tennis courts.
About 1,500 miles of roads had been constructed and 7,000 repaired or
improved; nearly 2,000 bridges had been built. Seven landing fields had
been constructed at airports. 188 miles of sewer and water lines had been
laid, and 6,200 sanitary privies built. Over 6.5 million articles of clothing
had been produced or renovated, nearly 2 million articles of furniture constructed or repaired, and 350,000 tools or other mechanical equipment constructed or repaired. 77.5 million school lunches had been served by NYA
youth; nearly 4 million pounds of foodstuffs had been produced and nearly
7 million pounds canned or preserved. Conservation activities had included
the construction or repair of 127 miles of levees and retaining walls and
15,700 check and storage dams.

(National Resources Planning Board 1942: 342, n. 5)

Not only did all these accomplishments widely improve the living conditions of
the U.S. population, but also these programs allowed millions of individuals to
maintain their skills and their income and brought an end to the employment
problem much more quickly than official data suggest. After one includes work
relief enrollees in the official data, the U.S. economy recovered its peak employment after seventy-eight months (instead of 136 months as often reported by
those who exclude New Deal jobs from the employment figures) and only three
years after the New Deal programs were implemented (Figure 5.5).

All these achievements were accomplished at a minimal labor cost, which
was the main cost. Wage payments to non-administrative employees (the overwhelming majority of employees) amounted to about $14 billion over ten
years for all federal work programs. Labor cost never represented more than 5
percent of GNP and was about 1.6 percent of GNP on average from 1933 to
1943 (Figure 5.5). If one includes all other costs (administrative, supervisory,
and non-labor costs), the total cost of the New Deal work programs was on
average 2.2 percent of GNP over the decade, and was at 1 percent of GNP on
average for an unemployment rate between 5 and 10 percent (Table 5.1). The
programs employed on average 34 percent of the unemployed (Tymoigne
2013).

Table 5.1 Total cost of work relief programs relative to the size of the economy (%)

Unemployment rate	5 or less	5 to 10	10 to 15	15 to 20	Over 20
Cost to GNP	0.32	1.03	2.42	2.64	2.12

Source: Gordon (1986), see Figure 5.4 and Tymoigne (2013).

Note
Cost drops above 20 percent unemployment because work programs just started to be implemented when this rate of unemployment was prevalent (1932–1933).

Of course, the New Deal programs had their shares of problems, from the lack of a training component and difficulties in setting the appropriate monthly wage, to the sometimes disruptive impacts on the private and public sectors or the occasional bad quality of some projects (National Resources Planning Board 1941, 1942; Salmond 1967; Schwartz 1984). As one must, expect given the novelty of the policy, some mistakes were made because of the lack of experience with implementing and managing such programs and because of the rushed implementation. A more serious issue was the lack of commitment to the cause, and the prevalent view in Washington that the work programs were of a temporary nature. This led to a lack of planning and a lack of accountability with comprehensive reports not published until the early 1940s, almost a decade after the implementation of work relief. As a consequence, there was sometimes a failure to detect problems early and to learn from successes (Macmahon *et al.* 1941). At the same time, however, the published reports show that the New Deal work programs were overall a success story, and an important means to tackle unemployment and its socio-economic consequences, while mostly providing relevant output of decent quality that was checked through quality controls. The reports also provide relevant insights on how to go (and not to go) about implementing a JG program.

In many important respects, America is broken again. Its infrastructure is not worthy of a rich, developed country, as recognized by President Obama in his 2012 "state of the union" address when he called for new investments to answer the challenges posed by China. Chapter 2 noted that the nation's public buildings, its roads, its bridges, its sewerage, its playgrounds and parks, and many of its schools are in need of repair and expansion. We do not want to overemphasize public infrastructure investment, however. The needs are at least as great in the area of public services, including aged care, preschools, playground supervision, clean-up of public lands, retrofitting public and private buildings for energy efficiency, and environmental restoration projections.

A new universal direct job creation program would improve working conditions in the private sector as employees would have the option of moving into the JG program. Hence, private sector employers would have to offer a wage and benefit package and working conditions at least as good as those offered by the JG program. The informal sector would shrink as workers become integrated into formal employment, gaining access to protection provided by labor laws.

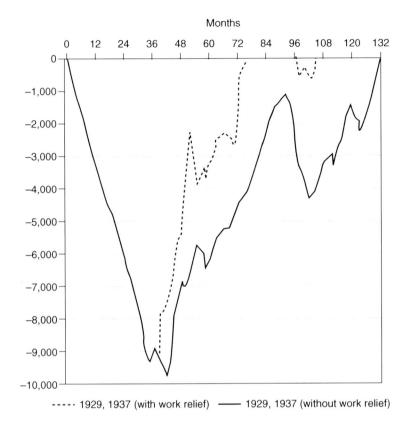

Figure 5.5 Difference between employment level and peak employment, nonfarm employment (thousands) (sources: Board of Governors of the Federal Reserve System 1941a, 1941b; see Figure 5.4).

There would be some reduction of racial and gender discrimination because unfairly treated workers would have the JG option. However, JG by itself cannot end discrimination.

Finally, a JG program with a uniform basic wage also helps to promote economic and price stability. The JG will act as an automatic stabilizer as employment in the program grows in recession and shrinks in economic expansion, counteracting private sector employment fluctuations. Furthermore, the uniform basic wage will reduce both inflationary pressure in a boom and deflationary pressure in a bust. In recession, workers down-sized by private employers can work at the JG wage, which puts a floor to how low wages and income can fall. In expansion, hiring workers out of the pool helps to check wage pressures.

However, some critics argue that a job guarantee would be inflationary (Sawyer 2003). Some argue that JG would reduce the incentive to work, raising private sector costs because of increased shirking, since workers would no longer

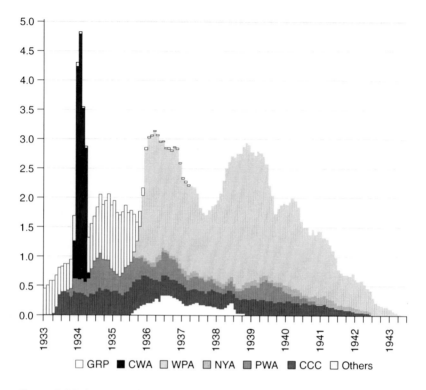

Figure 5.6 Labor cost of work relief programs relative to GNP (%) (sources: Gordon 1986; see Figure 5.4).

fear job loss. Workers would also be emboldened to ask for greater wage increases. Some argue that a JG program would be so big that it would be impossible to manage it; some fear corruption; others argue that it would be impossible to find useful things for JG workers to do. It has been argued that a national job guarantee would be too expensive, causing the budget deficit to grow on an unsustainable path (Aspromourgos 2000; King 2001). We will take up some of these criticisms next.

Feasibility issues: macroeconomic stability

A properly designed JG program would mitigate or eliminate these possible problems. This section will address issues surrounding macroeconomic stability, such as wage and price inflation and exchange rates. The next section will address affordability issues.

As mentioned earlier, the program would set a fixed (but periodically adjusted) basic compensation package. This will ensure that the JG wage will not pressure private wages in a competitive spiral. Such a wage would only set a floor below which private sector wages could not fall; thus, it operates like an agricultural commodity price floor—which does not cause prices to rise but only prevents them from falling. Indeed, a JG program designed along these lines can be analyzed as a buffer stock program that operates much like Australia's wool price stabilization program. The government purchases wool when the market price falls below the price support level, and sells wool when the market price rises above that level. By design, the program stabilizes wool prices in order to stabilize farm income and thus consumption by those who raise sheep.

In the JG program, government offers a floor price for labor, paying the program wage to participants. Government "sells" labor at any price above the JG wage to firms (and non-JG government employers). Just as in the case of a floor price for wool, a floor price for labor cannot directly generate inflationary pressures on the market wage. Indeed, so long as the buffer stock pool of labor is large enough, it will help to restrain market pressures on wages as government "sells" labor in a boom. Further, because labor is an input to all production, to the degree that wages are stabilized by JG, production costs will be more stable. Also, JG will directly stabilize income and consumption of JG workers, and if other wages and incomes become more stable because of JG, that will further enhance macroeconomic stability.

Critics fear that existence of JG will embolden workers, leading to rising wage demands and inflation. However, there are two reasons to doubt that this effect will be large. First, an effective labor buffer stock will dampen wage demands because employers always have the option of hiring out of the JG pool if the wage demands of non-JG workers are too high. The price demands of wool suppliers are attenuated by the government's buffer stock of wool; stubborn wool suppliers cannot raise wool prices much above the government's sell price. The second reason to doubt that obstinate workers will adopt accelerating wage demands is because the further their wages rise above the JG wage, the greater the costs to them of losing their higher-paying jobs. If the JG wage is $10 per hour, it may well be true that non-program workers earning $10.50 per hour will be emboldened to demand $10.75, but they are not likely to continue to demand ever-higher wages in subsequent years simply because they can fall back on a $10 per hour JG job. The cost of losing a $15 per hour job is not the same as the cost of losing a $10.50 per hour job. The JG pool acts as a "reserve army of the employed," helping to stabilize wages.

A related argument concerns the exchange rate: if jobs are created that provide income to the poor, consumption will rise, including purchases of imports. This will worsen the trade deficit, depreciate the currency, and possibly lead to accelerating inflation through an exchange rate "pass through" effect (import prices rise as the currency depreciates, adding to inflation of the price level of the domestic consumer basket). In other words, unemployment and poverty are viewed as the cost of maintaining not only low inflation, but also the value of the currency.

Two kinds of responses can be provided. The first is ethical. Should a nation attempt to maintain macroeconomic stability by keeping a portion of its population sufficiently poor that it cannot afford to consume? More generally, is unemployment and poverty an acceptable policy tool to be used to maintain currency stability? Are there other tools available to achieve these ends? If not, should policy makers accept some currency depreciation in order to eliminate unemployment and poverty? There are strong ethical arguments against using poverty and unemployment as the primary policy tools to achieve price and exchange rate stability. And even if currency stability is highly desired, it is doubtful that a case can be made for its status as a human right that trumps the internationally recognized right to work.

However, we can challenge the notion that JG actually threatens price and currency stability. To be clear, we do not argue that JG would have no effects on a particular index of prices (such as the CPI) or on the exchange rate. We argue instead that JG provides an anchor for the domestic and foreign value of the currency, hence, actually increases macroeconomic stability. As argued above, JG will not cause domestic inflation, although it can lead to a one-time wage and price increase, depending on where the JG wage is set. Similarly, if JG does increase income when implemented, this can lead to a one-off increase of imports. Even if the exchange rate does decline in response (and even if there is some pass-through inflation), the stable JG wage will prevent a wage-price spiral. If a nation is not prepared to allow its trade deficit to rise with rising employment and income in the JG program (some of which goes toward consumption of imports), it still has available all policy tools at its disposal with the lone exception of forcing the poor and unemployed to bear the entire burden. In other words, it can still use trade policy, import substitution, luxury taxes, capital controls, interest rate policy, turnover taxes, and so on, to minimize pressure on exchange rates if they should arise.

Feasibility of job guarantee: affordability issues

A sovereign nation operating with its own currency in a floating exchange rate regime can always financially afford a JG program (Wray 1998, 2012; Mitchell and Muysken 2008). So long as there are workers who are ready and willing to work at the program wage, the government can "afford" to hire them simply by crediting bank accounts. Thus there is no hard financial constraint on sovereign government. However, this does not mean that spending on the JG program will grow without limit. The size of the JG pool of workers will fluctuate with the cycle, automatically shrinking when the private sector grows. In recession, workers shed by the private sector find JG jobs, increasing government spending, and thereby stimulating the private sector so that it will begin to hire out of the JG pool.

A floating exchange rate provides the "degree of freedom" that allows the government to spend without worrying that increased employment and higher demand will threaten an exchange rate peg—by possibly increasing domestic inflation and/or increasing imports. Thus, fiscal policy is "freed" to pursue other objectives, rather than being held hostage to maintenance of the peg. By the same token, monetary policy can set the overnight interest rate to achieve other goals, rather than being determined by the rate consistent with pegging the exchange rate. This is not to imply that the government will necessarily avoid any consideration of impacts on exchange rates while forming fiscal and monetary policy. However, if achievement of full employment is believed to conflict with maintenance of a constant exchange rate, the government in a floating currency regime *can* choose full employment. On the other hand, on a fixed exchange rate, a government that has insufficient foreign exchange reserves may not be able to "afford" to spend to promote full employment if that might lead to loss of reserves.

Conclusion

There have been many job creation programs implemented around the world, some of which were narrowly targeted while others were broad based. The American New Deal included several moderately inclusive programs including the Civilian Conservation Corp and the Works Progress Administration. Sweden developed broad-based employment programs that virtually guaranteed access to jobs, until government began to retrench in the 1970s (Ginsburg 1983). In the aftermath of its economic crisis that came with the collapse of its currency board, Argentina created *Plan Jefes y Jefas* that guaranteed a job for poor heads of households (Tcherneva and Wray 2007). The program successfully created two million new jobs that not only provided employment and income for poor families, but also provided needed services and free goods to poor neighborhoods. More recently, India passed the National Rural Employment Guarantee Act (2005) that commits the government to providing employment in a public works project to any adult living in a rural area. The job must be provided within fifteen days of registration, and must provide employment for a minimum of 100 days per year (Hirway 2006).

If the goal of public policy is full employment the only way it can really be achieved and maintained is through direct job creation. A JG program will act as stabilizer during recessions but it can also be designed to tackle the question of structural unemployment by first employing and then training the long-term unemployed, on the job. This will increase their chance of being employed in the private sector again. It will provide every American who wants to work not with a job but with a decent job.

Many of the fears of the critics of JG have been shown to be fallacious both by theory and by real world exchanges. Job creation, even on a massive scale and under difficult circumstances, can be successful as the Jefes experience showed (Tcherneva and Wray 2007). Participants welcome the chance to work, viewing participation as empowering. The program can be democratically implemented, increasing participation in the political process, and with relatively few instances of corruption and bureaucratic waste. Useful projects can be undertaken—as the U.S. New Deal programs still show.

Conclusion

The Minsky half century

John Kenneth Galbraith's book, *The Great Crash*, argued that the economy on the verge of the Great Depression was so fragile that it was just waiting for some event to cause the crisis. It does not really matter what that triggering event was—it could have been anything—and we think that is also true of 2007. If one had to identify a primary weakness it was in the U.S. housing market, specifically the problem with mortgages underwritten on the basis of expected refinancing or home sales. While this was preeminent among the non-prime mortgages, prime mortgages were far from immune from this decline in the quality of underwriting. Some prime mortgages have recorded a default rate as high as that on subprime mortgages, and have recorded a rising default rate as early as subprime mortgages. Financial fragility spread to the rest of the financial system through the layering of debts promoted by securitization and derivatives. This layering of debts, combined with the poor quality of debts, made the U.S and some European countries prone to a debt deflation. Thus, while many have called the 2007 financial crisis a subprime crisis, it is more accurate to call it an underwriting crisis. Regardless of credit risk, expected repayment increasingly became dependent on a bonanza based on rising home prices and this is what made a debt deflation possible.

The triggering event was in early spring of 2007, when news came that homeowners were defaulting on their very first home payments, which had never happened before. For anyone paying attention that indicated something was really wrong. We had been warning about problems in real estate since 2000, and in 2005 had identified the relation between President Bush's "ownership society" and the housing bubble—arguing it would lead to a massive transfer of wealth to the rich when the bubble burst (Wray 2005). The rising default rate on mortgages triggered massive deleveraging and decline in asset prices that reinforced each other.

This book provides an explanation of the causes of the financial crisis from the point of view of Minsky's theoretical framework. The book argues that the economic changes that led to the Great Recession can be traced back to the 1970s, when a new form of capitalism progressively emerged to replace Managerial Capitalism—Money Manager Capitalism (MMC). MMC is a highly unstable form of capitalism with huge pools of funds under management by professionals, each seeking the highest return. Not only was the amount of funds massive but, managed money was largely unregulated, and was able to compete with the regulated banks. This played a role in the rise of what came to be called "shadow banks" and many have pointed to that portion of the financial system as an important contributor to the crisis. Indeed, much of the deregulation of banks was designed to allow them to compete with the less regulated, lower cost, and more highly leveraged shadow banks. To compete, banks created off-balance sheet entities that took huge risks without supervision. Those risks came back to banks when the crisis hit. It is difficult to imagine how we could have had the global financial crisis without the rise of money managers and the shadow banks.

This book shows that Ponzi finance is a central feature of MMC. As such, MMC requires rapid continuous growth in the price of some assets to be viable—commercial real estate in the 1980s, the stock market in the 1990s, housing in the 2000s, and now commodities. This rapid growth in asset prices probably ends up generating a bubble. However, this book also shows that Ponzi finance is a more important concept than bubbles for the purpose of economic stability. Ponzi finance means that leverage and asset prices end up going up together and feeding on each other. Higher leverage requires higher collateral value and so higher asset prices, and the funding of assets at a price that grows faster than income rises requires higher leverage. This is the crucial dynamic regardless of the correctness of the value of asset prices because, bubble or not, the size of a potential debt deflation grows with the duration of the use of Ponzi finance. Without Ponzi finance there cannot be a debt deflation because there is no leverage involved in the asset-price appreciation.

Chapter 1 presents the conceptual framework used in the rest of the book. This framework is not narrowed to changes in risk aversion of individuals and a tendency for irrational choices during a boom. While psychological propensities do affect debt aversion and risk aversion, they mostly reflect rational decisions in the sense that the information available and the prevailing incentives encourage economic units to take more risk on the liability and asset sides of their balance sheet. Large businesses have some profitability target to meet that is largely invariant with the growth of their assets thereby pushing them to innovate and to use leverage to reach that target. Periods of economic stability feed the models used by bankers to value assets and estimate creditworthiness with information that suggests that leverage is safe and risk-taking is warranted. In addition, policy decisions in terms of fiscal stand, interest rate, regulation, and supervision dramatically affect the growth of financial fragility. Given the trade deficit of a nation, fiscal austerity negatively impacts the finances of the domestic private sector, fine-tuning leads the central bank to raise its interest rate during a period of stability, and a lack of government regulation and supervision promotes dangerous financial innovations and fraud.

In the end, the core reason for instability has to be found in the nature of the economic system we use today and the failure to put in place means to constrain the destabilizing tendencies of market forces, and to promote market forces that contribute to a healthy cleansing of debts during periods of instability and long-term gains in well-being during periods of economic stability. Minsky argued that a big government (central bank and treasury) is needed to stabilize the economy, but he also understood that having a big government creates new problems by changing incentives and behaviors. A big government should account for these issues through proper regulation, supervision, and enforcement, and by ensuring that "a depression without a depression" (Minsky 1975b: 350) is possible, that is to say, that the economy can go through the cleansing effects of a depression (increase in prudence, increase in the liquidity of portfolios, decrease in leveraging, prosecution of frauds, and liquidation of unsound private companies) without the negative effects (widespread indiscriminate bankruptcies, high unemployment, wastage).

Chapter 2 explains how U.S. capitalism evolved after the Great Depression of the 1930s by using the stage approach developed by Minsky. Following the Great Depression and World War Two, the U.S. financial structure was tightly regulated, banks were flooded with default-free liquid treasury securities, and the federal government was actively present in the development of the economy. This led to a long period of economic stability characterized by strong and sustained economic growth and shared prosperity, in which businesses flourished and households made substantial economic gains. However, this long period of stability also set the stage for the emergence of an economic structure that contributes to economic instability by promoting the use of debt, and by making financial markets a central source of income for households and businesses on the basis of short-term economic results and capital gains. This tendency for instability was reinforced by the dismantlement of the financial regulatory structure of the New Deal that had become inadequate to deal with changes in the economic and policy environment, and by the pro-market policies that were put in place to replace New Deal regulations. This economic system puts money managers at the center of economic dynamics and is strikingly similar to Finance Capitalism that prevailed prior to the Great Depression, except for the size of government involvement in the economy. This size is what prevented the Great Recession from turning into a Great Depression.

Chapter 3 explains how Money Manager Capitalism is at the root of the current economic crisis. Policy makers continued the deregulatory and desupervisory trends of the 1970s and through fiscal austerity forced the domestic private sector to go into debt in order to sustain their standard of living. This led to a large increase in the use of debt and a dramatic decline in the quality of underwriting. The increase in the use of leverage was especially strong in the household and the financial sectors that both recorded rising debt-to-GDP ratios from the 1970s. What made things worse was that this leverage became tied to expectations of continuously rising asset prices. This created a debt inflation that became stronger and stronger as economic stability prevailed and economic units dared to venture in more risky financial practices.

When the upward dynamic stops a debt deflation occurs unless the government is willing (and able) to step in. However, more than just the size of the involvement of the government, the quality of this involvement is also important. Through regulation, supervision, and enforcement the government can limit this destabilizing feature of capitalism while promoting the cleansing elements of capitalism. And by intervening to sustain macroeconomic income and to limit the rise of the cost of debt, the government can break a debt deflation. Unfortunately, the responses of the Bush and Obama Administrations have been highly dissatisfactory because they have used big government to protect the bankers and financial markets that were at the core of the Great Recession, and have only paid lip-service to the nonfinancial sector, especially households. Thus, the short-term economic stability provided by big government has created huge moral hazard and so has increased the long-term instability of the economy. We did not have a "depression without a depression."

Chapters 4 and 5 provide some policy suggestions to use big government in a way that promotes long-term shared prosperity. Chapter 4 shows that two central principles that should guide financial policy should be the promotion of hedge finance and the detection of the growth of financial fragility as defined by the hedge/speculative/Ponzi classification. The chapter provides a measure of financial fragility for housing finance that shows that, from the late 1990s, in the U.S. there was a growing reliance on refinancing and asset liquidation to underwrite loans. The same was true in the UK and France even though France experienced a slower increase in fragility because some of the financial innovations in the mortgage industry did not exist there until 2005. This upward instability generated by the positive feedback loop between asset prices and debt is what ultimately led to the Great Recession. While the index was only applied to housing finance, the logic behind its construction can be applied to any economic activity. Beyond the detection of financial fragility, one must also put in place a financial structure that promotes economic stability. The current financial structure, with its reliance on giant Wall Street banks and financial-market-based retirement solutions, must go. Instead, one should promote small-to-medium size banks that are close to their community, and should boost Social Security benefits to guarantee a decent level of nominal income at retirement. People can still be free to use their savings as they wish but they should not expect any guarantee by government on financial market placements, nor should they receive tax benefits from saving. In order to sustain real income for the elderly, an investment program in infrastructures for elders is needed together with greater social services and an increase in the productivity of workers, through education and technological improvement.

While Chapter 4 proposes policy that affects the financial side of the economy, Chapter 5 focuses on the productive side of the economy and more specifically employment. Chapter 5 shows that putting in place a decentralized, federally funded, job guarantee program helps to promote stable full employment while also contributing to economic development and the improvement of the quality of the labor force. Work is the main source of income for the majority of the population, and it is also the main means to socialize and feel a sense of accomplishment. Through a job guarantee program, the government will contribute to maintain and improve the productivity, skills, and morale of the working age population, and will promote a shared prosperity through a provision of activities that are socially needed. The socio-economic benefits are numerous and go beyond the short-term stabilization of the economy.

Finally, Chapters 4 and 5 show that to stop a debt deflation one needs to care for both the liquidity crisis and the solvency crisis. The liquidity crisis is easy and quick to solve—just have the central bank act as lender of last resort. The solvency crisis requires more time to be solved but the starting point to deal with it should be the borrowers, not the lenders. Borrowers are the ones who cannot, or are unwillingly to, pay so one must first find a way to change that. The goal is to decrease the liquidation pressures by trying to make sure that borrowers can afford to hold onto their assets. This is done not only by sustaining their income through macroeconomic policies but also by lowering their debt service through a restructuring of debts. Restructuring of debts may not help all borrowers but it will usually help the majority of them. Once this problem is solved, lenders will return to long-term profitability even though they may have to accept a short-term loss following debt relief. This short-term loss may be so large that it can block the resolution of the solvency crisis; in that case, the government should step in to purchase old financial claims and to issue new ones on more affordable terms.

Unfortunately, the current approach of solving the housing crisis has mostly taken the exact opposite route. The goal has been to help the lenders in order to encourage them to lend more. But in a solvency crisis, one does not want to encourage more lending to already over-indebted economic units. The goal is to reduce leverage while also avoiding a massive liquidation of assets.

The relevance of Minsky's theoretical framework

As the 2007 global financial crisis unfolded and spread, it became evident that policy makers and most economists were not able to explain what was going on. Most academics had been using an economic framework that led them to conclude that the promotion of output-price stability by central banks had been a major contributor to financial stability and smooth economic growth. Together with policies focused on the promotion of economic liberalism (either through deregulation, desupervision, and/or deenforcement), output-price stability was seen as the main reason for the Great Moderation. Markets were supposed to allocate risks to the entities most able to bear them, funds were said to be allocated to the most deserving economic units, and a wider segment of the population was supposedly able to participate in the economic prosperity thanks to the flexibility and innovative characteristics of a freer financial sector.

Thus, the majority of economists, policy makers, and other pundits were not paying attention and were taken by surprise—or so they claim. That may be true, we do not know. Chairman Greenspan argued in 2004 that rising mortgage debt among U.S. households was not a problem because their wealth was rising thanks to rapidly rising home prices (Greenspan 2004). Similarly, Professor

Mishkin (then, a member of the Fed board) came to the Levy Economics Institute in April 2007 to give a talk, focused almost entirely on the dangers of inflation pressures. He argued that the economy had been growing too swiftly, proclaiming that

> Since the spring of 2006, however, the expansion of the U.S. economy appears to have been undergoing a transition to a more moderate and sustainable pace. Although such a transition will no doubt be marked by some bumps in the road, it represents a desired macroeconomic rebalancing that over the longer run can help ensure sustained noninflationary growth.
>
> (Mishkin in Levy Economics Institutes 2007: 18)

By that time there was a lot of evidence already accumulating that a debt deflation was coming, but Mishkin argued that any problems in subprimes would not spill over and said he preferred to focus on the "good news" in housing.

Hyman P. Minsky had long provided a theoretical framework that helps us to understand why major financial crises occur, and he rapidly became a "must read" as the financial crises grew in size. The global financial crisis was termed the "Minsky Moment" and Minsky was rapidly associated with bubbles, manias, and crashes. This book shows that Minsky's theoretical framework is much richer than that, and that the Minsky Moment is not where his main contribution can be found. The main point of his framework is to show that during periods of economic stability, economic units make sensible economic decisions that push them to use more leverage and decrease the quality of this leverage, while also engaging in more risky activities. The boom phase, with its highly inflated asset prices and disregard for risks on assets and liability sides, is only the end result of the earlier dynamics.

The reason why stability is destabilizing has many roots but Minsky was convinced that the nature of the current economic system had a lot to do with it. Capitalism, with its growth-oriented and money-oriented focuses, is an unstable economic system. This instability can be reduced through proper government involvement given a set of institutions but this gain of stability is only temporary. Capitalism is a highly innovative and constantly changing economic system and government involvement should account for those characteristics. Unfortunately, government usually does not do so and may actually promote instability by promoting policies that reinforce the destabilizing characteristics of capitalism, which is what has happened over the past forty years.

Minsky started writing about the inherent instability of capitalism in the late 1950s. He tracked the evolution of the economy, and argued that we were moving toward an economy where "it" (a Fisher's type debt deflation) could happen again. He continually adapted his theory to take account of what was going on. For example, his Financial Instability Hypothesis was originally more about the business cycle, but, later, by the end of the 1980s, it was more about this longer-term transformation of the economy. So the Financial Instability Hypothesis evolved to an explanation of a long-term transformation, not a business cycle explanation. This culminated in his development of the stages approach applied to the U.S.—the evolution from Hilferding's "Finance Capitalism" (that failed in 1929), the rise of "Managerial Capitalism" after World War Two with its New Deal protections, and finally to what he called the current stage; "Money Manager Capitalism."

Summary of the causes of the global financial crisis: a Minskyan view

The final report of the Financial Crisis Inquiry Commission (FCIC) makes a strong case that the global financial crisis was foreseeable and avoidable. It did not "just happen"; it had nothing to do with "black swans with fat tails"; it was not an extreme event that "Nature" drew randomly from a set of possible outcomes. Rather, it was created by the biggest banks, under the noses of our "public stewards" (the regulators). According to the FCIC Report, the global financial crisis represents a dramatic failure of corporate governance and risk management, in large part a result of an unwarranted and unwise focus by financial institutions on trading (actually, gambling) and rapid growth. We could go farther and note that, in all this, the biggest banks were aided and abetted by government "regulators" and "supervisors" who not only failed to properly oversee these institutions, but, indeed, continually pushed for deregulation and desupervision in favor of "self-regulation" and "self-supervision."

While the FCIC report does "name names" and accurately identifies practices and even individuals who are culpable, there is merit in the complaint made by the Republican minority report as well as by reviewers that there is some danger in focusing on "bad actors," bad financial practices, and "bad events" (Nocera 2011; Morgenson 2011) It is important to understand longer-term trends. We need to put the crisis in the context of the long-term postwar transformation of the financial system. In that sense, even if the "apples" were not bad, the system was.

The view taken in this book deviates somewhat from the FCIC report's conclusion: financial fragility had grown on trend, making "it" (in the words of Hyman P. Minsky, referring to a Fisher's type debt-deflation) likely to "happen again"—even without "bad" behaviors by institutions and their regulators. For that reason, we need to understand the "Minskyan" transformation—so that while the global financial crisis was not strictly inevitable, the financial structure made a crisis highly probable.

From Managerial Capitalism to Money Manager Capitalism: financialization of the economy and disengagement of the government

Financialization points to the rising role of finance in the economy, increasing leverage, increasing layering of debt on top of debt, and a greater share of GDP going to the financial system and to interest rather than profit. A telling measure of financialization is the ratio of financial-institution liabilities to GDP which indicates something new had occurred in recent years. We can think of this as financial layering: financial institutions borrowing from each other to lend. This led to complex linkages, such that failure of one financial institution (Bear Stearns or Lehman Brothers) would topple all the others that held its liabilities. This explanation clearly highlights one of the greatest indicators of financial fragility, and we think it is the closest to Minsky's explanation.

In order to understand why the financial sector gained such preeminence by the 1980s, one needs to go back over half a century. Following World War Two, Managerial Capitalism recorded a long period of shared economic prosperity until the end of the 1960s. There were some recessions but, similar to the later period of the Great Moderation, they were mild and short. This "Golden Age" period of prosperity provided the ideal conditions for financial and nonfinancial businesses to take more risk on the asset and liability sides of their balance sheet, because of declining risk perception and pressures from the profit motive. In addition, the Golden Age allowed many households to save substantial amounts of money and to look for higher returns than offered by savings accounts. Combined with policies that favored private pension funds, the growth of financial wealth led to the progressive emergence of money managers as a central component of economic dynamics.

After 1974, median male earnings stopped growing and began to fall, the social safety net was reduced, and unemployment came to be seen as something of a policy-making tool used to keep inflation down (the so-called "Phillips curve" trade-off). Given that income stagnated, some households had to rely on debt and draw down their savings in order to be able to afford expenses such as housing, health care, and education. This trend toward the higher use of debt to maintain or improve standards of living was further reinforced in the 1980s as the shared prosperity of the Golden Age was replaced with declining economic growth and rising inequalities and poverty. The 1990s fiscal austerity policies also pushed the domestic private sector to use more debt. With the growing use of debt, the role of money managers expanded even further, especially after banks tried to find means to unload illiquid financial claims from their balance sheets through securitization.

Finally, elected representatives and regulators slowly chipped away at the New Deal reforms that had promoted growth while providing social protection. Financial institutions were deregulated and desupervised, and their power began to grow in a self-reinforcing manner: as they were able to capture a greater share of profits, their political power increased, making it possible for them to further subvert or eliminate regulations to gain an even larger share of profits.

Money Manager Capitalism: rising inequalities and the promotion of Ponzi finance

By the time of the global financial crisis the financial sector accounted for 20 percent of U.S. national value added and 30 percent of corporate profits. By itself, the financial sector was an autonomous source of growth and also of rising inequality due to high compensation in the sector. Up to half of the college graduates from the elite colleges went into the financial sector because rewards there were far higher than in other sectors. Compensation at the very top quite simply exploded and shifted away from salary toward stocks and stock options.

Minsky called this new stage "Money Manager Capitalism" to draw attention to a characteristic feature: huge pools of funds under management by professionals—pension funds, sovereign wealth funds, hedge funds, university endowments, corporate treasuries, and so on. Every money manager had to beat the average return to retain clients, something that is, of course, statistically impossible. But the combination of such incentives and virtually no government regulation or oversight encouraged not only risky behaviors but also ethically compromised actions.

Moreover, a major problem from the point of view of economic stability was that the sheer volume of financial wealth under management outstripped socially useful investments. To keep returns high, money managers and bankers had to turn to increasingly esoteric financial speculation—in areas that not only failed to serve the public purpose but also actively subverted it. An example would be the rise of index speculation in commodities markets, which drives up global energy and food prices and ultimately leads to hunger and even starvation around the world. The dot-com bubble is another example: here, speculators drove up the stock prices of Internet companies with no business model or prospective profits. The inevitable crash wiped out hundreds of billions of dollars in wealth.

What was really important was the dynamic created by the shift of power away from banks and toward the very lightly regulated "money managers" at the "shadow banks." To compete, banks needed to subvert regulations through innovations and then to have regulations legislatively eliminated. This allowed banks to increase leverage ratios, and thus risk, in order to keep pace with shadow banking practices. There was a "Gresham's law" in operation: those institutions that could reduce capital ratios and loss reserves the most quickly were able to increase net earnings and thus rewards to management and investors. Further, there was a shift to maximization of share prices as one of the main goals of management—which supposedly aligned the interests of shareholders and top managers who received stock options in compensation. That in turn encouraged a short-term focus on performance in equity markets, which—as we already discovered in 1929—is accomplished through market manipulation (both legal and illegal).

Financial innovations emerged to bypass regulatory barriers, to find new profit opportunities, and to account for the great volatility of funding cost. It is not clear that many of these innovations serve a social purpose beyond making the top management of financial institutions incredibly rich. Indeed, many of the most celebrated "advances" have been the most subject to abuse. Both "junk bonds" and mortgage-backed securities, for example, were hailed as ways to limit risk through various types of portfolio diversification. In each case, however, the greater complexity of the transactions necessary to diversify the holdings made it easier to disguise market manipulation, customer deception, or outright fraud. For these new products to deliver their supposed advantages without undermining market stability would have required much greater oversight than the relatively more transparent transactions that preceded them.

In contrast, the New Deal reforms promoted stability by limiting commercial banks to activities that could be easily supervised—the distribution of toasters to attract depositors (a way to get around the Regulation Q restriction on using interest rates to attract customers) is much easier to oversee than a market for collateralized debt obligations. Some of the innovations had nothing to do with extending credit, but rather allowed speculators to bet on the failure of debtors to make promised payments; others allowed speculators to bet on inflation of food prices. As if it were not bad enough, speculation in these types of instruments could sometimes influence markets in a self-fulfilling manner: by betting on bankruptcy, speculators caused borrowing costs to rise on floating rate debt, thus ensuring that default was more likely.

At the same time, the structure of incentives and rewards was changed such that risky bets, high leverage ratios, and short-term profits were promoted over long-term firm survival and returns to investors. A good example of the transformation was the conversion of the venerable investment banks from partnerships to publicly held firms with hired and richly rewarded management. While the structure was somewhat different, the results were similar to those that led up to the 1929 crash—the "pump and dump" incentives through which management would "pump" asset and equity prices, and then sell out ("dump") their own positions before the speculative boom collapsed. By the early 2000s, the coalescence of three different phenomena made the positions taken by the biggest financial institutions precarious: (1) the return of "pump and dump" strategies; (2) the move from partnerships to corporate form, which increases the agency problems (institutions run in the interests of management, not owners); and (3) excessive executive compensation that was tied to short-term performance, which increases the pressures to do anything that justifies huge bonuses.

All these created an economic environment highly conducive to the emergence of Ponzi finance. In fact, financial engineers created financial instruments that required Ponzi finance to be profitable. The move of mortgage securitization from an income-based business to a capital-gain-based business is one of the most important evolutions toward the spread of Ponzi finance through the economy and it accumulated into the housing boom. Nothing is more emblematic of the speculative excess than the special collateralized debt obligations that allowed hedge fund managers to bet against homeowners and the holders of securitized mortgages. Financial institutions also placed lots of bets against American homeowners. And, finally, it was this demand by investment banks and other speculators for risky instruments on which they could place bets that generated the risky "subprime," "alt-A," and even "prime" mortgages that eventually brought on the global financial crisis.

Fraud

Fraud was involved at every step in the "home-finance food chain." The mortgage broker was rewarded for putting prospective homeowners into mortgages with the worst possible terms. Brokers often doctored the documents after signing—to make the terms even worse. Property appraisers were rewarded for overstating property values (so that mortgages would be larger than they should have been). The biggest financial institutions created the Mortgage Electronic Registry System (MERS) to evade fees owed to county recorders to register each sale of mortgages; MERS then apparently separated the mortgage "note" from the "deed," destroying a clear chain of title as it cut corners. The mortgage securitizers (investment banks) issued false "reps and warranties" in their descriptions of the mortgages backing the securities, and frequently failed to follow rules regarding the securitization process itself (the trustees apparently falsely asserted they held the mortgages—which in most cases were held by servicers, or intentionally destroyed).[1] Mortgage servicers hired "robo-signers" to manufacture documents needed for foreclosures; they have been accused of "losing" payments and falsely claiming that borrowers were delinquent, and they even tried to foreclose on homeowners who held no mortgage at all. Accountants signed off on fudged balances. Even though the Obama Administration has refrained from going after top management, the banks have been forced to pay fine after fine, and the attorney generals of the fifty states took action to force banks to pay billions in damages. As of Fall 2012, while few criminal investigations have begun, many civil cases have already been decided against financial institutions and hundreds of billions of dollars in damages remain on the line.

Goldilocks growth, government budgets, and financial balances

With worker income lagging behind, and with loss of U.S. manufacturing jobs, the financial sector played a big role in the Clinton recovery of the 1990s. Indeed, economic growth was sufficiently robust, and the boost to income at the very top caused federal government tax revenues to grow swiftly (it was called the Goldilocks economy—fast enough to create jobs but not so rapid as to generate inflation) (Godley and Wray 1999). The federal government's budget went into significant surplus for the first time since the late 1920s. While most economists thought that was good and praised President Clinton's projection that the surpluses would continue for at least fifteen years, allowing all federal debt to be retired, a few of us at the Levy Economics Institute (where Minsky worked until his death in 1996) argued that the surplus would be short lived, would kill the boom, and would cause a deep recession because of the negative impact on the finances of the domestic private sector (Wray 1999).

Wynne Godley at the Levy Institute had developed a "three balances" approach to macro analysis based on the accounting identity that the sum of the balances of the domestic private sector, the government sector, and the foreign sector must be zero. While any one of these could run a surplus, at least one of the others would have to run a deficit. In the case of the United States, by the late 1990s the government sector was running a surplus of about 2.5 percent of GDP, the foreign balance was 4 percent of GDP (meaning the U.S. was running a trade deficit), and so by identity the U.S. private sector (firms plus households) had a deficit of 6.5 percent (the sum of the other two). In other words the private sector was spending $106.50 for every $100 of income. Each year that the private sector spent more than its income, it went more deeply into debt.

This was in some sense the "ugly" side of MMC: the growth of financial assets under management was equal to the growth of financial liabilities of *somebody*. For every financial asset there is an equal financial liability. Godley projected that the private sector debt load would become too great, and when spending fell, the economy would slip into recession. That in turn would cause job losses and force defaults on some of the debt. Researchers at the Levy Economics Institute believed that that would set off a severe financial crisis (Godley 1999, 2000; Wray 1998; Godley and Wray 1999).

At the beginning of 2000 that appeared to be happening, but the crisis was not as severe as we expected. The private sector retrenched, spending less than its income, and the Clinton budget surpluses morphed into deficits. The dot-com bubble popped and stock markets tanked. The Fed responded by lowering interest rates as the big budget deficits helped to restore economic growth.

And then something amazing happened: the American consumer started borrowing again—at a pace even greater than during the Clinton boom years. Much of that borrowing took the form of "cash-out refinance" loans for big-ticket consumer items. In other words, the U.S. real estate boom had begun. For ten years, U.S. households would spend more than their incomes, with only a brief respite in the recession of 2001. Nothing like this had ever happened before. And it was aided and abetted by the practices of the money managers, inducing homeowners to go deeply into risky mortgage debt with bad terms that amounted to Ponzi finance.

By 2007, the U.S. ratio of financial liabilities to GDP reached an all-time peak of 500 percent; or, $5 of liability to service out of each $1 of income. While much public debate has been focused on the government debt ratio, the debt-to-GDP ratios of the household sector as well as the nonfinancial and financial business sectors were all much higher in 2007 as a percent of GDP, with government debt a small fraction of the total. Nonfinancial business debt was not a huge problem, since much of this was due to long-term finance of capital equipment—and after 2000, U.S. nonfinancial businesses actually did not borrow much. But household debt became a huge problem and still weighs heavily on consumers, preventing real recovery. What was particularly unusual, and had long been ignored, was the unprecedented rise of financial sector indebtedness, which reached almost 100 to 125 percent of GDP in 2007 depending on the measure of debt used.

The biggest political problem created from the experience of the Clinton years is that the wrong lesson was learned. Many continue to believe that the Clinton era budget surpluses were good for the economy, indeed, they argue that the Goldilocks growth was caused by surpluses and point to the Bush deficits that followed the recession in 2000 (and the Bush tax cuts that are purported to have contributed to "structural" deficits) as fiscally imprudent. And so when the global financial crisis hit the economy, the fiscal response was too small because of fears surrounding the impact of a larger stimulus on the budget deficit. When the economic slowdown lowered tax revenues, the new Obama Administration saw the budget deficit explode to 10 percent of GDP—the highest since World War Two. This generated even more fear about deficits that made it impossible to get additional support for stimulus on the necessary scale. As a result, the economy could not recover in a timely fashion.

Many other countries have experimented with the goal of reaching a government fiscal surplus. In most countries that has meant a drastic decline in the surplus of the private domestic sector and sometimes that sector became a net borrower (as in the U.S.). Prior to the creation of the euro, countries willing to be part of the Eurozone imposed on themselves a drastic decline in government deficit. They then went further and gave up their monetary sovereignty; thereby further limiting their capacity to respond to any economic crisis. This book argues that, for a monetarily sovereign government, the fiscal position of the government is not a proper policy goal even though it is often touted as a highly desired goal for political purposes. National governments should not aim to reach a surplus (or a deficit) but should concentrate on promoting stable full employment and shared prosperity, and should let the fiscal position of the government be whatever it needs to be. Indeed, the fiscal position is an endogenous variable that is ultimately set by the desired net saving of the domestic private sector and the rest of the world. If these desires are not fulfilled, aggregate income will fluctuate until net saving equals its desired level.

At the same time, the Great Recession has shown the dangers of letting domestic private net saving become negative. Indeed, that implies that the amount of net financial assets held by the domestic private sector is declining because borrowing grows faster than the accumulation of financial assets. As a consequence net worth declines unless the nominal value of real assets grows fast enough. This is exactly what happened during the 2000s housing boom when the growth of housing prices was rapid enough to sustain the wealth of households. However, this book also shows that the combined debt and asset-price dynamics generated by declining net financial assets is not sustainable because it involves Ponzi finance.

The lessons we should have learned (but probably did not) from the global financial crisis

1 The Great Recession did not happen by accident

Alan Greenspan compared the Great Recession to a "once-in-a-century credit tsunami." This is a telling analogy. Tsunamis are unpredictable and no one can proactively prevent tsunamis from occurring, or decrease their strength. One can build seawalls (i.e., capital requirement ratios for banks) that can protect against most tsunamis except rare extreme tsunamis, but one cannot blame policy makers for not trying to protect the public. Thus, by comparing the Great Recession to an extreme tsunami, Greenspan is basically saying that nothing could have been done to prevent the crisis because of its size and unpredictability.

This book argues that the Great Recession is, in an important sense, the result of the stability that prevailed during the Great Moderation and the Golden Age. The period of stability and shared prosperity recorded during the Golden Age increased the financial wealth of households, gave businesses and households the confidence to use debt, and promoted a return of free-market thinking as mainstream ideology. These trends led to a growth of the financial sector and a return of free-market thinkers to top government positions.

With the return of free-market thinkers in government, a process of disengagement of the government from economic affairs started as it reduced its purchases of goods and services, cut welfare spending, and deregulated, desupervised, and reduced enforcement. People (such as Greenspan) who did not believe in the benefit of government involvement in the economy (and in fact hated such involvement) were put in government positions that involved making decisions about the role of government in the economy. That could only end in a disaster. Once the top regulators set such a culture, competent and talented government employees who saw benefits in government involvement were soon discouraged and left public services as their actions and initiatives were not only not appreciated but also condemned.

Similar trends also occurred in financial businesses (and also nonfinancial business). Top managers and executives with a broad long-term vision of their business focused on going-concern were replaced by highly individualistic persons with a narrow and short-term vision oriented toward maximizing their personal benefit. The trading floor of financial institutions became a central profit-making machine and successful traders were promoted rapidly. Incentives were changed to make sure that the staff followed the new culture promoted by leadership. In the 1980s, the movie *Wall Street* embodied this trend with Gordon Gecko's famous sentence "Greed is Good." In the 2000s, Gordon came back with the exact same message. This is of course not true for all financial business, but it is true for all the major financial institutions in the U.S. and Europe. However, one has to be careful to avoid assuming that this crisis was due to a natural human propensity for greed. It was rather a planned move toward the promotion of greed and punishment of moderation that helped to create the conditions necessary for the crisis.

The return of free-market thinking also marked a decline in social benefits and working conditions. This led to decline or stagnation of real income and an increase of the financial burden for many families. By putting back on individuals a greater share of responsibilities, but not giving individuals the means to fund the implied financial burden, individuals had to turn to external sources of funds. For example, educational grants were replaced by student loans even as the cost of education soared as state governments decreased their support for public education. As a consequence, the dependence on the financial sector grew even larger as debt was seen (and promoted by bankers) as a means to maintain and increase one's living standard.

2 *The global financial crisis was not a "liquidity crisis"*

Many analysts have labeled the global financial crisis a liquidity crisis—which we think is highly misleading. Yes, there was a liquidity crisis and it took the Fed a long time to figure out what many of us knew: you quell a run to liquidity by lending reserves without limit at a penalty rate to any financial institution that needs them. Eventually the Fed did that (but without the penalty rate), ending that phase of the crisis. However, what we were actually experiencing was massive insolvency across at least the largest financial institutions (both banks and shadow banks) that led to the "run on liquidity." The banks had an insufficient supply of good assets to offer as collateral against loans; they just had trashy real estate derivatives and interbank loans, all backed by little more than a fog of deceit. And that is why it took tens of trillions of lending, spending, and guaranteeing of bad assets by Uncle Sam going beyond normal lender of last resort activities to stop the carnage. As of Fall 2012, the big banks are probably still insolvent. It is only the backing provided by the Treasury and the Fed as well as the "extend and pretend" policy adopted by regulators and government supervisors that keeps them open.

As we know from the Savings and Loan crisis of the 1980s, leaving insolvent institutions open tends to blow the hole bigger—especially when fraudsters are left in charge so they can run what criminologists call "control frauds." During the thrift fiasco, the fraudsters were finally shut down, more than 1,000 were jailed, and the Bush (senior) Administration resolved the crisis with an infusion of about $200 billion, using the Resolution Trust Authority. While that "bailout" was imperfect, at least it stopped the fraud, closed the worst thrifts, and jailed many of the crooks. So far, in this much bigger crisis we have done none of those things.

In order to deal with a solvency crisis, assets, debts, and net worth must be valued carefully, and an analysis of the cash inflows and cash outflows of the borrowers must be performed. The goal is to determine the exact nature and size of the insolvency in order to know what the best alternative is (such as debt renegotiation or debt discharge) to solve the problem. The Great Recession started with problems in the mortgage industry because homeowners could not repay and, as home prices declined, were not willing to repay. Thus, dealing with problems of borrowers should be at the core of any policy to deal with the Great Recession. Unfortunately, only marginal attention, and help, was provided to borrowers; instead most of the focus has been on lenders as trillions of dollars have been used by the government to purchase, or lend against, toxic bank assets at very favorable conditions that do not reflect the size of the problems in the mortgage market (because nothing had been done to carefully check borrowers' solvency).

3 *Underwriting matters*

Underwriting is the process of determining the creditworthiness of borrowers and putting in place incentives to ensure payments will be made as they come due. All the big institutions involved in home finance reduced or eliminated underwriting over the past decade. The Efficient Market Hypothesis said banks really do not need underwriting because markets will discover the proper prices for securitized loans; and lending was so much easier, quicker, and cheaper to do if lenders did not bother to check the financial capacity of the borrower. Hence, banks inevitably ended up making liar's loans and NINJA Loans (no income, no job, no assets, no problem!).

Indeed, if one looks closely at recent financial crises, one finds that the cause is usually deterioration of underwriting standards. Market discipline does not work because when some asset class is booming, lenders come to expect that prices of those assets will continue to rise. They will then lend more relative to value, current income, and expected cash flow because asset price appreciation makes most loans good. If things do not work out, loans can be refinanced, or the collateral can be seized and sold at profit. It goes on until someone questions the boom—and starts to sell assets or refuses to roll-over debt. The discovery that assets are probably overvalued causes prices to reverse course and then to collapse, so borrowers sink underwater and lenders are left insolvent. A run on uninsured liabilities then begins.

That leads to "fire sales" of assets, declining asset prices, and a general liquidity crisis. More importantly in 2008 in the U.S., it was recognized that assets had been tremendously overvalued—so even with Treasury extensions of guarantees (to money market mutual funds, for example) and trillions of dollars of lender of last resort activity by the Fed, no one wanted to refinance banks and shadow banks. Since they relied on each other (rather than on depositors), financial institutions discovered the dangers of "interconnectedness." They tried to delever, to sell toxic assets to the Fed, and to unwind positions.

It appears banks *have* retrenched, tightening standards and cutting off loans to all but the most creditworthy. They apparently learned their lesson? That always happens in the aftermath of a crisis. But the point is that there have been no significant regulatory and supervisory reforms put in place to deal with the next euphoric boom. Hence, underwriting standards will again decline—gradually at first and then with a rush to the bottom, with those lenders willing to adopt the lowest standards "winning." Market "discipline" is always perverse—there is no lending when it is most needed, and no underwriting when *that* is most needed. So, while banks are not lending, they have not been forced to learn any lessons from the global financial crisis.

The main lesson in terms of underwriting is that, for financial stability to prevail, underwriting must focus on the means used to repay debt rather than simply the capacity to repay. Income is the foundation upon which lending should be based if financial stability is to prevail. As long as this prevails and fraud is not prevalent, neither prime nor non-prime lending will promote financial instability if default occurs.

4 Lack of regulation, supervision, and enforcement leads to control frauds

Policy makers still do not want to recognize that fraud is everywhere. We know that the banks committed lender fraud on an unprecedented scale (the best estimate is that 80 percent of all mortgage fraud was committed by lenders); we know they continue to commit foreclosure fraud (and that their creation, MERS—Mortgage Electronic Registry System—has irretrievably damaged the nation's property records; this will take a decade to sort out); and we know they duped investors into buying toxic waste securities (using bait and switch—substituting the worst mortgages into the pools) and then bet against them using credit default swaps. Every time an investigator finally musters the courage to go after one of these banks, fraud is uncovered and a settlement is recovered.

It is apparent that fraud became normal business practice. We can compare the home-finance food chain to Shrek's onion: every layer was not only complex but also fraudulent, from the real estate agents to the appraisers and mortgage brokers who overpriced the property and induced borrowers into terms they could not afford, to the investment banks and their subsidiary trusts that securitized the toxic mortgages, to the credit ratings agencies and accounting firms that validated values and practices, to the servicers and judges who allowed banks to effectively steal homes, and to CEOs and lawyers who signed off on the fraud. To say that this is the biggest scandal in human history is an understatement. And the fraudsters are still running the institutions.

But the worst part is the cover-up. We should have known since the Watergate years that it is the cover-up that leads to the worst crimes.

If one considers the real estate food chain, it all begins with some lowly mortgage broker. He is told that if he can increase his throughput and induce borrowers to take more expensive loans than they actually qualify for, his rewards will be increased. The lender banks thus created Orwellian-named "affordability products" that insiders called neutron bomb mortgages (designed to blow up and kill the borrower, but leave the home standing) and told the brokers to make those and to refuse the usual documents required for loans—such as W-2 forms to verify income and bank account information to verify wealth. Why? Because then banks could claim they did not know they were making loans that could not be repaid.

Once a bank has made a Liar's Loan, every other link in the home finance chain *must be tainted*. The only questions remaining for everyone operating in that chain were these: how can we make a buck?, how can we get out of this pyramid scheme before it collapses?, and how can we stay out of jail? As we know, they made the bucks as they were rewarded with multi-million dollar bonuses. While most did not exit before the collapse, Uncle Sam covered their losses with trillions of dollars of bail-out. And now top bank management waits for the statute of limitations on their probable crimes to run out while the nation's top cops look the other way.

Unfortunately, we have not learned any of these lessons. We have done no reforming. We let the Ponzi schemes continue, run by the same crooks.

Are we actually on the road to recovery?

We believe reform will become possible when the next big crisis hits. That may be sooner than anyone expects because we reproduced the conditions of 2007, so this is similar to the 1929 situation analyzed by Galbraith: we are just waiting for a trigger. When it hits, the crisis is going to roll through the system again. The bail-out actually increased concentration and the linkages among the top four or five banks making the system even more fragile than it was in 2007. The next crisis could be worse than the previous one—which has been the general trend since the first postwar crisis in 1966. Let us see why.

Most of the private debt that we had in 2007 still exists. Households have repaid some, and they have defaulted on some, but most of it still exists. Meanwhile, households have lost their jobs, and a lot of them have lost their houses—which does not mean they have lost the debt because in a lot of cases they still owe the money but they do not have the house. House prices have declined by about a third across the country. So there is no way that households and firms are better off now than they were in 2007. Meanwhile, they have run up other kinds of debt—including student loans that now amount to $1 trillion. In most ways they are much worse. A wave of defaults on commercial real estate could be the next thing to hit. Or, student loans or credit card debts could trigger the next crisis as the value of those assets gets downgraded. That is one path back into crisis.

There is another avenue for contagion. Many people think that European banks are more fragile than American banks, so the problem could start in Europe, then spill over to the United States. For example, there is a path from U.S. money-market mutual funds' holdings of Eurobank assets to a global financial crisis. MMMFs have issued $3 trillion of extremely short-term liabilities that are like deposits but not insured. Last time, the U.S. government extended the guarantee to all of them; Dodd–Frank outlaws such intervention. So appearance of a problem among Eurobanks could bring down the MMMF market—about twice the size of the U.S. subprime mortgages that brought on the global financial crisis last time.

Ultimately, the trigger is really not that important, what matters is that the economic system that allowed financial instability to become prevalent has not been significantly transformed post-Great Recession. If anything, big banks have become bigger and their trading activity in exotic derivatives is as strong as ever; pension funds continue to grow in importance relative to public retirement programs like Social Security; income inequalities are still worsening. However, the growth model upon which the US has relied is broken—debt-led consumption and investment growth will not bring any major economic prosperity. We might have to wait for an actual new Great Depression for Money Manager Capitalism to fall definitively and, hopefully, for things to change for the best.

Appendix
Adjusted L5 data

For the government, net debt is approximated by taking "federal government total liabilities" and "state and local governments, excluding employee retirement funds total liabilities" and by removing any monetary, life insurance, and pension liabilities. For the private sector, the following steps were taken to retrieve domestic private total liabilities:

1   Take "domestic nonfinancial sectors total liabilities" from the flow of funds accounts. This is the total liabilities of the domestic economy (private and public) excluding the financial sector.
2   Remove "state and local governments, excluding employee retirement funds total liabilities" and "federal government total liabilities." This provides domestic private nonfinancial sectors total liabilities.
3   In order to find domestic private total liabilities, one needs to find the total liabilities of the financial sector. The Census Bureau calculates the latter by excluding bank deposits, bank notes in circulation, and pension and life insurance reserves of all sorts. This is done by:

   a   Taking "financial business total liabilities" from flow of funds data. It includes the liabilities monetary authorities, GSEs, and private financial sector. Liabilities do not include corporate equities.
   b   Removing all deposits, pension reserves, life insurance reserves, money market mutual funds shares, mutual funds shares, and total liabilities of government (monetary authorities, government pension funds reserves, treasury currency).

4   The sum of step 2 and step 3 are added to find total domestic private total liabilities.

Notes

1 The Minskian framework

1 In the U.S., Edward Bernays was a central figure in the creation and promotion consumerism (Curtis 2002).
2 Of course, the indirect legal, reputational, and financial costs of entering a Ponzi process may be immense, as their participants may end up figuring out that they are not going to be able to make it.
3 Some have argued that Hilferding's analysis applies directly only to the European situation (which relied on banks) and not to the U.S. (which was more "market oriented"). We will not go into that controversy because it is not important to our argument. The essential characteristics of early Finance Capitalism are: relatively small government, use of external finance, and growing concentration of economic power in the hands of "trusts"—or what we might today call megacorporations with varied interests and diverse affiliations across "industry," "finance," and "insurance."
4 Youngman (1906) provides an interesting account of the relative decline of the commercial paper around the turn of the last century (an instrument used for short-term lending to firms) and the rise of direct investments by financial institutions in stocks and bonds. She argues that

> the banks, far from acting independently, operate as part of a larger industrial and financial whole, and that the union of the principal banking, trust, and insurance companies of the country [...] merely reflects the trend of development of this more comprehensive alliance. It is, in fact but one aspect of the general movement toward an extension of investment interests together with a concentration of group control [...]. It is the necessary consequence, as it is the essential condition, of the effectual carrying through by large groups of investors of big railroad and industrial enterprises. Each group has its own financial backing which it brings to the support of any undertaking, and when several groups combine, their several financial interests also become allied.
>
> (Youngman 1906: 438–439)

She goes on to describe how investment banks that underwrite securities and stock issues end up accumulating positions in these assets—sometimes to keep prices up. Thus, the argument that the U.S. was more "market based" is perhaps overstated since banks held a lot of the "marketed" instruments.
5 Micromanagement would be left to individual initiatives. The goal of the government is to control the overall direction of the system, not all prices and production processes (Minsky 1986a: 293, 308).
6 This does not mean that welfare and Social Security should be eliminated. Future contributors (children) and past contributors (retirees) to the economic welfare of developed societies deserve to be helped. However, an opportunity to work should be

offered to those who are able and willing to contribute presently to the economic welfare of the society.

2 From Managerial Capitalism to Money Manager Capitalism

1 There was still one obstacle to full monetary sovereignty because of the Bretton Woods system. Under this system, the U.S. government managed the exchange rate between gold and the U.S. dollar, and allowed foreign governments to convert U.S. dollars into gold on demand. This fixed exchange rate regime constrained the degree of maneuver of the federal government because the latter had to be preoccupied by too large out-flows of dollars (through trade, income, or financial positions) relative to the dollar demand of the rest of the world. Fortunately for the United States, its gold hoards were substantial and dollar demand was large because of the role of the U.S. dollar in com-mercial transactions, and, more importantly, because of the role of the U.S. dollar in the Bretton Woods system. As a consequence, the United States has had to run a current account deficit to be able to meet the demand for U.S. dollars by the rest of the world, effectively taking the position of central banker of the world (Minsky 1986b). It takes "two to tango" to run a trade deficit—the U.S. wants consumer goods and the rest of the world wants U.S. dollars.

2 The payment of the fee depends on how subordinated the claim of the servicer is. Bank of America may take a fee upfront or the fee payment may depend on the existence of an excess spread, or a combination of both fee payment procedures may be used (Kothari 2006: 725).

3 The term asset-backed security is used more or less broadly. In the broadest sense, it means all securities issued by SPE (from mortgage-backed securities to structured finance collateralized debt obligations). In the strictest sense, it excludes resecuritiza-tion and mortgage-backed securities.

4 Unless the servicer can prove that repossession and liquidation of the underlying col-lateral (Joe's car) will not allow the servicer to recover the amount of advance pay-ments he is about to make.

5 The proportion of credit support to provide in order to obtain a specific rating, is deter-mined by credit rating agencies as a function of a multiple of the expected loss of capital on the pool expressed as a proportion of the par value of the pool. The expected loss (e.g., as commonly calculated by "value-at-risk") depends on the default prob-ability (p) (i.e., the capacity to recover the outstanding principal through the liquidation of the collateral), and the exposure (E) (i.e., amount advanced): the average expected loss equals $p(1-R)E$ (Kothari 2006: 221ff.; International Monetary Fund 2008a: 63ff.; Tavakoli 2001: 132).

5 Policy implications for employment

1 This chapter relies heavily on "Universal job guarantee program: Towards true full employment," a mimeograph by L.R. Wray and Y. Nersisyan.

Conclusion: the Minsky half-century

1 In one notorious case, Goldman Sachs let hedge fund manager John Paulson handpick the riskiest mortgages to put into securities that would be purchased by investors such as pension funds. Goldman then created CDOs that would pay off if the homeowners were not able to make their mortgage payments, meaning that the securities the inves-tors bought would fall in value. The investors would lose, the homeowners would lose their homes, and Paulson would win! Goldman, of course, won too—it got income in the form of fees for creating the securities, and also for creating the instrument that let Paulson win (Eisinger and Bernstein 2010; Financial Crisis Inquiry Commission 2011).

References

Adelson, A. (2005) "CDO/credit derivatives 2005: Conference notes," Nomura *Fixed Income Research*, April.

Adelson, A. (2006) "MBS basics," Nomura Securities International Inc., Research Paper, March.

Aglietta, M. (1998) *Le Capitalisme de Demain*, Paris: Fondation Saint-Simon.

Aglietta, M. (2000) "Shareholder value and corporate governance: Some tricky questions," *Economy and Society*, 29 (1): 146–159.

Appelbaum, B. (2009) "Fed held back as evidence mounted on subprime loan abuses," *Washington Post*, September 27.

Arza, V. and Español, P. (2008) "*Les Liaisons Dangereuses*: A Minskyan approach to the relation of credit and investment in Argentina during the 1990s," *Cambridge Journal of Economics*, 32 (5): 739–759.

Aspachs, O., Goodhart, C.A.E., Tsomocos, D.P., and Zicchino, L. (2007) "Towards a measure of financial fragility," *Annals of Finance*, 3 (Special Issue): 37–74.

Aspromourgos, T. (2000) "Is an employer-of-last-resort policy sustainable? A review article," *Review of Political Economy*, 12 (2): 141–155.

Associated Press (2009) "AP IMPACT: Gov't mortgage partners sued for abuses," *New York Times*, August 5.

Badger, A.J. (1989) *The New Deal: The Depression Years, 1933–1940*, Chicago, IL: Ivan R. Dee.

Bailey, S.K. (1950) *Congress Makes a Law: The Story Behind the Employment Act of 1946*, New York: Columbia University Press.

Baker, D. (2002) "The run-up in home prices: Is it real or is it another bubble?" Center for Economic and Policy Research, Briefing Paper, August.

Baltensperger, E. and Dermine, J. (1987) "Banking deregulation in Europe," *Economic Policy*, 2 (4): 63–109.

Bank for International Settlements (2008) *Credit Risk Transfer: Developments from 2005 to 2007*, Basel: Bank for International Settlements.

Bårdsen, G., Lindquist, K.-G., and Tsomocos, D.P. (2008) "Evaluation of macroeconomic models for financial stability analysis," *Journal of World Economic Review*, 3 (1): 7–32.

Barkin, S. (ed.) (1974) *Worker Militancy and Its Consequences: 1965–1975*, New York: Praeger Publishers.

Barth, J.R., Caprio Jr., G., and Levine, R. (2012) *Guardians of Finance: Making Regulators Work for Us*, Cambridge, MA: MIT Press.

Bell, J. (2000) "Leading indicator models of banking crises: A critical review," Bank of England *Financial Stability Review*, December: 113–129.

Bell, S.A. and Wray, L.R. (2000) "Financial aspects of the Social Security 'problem,'" *Journal of Economic Issues*, 34 (2): 357–364.

Bell, S.A. and Wray, L.R. (2004) "The war on poverty forty years on," *Challenge*, 47 (5): 6–29.

Berg, A., Borensztein, E., and Pattillo, C. (2005) "Assessing early warning systems: How have they worked in practice?" *IMF Staff Papers*, 52 (3): 462–502.

Bernanke, B.S. (2004) "The Great Moderation," remarks at the meetings of the Eastern Economic Association, Washington, DC, February 20.

Bernanke, B.S. and Gertler, M. (1990) "Financial fragility and economic performance," *Quarterly Journal of Economics*, 105 (1): 87–114.

Bernstein, J. and Eisinger, J. (2010) "Which CDOs and banks had deals with the most cross-ownership?" *ProPublica*, September 22.

Bezemer, D.J. (2010) "Understanding financial crisis through accounting models," *Accounting, Organizations and Society*, 26 (7): 676–688.

Black, W.K. (2005) *The Best Way to Rob a Bank is to Own One: How Corporate Executives and Politicians Looted the S&L Industry*, Austin, TX: University of Texas Press.

Black, W.K. (2009) "Those who forget the regulatory successes of the past are condemned to failure," *Economic and Political Weekly*, 44 (13): 80–86.

Blair Smith, E. (2008) "Bringing down Wall Street as ratings let loose subprime scourge," *Bloomberg News*, September 24.

Blankfein, L.C. (2009) "Do not destroy the essential catalyst of risk," *Financial Times*, February 9.

Bloomberg Businessweek (2006) "Phantom profits," September 10. www.businessweek.com/magazine/content/06_37/b4000010.htm.

Blundell-Wignall, A., Atkinson, P., and Lee, S.H. (2008) "The current financial crisis: Causes and policy issues," OECD *Financial Market Trends*, 95 (2): 1–21.

Board of Governors of the Federal Reserve System (1941a) "Seasonally adjusted estimates of nonagricultural employment," *Federal Reserve Bulletin*, June: 534–535.

Board of Governors of the Federal Reserve System (1941b) "Total nonagricultural employment," *Federal Reserve Bulletin*, September: 923.

Bond Market Association (2007) "CDO: A primer," in A. Taylor and A. Sansone (eds.) *The Handbook of Loan Syndications and Trading*, 709–784, New York: McGraw-Hill.

Bordo, M., Eichengreen, B., Klingebiel, D., and Martinez-Peria, M.S. (2001) "Is the crisis problem growing more severe?" *Economic Policy*, 16 (32): 51–82.

Boultwood, B. and Meissner, G. (2008) "The evolution of CDOs: From the BISTRO to CDO²," in G. Meissner (ed.) *The Definitive Guide to CDOs: Market, Application, Valuation, and Hedging*, 5–20, London: RISK books.

Boyer, R. (2000) "Is a finance-led growth regime a viable alternative to Fordism? A preliminary analysis," *Economy and Society*, 29 (1): 111–145.

Brown, C. (2007) "Financial engineering, consumer credit, and the stability of effective demand," *Journal of Post Keynesian Economics*, 29 (3): 427–450.

Bureau of Public Assistance (1943a) "A decade of public aid," *Social Security Bulletin*, 6 (February): 22–33.

Bureau of Public Assistance (1943b) "Termination of the federal public aid programs," *Social Security Bulletin*, 6 (August): 26–33.

Bussière, M. and Fratzscher, M. (2002) "Toward a new early warning system of financial crises," European Central Bank, Working Paper No. 145.

Campbell, C. and Minsky, H.P. (1987) "How to get off the back of a tiger or, do initial conditions constrain deposit insurance reform?" in Federal Reserve Bank of Chicago (ed.) *Proceedings of a Conference on Bank Structure and Competition*, 252–266, Chicago, IL: Federal Reserve Bank of Chicago.

Cargill, T.F. and Garcia, G.G. (1982) *Financial Deregulation and Monetary Control: Historical Perspective and Impact of the 1980 Act*, Stanford, CA: Hoover Institution Press.

Carter, J. and Osako, C. (2006) "CDO structures and definitions," FitchRating CDOs/ Global Special Report, July 19.

Cecchetti, S.G., Kohler, M., and Upper, C. (2009) "Financial crises and economic activity," National Bureau of Economic Research, Working Paper No. 15379.

Center for Public Integrity (2009) *Who is behind the Financial Meltdown? The Top 25 Subprime Lenders and their Wall Street Backers*, Washington, DC: Center for Public Integrity.

Center for Responsible Lending (2003) Letter to the Office of the Comptroller of the Currency titled "Re: OCC's proposal to preempt application of state anti-predatory lending and other laws," October 6.

Chandler, C. and Jobst, N. (2005) "CDO spotlight: Approach to rating leveraged super senior CDO notes," Standard & Poor's *Structure Finance Studies*, August 22.

Chittum, R. (2009) "Audit interview: James L. Bothwell, the author of a definitive '94 GAO derivatives report talks about industry pushback and financial-press complacency," *Columbia Journalism Review*, July 14.

Cho, D. (2007) "Pressure at mortgage firm led to mass approval of bad loans," *Washington Post*, May 7.

Chui, S. (2006) "Nontraditional mortgages: Appealing but misunderstood," Federal Reserve Bank of Chicago *Profitwise News and Views*, December: 2–11.

Civilian Conservation Corps (1944) *Civilian Conservation Corps Program of the United States Department of the Interior: March 1933–June 30, 1943*, Washington, DC: U.S. Government Printing Office.

Clark, E.H. (2007) "U.S. developments in synthetic securitization: Rampant growth and the spectre of SEC regulation," in J.J. de Vries Robbé and P.U. Ali (eds.) *Expansion and Diversification of Securitization, Yearbook 2007*, 25–40, London: Kluwer Law International.

Commons, J.R. (1934) *Institutional Economics*, New York: Macmillan. Reprinted in two volumes, vol. 1 (1959), Madison: University of Wisconsin Press.

Commons, J.R. (1934) *Institutional Economics*, New York: Macmillan. Reprinted in two volumes, vol. 2 (1961), Madison: University of Wisconsin Press.

Congressional Budget Office (2008) "Policy options for the housing and financial markets," Congressional Budget Office Paper, April.

Congressional Oversight Panel (2009a) *Assessing Treasury's Strategy: Six Months of TARP*, April Oversight Report, Washington, DC: Congressional Oversight Panel.

Congressional Oversight Panel (2009b) *Reviving Lending to Small Businesses and Families and the Impact of the TALF*, May Oversight Report, Washington, DC: Congressional Oversight Panel.

Congressional Oversight Panel (2010a) *Examining the Consequences of Mortgage Irregularities for Financial Stability and Foreclosure Mitigation*, November Oversight Report, Washington, DC: Congressional Oversight Panel.

Congressional Oversight Panel (2010b) *A Review of the Treasury's Foreclosures Prevention Programs*, December Oversight Report, Washington, DC: Congressional Oversight Panel.

Congressional Oversight Panel (2011) *The Final Report of the Congressional Oversight Panel*, March Oversight Report, Washington, DC: Congressional Oversight Panel.

Corelogic (2012) *Negative Equity Report*, First Quarter, Irvine, CA: Corelogic.

Coriat, B., Petit, P., and Schméder, G. (2006) *The Hardship of Nations: Exploring the Paths of Modern Capitalism*, Northampton, MA: Edward Elgar.

Counterparty Risk Management Policy Group III (2008) *Containing Systemic Risk: The Road to Reform*, New York: Counterparty Risk Management Policy Group III.

Creamer, D. and Bernstein, M. (1956) *Personal Income during the Business Cycle*, Princeton, NJ: Princeton University Press.

Creswell, J. (2007) "Web help for getting mortgage the criminal way," *New York Times*, June 16.

Crockett, R. (1995) *Thinking the Unthinkable: Think-Tanks and the Economic Counter-Revolution, 1931–1983*, London: Fontana.

Crotty, J.R. (1992) "Neoclassical and Keynesian approaches to the theory of investment," *Journal of Post Keynesian Economics*, 14 (4): 483–496. Reprinted in P. Davidson (ed.) (1993) *Can the Free Market Pick Winners*, 61–74, Armonk: M.E. Sharpe.

Crotty, J.R. (2009) "Structural causes of the global financial crisis: A critical assessment of the 'new financial architecture,'" *Cambridge Journal of Economics*, 33 (4): 563–580.

Curtis, A. (2002) *The Century of the Self, Part 1: Happiness Machines*, BBC documentary, Big D Film.

D'Arista, J.W. and Schlesinger, T. (1993) "The parallel banking system," Economic Policy Institute, Briefing Paper No. 37.

Das, S. (2006) *Traders, Guns and Money: Knowns and Unknowns in the Dazzling World of Derivatives*, New York: Prentice Hall.

Davidoff, S.M. and Zaring, D.T. (2009) "Regulation by deal: The government's response to the financial crisis," *Administrative Law Review*, 61 (3): 463–542.

Davidson, P. (1978) *Money and the Real World*, 2nd edn., London: Macmillan.

Davies, P.J. (2008) "Lenders line up for central bank bond swaps," *Financial Times*, May 17.

Davis, E.P. (1995) *Debt, Financial Fragility, and Systemic Risk*, 2nd edn., Oxford: Oxford University Press.

De Bondt, W.F.M. and Thaler, R.H. (1985) "Does the stock market overreact?" *Journal of Finance*, 40 (3): 794–805.

De Bondt, W.F.M. and Thaler, R.H. (1995) "Financial decision making in markets and firms: A behavioral perspective," in R. Jarrow, V. Maksimovic, and W.T. Ziemba (eds.) *Handbook in Operations Research and Management Science*, vol. 9, 385–410, San Diego, CA: Elsevier.

De Paula, L.F.R. and Alves Jr., A.J. (2000) "External financial fragility and the 1998–1999 Brazilian currency crisis," *Journal of Post Keynesian Economics*, 22 (4): 589–617.

De Long, B.J. and Summers, L.H. (1988) "How does macroeconomic policy affect output?" *Brookings Papers on Economic Activity*, 2: 433–494.

de Vries Robbé, J.J. (2006) "That's one small step for man…Securitizing commodity risk through Apollo," in J.J. de Vries Robbé and P.U. Ali (eds.) *Innovations in Securitisation, Yearbook 2006*, 71–84, London: Kluwer Law International.

de Vries Robbé, J.J. and Ali, P.U. (eds.) (2007) *Expansion and Diversification of Securitization, Yearbook 2007*, London: Kluwer Law International.

Demirgüç-Kunt, A. and Detragiache, E. (1998) "The determinants of banking crises in developing and developed countries," *IMF Staff Papers*, 45 (1): 81–109.

Department of Labor (2000a) "Proposed amendment to prohibited transaction exemption (PTE) 97–34 involving Bear, Stearns & Co. Inc., Prudential Securities Incorporated, *et al.*, (D-10829); notice," *Federal Register*, 65 (164): 51454–51494.

Department of Labor (2000b) "Amendment to prohibited transaction exemption (PTE) 97–34 involving Bear, Stearns & Co. Inc., Prudential Securities Incorporated, *et al.* (D-10829)," *Federal Register*, 65 (219): 67765–67774.

Department of the Treasury (2008) *Blueprint for a Modernized Financial Regulatory Structure*, Washington, DC: Department of the Treasury.

Der Hovanesian, M. (2006) "Nightmare mortgages," *Bloomberg Business Week*, September 10. www.businessweek.com/magazine/content/06_37/b4000001.htm.

Dugger, W.M. (1996) "Redefining economics: From market allocation to social provisioning," in C.J. Whalen (ed.) *Political Economy for the 21st Century*, 31–43, Armonk, NY: M.E. Sharpe.

Dugger, W.M. and Peach, J.T. (2008) *Economic Abundance: An Introduction*, Armonk, NY: M.E. Sharpe.

Duhigg, C. (2006) "Fast credit, easy terms, buy now," *New York Times*, November 21.

Edison, H.J. (2003) "Do indicators of financial crises work? An evaluation of an early warning system," *International Journal of Finance and Economics*, 8 (1): 11–53.

Eisinger, J. and Bernstein, J. (2010) "The Magnetar trade: How one hedge fund helped keep the bubble going," *ProPublica*, April 13.

Eisner, R. (1998) "Save social security from its saviors," *Journal of Post Keynesian Economics*, 21 (1): 77–92.

Elul, R. (2006) "Residential mortgage default," Federal Reserve Bank of Philadelphia *Business Review*, Third Quarter: 21–30.

Emergency Conservation Work (1935) *Summary Report of the Director of Emergency Conservation Work on the Operations of Emergency Conservation Work for the Period Extending from April 1933, to June 30, 1935*, Washington, DC: U.S. Government Printing Office.

Epstein, G.A. (ed.) (2005) *Financialization and the World Economy*, Northampton, MA: Edward Elgar.

Erturk, K.A. (2006) "Asset price bubbles, liquidity preference and the business cycle," *Metroeconomica*, 57 (2): 239–256.

Erturk, K.A. (2007) "On the Minskyan business cycle," in P. Arestis and G. Zezza (eds.) *Advances in Monetary Policy and Macroeconomics*, 158–173, New York: Palgrave Macmillan.

Estenson, P.S. (1987) "Farm debt and financial instability," *Journal of Economic Issues*, 21 (2): 617–627.

Evans, D. (2007) "Banks sell 'toxic waste' CDOs to Calpers, Texas teachers fund," *Bloomberg News*, June 1.

Fabozzi, F.J. and Dunlevy, J. (2002) "Nonagency MBS and real estate-backed ABS," in F.J. Fabozzi (ed.) *The Handbook of Financial Instruments*, 367–398, Hoboken, NJ: Wiley.

Fama, E.F. (1970) "Efficient capital markets: A review of theory and empirical work," *Journal of Finance*, 25 (2): 383–417.

Fazzari, S. (1993) "The investment–finance link," Levy Economics Institute, Public Policy Brief No. 9/1993.

Federal Open Market Committee (1999) Transcripts of the Meeting of the Federal Open Market Committee, February 2–3, Washington, DC: Board of Governors of the Federal Reserve System.

Federal Security Agency (1944) *Final Report of the National Youth Administration, Fiscal Years 1936–1943*, Washington, DC: U.S. Government Printing Office.

Federal Works Agency (1941) *Summary of Relief and Federal Work Program Statistics: 1933–1940*, Washington, DC: U.S. Government Printing Office.

Federal Works Agency (1942) *Final Statistical Report of the Federal Emergency Relief Administration*, Washington, DC: U.S. Government Printing Office.

Federal Works Agency (1947) *Final Report on the WPA Program: 1935–43*, Washington, DC: U.S. Government Printing Office.

Felkerson, J.A. (2011) "$29,000,000,000,000: A detailed look at the Fed's bailout by funding facility and recipient," Levy Economics Institute, Working Paper No. 698.

Fell, J. and Shinasi, G. (2005) "Assessing financial stability: Exploring the boundaries of analysis," *National Institute Economic Review*, 192 (1): 102–116.

Ferrer Sr., R., González, C., and Jordá, P. (2006) "Integration of mortgage and capital markets: Evidence in the Spanish case," Mimeograph, University of Valencia (Spain), February.

Field, A.J. (2011) *A Great Leap Forward: 1930s Depressions and U.S. Economic Growth*, New Haven, CT: Yale University Press.

Financial Crimes Enforcement Network (2008) *Mortgage Loan Fraud: An Update of Trends Based upon an Analysis of Suspicious Activity Reports*, Washington, DC: Financial Crimes Enforcement Network.

Financial Crisis Inquiry Commission (2011) *Final Report of the National Commission on the Causes of the Financial and Economic Crisis in the United States*, Washington, DC: Financial Crisis Inquiry Commission.

Fishbein, A.J. and Woodall, P. (2006) "Exotic or toxic? An examination of the non-traditional mortgage market for consumers and lenders," Studies, May 22, Washington, DC: Consumer Federation of America.

Fisher, I. (1932) *Booms and Depressions: Some First Principles*, New York: Adelphy.

Fisher, I. (1933) "The debt-deflation theory of great depressions," *Econometrica*, 1 (4): 337–357.

Flanagan, C., Asato, R., and Reardon, E. (2005) "Single name CDS of ABS: Next step in the evolution of the ABS market," JP Morgan *Global Structured Finance Research*, March 17.

Foley, D.K. (2003) "Financial fragility in developing countries," in A. Dutt and J. Ros (eds.) *Development Economics and Structuralist Macroeconomics: Essays in Honour of Lance Taylor*, 157–168, Cheltenham: Edward Elgar.

Forrester, J.P. (2006) "Still mortgaging the American dream: Predatory lending, preemption, and federally supported lenders," *University of Cincinnati Law Review*, 74 (4): 1303–1371.

Forstater, M. (1999) "Full employment and economic flexibility," *Economic and Labour Relations Review*, 11 (supplement): 69–88.

Foster, J.B. and Magdoff, F. (2009) *The Great Financial Crisis: Causes and Consequences*, New York: Monthly Review Press.

Foust, D. and Pressman, A. (2008) "Credit scores: Not-so-magic numbers," *Business Week*, February 18.

Frazis, H. and Stewart, J. (2010) "Why do BLS hours series tell different stories about trends in hours worked?" Bureau of Labor Statistics, Working Paper No. 433.

Friedman, M. (1962) *Capitalism and Freedom*, Chicago, IL: University of Chicago Press.

Froeba, M. (2010) Testimony before the Financial Crisis Inquiry Commission, The New School, Arnhold Hall, New York, June 2.

Froud, J., Johal, S., Leaver, A., and Williams, K. (2006) *Financialization and Strategy: Narrative and Numbers*, New York: Routledge.

Frydman, C. and Jenter, D. (2010) "CEO compensation," *Annual Review of Financial Economics*, 2: 75–102.

Fullwiler, S.T. (2007) "Macroeconomic stabilization through an employer of last resort," *Journal of Economic Issues*, 41 (1): 93–134.

Galbraith, James K. (2008) *The Predator State: How Conservatives Abandoned the Free Market and Why Liberals Should Too*, New York: Free Press.

Galbraith, James K. (2009) "Who are these economists, anyway?" *Thought and Action*, Fall: 85–97.

Galbraith, John K. (1958) *The Affluent Society*, Cambridge, MA: Riberside Press.

Galbraith, John K. (1961) *The Great Crash*, 3rd edn., Cambridge, MA: Riberside Press.

Galbraith, John K. (1967) *The New Industrial State*, Boston, MA: Houghton-Mifflin.

Gaytàn, A. and Johnson, C.A. (2002) "A review of the literature on early warning systems for banking crises," Central Bank of Chile, Working Paper No. 183.

Gertler, M. (1988) "Financial structure and aggregate economic activity: An overview," *Journal of Money, Credit and Banking*, 20 (3), Part 2: 559–588.

Ginsburg, H. (1983) *Full Employment and Public Policy: The United States and Sweden*, Lexington, MA: Lexington Books.

Glickman, M. (1994) "The concept of information, intractable uncertainty, and the current state of the 'efficient market' theory: A post Keynesian view," *Journal of Post Keynesian Economics*, 16 (3): 325–349.

Godley, W. (1999) "Seven unsustainable processes: Medium-term prospects and policies for the United States and the world," Levy Economics Institute, Strategic Analysis, January.

Godley, W. (2000) "Drowning in debt," Levy Economics Institute, Policy Note No. 2000/6.

Godley, W. and Lavoie, M. (2007) *Monetary Economics: An Integrated Approach to Credit, Money, Income, Production and Wealth*, New York: Palgrave Macmillan.

Godley, W. and Wray, L.R. (1999) "Can Goldilocks survive?" Levy Economics Institute, Policy Note No. 1999/4.

Goldstein, M., Kaminsky, G., and Reinhart, C.M. (2000) *Assessing Financial Vulnerability: An Early Warning System for Emerging Markets*, Washington, DC: Peterson Institute for International Economics.

Gonzalez-Hermosillo, B. (1999) "Developing indicators to provide early warnings of banking crises," *Finance and Development*, June: 36–42.

Goodhart, C.A.E., Sunirand, P., and Tsomocos, D.P. (2006) "A time series analysis of financial fragility in the UK banking system," *Annals of Finance*, 2 (1): 1–21.

Goodman, L.S. (2001) "Synthetic CDOs," in F.J. Fabozzi and Goodman, L.S. (eds.) *Investing in Collateralized Debt Obligations*, 141–155, Hoboken, NJ: Wiley.

Goodman, P.S. (2009) "Lucrative fees may deter efforts to alter loans," *New York Times*, July 29.

Gordon, R.J. (ed.) (1986) *The American Business Cycle: Continuity and Change*, Chicago, IL: University of Chicago Press.

Government Accountability Office (1994) "Financial derivatives: Actions needed to protect the financial system," Report No. GAO/GGD-94-133, May.

Government Accountability Office (1997) "Downsizing at the U.S. Government Accountability Office," Report by the Personal Appeals Board, September 30. www.pab.gao.gov/oversight.php.

Government Accountability Office (2011) "Mortgage foreclosures: Documentation problems reveal need for ongoing regulatory oversight," Report No. GAO-11-433, May.

Grabel, I. (2003) "Predicting financial crisis in developing economy: Astronomy or astrology," *Eastern Economic Journal*, 29 (2): 243–258.

Graybow, M. and Keating, G. (2008) "Countrywide sued for unfair lending; buyout approved," *Reuters*, June 25.

Greenspan, A. (1999) "Financial derivatives," remarks before the Futures Industry Association, Boca Raton, FL, March 19.

Greenspan, A. (2002) "International financial risk management," remarks before the Council on Foreign Relations, Washington, DC, November 19.

Greenspan, A. (2004) "The mortgage market and consumer debt," remarks at America's Community Bankers Annual Convention, Washington, DC, October 19.

Greider, W. (1987) *Secrets of the Temple: How the Federal Reserve Runs the Country*, New York: Simon and Schuster.

Guttman, R. (2008) "A primer on finance-led capitalism and its crisis," *Revue de la Regulation*, No. 3/4: 1–19.

Hadley, K.L. and Touhey, A.T. (2006) "An assessment of traditional liquidity ratios," *FDIC Outlook*, Fall: 11–16.

Hadley, K.L. and Touhey, A.T. (2007) "Liquidity analysis: Decades of change," *FDIC Supervisory Insights*, 4 (2): 4–11.

Han, S. and Mulligan, C.B. (2008) "Inflation and the size of the government," Federal Reserve Bank of St. Louis *Review*, May/June: 245–267.

Harvey, J. (1998) "Heuristic judgment theory," *Journal of Economic Issues*, 32 (1): 47–64.

Harvey, P.L. (1989) *Securing the Right to Full Employment: Social Welfare Policy and the Unemployed in the United States*, Princeton, NJ: Princeton University Press.

Harvey, P.L. (1999) "Liberal strategies for combating joblessness in the twentieth century," *Journal of Economic Issues*, 33 (2): 497–503.

Harvey, P.L. (2000) "Combating joblessness: An analysis of the principal strategies that have influenced the development of American employment and social welfare law during the 20th century," *Berkeley Journal of Employment and Labor Law*, 21 (2): 677–758.

Harvey, P.L. (2002) "Human rights and economic policy discourse: Taking economic and social rights seriously," *Columbia Human Rights Law Review*, 33 (2): 364–471.

Harvey, P.L. (2011) "Back to work: A public jobs proposal for economic recovery," Dçmos *Report*, March 7.

Hein, E., Niechoj, T., Spahn, P., and Truger, A. (eds.) (2009) *Finance-Led Capitalism? Macroeconomic Effects of Changes in the Financial Sector*, 2nd edn., Marburg: Metropolis-Verlag.

Hilferding, R. (1910) *Finance Capital: A Study of the Latest Phase of Capitalist Development*, English edition, T. Bottomore (ed.) (1981), London: Routledge & Kegan Paul.

Hirway, I. (2006) "Enhancing livelihood security through the National Employment Guarantee Act: Toward effective implementation of the Act," Levy Economics Institute, Working Paper No. 437.

House of Commons (2011) "Appointment of Dr. Donald Kohn to the Interim Financial Policy Committee," Thirteenth Report of Session 2010–12, Volume 2, London: Stationery Office Limited

Hu, H.T.C. and Black, B.S. (2008) "Equity and debt decoupling and empty voting II: Importance and extensions," *University of Pennsylvania Law Review*, 156 (3): 625–739.

Hume, M.J. and Sentence, A. (2009) "The global credit boom: Challenges for macroeconomics and policy," *Journal of International Money and Finance*, 28 (8): 1426–1461.

Hurst, R.R. (2001) "CDOs backed by ABS and commercial real estate," in F.J. Fabozzi and L.S. Goodman (eds.) *Investing in Collateralized Debt Obligations*, 114–140, Hoboken, NJ: Wiley.

International Labour Organization (2007) *Global Employment Trends Brief*, January, Geneva: International Labour Organization.

International Labour Organization (2012) *World of Work Report 2012*, Geneva: International Labour Organization.

International Monetary Fund (2007) *Financial Market Turbulence: Causes, Consequences, and Policies.* International Monetary Fund *Global Financial Stability Report*, October, Washington, DC: International Monetary Fund.

International Monetary Fund (2008a) *Containing Systemic Risks and Restoring Financial Soundness.* International Monetary Fund *Global Financial Stability Report*, April, Washington, DC: International Monetary Fund.

International Monetary Fund (2008b) *Financial Stress and Deleveraging: Macrofinancial Implications and Policy.* International Monetary Fund *Global Financial Stability Report*, October, Washington, DC: International Monetary Fund.

International Monetary Fund (2009) *Responding to the Financial Crisis and Measuring Systemic Risks.* International Monetary Fund *Global Financial Stability Report*, April, Washington, DC: International Monetary Fund.

Isenberg, D.L. (1988) "Is there a case for Minsky's financial fragility hypothesis in the 1920s?" *Journal of Economic Issues*, 22 (4): 1045–1069.

Isenberg, D.L. (1994) "Financial fragility and the Great Depression: New evidence on credit growth in the 1920s," in G.A. Dymski and R. Pollin (eds.) *New Perspectives in Monetary Macroeconomics: Explorations in the Tradition of Hyman P. Minsky*, 201–229, Ann Arbor, MI: University of Michigan Press.

Jobst, N. (2007) "Recent and not so recent developments in synthetic collateral debt obligations," in A. de Servigny and J. Norbert (eds.) *The Handbook of Structured Finance*, 465–542, New York: McGraw-Hill.

Jones, S. (2009) "The formula that felled Wall St," *Financial Times*, April 24.

JP Morgan (2000) *The J.P. Morgan Guide to Credit Derivatives*, New York: JP Morgan.

Kaboub, F. (2008) "Employment guarantee programs: A survey of theories and policy experiences," Levy Economics Institute, Working Paper No. 498.

Kaboub, F. (2013) "Low cost of full employment in the United States," in M.J. Murray and M. Forstater (eds.) *The Job Guarantee Program: Toward True Full Employment*, New York: Palgrave Macmillan.

Kalecki, M. (1971) "The determinants of profits," in M. Kalecki (ed.) *Selected Essays on the Dynamics of the Capitalist Economy*, 78–92, Cambridge: Cambridge University Press.

Kalser, K. and Puwalski, A. (1998) "CLOs lure another major bank asset off the balance sheet," *FDIC San Francisco Regional Outlook*, Third Quarter. www.fdic.gov/bank/analytical/regional/ro19983q/sf/infocus2.html.

Kedrosky, P. and Stangler, D. (2011) "Financialization and its entrepreneurial consequences," Kauffman Foundation Research Series, March, Kansas City: Ewing Marion Kauffman Foundation.

Keynes, J.M. (1930) *A Treatise on Money*, London: Macmillan. Reprinted in D.E. Moggridge (ed.) (1971) *The Collected Writings of John Maynard Keynes*, vol. 5 and vol. 6, London: Macmillan.

Keynes, J.M. (1933a) "A monetary theory of production." Reprinted in D.E. Moggridge (ed.) (1973) *The Collected Writings of John Maynard Keynes*, vol. 13, 408–411, London: Macmillan.

Keynes, J.M. (1933b) "The characteristics of an entrepreneur economy." Reprinted in D.E. Moggridge (ed.) (1979) *The Collected Writings of John Maynard Keynes*, vol. 29, 87–101, London: Macmillan.

Keynes, J.M. (1933c) "The distinction between a co-operative economy and an entrepreneur economy." Reprinted in D.E. Moggridge (ed.) (1979) *The Collected Writings of John Maynard Keynes*, vol. 29, 76–87, London: Macmillan.

Keynes, J.M. (1936) *The General Theory of Employment, Interest, and Money*, New York: Harcourt Brace. Reprinted in D.E. Moggridge (ed.) (1971) *The Collected Writings of John Maynard Keynes*, vol. 7, London: Macmillan.

Keynes, J.M. (1937a) "The general theory of employment," *Quarterly Journal of Economics*, 51 (2): 209–223. Reprinted in D.E. Moggridge (ed.) (1973) *The Collected Writings of John Maynard Keynes*, vol. 14, 109–123, London: Macmillan.

Keynes, J.M. (1937b) "How to avoid the slump," *The Times*, January 12–14. Reprinted in D.E. Moggridge (ed.) (1973) *The Collected Writings of John Maynard Keynes*, vol. 21, 384–395, London: Macmillan.

King, J.E. (2001) "The last resort? Some critical reflections on ELR," *Journal of Economic and Social Policy*, 5 (2): 72–76.

Kiyotaki, N. and Moore, J. (1997) "Credit cycles," *Journal of Political Economy*, 105 (2): 211–248.

Klein, A. and Goldfarb, Z.A. (2008) "The bubble," *Washington Post*, June 15, 16, 17.

Klein, L.R. and Shabbir, T. (2003) "Asia before and after the financial crisis of 1997–98: A retrospective essay," in L.R. Klein and T. Shabbir (eds.) *Recent Financial Crises: Analysis, Challenges and Implications*, 23–68, Cheltenham: Edward Elgar.

Kolchinsky, E. (2010) Testimony before the Financial Crisis Inquiry Commission, The New School, Arnhold Hall, New York, June 2.

Kolker, C. and Voreacos, D. (2009) "UBS employee called CDO 'vomit' in 2007 e-mail (Update1)," *Bloomberg News*, September 11.

Kothari, V. (2006) *Securitization: The Financial Instrument of the Future*, Hoboken, NJ: Wiley.

Kregel, J.A. (1976) "Economic methodology in the face of uncertainty: The modeling methods of Keynes and the Post-Keynesians," *Economic Journal*, 85 (342): 209–225.

Kregel, J.A. (1986) "Conceptions of equilibrium: The logic of choice and the logic of production," in I. Kirzner (ed.) *Subjectivism, Intelligibility, and Economic Understanding: Essays in Honor of Ludwig M. Lachmann on his Eightieth Birthday*, 157–170, New York: New York University Press. Reprinted in P. Boettke and D. Prychitko (eds.) (1998) *Market Process Theories, Volume 2: Heterodox Approaches*, 89–102, Northampton, MA: Edward Elgar.

Kregel, J.A. (1992) "Minsky's 'two price' theory of financial instability and monetary policy: Discounting vs. open market intervention," in S. Fazzari and D.B. Papadimitriou (eds.) *Financial Conditions and Macroeconomic Performance*, 85–103, Armonk, NY: M.E. Sharpe.

Kregel, J.A. (1997) "Margins of safety and weight of the argument in generating financial fragility," *Journal of Economic Issues*, 31 (2): 543–548.

Kregel, J.A. (1998a) *The Past and Future of Banks*, Quaderni di Ricerche, No. 21, Rome: Ente Luigi Einaudi.

Kregel, J.A. (1998b) "Derivatives and global capital flows: Applications to Asia," *Cambridge Journal of Economics*, 22 (6): 677–692.

Lamoussière-Pouvreau, C. and Masset-Denèvre, E. (2007) "L'hypothèque rechargeable," *INC Hebdo*, No. 1437.

Lavoie, M. (1986) "Minsky's law or the theorem of systemic financial fragility," *Studi Economici*, 41 (29): 3–28.

Lavoie, M. (1987) "Monnaie et production: Une synthèse de la théorie du circuit," *Economies et Sociétés*, 20 (9), MP 4: 65–101.

Lavoie, M. (1992) *Foundations of Post Keynesian Economic Analysis*, Aldershot: Edward Elgar.

Lavoie, M. (1997) "Loanable funds, endogenous money, and Minsky's financial fragility hypothesis," in A.J. Cohen, H. Hagemann, and J. Smithin (eds.) *Money, Financial Institutions, and Macroeconomics*, 67–82, Boston, MA: Kluwer Nijhoff.

Lestano, J. and Kuper, G.H. (2003) "Indicators of financial crises do work! An early-warning system for six Asian countries," University of Groningen, CCSO Centre for Economic Research, Working Papers No. 200313.

Levy, D. (2009) "California foreclosure center shows Obama challenge (update 2)," *Bloomberg News*, February 18.

Levy Economics Institute (2007) *Conference Proceedings, 16th Annual Hyman P. Minsky Conference on the State of the U.S. and World Economies*, Blithewood, NY: Levy Economics Institute.

Logie, M.J. and Castagnino, J.-P. (2006) "Equity default swap and the securitization of risk," in J.J. de Vries Robbé and P.U. Ali (eds.) *Innovations in Securitisation, Yearbook 2006*, 41–70, London: Kluwer Law International.

Lowenstein, R. (2008) "Triple-A failure," *New York Times*, April 27.

Lucas, D.J., Goodman, L.S., and Fabozzi, F.J. (2006) *Collateralized Debt Obligations: Structure and Analysis*, 2nd edn., Hoboken, NJ: Wiley.

Lui, D. (2005) "Interest-only ARMs," in F.J. Fabozzi (ed.) *The Handbook of Mortgage-Backed Securities*, 333–362, Hoboken, NJ: Wiley.

McCulley, P. (2007a) "The plankton theory meets Minsky," PIMCO *Global Central Bank Focus*, March.

McCulley, P. (2007b) "A reverse Minsky journey," PIMCO *Global Central Bank Focus*, October.

Macmahon, A.W., Millett, J.D., and Ogden, G. (1941) *The Administration of Federal Work Relief*, Chicago, IL: Public Administration Service.

Majewski, R. (2004) "Simulating an employer of last resort program," in G. Argyrous, M. Forstater, and G. Mongiovi (eds.) *Growth, Distribution, and Effective Demand: Alternatives to Economic Orthodoxy, Essays in Honor of Edward J. Nell*, 163–180, Armonk, NY: M.E. Sharpe.

Marx, K. (1894) *Capital: A Critique of Political Economy*, Vol. 3, 1906 English translation, New York: Charles H. Kerr & Co.

Mayer, G. (2004) "Union membership trends in the United States," Congressional Research Service, *Federal Publications*, Paper 174.

Mayer, R. (2003) "Casting for returns," *CFO Magazine*, 19 (10): 49.

Medova, E.A. and Smith, R.G. (2006) "A structural approach to EDS pricing," *Risk*, 19 (4): 84–88.

Minsky, H.P. (1957) "Central banking and money market changes," *Quarterly Journal of Economics*, 71 (2): 171–187.

Minsky, H.P. (1962) "Financial constraints upon decisions, an aggregate view," *Proceedings of the Business and Economic Statistics Section*, 256–267, Washington, DC: American Statistical Association.

Minsky, H.P. (1963) "Financial institutions and monetary policy: discussion," *American Economic Review*, 53 (2): 401–412.

Minsky, H.P. (1964) "Financial crisis, financial system and the performance of the economy," in Commission on Money and Credit (ed.) *Private Capital Markets*, 173–380, Englewood Cliffs, NJ: Prentice-Hall.

Minsky, H.P. (1967a) "Money, other financial variables, and aggregate demand in the short run," in G. Horwich (ed.) *Monetary Process and Policy: A Symposium*, 265–293, Homewood, IL: Richard D. Irwin.

Minsky, H.P. (1967b) "Financial intermediation in the money and capital markets," in G. Pontecorvo, R.P. Shay, and A.G. Hart (eds.) *Issues in Banking and Monetary Analysis*, 31–56, New York: Holt, Rinehart and Winston, Inc.

Minsky, H.P. (1969) "The new uses of monetary power," *Nebraska Journal of Economics and Business*, 8 (2): 3–15. Reprinted in H.P. Minsky (ed.) (1982) *Can "It" Happen Again?* 179–191, Armonk, NY: M.E. Sharpe.

Minsky, H.P. (1972) "Financial instability revisited: The economics of disaster," in Board of Governors of the Federal Reserve System (ed.) *Reappraisal of the Federal Reserve Discount Mechanism*, vol. 3, 95–136, Washington, DC: Board of Governors of the Federal Reserve System.

Minsky, H.P. (1974) "The modeling of financial instability: An introduction," *Modeling and Simulation*, 5, Part 1: 267–272. Reprinted in Committee on Banking, Housing, and Urban Affairs (ed.) (1975) *Compendium of Major Issues in Bank Regulation*, 354–364, Washington, DC: U.S. Government Printing Office.

Minsky, H.P. (1975a) *John Maynard Keynes*, Cambridge: Cambridge University Press.

Minsky, H.P. (1975b) "Financial instability, the current dilemma, and the structure of banking and finance," in Committee on Banking, Housing, and Urban Affairs (ed.) *Compendium of Major Issues in Bank Regulation*, 310–353, Washington, DC: U.S. Government Printing Office.

Minsky, H.P. (1975c) "Suggestions for a cash flow-oriented bank examination," in Federal Reserve Bank of Chicago (ed.) *Proceedings of a Conference on Bank Structure and Competition*, 150–184, Chicago, IL: Federal Reserve Bank of Chicago.

Minsky, H.P. (1977a) "Banking and a fragile financial environment," *Journal of Portfolio Management*, Summer: 16–22.

Minsky, H.P. (1977b) "The financial instability hypothesis: An interpretation of Keynes and an alternative to 'standard' theory," *Nebraska Journal of Economics and Business*, 16 (1): 5–16. Reprinted in *Challenge* 20 (1), March–April 1977: 20–27, and in H.P. Minsky (ed.) (1982) *Can "It" Happen Again?* 59–70, Armonk, NY: M.E. Sharpe.

Minsky, H.P. (1977c) "A theory of systemic fragility," in E.I. Altman and A.W. Sametz (eds.) *Financial Crises: Institutions and Markets in a Fragile Environment*, 138–152, New York: Wiley.

Minsky, H.P. (1980a) "Finance and profit: The changing nature of American business cycle," in Joint Economic Committee (ed.) *The Business Cycle and Public Policy, 1929–1980*, Washington, DC: U.S. Government Printing Office. Reprinted in H.P. Minsky (ed.) (1982) *Can "It" Happen Again?* 14–59, Armonk, NY: M.E. Sharpe.

Minsky, H.P. (1980b) "Capitalist financial processes and the instability of capitalism," *Journal of Economic Issues*, 14 (2): 505–523.

Minsky, H.P. (1982) "The financial-instability hypothesis: Capitalist process and the behavior of the economy," in C.P. Kindleberger and J.-P. Lafargue (eds.) *Financial Crises: Theory, History, and Policy*, 13–39, New York: Cambridge University Press.

Minsky, H.P. (1983a) "Institutional roots of American inflation," in N. Schmukler and E. Marcus (eds.) *Inflation through the Ages: Economic, Social, Psychological and Historical Aspects*, 266–277, New York: Brooklyn College Press.

Minsky, H.P. (1983b) "Pitfalls due to financial fragility," in S. Weintraub and M. Goodstein (eds.) *Reaganomics in the Stagflation Economy*, 104–119, Philadelphia, PA: University of Pennsylvania Press.

Minsky, H.P. (1984a) "Financial innovations and financial instability: Observations and theory," in Federal Reserve Bank of St. Louis (ed.) *Financial Innovations*, 21–45, Boston, MA: Kluwer-Nijhoff.

Minsky, H.P. (1984b) "Banking and industry between the two wars: The United States," *Journal of European Economic History*, 13 (Special Issue): 235–272.

Minsky, H.P. (1986a) *Stabilizing an Unstable Economy*, New Haven, CT: Yale University Press.

Minsky, H.P. (1986b) "Global consequences of financial deregulation," *Marcus Wallenberg Papers on International Finance*, 2 (1): 1–19.

Minsky, H.P. (1990a) "Sraffa and Keynes: Effective demand in the long run," in K. Bharadwaj and B. Schefold (eds.) *Essays on Piero Sraffa: Critical Perspectives on the Revival of Classical Theory*, 362–371, London: Unwin Hyman.

Minsky, H.P. (1990b) "Money manager capitalism, fiscal independence and international monetary reconstruction," in M. Szabó-Pelsőczi (ed.) *The Future of the Global Economic and Monetary System*, 209–218, Budapest: Institute for World Economics of the Hungarian Academy of Sciences.

Minsky, H.P. (1990c) "Schumpeter: Finance and evolution," in A. Heertje and M. Perlman (eds.) *Evolving Technology and Market Structure*, 51–74, Ann Arbor, MI: University of Michigan Press.

Minsky, H.P. (1992a) "Reconstituting the United States' financial structure: Some fundamental issues," Levy Economics Institute, Working Paper No. 69.

Minsky, H.P. (1992b) "The capital development of the economy and the structure of financial institutions," Levy Economics Institute, Working Paper No. 72.

Minsky, H.P. (1992c) "Reconstituting the financial structure: The United States," Mimeograph, Hyman P. Minsky Archive, Paper 18. http://digitalcommons.bard.edu/hm_archive/18.

Minsky, H.P. (1993a) "Schumpeter and finance," in S. Biasco, A. Roncaglia, and M. Salvati (eds.) *Market and Institutions in Economic Development*, 103–115, New York: St. Martin's Press.

Minsky, H.P. (1993b) "On the non-neutrality of money," Federal Reserve Bank of New York *Quarterly Review*, 18 (1): 77–82.

Minsky, H.P. (1993c) "The economic problem at the end of the second millennium: Creating capitalism, reforming capitalism and making capitalism work," Mimeograph, *Hyman P. Minsky Archive*, Paper 101. http://digitalcommons.bard.edu/hm_archive/101.

Minsky, H.P. (1993d) "Full employment and resource creation rather than inflation containment as the objectives of economic policy: Some thoughts on the limits of capitalism," Mimeograph, *Hyman P. Minsky Archive*, Paper 44 (10–27–93 version) http://digitalcommons.bard.edu/hm_archive/44.

Minsky, H.P. (1994a) "Financial instability and the decline (?) of banking public policy implications," in Federal Reserve Bank of Chicago (ed.) *Proceedings of a Conference on Bank Structure and Competition*, 55–64, Chicago, IL: Federal Reserve Bank of Chicago.

Minsky, H.P. (1994b) "Full employment and economic growth as objectives of economic policy: Some thoughts on the limits of capitalism," Mimeograph, *Hyman P. Minsky Archive*, Paper 44. http://digitalcommons.bard.edu/hm_archive/44.

Minsky, H.P. (1995) "Financial factors in the economics of capitalism," *Journal of Financial Services Research*, 9 (3–4): 197–208. Reprinted in H.A. Benink (ed.) (1995) *Coping with Financial Fragility and Systemic Risk*, 3–14, Boston, MA: Ernst and Young.

Minsky, H.P. (1996) "The essential characteristics of Post-Keynesian economics," in G. Deleplace and E.J. Nell (eds.) *Money in Motion: The Post Keynesian and Circulation Approaches*, 70–88, New York: St. Martin's Press.

Minsky, H.P. and Whalen, C.J. (1996) "Economic insecurity and the institutional pre-requisites for successful capitalism," *Journal of Post Keynesian Economics*, 19 (2): 155–170.

Minsky, H.P., Papadimitriou, D.B., Phillips, R.J., and Wray, L.R. (1993) "Community development banking: A proposal to establish a nationwide system of community development banks," Levy Economics Institute, Public Policy Brief No. 3/1993.

Mishel, L. and Shierholz, H. (2011) "Sustained, high joblessness causes lasting damage to wages, benefits, income and wealth," Economic Policy Institute, Briefing Paper No. 324.

Mishkin, F.S. (1991) "Asymmetric information and financial crises: A historical per-spective," in R.G. Hubbard (ed.) *Financial Markets and Financial Crises*, 69–108, Chicago, IL: University of Chicago Press.

Mitchell, W.F. and Muysken, J. (2008) *Full Employment Abandoned: Shifting Sands and Policy Failures*, Cheltenham: Edward Elgar

Mohebbi, C., Li, G., and White, T. (2005) "Stripped mortgage-backed securities," in F.J. Fabozzi (ed.) *The Handbook of Mortgage-Backed Securities*, 465–480, Hoboken, NJ: Wiley.

Moore, P. (2004) *The ABC of CDO: The Credit Guide to Collateralised Debt Obliga-tions*, London: Incisive Media Investments Ltd.

Morgenson, G. (2007) "Judge demands documentation in foreclosure," *New York Times*, November 17.

Morgenson, G. (2008) "A road not taken by lenders," *New York Times*, April 6.

Morgenson, G. (2011) "A bank crisis whodunit, with laughs and tears," *New York Times*, January 29.

Morgenson, G. and Van Natta Jr., D. (2009) "During crisis, Paulson's calls to Goldman posed ethics test," *New York Times*, August 8.

National Association of Mortgage Brokers (2006) "The regulation & oversight of the mortgage broker industry," *Word from Washington*, November. www.namb.org/namb/20062.asp.

National Resources Planning Board (1941) *Development of Resources and Stabilization of Employment in the United States*, Washington, DC: U.S. Government Printing Office.

National Resources Planning Board (1942) *Security, Work, and Relief Policies*, Washing-ton, DC: U.S. Government Printing Office.

Nelken, I. (1999) *Implementing Credit Derivatives: Strategies and Techniques for Using Credit Derivatives in Risk Management*, New York: McGraw-Hill.

Nersisyan, Y. and Wray, L.R. (2010) "The trouble with pensions," Levy Economics Insti-tute, Public Policy Brief No. 109/2010.

Niggle, C.J. (1989) "The cyclical behavior of corporate financial ratios and Minsky's fin-ancial instability hypothesis," in W. Semmler (ed.) *Financial Dynamics and Business Cycles: New Perspectives*, 203–220, Armonk, NY: M.E. Sharpe.

Nocera, J. (2011) "Inquiry is missing bottom line," *New York Times*, January 26.

O'Kane, D. (2001) "Credit derivatives explained: Market, products, and regulations," Lehman Brothers *Structured Credit Research*, March.

Obay, L. (2000) *Financial Innovation in the Banking Industry: The Case of Asset Securi-tization*, London: Routledge.

Office of the Comptroller of the Currency (2008) *OCC and OTS Mortgage Metrics Report*, Third Quarter, Washington, DC: Office of the Comptroller of the Currency.

Office of the Comptroller of the Currency (2009) *OCC and OTS Mortgage Metrics Report*, First Quarter, Washington, DC: Office of the Comptroller of the Currency.

Office of the Comptroller of the Currency (2012) *Mortgage Metrics Report*, First Quarter, Washington, DC: Office of the Comptroller of the Currency.

Orléan, A. (1999) *Le Pouvoir de la Finance*, Paris: Odile Jacob.

Palley, T.I. (1994) "Debt, aggregate demand, and the business cycle: An analysis in the spirit of Kaldor and Minsky," *Journal of Post Keynesian Economics*, 16 (3): 371–390.

Papadimitriou D., Chilcote, E., and Zezza, G. (2006) "Are housing prices, household debt, and growth sustainable?" Levy Economics Institute, Strategic Analysis, January.

Papadimitriou, D., Shaik A., dos Santos, C., and Zezza, G. (2002) "Is personal income sustainable?" Levy Economics Institute, Strategic Analysis, November.

Parguez, A. (1984) "La dynamique de la monnaie," *Economies et Sociétés*, 18 (4), MP 1: 83–118.

Pendley, M.D., Costello, G., and Kelsh, M. (2007) "The impact of poor underwriting practices and fraud in subprime RMBS performance," FitchRating, U.S. Residential Mortgage Special Report, November 28.

Polizu, C. (2007) "An overview of structured investment vehicles and other special purpose companies," in A. de Servigny and J. Norbert (eds.) *The Handbook of Structured Finance*, 621–674, New York: McGraw-Hill.

Pollin, R. and Dymski, G.A. (1994) "The costs and benefits of financial instability: Big government capitalism and the Minsky paradox," in G.A. Dymski and R. Pollin (eds.) *New Perspectives in Monetary Macroeconomics*, 369–401, Ann Arbor, MI: University of Michigan Press.

Porter, K.M. (2007) "Misbehavior and mistake in bankruptcy mortgage claims," University of Iowa, Legal Studies Research Paper No. 07-29.

Reinhart, C.M. and Rogoff, K.S. (2009) "The aftermath of financial crises," *American Economic Review*, 99 (2): 466–472.

Renault, O. (2007) "Cash and synthetic collateral debt obligations: Motivations and investment strategies," in A. de Servigny and J. Norbert (eds.) *The Handbook of Structured Finance*, 372–396, New York: McGraw-Hill.

Ricks, M. (2011) "Regulating money creation after the crisis," *Harvard Business Law Review*, 1 (18): 75–143.

Ritter, L.S. (1963) "An exposition of the structure of the flow-of-funds accounts," *Journal of Finance*, 18 (2): 219–230.

Robins, L. (1945) *An Essay on the Nature and Significance of Economic Science*, 2nd edn., London: Macmillan.

Rojas-Suarez, L. (2002) "Rating banks in emerging markets: What banks should learn from financial indicators," in R.M. Levich, G. Majnoni, and C.M. Reinhart (eds.) *Ratings, Rating Agencies and the Global Financial System*, 177–201, New York: Springer.

Rosen, K.T. (2007) "Anatomy of the housing market boom and correction," Haas School of Business, University of California, Berkeley, Fisher Center for Real Estate & Urban Economics, Working Paper No. 306.

Salmond, J.A. (1967) *The Civilian Conservation Corps, 1933–1942*, Durham, NC: Duke University Press.

Santoni, G.J. (1986) "The Employment Act of 1946: Some history notes," Federal Reserve Bank of St. Louis *Review*, November: 5–16.

Sawyer, M. (2003) "Employer of last resort: Could it deliver full employment and price stability?" *Journal of Economic Issues*, 37 (4), 881–908.

Schinasi, G.J. (2006) *Safeguarding Financial Stability: Theory and Practice*, Washington, DC: International Monetary Fund.

Schroeder, S.K. (2008) "The underpinnings of country risk assessment," *Journal of Economic Surveys*, 22 (3), 498–535.

Schroeder, S.K. (2009) "Defining and detecting financial fragility: New Zealand's experience," *International Journal of Social Economics*, 36 (3): 287–307.

Schwartz, A.J. (1988) "Financial stability and the federal safety net," in W.S. Haraf and R.M. Kushmeider (eds.) *Restructuring Banking and Financial Services in America*, 34–62, Washington, DC: American Enterprise Institute for Public Policy and Research.

Schwartz, A.J. (1998) "Why financial stability depends on price stability," in G. Wood (ed.) *Money, Prices and the Real Economy*, 34–41, Northampton, MA: Edward Elgar.

Schwartz, B.F. (1984) *The Civil Works Administration, 1933–1934: The Business of Emergency Employment in the New Deal*, Princeton, NJ: Princeton University.

Schwartz, N.D. (2007) "Can the mortgage crisis swallow a town?" *New York Times*, September 2.

Seccareccia, M. (1988) "Systemic viability and credit crunches: An examination of recent cyclical fluctuations," *Journal of Economic Issues*, 22 (1): 49–77.

Segoviano, M.A. and Goodhart, C.A.E. (2009) "Banking stability measures," International Monetary Fund, Working Paper No. 09/4.

Sen, S. (2010) "The meltdown of the global economy: A Keynes–Minsky episode?" Levy Economics Institute, Working Paper No. 677.

Shiller, R.J. (1999) "Human behavior and the efficiency of the financial system," in J.B. Taylor and M. Woodford (eds.) *Handbook of Macroeconomics*, vol. 1c, 1305–1340, Amsterdam: North-Holland Publishing Co.

Shiller, R.J. (2000) *Irrational Exuberance*, Princeton, NJ: Princeton University Press.

SIGTARP (2009) *Quarterly Report to Congress*, July 21, Washington, DC: Office of the Special Inspector General for the Troubled Asset Relief Program.

SIGTARP (2010) *Quarterly Report to Congress*, July 21, Washington, DC: Office of the Special Inspector General for the Troubled Asset Relief Program.

Sinai, A. (1976) "Credit crunches: An analysis of the postwar experience," in O. Eckstein (ed.) *Parameters and Policies in the U.S. Economy*, 244–274, Amsterdam: North-Holland Publishing Co.

Sinkey, J.F. (1977) "Problem and failed banks, bank examinations, and early warning systems: A summary," in E.I. Altman and A.W. Sametz (eds.) *Financial Crises: Institutions and Markets in a Fragile Environment*, 23–47, New York: Wiley.

Steinhauer, J. (2009) "A cul-de-sac of lost dreams, and new ones," *New York Times*, August 22.

Sterman, J.D. (2000) *Business Dynamics: Systems Thinking and Modeling for a Complex World*, Boston, MA: McGraw-Hill.

Stiglitz, J.E. (2010) *Freefall: America, Free Markets, and the Sinking of the World Economy*, New York: W.W. Norton & Co.

Stock, J.H. and Watson, M.W. (2002) "Has the business cycle changed and why?" *NBER Macroeconomics*, 17: 159–218.

Stock, J.H. and Watson, M.W. (2005) "Understanding changes in international business cycle dynamics," *Journal of the European Economic Association*, 3 (5): 968–1006.

Stockhammer, E. (2004) "Financialization and the slowdown of accumulation," *Cambridge Journal of Economics*, 28 (5): 719–741.

Strange, S. (1986) *Casino Capitalism*, Oxford: Basil Blackwell.

Streitfeld, D. (2009) "In appraisal shift, lenders gain power and critics," *New York Times*, August 18.

Suarez, J. and Sussman, O. (1997) "Endogenous cycles in a Stiglitz-Weiss economy," *Journal of Economic Theory*, 76 (1): 47–71.

Suarez, J. and Sussman, O. (2007) "Financial distress, bankruptcy law and the business cycle," *Annals of Finance*, 3 (1): 5–35.

Talberth, J., Cobb, C., and Slattery, N. (2007) *The Genuine Progress Indicator 2006: A Tool for Sustainable Development*, Oakland, CA: Redefining Progress.

Tavakoli, J.M. (2001) *Credit Derivatives and Synthetic Structures: A Guide to Instruments and Applications*, Hoboken, NJ: Wiley.

Taylor, N. (2008) *American-Made: The Enduring Legacy of the WPA: When FDR Put the Nation to Work*, New York: Bantam Books.

Tcherneva, P.R. (2012) "Permanent on-the-spot employment: The missing Keynes plan for full employment and economic transformation," *Review of Social Economy*, 70 (1): 57–80.

Tcherneva, P.R. and Wray, L.R. (2007) "Public employment and women: The impact of Argentina's *Jefes Program* on female heads of poor households," Levy Economics Institute, Working Paper No. 519.

Thomson, J.B. (1991) "Predicting bank failures in the 1980s," Cleveland Federal Reserve *Economic Review*, 27 (1): 9–20.

Tobin, J. (1969) "A general equilibrium approach to monetary theory," *Journal of Money, Credit and Banking*, 1 (1): 15–29.

Troy, L. (1965) *Trade Union Membership, 1897–1962*, New York: National Bureau of Economic Research.

Turner, A. (2009) Mansion House speech, City Banquet, Mansion House, London, September 22.

Tversky, A. and Kahneman, D. (1974) "Judgment under uncertainty: Heuristics and biases," *Science*, 185 (27 September): 1124–1131.

Tymoigne, E. (2007a) "A hard-nosed look at worsening U.S. household finance," *Challenge*, 50 (4): 88–111.

Tymoigne, E. (2007b) "Improving financial stability: Uncertainty versus imperfection," *Journal of Economic Issues*, 41 (2): 503–511.

Tymoigne, E. (2009) *Central Banking, Asset Prices and Financial Fragility*, London: Routledge.

Tymoigne, E. (2010) "Minsky and economic policy: 'Keynesianism' all over again?" in D.B. Papadimitriou and L.R. Wray (eds.) *The Elgar Companion to Hyman Minsky*, 47–83, Northampton. MA: Edward Elgar.

Tymoigne, E. (2012a) "Measuring macroprudential risk through financial fragility: A Minskyan approach," Levy Economics Institute, Working Paper No. 716.

Tymoigne, E. (2012b) "Expectations," in J.E. King (ed.) *The Elgar Companion to Post Keynesian Economics*, 2nd edn., 190–196, Northampton, MA: Edward Elgar.

Tymoigne, E. (2013) "The cost of Job Guarantee in the United States: Insights from the 1930s work programs," forthcoming in the *Review of Radical Political Economy*.

UBS Investment Research (2007) "Investment strategist," *Digital Newsletter*, November 27.

U.S. Congress (2010) *Dodd–Frank Wall Street Reform and Consumer Protection Act*, Washington, DC: U.S. Government Printing Office.

U.S. House of Representatives (2008a) *Credit Rating Agencies and the Financial Crisis*. Hearing before the Committee on Oversight and Government Reform, October 22, Serial No. 110-155, Washington, DC: U.S. Government Printing Office.

U.S. House of Representatives (2008b) *The Financial Crisis and the Role of Federal Regulators*. Hearing before the Committee on Oversight and Government Reform, October 23, Serial No. 110-209, Washington, DC: U.S. Government Printing Office.

U.S. House of Representatives (2008c) *Hearing to Review the Role of Credit Derivatives in the U.S. Economy*. Hearing before the Committee on Agriculture, October 15, November 20, and December 8, Serial No. 110-49, Washington, DC: U.S. Government Printing Office.

U.S. House of Representatives (2009a) *Assessing the Madoff Ponzi Scheme and Regulatory Failures*. Hearing before the Committee on Financial Services, March 1, Serial No. 111-2, Washington, DC: U.S. Government Printing Office.

U.S. House of Representatives (2009b) *Mark-to-Market Accounting: Practices and Implications*. Hearing before the Committee on Financial Services, March 12, Serial No. 111-12, Washington, DC: U.S. Government Printing Office.

U.S. House of Representatives (2010) *Public Policy Issues Raised by the Report of the Lehman Bankruptcy Examiner*. Hearing before the Committee on Financial Services, April 20, Serial No. 111-124, Washington, DC: U.S. Government Printing Office.

U.S. Senate (1934) *Gold Reserve Act of 1934*. Hearings before the Committee on Banking and Currency, Second Session on S. 2366, January 19 to 23, Washington, DC: U.S. Government Printing Office.

U.S. Senate (2006) *Calculated Risk: Assessing Non-Traditional Mortgage Products*. Hearing before the Subcommittee on Housing and Transportation, and Subcommittee on Economic Policy Committee on Banking, Housing and Urban Affairs, September 20, Senate Hearing No. 109-1083, Washington, DC: U.S. Government Printing Office.

U.S. Senate (2008) *High Price of Commodities: 2008*. Hearings before the Senate Committee on Homeland Security and Governmental Affairs, May 7, May 20, and June 24, Senate Hearing No. 110-705, Washington, DC: U.S. Government Printing Office.

U.S. Senate (2009) *Modernizing the U.S. Financial Regulatory System*. Hearing before the Senate Committee on Banking, Housing, and Urban Affairs, February 4, Senate Hearing No. 111-42, Washington, DC: U.S. Government Printing Office.

U.S. Senate (2011) *Wall Street and the Financial Crisis: Anatomy of a Financial Collapse*. Permanent Subcommittee on Investigations, New York: Cosimo.

van Treeck, T. (2009) "The political economy debate on 'financialization': A macroeconomic perspective," *Review of International Political Economy*, 16 (5): 907–944.

Veblen, T.B. (1898) "Why is economics not an evolutionary science?" *Quarterly Journal of Economics*, 12 (4): 373–397.

Veblen, T.B. (1899) *The Theory of the Leisure Class*, New York: Macmillan.

Veblen, T.B. (1904) *The Theory of Business Enterprise*, New York: Charles Scribner's Sons.

Veblen, T.B. (1921) *The Engineers and the Price System*, New York: B.W. Huebsch.

Wärneryd, K.-E. (2001) *Stock-Market Psychology: How People Value and Trade Stocks*, Northampton, MA: Edward Elgar.

Watterson Jr., P.N. (2005) "The evolution of the CDO squared," *Journal of Structured Finance*, 11 (1): 6–12.

Watts, M.J. and Mitchell, W.F. (2000) "The cost of unemployment in Australia," *Economic and Labour Relations Review*, 11 (2): 180–197.

Western, B. and Rosenfeld, J. (2011) "Unions, norms, and the rise in American wage inequality," *American Sociological Review*, 76 (4): 513–537.

Whalen, C.J. (1997) "Money-manager capitalism and the end of shared prosperity," *Journal of Economic Issues*, 31 (2): 517–525.

Whalen, C.J. (2001) "Integrating Schumpeter and Keynes: Hyman Minsky's theory of capitalist development," *Journal of Economic Issues*, 35 (4): 805–823.

Whetten, M. (2005) "Anatomy of credit CPPI," Nomura Fixed Income Research, September 2005.

Wojnilower, A.M. (1977) "L'envoi," in E.I. Altman and A.W. Sametz (eds.) *Financial Crises: Institutions and Markets in a Fragile Environment*, 234–237, New York: Wiley.

Wojnilower, A.M. (1980) "The central role of credit crunches in recent financial history," *Brookings Papers on Economic Activity*, 2: 277–339.

Wolfson, M.H. (1994) *Financial Crises: Understanding the Postwar U.S. Experience*, 2nd edn., Armonk, NY: M.E. Sharpe.

Works Progress Administration (1939) *Analysis of Civil Works Program Statistics*, Washington, DC: U.S. Government Printing Office.

Wray, L.R. (1991) "Can the Social Security Trust Fund contribute to savings?" *Journal of Post Keynesian Economics*, 13 (2): 155–170.

Wray, L.R. (1998) *Understanding Modern Money: The Key to Full Employment and Price Stability*, Northampton, MA: Edward Elgar.

Wray, L.R. (1999) "Surplus mania: A reality check," Levy Economics Institute, Policy Note No. 1999/3.

Wray, L.R. (2003) "Social Security: Truth or convenient fictions?" in M. Tool and P. Bush (eds.) *Institutional Analysis and Economic Policy*, 219–249, Norwell, MA: Kluwer Academic Publishers.

Wray, L.R. (2005) "The ownership society: Social security is only the beginning...," Levy Economics Institute, Public Policy Brief No. 82/2005.

Wray, L.R. (2006) "Social Security in an aging society," *Review of Political Economy*, 18 (3): 391–412.

Wray, L.R. (2007) "The employer of last resort programme: Could it work for developing countries?" International Labour Office, Economic and Labour Market Paper No. 2007/5.

Wray, L.R. (2008a) "Lessons from the subprime meltdown," *Challenge*, 51 (2): 40–68.

Wray, L.R. (2008b) "The commodities market bubble: Money manager capitalism and the financialization of commodities," Levy Economics Institute of Bard College, Public Policy Brief No. 96/2008.

Wray, L.R. (2009) "The rise and fall of money manager capitalism: A Minskian approach," *Cambridge Journal of Economics*, 33 (4): 807–828.

Wray, L.R. (2010a) "Anatomy of mortgage fraud, part I: MERS's smoking gun," *Huffington Post*, December 9.

Wray, L.R. (2010b) "Anatomy of mortgage fraud, part II: The mother of all frauds," *Huffington Post*, December 13.

Wray, L.R. (2010c) "Anatomy of mortgage fraud, part III: MERS's role in facilitating the mother of all frauds," *Huffington Post*, December 16.

Wray, L.R. (2011) "The Job Guarantee: A government plan for full employment," *The Nation*, June 8.

Wray, L.R. (2012) *Modern Money Theory: A Primer on Macroeconomics for Sovereign Monetary Systems*, New York: Palgrave Macmillan.

Youngman, A. (1906) "The growth of financial banking," *Journal of Political Economy*, 14 (7): 435–443.

Zabel, R.R. (2008) "Credit default swaps: From protection to speculation," *Pratt's Journal of Bankruptcy Law*, 4 (6): 546–552.

Zelman, I.L. (2007) "Mortgage liquidity du jour: Underestimated no more," Credit Suisse *Equity Research*, March.

Index

Page numbers in *italics* denote tables, those in **bold** denote figures.

Pension Benefit Guarantee Corporation
211

pension funds 78, 79–80, 81, **82**; and asset
classes 212–13; and commodity futures
indexes 213; and financial markets
213–14; growth in 261; investment in
commodities 212–13; and IRAs 211;
management 214; Minsky's views 211;
regulation changes 112, 114; and
securitization 114, 145; threat to
solvency 156; and Treasuries 214; and
unrated equity tranches of CDOs 145–6

perfect competition 8, 9, 14

perfect mobility 8, 9

personal consumption expenditure price
index (PCE) 68

Phillips curve 251

Phillips, Ronnie 207, 208

PIMCO 169

Ponzi, Charles 45

Ponzi finance 22; and amortization rate 34;
asset-based lending 193, 194, 199, 200;
in boom period 30; collateral-based
25–6, 30, 40; concept of 25; and debt
deflation 22, 28, 183, 193–4, 245; and
debt servicing 25, 40, 193; and default
probability 199; and (defensive)
position-making operations 24, 194;
deregulation and desupervision 105;
different from poor credit 27; different
from speculation 26; discouragement of
218–19; and financial fragility 22, 192;
and fraud 151; growth in household
sector 37, 105; income-based 30,
199–200; and interest rates increase
39–40; and investment-led growth 216;
and liquidation/servicing financial
commitments 26; long-term upward
trend 128; and Money Manager
Capitalism 245; and mortgages 154, 201;
move towards 2, 36–7, 40, 153; and
position-making operations 23, 26, 192;
and practices 154; processes (economic
activities) 25; pyramid schemes 25, 26;
and refinancing 23, 25–6, 193; reliance
on 183; and securitization 131–2, 146,
220; and underwriting 117–21;
unsustainable financial process 23–4

Porter, K.M. 176, 177

Portugal 108, **111**

poverty: and capitalism 10, 224, 241–2; in
Golden Age 59–60, 62, 105; and job
programs 232, 234; rate **63**; rise in 73,
112, 251

price speculation, in boom period 30

price stability, and structural programs 5

private financial businesses 100, **100**

private sector: debt 107–12, 187, 262; and
debt dependency 3, 246, 251; deficit 19;
indebtedness 4, 5, 99; as net borrower
107–8; and surpluses 19, 254, 255

private-label mortgage-backed securities
(PL MBSs) 119, 132, 133, 144, 176

profit: and cash commitments equation
36–7; and government deficit 37;
Kalecki's equation 33–4, 36, 43; and
trade balance 37

profit rate, decomposition 32–3

profitability, as central regulatory criterion
76, 77

Project Lifeline 176

promissory notes 57, 83–6, 88

public-private partnerships 211

pump and dump schemes 94, 155, 178,
253

pyramid schemes 25, 45, 151, 155, 193

Quantitative Easing 165

Raiter, Frank 143

Rand, Ayn 117

Reagan Administration 219

Reagan, Ronald 51

Real Estate Settlement Procedures Act
(RESPA) 115

real exchange economy 2, 7–9

recessions: in 1970s and 1980s 74; in 2001
108, 124, 129, 147; explanation 189;
frequency of occurence 52, 229; and
government surpluses 254; product of
specific form of capitalism 5; and
unemployment 227–8

regulation: approach to 184; challenges to
106; and credit rating 144; dismantling
of 35, 246, 251; and financial crisis 161;
and financial fragility 185; and financial
innovations 200–1; and need for 76–7

Regulation D 92

Regulation Q 35, 65, 72, 92, 253

regulatory agencies, and subprime
mortgages 152–3

regulatory framework 217–18

regulatory policies 34, 35; changes 113;
Federal Reserve as umbrella supervisor
112–13; and government oversight 76;
leniency of 106; profitability as criterion
76; self-regulation 76, 77, 146

Reinhart, C.M., and Rogoff, K.S. 187

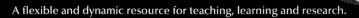